STUDIES IN MANUSCRIPT ILLUMINATION

NUMBER 2

STUDIES IN MANUSCRIPT ILLUMINATION

KURT WEITZMANN, *GENERAL EDITOR*

1. AN EARLY MANUSCRIPT OF
THE AESOP FABLES OF AVIANUS AND RELATED MANUSCRIPTS
BY ADOLPH GOLDSCHMIDT

2. ILLUSTRATIONS IN ROLL AND CODEX
A STUDY OF THE ORIGIN AND METHOD OF TEXT ILLUSTRATION
BY KURT WEITZMANN

3. THE JOSHUA ROLL
A WORK OF THE MACEDONIAN RENAISSANCE
BY KURT WEITZMANN

4. GREEK MYTHOLOGY IN BYZANTINE ART
BY KURT WEITZMANN

5. THE ILLUSTRATION OF
THE HEAVENLY LADDER OF JOHN CLIMACUS
BY JOHN RUPERT MARTIN

6. THE ILLUSTRATIONS OF
THE LITURGICAL HOMILIES OF GREGORY NAZIANZENUS
BY GEORGE GALAVARIS

—————

PUBLISHED FOR THE
DEPARTMENT OF ART AND ARCHAEOLOGY
PRINCETON UNIVERSITY

ILLUSTRATIONS
IN ROLL AND CODEX

A STUDY OF
THE ORIGIN AND METHOD OF
TEXT ILLUSTRATION

———

By Kurt Weitzmann

PRINCETON

PRINCETON UNIVERSITY PRESS

1970

MANUFACTURED IN THE UNITED STATES OF AMERICA BY
PRINCETON UNIVERSITY PRESS AT PRINCETON, NEW JERSEY

PREFACE

THE present study of the origin and the method of text illustration has a twofold origin. In part, it grew out of a lecture course, delivered jointly with Professor A. M. Friend, to graduate students of the Art Department of Princeton University. The series of lectures was revised every year in constant collaboration with Friend, and in the form in which it is now published it is the result of a continuous exchange of thoughts with him. Inasmuch as the author's part of the lecture series dealt only with cycles of text illustrations and was supplementary to Friend's lectures on illustrations of portraits in manuscripts, this study does not cover the whole field of the earliest book illumination but is confined to those illustrations that are intercalated in the text; a corresponding study by Friend will deal with the problem of the origin of the author portraits.

Secondly, this study grew out of the work on the corpus of the Septuagint manuscripts published under the auspices of the Department of Art and Archaeology of Princeton University. The occupation with the iconography of the Old Testament and its origin led necessarily to an investigation of classical book illustration at the time of the first illustration of the Bible, and of the question of how much the first Bible illustrators owed to their pagan forerunners in the same medium as far as the distribution of the pictures, their compositional schemes, figure types and other features are concerned.

The comparison of secular as well as biblical miniature cycles with their underlying texts posed the problem of how miniature and text are related to each other in principle. The present study is an attempt to deal with this problem in a systematic manner, so that the results may not only constitute a kind of prolegomenon to the history of the Septuagint illustration, but also an outline of the method which can be applied to similar iconographic studies in the field of manuscript illumination.

The writer owes to his colleague, Professor Friend, the greatest gratitude for never-failing help and inspiration through all the years of work on this subject. Were it not that he is the editor of this series of studies, nothing would be more appropriate than to dedicate this piece of writing to him, as a sign of the writer's highest appreciation. To Miss Margot Cutter of the Princeton University Press the author is much indebted for her help in improving the English.

KURT WEITZMANN

Princeton, New Jersey
June 1945

PREFACE TO THE SECOND PRINTING

When *Roll and Codex* appeared, shortly after the end of World War II, no one could have foreseen what the market for a book of this nature would be. The author alone is to blame that the book was not reprinted as soon as the considerable demand for it became apparent.

My own research has continued along the line laid down in *Roll and Codex* in a series of articles as well as in the book *Ancient Book Illumination*. In the latter an attempt was made to go beyond the formulation of the principles of ancient book illumination and, though only in the sketchy form of a lecture series, to circumscribe in some detail which kinds of texts were chosen for illumination in classical antiquity. At the same time some new papyrus fragments with pictures came to light and also some more derivative material in other media from classical antiquity. These further support the idea of how extensively book illustration had spread at that time.

The point of departure of the *Roll and Codex* study was the attempt to explore the sources which led to the illustration of the Bible. The indications were that from the very beginning individual books of the Bible were illustrated with enormously rich miniature cycles; this seems to suggest that the early Christians were not timidly starting a new branch of art but making use of an established tradition, which only could have been illustrated classical texts. Not long after the publication of *Roll and Codex*, however, it became clear that the history of early book illumination was even more complex than could have been anticipated. A group of scholars, including the author, brought forth diverse evidence that Hellenized Jews must at an early time have had illustrated books of various types which dealt with the stories of the Old Testament, and that consequently the Christians relied not only on illustrated classical texts but on illustrated Jewish writings as well.

To incorporate all the new material and new ideas in a revised edition of *Roll and Codex* turned out to be impossible since it threatened to change the character of the book as primarily methodological and only secondarily historical. At the same time I have seen no reason to change any of the basic tenets of the methodological discussion concerning the relation of picture and text. Thus I decided to have the text reprinted in its original form so that it does not lose whatever conciseness it has and to provide addenda, which follow the index. As for the monuments themselves, I have added only a few illustrated papyri that have appeared in the meantime since they are essential to strengthen the primary evidence of ancient book illumination.

When *Roll and Codex* appeared in 1947, it was planned that Professor Friend would write a volume from a similar point of view on the author portraits in manuscripts. When he died in 1956, he left his study on this subject only in the form of lectures. Now, after having taken over the editorship of the Studies in Manuscript Illumination, I hope to publish Friend's study posthumously in this series.

I wish to express my sincere thanks to the Department of Art and Archaeology of Princeton University and to the Princeton University Press for encouraging me to have *Roll and Codex* reprinted.

KURT WEITZMANN

Princeton, New Jersey
January 1969

CONTENTS

CONTENTS

ILLUSTRATIONS IN ROLL AND CODEX

INTRODUCTION

THE remains of classical book illumination from the period in which the papyrus roll was the predominant medium, are pitifully few. Most of its history must be reconstructed on the basis of contemporary copies in other media on the one hand, and of mediaeval copies of parchment codices on the other. The loss of the bulk of the original documents easily explains why the subject was hitherto treated in a peripheric manner by scholars whose chief interest lay either in the general subject of book production and book writing or in the particular subjects of classical philology and archaeology, or in papyrology, or in mediaeval art history as far as the latter had centered upon book illumination. Valuable contributions have been made by these scholars to what from their viewpoint was a border field. In making classical book illumination the center of a study, the point of departure had to be the correlation of the results gained thus far from widely varied groups of scholars. Because of the diversity of their contributions the writer may be permitted to present here a short review of the essential bibliography.

One branch, containing valuable information regarding pictures in roll and codex, comprises the handbooks dealing with production and book writing in general, in which, among many different items, a chapter about illumination was appropriate. The first person to collect all available literary as well as documentary evidence in such a chapter was Wilhelm Wattenbach,[1] a scholar who typifies the well-read universal historian, philologist and antiquarian of his time. The subject of book production was merely ancillary to his wide historical studies, and the illumination of books was to him a mere tangent to a border field. All the more remarkable, therefore, is his broad view of this subject. He collected the most important quotations of classical writers concerning pictures in roll and codex, he knows the Eudoxus Roll in Paris as the oldest illustrated Greek papyrus (p. 49 and fig. 37), he enumerates the various categories of manuscripts which reflect ancient illumination, such as those of Homer, Virgil, Dioscurides, Terence, Aratus and others, and he even refers to Jahn's study of the *Bilderchroniken* as reflections of illustrated rolls in another medium. In so doing he actually touches all essential branches upon which a special study of classical book illumination has to be built up, and in this respect this very first sketch is more comprehensive than most of the later more specialized treatments.

By the time Theodor Birt wrote the next important handbook with a chapter on book illumination,[2] not only had the material referring to our subject

---

[1] W. Wattenbach, *Das Schriftwesen im Mittelalter*, 2nd ed., Leipzig 1875, pp. 291ff.
[2] Th. Birt, *Die Buchrolle in der Kunst*, Leipzig 1907, pp. 269ff.

considerably increased, but some art-historical literature had also appeared, notably Strzygowski's study on the Alexandrian World Chronicle. Under this influence Birt engages in building up a theory about the formal aspect of ancient roll illustration and its development. The title of his chapter, "Die Trajanssäule und das Bilderbuch," indicates clearly what he considers to be the basic monument on which his theory rests. According to Birt the illustrated roll consisted primarily of an uninterrupted picture frieze with little or no text, the best evidence for it being the Trajan's Column and the Vatican Joshua Roll (figs. 110 and 111). Because of the widespread acceptance of this theory, which seems never to have been seriously contested by art historians, we shall have to deal with it more explicitly in the chapter on frieze illustration (p. 123).

The specialization in the field of book production in the last decades has not much advanced the study of ancient book illumination. In Milkau's *Handbuch der Bibliothekswissenschaft*[3] the authors who contributed special chapters on script and papyrology felt themselves excused from the obligation of dealing with illustrations because a special chapter was to be devoted to them. This chapter, however, save for some conventional sentences based upon Birt's theory, starts out with the period of the earliest surviving codices. As so often is the case in handbooks written by several authors, their results are not sufficiently correlated, and what the archaeologist, the philologist and the papyrologist could have supplied was not taken into consideration by the art historian. Thus Birt's book, though it should be used with caution where he embarks on formal problems and theories about illumination, must still be considered an outstanding attempt to collect the evidence for roll illustration from as many angles as possible.

Among the scholars who have studied special groups of documents credit should be given first to the classical philologists who dealt with those illustrated codices which they rightly considered to be copies of lost archetypes of the classical period. Georg Thiele has made these the subject of a thesis, the four chapters of which, however, are somewhat uneven.[4] Actual research is concentrated on the first and last chapters about the Aratea and the Aesop Fables, chapters to be understood as preparatory to two special monographs which became the bases for all further studies on Aratus and Aesop illustration.[5] The other two chapters of the thesis, the one on the epic poems, i.e. the two Vatican Virgil codices and the Milan Iliad, together with the Ter-

---

[3] Vol. 1: *Schrift und Buch*, Leipzig 1931. Cf. especially chaps. II-V.

[4] G. Thiele, *De Antiquorum Libris Pictis Capita Quattuor*, Marburg 1897.

[5] G. Thiele, *Antike Himmelsbilder, mit Forschungen zu Hipparchos, Aratos und seinen Fortsetzern und Beiträgen zur Kunstgeschichte des Sternhimmels*, Berlin 1898.—Idem, *Der Illustrierte Lateinische Aesop in der Handschrift des Ademar* (Codices Graeci et Latini, suppl. III), Leyden 1905.

ence manuscripts, the other on herbals and medical treatises, are of a rather summary and conventional nature, and thus the study is not quite as comprehensive as the title might suggest. In all of Thiele's studies, the interpretive or hermeneutic problems prevail over the formal and stylistic ones.

Similar, in this respect, to Thiele's treatment of the subject is that of Erich Bethe. In the text to the facsimile publication of the Terence manuscript in Milan[6] he devotes a special paragraph to those classical texts which were illustrated before the time of the Birth of Christ, in order to give a more general background to the illustration of the Terence manuscripts. In this rather summary sketch he picks out classical authors such as Varro, Crateuas, Apollonius of Citium, Aratus and Nicander, some of which are preserved in later manuscript copies, while others are known only by literary references to have been illustrated. The work of these two philologists by no means exhausts the contributions to the reconstruction of ancient book illumination by scholars in this field. One could easily add a list of excellent publications dealing with single manuscripts or certain recensions, most of which will be quoted in the present study, but Thiele and Bethe are the only two who tried to integrate the results, gained from individual recensions, into the history of early book illustration in general.

It will be one of our chief aims to demonstrate that for the reconstruction of ancient book illumination the later codices, though they are very important indeed, are by no means the only group of documents. In the Hellenistic and Roman periods illustrations of papyrus rolls were copied in other media to an apparently considerable extent, and quite a number of these copies are earlier in date than the oldest existing illustrated Greek roll fragment. This material has to be used critically and with proper caution, by taking into consideration the transformations that occur in the shift from one medium into another. In spite of excellent preliminary studies from the point of view of classical archaeologists, further individual studies in this field will have to be made before a sufficient basis is created for the writing of a more comprehensive history of classical book illustration, which would take this source fully into account.

The first archaeologist to connect a group of classical monuments with book illustration was Otto Jahn in a basic study about the so-called *Iliac tablets*,[7] and although he expressed this idea with great caution and reservation, most scholars who added new material to this group of monuments have adopted his suggestion. The most extensive groundwork for all future studies about reflections of book illumination in other media has been laid

[6] E. Bethe, *Terentius Codex Ambrosianus H. 75 inf.* (Codices Graeci et Latini, vol. VIII), Leyden 1903, cols. 54 ff.

[7] O. Jahn, *Griechische Bilderchroniken*, Bonn 1873.

down in the various writings of Carl Robert. Touching the problem only slightly in his masterly early study *Bild und Lied*,[8] where monuments with cyclic illustrations were paralleled with the "moderne Klassiker-Illustra-tionen," Robert became more precise when he dealt with the most important of all classical monuments reflecting book illustration, the group of Hel-lenistic terra cotta bowls which in a basic study he called *Homerische Becher*.[9] Here, and more particularly in a later article about two bowls with scenes from the *Phoenissae* of Euripides,[10] he refers to them as transformations of book illustrations, and he assumes an illustrated edition of the Euripidean dramas not perhaps as the immediate but certainly ultimate source for the terra cotta workers. Already ten years earlier Wilamowitz had for the first time introduced the idea of illustrated editions of the classics in a lecture on "Griechische Illustrierte Volksbücher,"[11] but hardly any archaeologist, with the exception of Carl Robert, realized that in this short report Wilamowitz had planted the seed for a new chapter in classical archaeology. Wherever the subject of the terra cotta bowls with scenic illustrations was again treated, the question of their relationship to illustrated rolls as models could not be avoided; most scholars confirmed Robert's viewpoint and introduced new cups into the discussion that not only expanded our knowledge of the material as such, but of the textual sources involved as well.[12]

It is the merit of Robert to have analysed also other classical monuments from the viewpoint of their being reflections of illuminated books, partic-ularly a large group of Roman frieze sarcophagi which for their mythologi-cal cycles he believed to be largely dependent on illustrated Euripides rolls.[13] Furthermore the numerous representations of groups of masks on Pompeian frescoes and Roman mosaics were considered by him to be copies of title miniatures of illustrated dramatic rolls, reflections of which are found in the later Terence manuscripts.[14] Finally, when Robert, at the end of his

[8] C. Robert, *Bild und Lied. Archaeologische Beiträge zur Geschichte der Griechischen Heldensage* (Philologische Untersuchungen hersg. von A. Kiessling und U. v. Wilamowitz-Moellendorff, vol. v), Berlin 1881.

[9] C. Robert, *Homerische Becher* (50. Berliner Winckelmannsprogramm), Berlin 1890.

[10] C. Robert, "Homerische Becher mit Illustrationen zu Euripides' Phoinissen," *Jahrb. d. Inst.*, XXIII, 1908, pp. 192ff. and p. 201.—*Idem, Oidipus*, Berlin 1915, p. 451.

[11] U. von Wilamowitz-Moellendorff, *Arch. Anz.*, XIII, 1898, p. 228.

[12] E.g. A. von Salis, "Sisyphos," *Corolla, Ludwig Curtius zum 60. Geburtstag*, Stuttgart 1937, pp. 161, 166.—M. Rostovtzeff, "Two Homeric Bowls in the Louvre," *Am. Journ. Arch.*, XLI, 1937, pp. 86ff. and esp. p. 93.

[13] C. Robert, *Die antiken Sarkophag-Reliefs*, vols. II and III, 1-3, Berlin 1890-1919. Cf. esp. III, 3, p. 500.

[14] C. Robert, "Maskengruppen. Wandgemälde in Pompeji," *Arch. Zeit.*, XXXVI, 1878, pp. 13 and esp. 24.—*Idem, Die Masken der neueren attischen Komoedie* (25. Hallisches Winckelmannspro-gramm), Halle 1911, pp. 86ff.

career, summed up the experiences of his lifetime, he reviewed once more the problem of the relationship between illustrated rolls and their copies in other media, and this time in a more comprehensive way than ever before. He looked at the Homeric bowls, the Iliac tablets and the sarcophagi from a common angle as the chief groups that reflect those assumed, but now lost, rolls.[15] Though Robert never attempted to make book illustration the center of a special study and never tried to investigate the classical material systematically from this viewpoint, nevertheless, with wide knowledge as well as imagination, he did concentrate on those very groups of monuments which, in addition to later manuscript copies, will constitute the center of any study of classical book illumination.

The actual remains of illustrated papyri which, judging from later manuscript copies as well as from the derivative material in other media, must have played such an important role, are extremely few and, as will be seen, artistically utterly insignificant. Therefore one should not be astonished that the papyrologists paid only slight attention to this angle of their scattered material, or that some of the greatest scholars in this field even ignored it entirely. The few fragments with illustrations are so casual that no attempt can be made for the time being to relate them to each other from the viewpoint of an historical or artistic development. All that could be done so far was the collecting and recording of the fragments in a descriptive way. This was done by Wilhelm Schubart[16] and Karl Preisendanz,[17] whose comprehensive studies provide the most complete lists of illustrated papyri and, therefore, the bases for further studies of this subject. They also have to be consulted wherever a technical question about papyrus is involved that might aid in the reconstruction of lost illustrated rolls.

The first scholar to embark on the problem of ancient book illumination from the art-historical point of view was Josef Strzygowski, in his publication of the Alexandrian World Chronicle.[18] In a chapter on stylistic criticism he establishes two categories of illustration that start out separately but later merge into each other: one is the *papyrus type* and the other the *parchment type*. The former originates in Egypt and is characterized by scenic illustrations (which according to Strzygowski's aesthetic criticism cannot be labeled as art at all, since art as he understands it is expressive in ornament only), while the other is characterized by isolated pictures, such as those of the Paris Psalter, together with rich ornamentation, and, coming from Persia,

[15] C. Robert, *Archaeologische Hermeneutik*, Berlin 1919, pp. 176, 186, 197.

[16] W. Schubart, *Das Buch bei den Griechen und Römern*, 2nd ed., Berlin 1921, pp. 108 and 140.

[17] K. Preisendanz, *Papyrusfunde und Papyrusforschung*, Leipzig 1933, p. 309.

[18] Adolf Bauer and Jos. Strzygowski, *Eine Alexandrinische Weltchronik* (Denkschriften der K. Akademie d. Wissenschaften, Phil.-hist. Kl., vol. LI, Abh. 2), Vienna 1906, pp. 169ff.

penetrates via Mesopotamia, Armenia, Asia Minor, Syria and Egypt into Byzantium and the North. This concept is based on an antihistoric as well as on an anti-Greek attitude. In juxtaposing the two types of illustrations Strzygowski creates the impression, though avoiding suggestions on date as far as possible, that they existed side by side from the very beginning as expressions of two different cultural areas. It will be one of our aims to demonstrate that the parchment type grows out of the papyrus type in the course of an evolutionary process. Though Strzygowski does not entirely eliminate, but tries to diminish, the role which Hellenistic art played in the process of the creation of illustrated books, his anti-Greek attitude becomes manifest in such categorical statements as that the papyrus roll was used by the Greeks down to the Roman period for text writing exclusively.[19] He thus does not take notice of the contributions which Jahn, Robert and Wilamowitz had made previously concerning the reflections of Hellenistic and Roman roll illustration. But, aside from its prejudiced general theories, Strzygowski's chapter is valuable as a documentary publication of quite a number of scattered illustrated papyrus fragments which he introduced for the first time into the art-historical literature.

One would, of course, expect to find preliminary work about the illustration of rolls in the writings of those scholars who have specialized in book illumination and tried to investigate the foundation and sources of their proper field. But they usually begin with a chapter that merely records and describes the earliest illustrated codices in existence, such as the Milan Iliad, the two Vatican Virgil manuscripts and others, and they consider them the earliest illustrated manuscripts ever made, not realizing that only a long development could have produced such advanced works as all these earliest codices.[20] An exception is Hans Gerstinger, who in his history of Greek book illumination[21] devoted a whole chapter to classical antiquity. Though he confines himself to repeating in a descriptive way the current theories, such as Bethe's not too fortunate idea about the *schoolbook* as a point of departure for illustration, or Birt's disputable assumption of textless picture rolls, his chapter as a whole is a competent recapitulation of the research on the origin of book illustration.

The first and hitherto the only monograph which deals with ancient book illumination as a central theme was written by the Polish scholar Gasio-

[19] *Op. cit.*, p. 175.

[20] J. A. Herbert, *Illuminated Manuscripts*, New York 1911, chap. 1.—Boeckler, *Abendländische Miniaturen bis zum Ausgang der Romanischen Zeit* (Tabulae in usum scholarum, vol. 10), Berlin 1930, and others.

[21] H. Gerstinger, *Die Griechische Buchmalerei*, Vienna 1926, pp. 9-11.

rowski.[22] This study is a collection and investigation of later manuscripts which hark back to an archetype of the classical period, but it gives only slight consideration to the extant illustrated papyrus fragments and none at all to the classical monuments in other media related to book illumination. The basis for his collection is the classical text, regardless of whether the miniatures have iconographically a classical ancestry or not. Therefore Gothic and Renaissance miniature cycles are included that have no pictorial archetype in the Graeco-Roman period, and now and then we are confused as to whether a later copy reveals a recognizable trace of the classical representational tradition, or whether it is an entirely new mediaeval creation. Another difficulty lies in the grouping of the material according to languages and in placing the Latin before the Greek. The consequence of this division is, to quote only one example, that the copies of the herbal of Pseudo-Apuleius are treated ahead of the Greek Dioscurides manuscripts upon which they depend, while both, of course, as products of the same pictorial tradition, should have been treated together. The study is a lining-up of various illustrated recensions, each investigated separately as to the age of its archetype, following in this respect Thiele's earliest study *De Antiquorum Libris Pictis*. This manner of treating each recension as a unit in itself will always remain a sound basis for further studies in the field, but what still remains to be done is the co-ordination of the results gained from each recension and their corroboration with the miniature copies in other media and in the papyrus fragments. Gasiorowski's general concept of the formal structure of early rolls and codices again depends chiefly on Birt's theory of the continuous picture roll without a text.

While reading proof on the present study, a copy of Bethe's posthumous book on ancient book illumination, which was published shortly before the end of the war, fell into our hands.[23] Since this is the only other attempt, besides Gasiorowski's, to deal with this subject in the form of a monograph, we are glad to be able to insert this stimulating and learned piece of writing in our bibliographical survey. Bethe's leading idea is to prove that book illumination did not start with the period from which we have the earliest extant codices, i.e. the fourth century A.D., but that it was a well-established though as yet little-known branch of classical art. The proof of his argument rests primarily on the scientific treatises, mechanical, zoological, medical, botanical and astronomical, the origin of which he tries to take back even into the pre-Hellenistic period, reasoning rightly that many scientific texts require illustrations from the very beginning in order to be fully un-

[22] Stan. J. Gasiorowski, *Malarstwo Minjaturowe Grecko-Rzymskie*, Cracow 1928 (with English résumé).

[23] Erich Bethe, *Buch und Bild im Altertum*, (aus dem Nachlass hersg. von Ernst Kirsten) Leipzig 1945.

derstood. From these illustrated texts (=Bilderbücher) he distinguishes those books in which pictures are predominant, being either separated from the text, as in the case of frontispieces, or having only little or no text at all added to them (=Buchbilder). This latter principle he considers typical for the illustration of epic poems and other literary texts and at the same time a Roman invention. At the root of this thesis of the Roman origin lies once more Birt's controversial concept of the roll with a continuous picture frieze, similar to the triumphal columns and the Vatican Joshua Rotulus, as the characteristic form of ancient book illustration. In linking the illustration of literary texts with this idea of a continuous picture frieze, Bethe comes to the conclusion that the Greeks never illustrated their literary texts, that this was even contrary to their artistic genius which kept literature and representational arts apart, and that for this reason they confined themselves to the illustration of scientific treatises and didactic poems. Associating in this manner the formal problem of the distribution of pictures with different types of texts—categories which have no common denominator and should be kept apart—Bethe disregarded the possibility of literary texts ever having been illustrated in the same manner as didactic works with intercalated pictures. It is to be regretted that the distinguished philologist and Homer critic, in not following the path prepared by Jahn, Wilamowitz and Robert, deprived himself of the opportunity to investigate in an unbiased way the problem of the illustration of the Homeric poems and other literary texts in the Hellenistic period. In spite of the penetrating treatment of the scientific treatises and the didactic poems, Bethe's book cannot be considered as comprehensive since, as we shall try to demonstrate in the following pages, the great classics, not only for the ancient reader but for the illustrator as well, were, from the Hellenistic period on, Homer and Euripides, and not Nicander, Oppian and the like.

Our present study is not another attempt to write a comprehensive history of ancient book illumination, but is confined to an investigation of various methods and principles which, we hope, will aid the writing of such a history in the future. Therefore no attempt has been made to collect all existing monuments that might have a bearing upon our problems, nor even to discuss one example out of each recension which has been illustrated in classical antiquity. Moreover, it will be noticed that a comparatively greater emphasis is placed upon the Greek manuscripts than on the Latin. To begin with, all preserved papyrus fragments with illustrations are Greek, though this, of course, is only accidental and explained by the fact that Hellenized Egypt is the only place where they were and will be found. It can be surmised that a great production of illustrated Latin papyri also existed, but we have every reason to believe that, like much of Roman poetry and science to which the illustrations were attached, they were dependent on Greek models. We see this dependence still clearly reflected in many later Latin codices whose illustrations stay in a tradition which ultimately harks back to a Greek model. At the same time the Latin illuminator is more inclined to change iconographic features of his model, while his Greek colleague is generally more conservative and pays comparatively greater attention to the preservation of the iconography, though naturally also in the Greek world numerous cases of iconographic negligence and corruption do occur in a long process of copying. If, nevertheless, a certain number of Latin manuscripts are introduced into the present study, it is for the reason that of many picture recensions only Latin copies are preserved or known at the present time, while the corresponding Greek ones have perished.

I. THE GENERAL RELATION BETWEEN LITERATURE AND THE REPRESENTATIONAL ARTS

A. THE THREE METHODS OF RENDERING THE LITERARY CONTENT

EARLY in Greek history, not long after the geometric style had adopted the human figure into its repertory, a representational art gradually developed, the subject matter of which was drawn not so much from the observation of the daily life of the artist's environment, but rather from his imagination, which was inspired either directly by the popular myths of the gods and the heroes, or by the form in which the epic poem had shaped the mythological tradition. The relation between pictorial representations and works of literature is quite vague at the beginning, but as time goes on becomes closer until, in a final stage, the pictorial representation even adopts from literature a fundamental principle which in the earlier centuries apparently had been contradictory to those of the fine arts, namely that of *progressive narration*. The closest union was achieved when both picture and literature were physically united in the illustrated papyrus roll, and the text and the picture intermingled. This development required a long time and covered practically the entire range of Greek history in its most productive centuries, i.e. from the archaic to the Hellenistic period.

Three stages of this development were distinguished by Carl Robert, who in *Bild und Lied* analysed them with great precision and clarity, so that any further investigation of this subject must take this study as a point of departure. Most of Robert's research in one way or another takes into consideration the distinctions laid down in this early work and when, at the end of his life, he elaborated on some points, in his *Archaeologische Hermeneutik*, he did not need to change the original concept in any essential feature. The common trend of development, which focused the research of the fine arts more and more on the problems of style rather than interpretation, prevented the full exploitation of Robert's basic studies by his contemporaries and followers; Robert, therefore, never had the success of Franz Wickhoff, who, sometime after him, treated the same problem of relationship between picture and text in his book on the Vienna Genesis.[1] Wickhoff, too, distinguishes three stages in the development of the relation between literature and representational art, which coincide more or less with those established by Robert, and he calls the methods which prevail in each of the three periods the *complementary*, the *isolating* and the *continuous*—as the German terms *completirend*, *distinguirend* and *continuirend* were translated in

---

[1] W. Ritter von Hartel and Fr. Wickhoff, *Die Wiener Genesis*, Vienna 1895.

12

the English edition[2]—terms which for special reasons we have not accepted for the present study.

1. *The Simultaneous Method*

The influence of literature upon the representational arts, which can be found sporadically already in geometric pottery and metalwork,[3] increases rapidly in the archaic period, as is most clearly recognizable in black-figured vases. Here literary themes occur for the first time in large numbers and their representations show a decisive gain in the individualization of the subject matter. The most powerful influence is exerted by the epic poems, and a marked emphasis is already placed upon Homer's Iliad and Odyssey, of which, however, only the most striking or dramatic scenes attracted the painters of this period. It is, therefore, not arbitrary that we should begin an analysis of the archaic method of rendering a literary content by pictorial means with an illustration of the Odyssey, choosing the same example that Robert used for his demonstration. A Spartan cup from the sixth century B.C., now in the Bibliothèque Nationale in Paris,[4] illustrates Odysseus' adventure with the Cyclopes (fig. 1). Polyphemus sits upright and holds the legs of one of Odysseus' companions whom he has just devoured (IX, 292ff.). In front of him stands Odysseus, who offers a cup of wine in order to intoxicate him (IX, 347ff.), but the giant obviously is unable to take the cup, since he has no hand free. Furthermore, the same Odysseus who offers the drink with one hand already holds with the other the beam which he is going to thrust into the giant's one eye (IX, 375ff.), and he is accompanied by three companions (instead of four as the text requires). With a naïve gaiety the archaic artist depicts three moments of the tale as one single scene without repeating any of its participants, thereby transgressing the limitations of the unity of time, which later on were so much respected by the representational arts.

Not always does archaic art weld together various happenings in such a primitive manner as in the Polyphemus cup, where the actions conflict with each other. In the representation of the killing of Troilus on the François Vase in Florence (fig. 2),[5] the literary source of which is the lost epic poem *Cypria*, the archaic painter was able to handle the method described above

[2] E. Strong, *Roman Art; Some of its Principles and their Application to Early Christian Painting*, London-New York 1900.

[3] Roland Hampe, *Frühe Griechische Sagenbilder in Böotien*, Athens 1936.

[4] *Monumenti inediti*, I, 1829-33, pl. VII, no. 1—Robert, *Bild und Lied*, p. 19; *Hermeneutik*, p. 182, fig. 141.—*Corpus Vasorum Antiquorum*, France, fasc. 7; Paris-Bibliothèque Nationale, Paris 1928, p. 18 and pl. 22, no. 4; pl. 23, no. 5 (here more complete bibliography).

[5] Robert, *Bild und Lied*, p. 16; *Hermeneutik*, p. 182 and fig. 142.—Furtwängler-Reichhold, *Griechische Vasenmalerei*, ser. I, Munich 1904, p. 55 and pls. 11-12.

13

in a more subtle manner. In a friezelike composition the center is occupied by Achilles (mostly destroyed), who pursues Troilus on horseback, while Polyxena, having dropped her hydria, runs away in front of the horses. Athena, Hermes and Thetis are standing as the protecting gods behind Achilles. So far the unity of time is maintained. But at both sides are more figures that are intimately related to the center and supposed to be seen by the beholder as a compositional unit with the Troilus scene. At the right Antenor announces the catastrophe of Troilus' death to Priam even before it has taken place, and while Priam is hearing the tragic news, Polites and Hector are already storming out of Troy in order to avenge the younger brother, before the news could have reached them. Thus the additional figures at the right point far into the future, while the left part represents a situation which precedes the central action: in a well-house a Trojan boy and girl are peacefully drawing water as could have happened only before Achilles had entered and perturbed the scene. By avoiding any caesura or the repetition of any participant, and by using other devices, such as turning the heads of the water-girl and presumably also that of Antenor (now lost) toward the center, so as to make them observers of the imminent catastrophe, the painter has done everything in his power to create the impression of a single scene in which the time is not fixed, but transitory. If the archaic method thus described is to be characterized by a single term, that word must imply that within the limits of a single scene several actions take place at the same time, i.e. simultaneously. Thus we might speak of a *simultaneous method*, a method which was predominant for only a short while. In the fifth century B.C. a new method is already in use that quickly supersedes the older one.

2. *The Monoscenic Method*

The new method of expressing a literary content in the representational arts is based on the principle of the unity of time and place. Now only one single action is represented in a picture, and the increasingly expressive and individualized attitudes and gestures of all the participants are related to one precise moment. This method, already becoming clear at the end of the archaic period, is predominant during the fifth and fourth centuries B.C., and continues in use, even after the invention of a third method in the Hellenistic period, throughout the history of art. Robert realized that the new rational principle of the unity of time and place appears in the representational arts about the same period in which the classical drama, which adheres so strongly to the same principle, came into existence, and he infers an interrelation between painting and drama in this respect. Also, the greater expressiveness in the gesticulation of painted figures can be ascribed to a strong influence from the drama, though it must be made clear that throughout the fifth century B.C. it is only this general principle and not the actual text of the drama which influences the fine arts. According to Robert there is no fifth century vase painting known which can be established beyond doubt as having an iconographic connection with any play of the great tragedians;[6] most vase paintings of that early period which Séchan[7] tries to connect with Sophoclean and Euripidean tragedies remain questionable and indeed justify Robert's caution in this regard. Once more it is primarily the epic poem whose events are depicted in a newly dramatized way.

Again a scene from the Odyssey may be used to illustrate the new method. A skyphos in Berlin from about the middle of the fifth century B.C. represents the slaying of the wooers by Odysseus according to Book XXII (fig. 3).[8] One wooer is already hit by an arrow, while Odysseus is bending his bow and aiming at one of the two other wooers, who try to protect themselves. All four persons described thus far illustrate a very precise moment of the fight and there is no action involved which interferes with the principle of unity of time such as one would expect from a monument in simultaneous method. Moreover, behind Odysseus stand two women with an expression of horror upon their faces, apparently two of the twelve shameless women (XXII, 424) who were sympathetic to the wooers, but according to the Homeric text were not present in the hall during the killing. The painter, deviating from the text, added them on his own account, relating their concern to the catastrophe just taking place before their eyes, and therefore he wants them to be understood as actual participants. In this manner he preserved strictly the unity of time and place. These women are *complementary* to the nucleus of the scene, a term which Robert uses in order to describe figures which are additional to those required by the text. Still another point may be learned from this vase painting. Between Odysseus and the wooers is a palmette ornament which, from the formal point of view, divides the scene, though it is iconographically a unit, in two parts covering two opposite sides of the surface of the vase. This shows clearly that formal and iconographic units do not necessarily coincide, though in most instances they do.

If a painter of this period wanted to represent more of the content of his literary source than could be included in a single scene, without impairing the unity of time and place, he had no other choice than to invent as many

[6] Robert, *Bild und Lied*, pp. 129ff.

[7] L. Séchan, *Études sur la tragédie grecque dans ses rapports avec la céramique*, Paris 1926.

[8] Furtwängler-Hauser-Reichhold, *Griechische Vasenmalerei*, ser. III, Munich 1932, p. 102 and pl. 138, no. 2. (here the older literature).—Fr. Müller, *Die antiken Odyssee-Illustrationen*, Berlin 1913, p. 96.—E. Pfuhl, *Malerei und Zeichnung der Griechen*, Munich 1923, vol. II, p. 566; vol. III, pl. 219, fig. 559.

independent iconographic units as there were actions to be represented, and in each unit the chief actors had to be repeated. The vase painting of the fifth and fourth centuries B.C. shows a number of instances of this kind, though they are not very frequent. Robert describes a cylix of Duris, in Vienna,[9] whose outer frieze shows two separate scenes based upon the lost *Aethiopis* of Arctinus. On one side (fig. 4a) the fight between Ajax and Odysseus over the arms of Achilles is depicted at a very precise moment of the action, upon which also the figures behind the two contenders are focused. The outcome of the fight is rendered on the opposite side of the cylix (fig. 4b), where the Achaeans cast dice, voting to whom the arms of Achilles shall belong, and it is clear already from the gestures and the uneven distribution of the dice that Odysseus will emerge as the victor. The painter created a second scene, with its own concentration upon a highly dramatic moment, which is iconographically so much of a unit in itself that it can be fully appreciated even without glancing at the first scene. And in the same manner he painted a third iconographic unit on the inner side of the cylix, representing Odysseus as he gives Achilles' weapons back to Neoptolemus (fig. 4c).

For this method, as analyzed on the preceding two red-figured vases of the fifth and fourth centuries B.C., Robert has no specific term. Occasionally he speaks of *Situationsbilder*, i.e. iconographic units in which the pictorial features of each are related to one very specific situation. Since the new method, as demonstrated above, is characterized by the concentration on a single action within the limits of one scene, we may call it the *monoscenic method*, a term which stresses an iconographic rather than formal connotation.

Not before the fourth century B.C. does the drama have any considerable influence on the iconography of vase painting. This influence is best revealed in the huge Tarentine amphorae,[10] most of which display very complex compositions involving many more figures than participate in the action or are even mentioned in the drama on which the vase depends. On an amphora from Canosa, now in Munich (fig. 5), with a figural composition based upon the *Medea* of Euripides,[11] the center is occupied by a representation of the

---

[9] In the Oesterreich. Museum für Kunst und Industrie. Robert, *Bild und Lied*, pp. 29ff.—Furtwängler-Reichhold, *op. cit.*, ser. I, p. 267 and pl. 54.—J. Cl. Hoppin, *A Handbook of Attic Red-figured Vases*, vol. I, Cambridge, Mass. 1919, p. 269 (here the older literature).—Pfuhl, *op. cit.*, vol. I, p. 478; vol. III, pls. 160-162, nos. 459, 460 and 463.

[10] Watzinger, *Studien zur unteritalischen Vasenmalerei*, Bonner Dissertation, Darmstadt 1899.—Pfuhl, *op. cit.*, II, pp. 575f., 718f.

[11] Robert, *Bild und Lied*, p. 37; *Hermeneutik*, p. 159, fig. 130.—Furtwängler-Reichhold, *Griechische Vasenmalerei*, ser. II, Munich 1909, pp. 161ff. and pl. 90.—Séchan, *op. cit.*, p. 405, pl. VIII (here the older literature).—Pfuhl, *op. cit.*, III, pl. 353, fig. 795.

death of Creon's daughter in the presence of her desperate father, while in the lower part Medea is just about to kill her own children. This nucleus is surrounded by *complementary* figures that are not based upon the Euripides text, relatives such as Hippotes, Merope, Aeetes, gods like Athene, Heracles and the Dioscuri, servants, and finally Oistros, the personification of frenzy. Actually there are two different moments represented: the death of Creon's daughter, and the killing of Medea's children. In this respect the composition is in accordance with the older simultaneous method, the more so in that the painter carefully avoids the repetition of any participant. But at the same time he imposes the new principle of unity of time and place upon the complex composition by trying to convey the impression of isochronism of the two actions involved. Whereas in archaic art only consecutive actions are shown simultaneously in an anachronistic fashion, the painter of the Canosa vase placed two actions together which from a rational viewpoint *could* actually have taken place at the same time without mutual interference. Furthermore, he allows persons to go from the lower frieze to the upper one and vice versa, in order to create a unified plane and to relate the scenes spatially. Nevertheless the impression is that the painter, though trying his utmost in a quite sophisticated way not to offend against the unity of time and place, has to some extent already overstepped it. Clearly a limit has been reached in the grouping of many elements together in a single iconographic unit, and this is a transitional stage leading to a new method which will enable the painter to express pictorially a steadily increasing amount of literary content without falling back into the primitive simultaneous method.

3. *The Cyclic Method*

In the Hellenistic period a new method was invented by which the content of a literary source could be rendered in the representational arts on an ever-increasing scale without impairing the clarity of the pictorial composition. By conceiving each changing situation of the text as a picture in itself, the artist creates now a series of consecutive compositions with separate and centered actions, repeating the actors in each and so observing at the same time the rules of the unity of time and place. In this manner the shortcomings of the simultaneous method are avoided, as well as the limitations imposed by the monoscenic method on the number of different actions which could be represented. Moreover, beyond the mere increase in iconographic subject matter, the representational arts become still more closely related to the literary sources by adapting from literature the transitory element, which was hitherto confined to the written word. As the eye in reading a text moves from one writing column to another, so it moves now from one picture to the next, *reading* them, so to speak, and the beholder visualizes in his mind the changes which took place between the consecutive scenes. In other words, the single scenes in a sequence contain elements which stimulate in the beholder a certain creativeness in imagining those actions which lie between the painted scenes, since these never follow each other as closely as the shots of a motion picture camera. But as the number of scenes increases there is a clearly recognizable tendency to treat each single one in a more economical way and to confine it to the most essential figures in order to counterbalance to some extent the numerical expansion of iconographic units. Thus we can observe a decrease in complementary figures, though they by no means disappear entirely from works executed in the new method.

The group of monuments which for the first time in Greek art show clearly the new method of consecutive scenes are the terra cotta cups which Robert called *Homerische Becher*[12] in accordance with the chief subject matter represented on them, while the entire group is generally known as *Megarian bowls*. Robert dates the earliest group of them in the third century B.C., while Courby[13] suggests even the end of the fourth. Thus one finds this new method in existence not long after the flourishing period of the Tarentine vases and consequently it can be assumed that it was invented during the comparatively short period which lies between these fourth century vases and the earliest bowls, i.e. at the very beginning of the Hellenistic period. The first example, chosen as before from the Odyssey, is a cup in Berlin (fig. 6)[14] which represents on its outer surface three scenes of the twenty-second book. In the first (at the left) Eumaeus and Philoetius fetter the feet and arms of the unfaithful goatherd Melanthius (v. 161ff.). In the next (at the right) the two faithful servants Eumaeus and Philoetius stand before Melanthius, whom they hanged head down on a twisted rope, thus fulfilling their task in getting rid of the goatherd (v. 192ff.). Then follows a third scene (in the center), in which Athena incites Odysseus and Telemachus to fight against the wooers (v. 205ff.). Each of these three scenes is as close to the text as compositions of the monoscenic method, but while in the latter the artist selected freely the situations he considered of paramount importance, the artist of the cup, in covering each quickly changing action of the text, largely sacrifices the freedom of choice; in trying to deal with every situation in the text he becomes dependent on it as no artist had been hitherto. The result is a tremendous increase in iconographic themes; theoretically speaking, every situation described in an epic poem is now adaptable for the representational arts, whether it be highly dramatic or

---

[12] C. Robert, *Homerische Becher* (50. Berliner Winckelmannsprogramm), Berlin 1890.

[13] F. Courby, *Les vases grecs à reliefs*, Paris 1922, chap. XIX, pp. 281ff.

[14] Robert, *op. cit.*, p. 8 and fig. A.

static with little or no action at all. This does not mean, however, a complete break in the iconographic tradition. A classical, and for that matter also a mediaeval, artist invents only where he has to do so because of lack of models, while he will try to copy earlier models wherever they are available.

The enormous increase in Homeric iconography, in this period, becomes evident when one realizes that other episodes were illustrated with the same density of consecutive moments as the Melanthius episode. Another Megarian bowl, likewise in Berlin, contains three more scenes from the same twenty-second book of the Odyssey (fig. 7).[15] In the first (center) Odysseus is seen stabbing Leiodes in the back, the seer grasping in vain the hero's knee to implore his mercy (v. 310ff.). In the next (at the right) Odysseus is repeated just about to kill Phemius, who likewise embraces his knee, while Telemachus intervenes in favor of the threatened minstrel and effects his pardon (v. 330ff.). Finally (at the left) one recognizes once more Odysseus and Telemachus pardoning the minstrel Medon, who comes from underneath the chair that had served as his hiding place (v. 361ff.). It seems to be merely accidental that so many scenes from only the twenty-second book of the Odyssey have come down to us. There is every reason to believe that the other books of the same poem were just as extensively illustrated and that the same was true for the twenty-four books of the Iliad as well.

The terra cotta bowls are by no means the only group of monuments in which the expansion of Homeric iconography has left its traces. Another important class is the so-called *Tabulae Iliacae*, small plaques in *piombino* from the first century, in which illustrations of the Iliad predominate, though Odyssey scenes also occur, as can be seen in a tablet, formerly in the Rondanini Collection and now lost, which contains three scenes from the tenth book (fig. 8).[16] They illustrate the Circe adventure, and moving from one scene to the next, the picture narrative can be easily read as follows: first, Odysseus in front of Circe's palace is approached by Hermes who gives him the moly, the herb which will make him immune against Circe's sorcery (v. 278ff.). In the next scene, which takes us inside the palace, Odysseus threatens Circe with his sword after her attempt to bewitch him had failed (v. 314ff.), and in the third and last, Circe raises her magic wand to disenchant Odysseus' companions who had been transformed into animals (v. 388ff.). The Circe adventure was very popular in Greek art from the archaic period, but the black-figured vases[17] confine themselves exclusively to the meta-

---

[15] *Ibid.*, p. 14 and fig. B.

[16] Otto Jahn, *Griechische Bilderchroniken*, Bonn 1873, pp. 6, 38 and pl. IV, no. H. For another Odyssey plaque, cf. K. Weitzmann, "A Tabula Odysseaca," *Am. Journ. Arch.*, XLV, 1941, pp. 166ff.

[17] Müller, *Odyssey-Illustrationen*, pp. 47ff.

morphosis of the companions as the most striking moment. It is only since the Hellenistic period that this episode is expanded into a number of iconographic units which represent consecutively its various phases.

The same phenomenon of expanding iconography can be observed in the illustration of the drama. While in the Apulian vases of the fourth century, like the Medea vase of Canosa (fig. 5), as much of the content as possible of the whole drama is compressed into one complex composition, the Megarian bowls depict a series of small scenes which can be read as a narrative, like the drama from which they are made up. The Antiquarium in Berlin, e.g., possesses a bowl with no less than five scenes from Euripides' *Iphigenia at Aulis* (fig. 10).[18] In the first (at the right) Iphigenia has just arrived in the camp of the Achaeans with her little brother Orestes and her mother Clytaemnestra, and she runs happily toward Agamemnon, who sits on the throne in a grieving attitude (v. 631ff.). Next to this scene a discourse takes place between Clytaemnestra and Achilles, in which the latter shows openly his displeasure about the falsely planned marriage between Iphigenia and himself (v. 819ff.). Then there follows the old servant's revelation about the real intentions of Agamemnon, which he tells with dramatic gestures to Clytaemnestra standing in front of him (v. 866ff.). In the fourth scene (which, resulting from a confusion of the original order, is at the extreme left) Iphigenia, accompanied by the little boy Orestes, is represented kneeling before her veiled father and pleading for her life, while Clytaemnestra turns away in a sorrowful attitude (v. 1211ff.). Finally, in the last scene, Achilles has come to offer his services to defend Iphigenia, but she, as well as Clytaemnestra, turns away from him (v. 1338ff.).

These five scenes are not all the illustrations for this one drama. A Megarian bowl recently acquired by the Metropolitan Museum in New York (figs. 9a-e)[18a] has five more scenes representing events which precede those rendered on the Berlin cup. In the first (fig. 9a)[19] Agamemnon entrusts to his old servant a letter for Clytaemnestra, instructing her not to bring Iphigenia to Aulis as previously planned (v. 111ff.). This letter, which has the shape of a diptych, is forcibly snatched from the servant's hand by Menelaus (fig. 9b).[20] Then follows a scene (fig. 9c) in which a messenger approaches hurriedly to announce to Agamemnon the arrival of his family,[21] which itself is represented in the next picture (fig. 9d). A cart has arrived drawn

---

[18] Robert, *op. cit.*, p. 51 and fig. L. He mentions two more copies from the same model, one in Athens and the other in Brussels.

[18a] Photographs by courtesy of the Metropolitan Museum of Art.

[19] The inscriptions read: ΕΠΙΣΤΟΛΟΦΟΡΟΣ ΠΡΟΣ ΚΛΥΤΑΙΜΝΗΣΤΡΑΝ and ΑΓΑΜΕΜΝΩΝ

[20] Inscription: ΜΕΝΕΛΑΟΣ

[21] Inscriptions: ΑΓΓΕΛΟΣ ΠΕΡΙ ΤΗΣ ΠΑΡΟΥΣΙΑΣ ΤΗΣ ΙΦΙΓΕΝΕΙΑΣ and ΑΓΑΜΕΜΝΩΝ

by two horses which a groom holds by the bridle and in the cart itself one recognizes Orestes and Iphigenia, who is about to descend from the vehicle, aided by another woman who is not inscribed and may be either a servant or Clytaemnestra after she had left the cart (v. 416ff.).[22] In the fifth scene, finally (fig. 9e), Menelaus with the fateful letter in his hand reproaches Agamemnon for his attempt to keep Iphigenia away from Aulis (v. 322ff.),[23] a scene which should have preceded the two previous ones, since it interrupts the original sequence. It must be noted that the most important event of the whole drama is not among the representations of the two cups just described, namely the actual sacrifice of Iphigenia. This scene hardly could have been omitted in a complete narration of the drama, and therefore it can be surmised that the ten scenes preserved do not comprise the full number of illustrations which Hellenistic art had invented, and that there must have existed still a third bowl with illustrations from the end of the drama. On the earlier Apulian amphorae one finds, typically enough, only one scene, namely the Sacrifice of Iphigenia,[24] and it is questionable whether pre-Hellenistic art ever transformed any other scene from the *Iphigenia at Aulis* into painting.

Although the new method appears in its purest form on the Megarian bowls and Iliac tablets, there are other groups of classical monuments in which it has been adapted to a greater or lesser degree, as e.g. the sarcophagi of the Roman period. These too depend, as far as the literary source is concerned, predominantly on the drama and, like the bowls, chiefly on Euripides, as Robert has convincingly shown in his corpus. In still other media new illustrated texts begin to stimulate the artist, be it lyric poetry or various kinds of prose texts or scientific treatises. This means that not only each situation of an epos or drama is convertible into a series of pictures, but, theoretically speaking, every text of any standard or great popularity is now adaptable for the painter.

In contradistinction to the *monoscenic method*, a sequence of several scenes might be called *polyscenic*. But since this term in its proper sense would include any combination of single scenes, no matter whether they are iconographically connected or not, a term should be chosen that suggests iconographic coherence as well as dependence upon a uniform textual source. A series of pictures related in this way can be described as a *cycle*, and the new method thus be called *the cyclic method*.

The cyclic method, as we have already suggested, does not appear in its fully developed form until the Hellenistic period, but there are, nevertheless, preliminary steps leading up to it. In two notable instances the ad-

[22] Inscriptions: ΟΡΕΣΤΗΣ and ΙΦΙΓΕΝΕΙΑ   [23] Inscriptions: ΜΕΝΕΛΑΟΣ and ΑΓΑΜΕΜΝΩΝ
[24] London, British Museum. Séchan, *op. cit.*, p. 372 and fig. 108.

ventures of a hero are represented in a manner which resembles fairly closely the cyclic method, namely the series of Deeds of Heracles and of Theseus, both of which occur in various media. Whether on the metopes of a temple or elsewhere, each of the Deeds is usually rendered by one single scene, depicting the decisive moment of the exploit. On a relief amphora in Berlin (fig. 11), which Furtwängler[25] dates at the end of the fifth century B.C., while Courby[26] classifies it among the products of the fourth century B.C., six Deeds are lined up in a frieze (the Nemean Lion, the Stymphalian Birds, the Golden Apples of the Hesperides, the Cerynitian Hind, the Cerberus, the Lernaean Hydra), and another similar vase contained most likely the remaining six Labors of the so-called dodecathlos. From the merely formal viewpoint, as one scene is placed alongside the next, the relief vase shows an arrangement not unlike that of the Megarian bowls, but with regard to the method of illustration there is a fundamental difference between them. While in the Berlin amphora each single combat constitutes an iconographic entity, in the genuine cyclic method there would be represented several scenes, leading up to or following the most dramatic moment of the episode. This expansion can best be demonstrated again on a Megarian bowl. The Louvre possesses a piece (fig. 12)[27] whose inscription ἆθλος πέμπτος makes it clear that all its representations fall within the time limits of a single exploit. First Hephaestus is depicted forging the club for Heracles, then Athena follows offering this club to Heracles, and finally Heracles is shown carrying the subdued Erymanthian Boar to Mycenae. By analogy to the Odyssey and the Iphigenia bowls (figs. 6-7 and 9-10) which follow extremely closely the text of Homer and Euripides, we can assume that the scenes of the Heracles bowl are also faithful to a narrative text, which, however, is not known. Most likely there existed other Heracles cups, each of them illustrating only one labor in several scenes.

The pre-Hellenistic series of the Contests of Theseus are best represented in a group of red-figured cylices of the severe style. One such cylix in London (figs. 13a-b)[28] contains no less than five Deeds of Theseus occupying the outer frieze, and other vases of the same kind show even more. On the one side we see the combats with Procrustes, Cercyon and the Minotaur, and on the other the fight with the Marathonian Bull and the Sow of Crommyon. Again one expects that a Hellenistic or Roman artist would elaborate on a single contest and turn it into a series of consecutive scenes in a true cyclic

[25] A. Furtwängler, *Die Sammlung Sabouroff*, vol. I, Berlin 1883-87, pl. LXXIV.

[26] F. Courby, *op. cit.*, p. 195 and fig. 31.

[27] M. Rostovtzeff, "Two Homeric Bowls in the Louvre," *Am. Journ. Arch.*, XLI, 1937, p. 90 and figs. 3-4.

[28] C. H. Smith, *Catalogue of the Greek and Etruscan Vases in the British Museum*, III, London 1896, p. 62, no. E36 and pl. II.

manner. A reflection of this kind of illustration is indeed preserved in a Roman mosaic from Salzburg (figs. 14a-d)[29] in which the Ariadne episode alone is rendered in four consecutive scenes: (1) Ariadne gives Theseus a clue to find the way through the labyrinth; (2) Theseus battles with the Minotaur; (3) Theseus and Ariadne board a ship; and (4) Ariadne finds herself forsaken. The earlier series of the Deeds of Heracles and Theseus can at best be defined as the rudimentary stage of the cyclic method,[30] and are therefore only seemingly exceptions to the statement that the cyclic method is no older than the Hellenistic period. The way in which iconographic expansion occurs in both sets of Deeds after the third century B.C. is further confirmation of the Hellenistic origin of the new method.

In order to illustrate a certain text, whether an epic poem or a drama, to the fullest extent, the cyclic method requires a very considerable number of scenes. One has only to imagine the whole twenty-second book of the Odyssey illustrated on the same scale as the Homeric bowls described above (p. 18), each of which covers only a small portion of the text, to realize that in most media of classical art the amount of space required was not available. Therefore most artists had to confine themselves to an excerpt of a larger picture cycle, which could be obtained in two ways.

In the first the artist, preserving the original sequence of scenes, copied only a *section of a full cycle*. Such is the case in the Odyssey cups (figs. 6-7), in each of which only seventy to eighty verses of the twenty-second book were illustrated. If the artist wanted to represent more scenes of the same book, he had to copy more sections in the same manner and to distribute them over similar cups. But this system was unsatisfactory if the artist wanted to include on a single monument both the beginning and the end of the story. In this second case he had to make a selection on the basis of those scenes which he considered more important or more easily understandable to the beholder. Such a selection of scenes out of a larger context might be called an *epitomized cycle*.

On most of the Roman frieze sarcophagi, for instance, the available surface was not large enough to reproduce a complete cycle, and the sculptors adapted the epitomizing method, as can be demonstrated on a group of sarcophagi with scenes from Euripides' *Iphigenia among the Taurians*. The copy in Munich[31] illustrates on the right short-side (fig. 15c) the recognition of Orestes by Iphigenia, who holds the tablet-shaped letter in her raised hand. This same scene occurs also on the sarcophagi in Weimar (fig. 16)[32]

[29] A. von Salis, *Theseus und Ariadne*, Berlin 1930, p. 18, fig. 14 and pls. I-II.
[30] Robert, *Bild und Lied*, p. 46.
[31] C. Robert, *Die Antiken Sarkophag-Reliefs*, vol. II, p. 177, no. 167 and pl. LVII.
[32] *Ibid.*, vol. II, p. 183, no. 172 and pl. LVIII.

23

and Berlin (fig. 17)[38] on the front-sides at the left and in so similar a compositional arrangement that there can be no doubt that all three sarcophagi hark back to the same iconographic archetype. In reconstructing the archetype from these three sarcophagi, the following series of scenes can be constituted in its original sequence:

(1) The madness of Orestes (v. 260ff.) (fig. 15a in the middle).
(2) Orestes and Pylades brought as prisoners before Iphigenia (v. 467-481) (fig. 16 in the middle).
(3) The farewell of the two friends (v. 657ff.) (fig. 17 in the middle).
(4) The recognition of Orestes by Iphigenia (v. 725ff.) (figs. 15c and abbreviated on 15b; 16 at the left, 17 at the left).
(5) Iphigenia taking the image out of the temple (v. 1056-1088) (fig. 15a at the left).
(6) Iphigenia asks Thoas for permission to go to the seashore (v. 1152ff.) (fig. 17 at the right).
(7) The fight at the seashore (v. 1354ff.) (fig. 15a second scene from the right).
(7a) The pause in the fight (fig. 16, second scene from the right).
(8) Iphigenia boarding the ship (v. 1379ff.) (fig. 16 at the right).
(8a) Orestes retreating to the ship and going on board (fig. 15a at the right).

Altogether there are eight scenes (or ten, counting the subdivided ones), a number apparently too great to be represented on any single sarcophagus. Consequently there must have been a model with a larger cycle which could comprise this number of scenes and which was at the disposal of the sculptors of the sarcophagi. This model, then, was excerpted or *epitomized* by each of the copyists in a different way, which accounts for the variations among the sarcophagi. But that the eight to ten scenes listed above constitute the complete cycle of the assumed model is by no means sure, for the possibility remains either that not all scenes of the model were taken over into the sarcophagi or that some of them were perhaps on sarcophagi now lost.

To condense a model with a fuller cycle the artist has still other means than epitomizing, namely the *conflation* of scenes, as can be demonstrated by two sarcophagi with scenes from Euripides' *Alcestis*. One in Cannes (figs. 18a-c)[34] contains five scenes which do not follow each other in the sequence of the text, but are rearranged in order to distinguish between scenes of greater or lesser importance, placing the former on the front-side and the latter on the two short-sides. Their original sequence is as follows:

[38] *Ibid.*, vol. II, p. 186, no. 177 and pl. LIX. [34] *Ibid.*, vol. III, 1, p. 26, no. 22 and pl. VI.

(1) Admetus tries to persuade his parents to die in his place (v. 15-18) (fig. 18a at the left).

(2) The death of Alcestis (v. 280-390) (fig. 18a in the center).

(3) Alcestis before the gods of the lower world (fig. 18b).

(4) Alcestis brought back to the upper world by Heracles (fig. 18c).[35]

(5) Heracles' farewell to the reunited married couple (v. 1149-1158) (fig. 18a at the right).

A second sarcophagus, now in the Vatican (fig. 19),[36] confines its decoration to the front-side and condenses the whole Alcestis story into two scenes only. The left one represents the death of Alcestis with so many complementary figures that it takes the whole space up to the left corner, so that the scene of the dispute between Admetus and his parents had to be dropped altogether. The scene at the right is made up by a conflation of scenes 3, 4 and 5 of the Cannes sarcophagus. At the corner sit the gods of the lower world, with Pluto stretching his hand out toward Alcestis as on the short-side of the Cannes sarcophagus (fig. 18b). But Alcestis, instead of facing him, turns around and follows Heracles, forming with him a group which corresponds to scene 4 of the former piece (fig. 18c). Furthermore, the same Heracles who leads Alcestis out of the lower world is at the same time stretching his hand out toward Admetus in a farewell gesture (cf. fig. 18a at the right). Thus the right scene of the Vatican sarcophagus, in which the sculptor obviously intended to represent one single situation, actually contains elements of three different actions. In other words, we deal with a case of *simultaneous method*, not in its primitive form with its conflicting moments as on the Polyphemus cup (fig. 1), but resembling more closely the subtle variant as exemplified by the Troilus scene of the François Vase (fig. 2). Just as in the latter one situation changes smoothly into another regardless of the unity of time and place, so in the sarcophagus action and locality gradually shift from Hades to the residence of Admetus. But in spite of the fact that the results are similar, it must be emphasized that the artists of the two monuments proceeded differently: while in the archaic vase the scene is from the very outset conceived in the simultaneous method, the composition of the Vatican sarcophagus is obviously the result of a conflation of several scenes which, like those of the Cannes sarcophagus, were, to begin with, independent iconographic units. Even in this conflation the succession of three different actions is still felt, in distinct contrast to the François Vase where the additional figures at both sides are so intimately related to the center that the impression remains that of a single scene.

[35] As to the relationship of scenes 3-4 to Euripides, cf. *Ibid.*, vol. III, I, p. 25.

[36] *Ibid.*, vol. III, I, p. 31, no. 26 and pl. VII.

There are other sarcophagi where the *conflating method* has been used, though only in rare cases is it possible to dissolve the conflated scenes and to reconstruct the earlier stage in which the various actions were still separated. Hence wherever, after the beginning of the Hellenistic period, the simultaneous method occurs—and not only on sarcophagi—it is not always clear whether the original archaic form has survived or whether, as seems to have happened much more frequently, a conflation as just described has taken place.

Thus far we have dealt with epitomized picture cycles, the full archetype of which corresponds either with a single book of an epos or a single drama. However, there are instances where the copyist selects a few scenes from larger literary units such as a whole epic poem or the complete *œuvre* of one dramatist in order to make up an epitomized cycle, and in its extreme form he may even choose only one scene out of each epic book or drama. A Homeric bowl in Berlin (fig. 20)[37] may demonstrate this point for the epos. Three scenes make up its frieze, each of them taken from a different book of the Iliad:

(1) Book XIX: Achilles urges Agamemnon to let him resume the fight while Odysseus gives the warning (v. 155ff.).

(2) Book XX: Achilles pursues Aeneas, who is saved by Poseidon (v. 318-329).

(3) Book XXI: Achilles' fight against Lycaon near the Scamander (v. 34ff.).

On this scale the sculptor was able to compress the content of the whole Iliad into eight cups, the one in Berlin being the seventh in such a set. If one compares this piece with the earlier Odyssey cups (figs. 6-7), the outer surface of which was occupied by the illustration of only a small section of one book, one can measure the extreme condensation which has taken place.

A similar condensation can be shown for the illustrations of the drama. Along with those bowls on which only a section of a drama found its place, like the two Iphigenia bowls (figs. 9-10), there are others with single scenes from different plays, like the Greco-Bactrian silver bowl which was found in Russia and is now in the Hermitage in Leningrad (figs. 21a-e).[38] It is

[37] C. Robert, "Zwei Homerische Becher," *Jahrb. d. Inst.*, XXXIV, 1919, pp. 65ff. and pl. 5.—K. Bulas, *Les illustrations antiques de l'Iliade*, Lwow 1929, p. 119 and fig. 60.

[38] Я. И. СМИРНОВЪ, Восточное Серебро, S. Petersburg 1909, Atlas, pl. CXIII, no. 284.—M. Rostovtzeff, "Some New Aspects of Iranian Art," *Seminarium Kondakovianum*, VI, 1933, pp. 175ff. and pl. XIII, nos. 1-2 (here explained as illustrations of Iranian history).—К. В. ТРЕВЕР, Памятники Греко-Бактрийского Искусства, Moscow 1940, p. 71, no. 15 and pls. 15-17 (here explained as illustrations of Indian Saga).—K. Weitzmann, "Three 'Bactrian' Silver Vessels with Illustrations from Euripides," *Art Bull.*, XXV, 1943, p. 290 and figs. 1, 5-8.

26

apparently a copy from a Hellenistic model of the same class of silver vessels, of which the Megarian bowls are only cheap replicas in terra cotta. The following Euripidean tragedies are represented:

(1) *The Alcestis* (fig. 21a). Scene A: Admetus tries to lift the chin of his wife who is about to be taken to the lower world by Hermes psychopompus (v. 250ff.). Scene B: Apollo in a worker's tunic behind Admetus, probably illustrating the prologue (v. 8ff.).

(2) *The Alope* (fig. 21b). The two shepherds, with the child Hippothoon between them, arguing before the judge, who is here replaced by an oriental goddess with a cornucopia.

(3) *The Ion*. Scene A (fig. 21c): Ion comes out of the temple of the Delphian Apollo, sings a hymn in honor of the laurel branch (v. 111ff.) and meets the leader of the chorus (v. 226ff.) and his mother Creusa (v. 237ff.). Scene B (fig. 21e): Creusa gives her devoted servant poison with which to get rid of Ion (v. 1029ff.).

(4) *The Bacchae* (fig. 21d). Pentheus angrily reproaches Cadmus and Tiresias, who had just been introduced into the Bacchic rites, and they dance together (v. 248ff.).

In both the Homeric and the Euripidian bowl, the original narrative element, from which the cyclic method had started out and which is its essential quality, has disappeared. Since the Iliad cup with the scenes from Books XIX-XXI is apparently not much later in date than the two Odyssey cups with the section of a full cycle (figs. 6-7), this process of *extreme epitomizing* must have taken place comparatively soon after the invention of the huge picture cycles themselves.

In all instances discussed so far, each pictorial cycle coincided with a certain textual unit. However, not very long after the cyclic method was introduced into the representational arts under the influence of literary narration, artists learned to use this method with increasing independence from the textual units, selecting pictures from various texts and mixing them up. Usually there is a guiding idea behind their selections. When e.g. the maker of a Megarian bowl in Berlin[39] combined a scene from the twenty-fourth book of the Iliad with two scenes from the *Aethiopis* of Arctinus, he must have used two different texts as sources, but as all three scenes center around Achilles, the life of this hero was apparently the basis for their selection. A picture series collected from this viewpoint may be called a *biographical cycle*,[40] i.e. a cycle in which the *bios* of a god or hero was taken as

[39] Robert, *Homerische Becher*, p. 26 and fig. D.
[40] Lehmann-Hartleben, "Two Roman Silver Jugs," *Am. Jour. Arch.*, XLII, 1938, pp. 87ff.— *Idem*, "The *Imagines* of the Elder Philostratus," *Art Bull.*, XXIII, 1941, p. 42.

the dominating theme. But along with those biographical cycles made up from different sources, there existed in all probability others which actually did coincide with a single literary unit, particularly since in the Hellenistic period biography had become an important and influential branch of literature.

Besides the *bios* there are many other leading motifs which an artist could use as a basis for making up a picture cycle of his own, such as abstract ideas of all kinds. To illustrate, for instance, in cyclic form the *power of love*, one of the most popular themes in classical art, a painter could easily find any number of mythological scenes and join them in a cycle. The variations in the selection of the scenes are, of course, unlimited, as each painter may either freely select all his examples from a single literary source or make his individual choice from several.

The former case can be demonstrated by a floor mosaic in Antioch[41] which consists of five panels illustrating Aphrodite's destructive power of inciting mad love. All examples are chosen from Euripides:

(1) *The Hippolytus*. The chaste hero is repudiating Phaedra's love-proposal (v. 601ff.).
(2) *The Meleager*. The fight between the hero and his uncles over the allotment of the bearskin to Atalanta.
(3) *The Stheneboea*. Bellerophon is repudiating Stheneboea's advances.
(4) *The Troades*. Helen, driven by Aphrodite, is approaching Paris (v. 943ff.).
(5) *The Medea*. The Colchian sorceress appeals to Jason's love for his children (v. 894ff.).

A similar love motif was chosen as the central theme by the painter who decorated the "Room of Aphrodite" which Lehmann-Hartleben reconstructed on the basis of the Elder Philostratus' description in his *Imagines*.[42] As the ancient beholder went around the room he saw the following subjects depicted on the walls in fresco:

(1) The procession of Aphrodite.
(2) The death of Hippolytus.
(3) Rhodogoune (or Hippolyte?).
(4) Krithis and Meles.
(5) The suicide of Panthea.
(6) The death of Cassandra.

[41] K. Weitzmann, "Illustrations of Euripides and Homer in the Mosaics of Antioch," *Antioch-on-the-Orontes* III, *The Excavations of 1937-1939*, Princeton 1941, p. 233, pls. 66-68.

[42] *Art Bull.*, XXIII, 1941, pp. 31ff. Lehmann-Hartleben fittingly called this kind of combination a *moralizing combination of mythological scenes*.

In this instance, however, a single literary source which might have contained all six subjects together has not been identified, and most likely never existed. With all probability the set of frescoes decorating the Room of Aphrodite is an instance of a painter choosing his examples at random from *various* sources. From the merely literary angle, one may well consider this program a thorough disintegration of the cyclic method.

So much for the cyclic method as far as its relation to literature is concerned. There is also a purely formal problem involved that deals with the distribution of scenes or with what might be called their *physical relation*, for which classical art had found different solutions.

The simplest and most frequently applied system lines up the scenes of a cycle in frieze form, so that all figures share with each other a common groundline. This is obviously the most convenient arrangement with regard to a beholder, who, unassisted by a text, likes to read a story in picture language. His eye glides smoothly from one scene to the next, and he is enabled to measure easily the progress of action which reveals itself in each consecutive picture. A series of pictures could be lined up in frieze form in various ways:

(a) Scene may follow scene without any intersecting motifs either to divide or connect. The beholder, on whose knowledge of the underlying text the artist counts, is supposed to find out by himself where one scene ends and the next starts. Only partially is he aided by the artist, who frequently turns the backs of two figures toward each other in order to mark the end and the beginning of two consecutive scenes. This system is most frequently applied on the Homeric bowls and on the sarcophagi (figs. 6-7, 9-10, 12, 15-21).

(b) The artist may surround each single scene by a frame of its own and thus separate it from the next, as is the case in the bronze reliefs of the Palazzo dei Conservatori which cover a triumphal chariot known as the Tensa Capitolina (fig. 22).[48] Each of its twelve scenes from the life of Achilles (his riding on Chiron's back and hunting a bear, his sojourn at the court of Lycomedes, his discovery by Odysseus, and other events from his birth to his death which constitute one of the biographical cycles we discussed above) is placed separately under an aedicula of its own, in such a way that one column supports two adjacent gables. In this manner the picture cycle is subjugated to a strong architectural system which tends to isolate the pictures within a unifying structure.

(c) The artist tries to interrelate instead of divide the scenes. Wherever possible he connects them with each other by common background features,

[48] F. Staehlin, "Die Thensa Capitolina," *Röm. Mitt.*, XXI, 1906, pp. 335ff.—H. Stuart Jones, *Catalogue of the Sculptures of the Palazzo dei Conservatori*, Oxford 1926, pp. 179ff. and pls. 68-73.

thus dissolving somewhat the unity of space with regard to each individual picture but at the same time unifying the frieze as a whole. One of the earliest monuments which shows this interrelation in an initial stage, is the well-known Telephus Frieze of Pergamon, from the beginning of the second century B.C. The example chosen for illustration represents an assembly of seated heroes, the one at the right being Telephus who shows his wound (fig. 23).[44] The scene is framed by two pilasters, the right one being more clearly visible. This pilaster serves as an intersection-motif separating as well as uniting the central scene from the right one, of which only a part of a bending figure is preserved, identified by Robert as Achilles in a scene with the Healing of Telephus,[45] while Schrader does not propose any name.[46] In addition the sculptor uses still other means to create a formal connection between these two neighboring scenes: in front of the pilaster he places a servant facing the beholder and carrying a fruit bowl in his hands. The artistic function of this figure is to smooth the sharp division created by the pilaster as well as by the turning of the two backs to each other; but although from a purely formal viewpoint the figure links two scenes, he belongs iconographically exclusively to the left one, toward which he takes a slight turn. These and other devices of a great variety occur throughout classical and mediaeval art, wherever an artist has to relate successive scenes by connecting features.

A second system of arranging the pictures of a cycle is by distributing them in a decorative system, where they become subordinated to an ornamental pattern. Here the possibilities of distributing the scenes are just as manifold as there are variations of ornamental schemes. In this category belongs the Antioch mosaic with the five panels illustrating Euripidean tragedies (p. 28): the Medea scene occupies the center and the other four are grouped around it in the form of a cross so that each picture changes the orientation of the groundline, forcing the beholder to walk around in a circle. In the Theseus mosaic from Salzburg (p. 23)[47] the panels, though preserving the orientation in one direction, are widely scattered and separated by large areas of ornamental patterns, so that some iconographic knowledge on the part of the spectator is required to find the beginning of the cycle and the direction the eye has to follow in order to read the story coherently, starting at the left, turning to the center, moving upward and

[44] H. Winnefeld, *Die Friese des Grossen Altars* (Altertümer von Pergamon, vol. III, 2), Berlin 1910, p. 188 and pl. XXXIII, no. 3.

[45] Robert, "Beiträge zur Erklärung des Pergamenischen Telephosfrieses," *Jahrb. d. Inst.*, II, 1887, p. 250.

[46] Schrader, "Die Anordnung und Deutung des Pergamenischen Telephosfrieses," *Jahrb. d. Inst.*, XV, 1900, p. 117.

[47] A. von Salis, *Theseus und Ariadne*, fig. 14.

ending at the right. From the cyclic viewpoint such decorative arrangements mean an encroachment upon the legibility of the literary content.

A third way of distributing the pictures of a cycle can be seen in the few classical manuscripts we possess, such as the Iliad in Milan (figs. 32-34, 159, 160, 168, 176) or the Aeneid in the Vatican (figs. 91, 144) and in the numerous mediaeval manuscripts which are copies of classical models (figs. 56-60). Though we will deal later on with this problem at great length this much can be said with regard to the most general principle of distribution of miniatures: the control over their disposition has passed from the artist into the hands of the scribe. In writing a text the scribe leaves an open space in the column wherever he wants to have a picture inserted. His chief concern is the close physical connection of the miniature with the particular passage it illustrates. The result is usually a very irregular spacing of the pictures, leaving the painter no chance to relate them formally to each other. But at the same time this method offers an advantage to the reader who wants to enjoy text and picture at the same time, conceiving them as a unity in which the written word is supplemented by the picture and vice versa.

The fourth and last step in the formal development of the picture cycle leads to its complete disintegration, i.e. to a stage in which each scene becomes isolated and is represented on a separate object. This means a falling back into the *monoscenic* method, at least in its material form. But whereas in the genuine monoscenic method each picture is conceived as a compositional and iconographic entity, the scene which is isolated out of a cycle still remains at least in content a part of a larger iconographic context. It is not always easy, and sometimes even impossible, to prove that a scene has been singled out from a larger cycle.

The cyclic origin of an isolated scene may be determined, first, by an iconographic parallel which is still a link in a cycle. For instance, on a lamp handle in the British Museum, Achilles dragging Hector's corpse behind the chariot around the walls of Troy (fig. 24)[48] is depicted in the same iconography as on the Tabulae Iliacae (fig. 25),[49] where it occurs among other representations of the twenty-second book of the Iliad, or as on the Tensa Capitolina, already mentioned, where it is a part of the biographical cycle of episodes from the life of Achilles (fig. 26).[50] In this case one can rightly suspect that the maker of the lamp singled out the scene from a cycle which was either an illustrated Iliad or a biographical series of Achilles episodes.

Secondly, it may be shown that a single scene has been isolated from a

[48] H. B. Walters, *Catalogue of the Greek and Roman Lamps in the British Museum*, London 1914, p. 133, no. 876 and fig. 171.—K. Bulas, *op. cit.*, p. 93 and fig. 43.

[49] Jahn, *op. cit.*, pl. I, no. A.

[50] Stuart Jones, *Cat. Pal. Conserv.*, pl. 73 B.—F. Staehlin, *op. cit.*, p. 347, fig. 5.

cycle by searching in the same class of monuments for more scenes which may go back to the same cyclic model. There are, for instance, several Etruscan urns, each of which depicts a different phase of the Polyphemus adventure according to Book IX of the Odyssey. Placed side by side (figs. 27-29) they clearly form a *section* or an *epitome* of a cycle, with scenes as follows:

(1) Florence, Museo Archeologico (fig. 27):[51] Odysseus presents a winecup to Polyphemus in order to make him drunk (v. 345ff.).

(2) Volterra, Museo Guarnacci (fig. 28).[52] The blinding of Polyphemus (v. 382ff.).

(3) Leyden, Rijksmuseum van Oudheden (fig. 29):[53] Polyphemus throws a rock after Odysseus and his companions, who escape in their boat (v. 474ff.).

This example suggests that the Etruscan sculptors already used coherent picture cycles as models, like their successors, the sculptors of the Roman sarcophagi. But while the latter had a more extended surface at their disposal, where they could place several scenes side by side, the makers of the urns had only space for one iconographic unit,[54] and therefore had to distribute the various scenes over a greater number of objects. It is quite possible that even more scenes of the Polyphemus adventure were copied on urns now lost. The first two scenes just described (figs. 27-28) follow each other very closely in the text of the Odyssey, with less than forty verses in between, while the third is farther removed.

The splitting up a cycle over a number of isolated objects is by no means confined to Etruscan urns but, dated as far back as the third century B.C., they are one of the earliest examples. Cycles were dissolved in much the same way at various times and in different media, and there may be mentioned, by way of example, a set of nine silver plates which belong to the sixth or seventh century A.D. and were discovered in Cyprus. Six of them are now in the Metropolitan Museum in New York,[55] while three are still in Nicosia on Cyprus,[56] and each of them contains one scene from the life of David, with

[51] E. Brunn, *I rilievi delle urne etrusche*, vol. I, Rome 1870, p. 114 and pl. LXXXVI, no. 2.—F. Müller, *Odyssee-Illustrationen*, p. 17.

[52] Brunn, *op. cit.*, vol. I, p. 115 and pl. LXXXVII, no. 3.—Müller, *op. cit.*, p. 10.

[53] Brunn, *op. cit.*, vol. I, p. 116 and pl. LXXXVII, no. 4.—Müller, *op. cit.*, p. 30.

[54] This is the general rule, though there are a few cases where at least two scenes occur on one urn. Robert, *Hermeneutik*, pp. 288ff. and figs. 218-219.

[55] O. M. Dalton, "Byzantine Plate and Jewellery from Cyprus in Mr. Morgan's Collection," *Burl. Mag.*, x, 1906-7, pp. 355ff. and pls. I-II.—M. Rosenberg, *Der Goldschmiede Merkzeichen*, vol. IV, 3rd ed., Berlin 1928, pp. 636-647.

[56] O. M. Dalton, "A Second Silver Treasure from Cyprus," *Archaeologia*, LX, pt. 1, 1906, pl. II and figs. 4a-b.—Rosenberg, *op. cit.*, pp. 648-653.

the exception of one larger plate which has three consecutive scenes with the fight between David and Goliath as its center.[57] This David fight corresponds iconographically so closely to the same scene in the well-known Psalter manuscript in Paris, cod. gr. 139,[58] that there remains little doubt that the silversmith drew upon a miniature cycle similar to, but of an earlier date than, that of the Paris manuscript. He adapted his model so that each plate would correspond to a miniature, with the one exception where he compressed the iconography of three miniatures onto one big plate. We are fortunate in having this large set of plates, for if only one of them had been preserved, the cyclic implications might very well have been obscured and difficult to prove.

These silver plates are only one example showing that the various relations between picture cycles and textual units, as well as the formal principles of cyclic representations which we demonstrated on Hellenistic and Roman material, are equally applicable to all phases and media of the mediaeval period.

B. A CRITICISM OF WICKHOFF'S TERMINOLOGY

The distinction of the three methods, which we termed the *simultaneous*, the *monoscenic* and the *cyclic*, is based, we repeat, chiefly on those documents and observations which Carl Robert had used in his early study *Bild und Lied*. We have also previously referred to the fact that Franz Wickhoff, too, dealt with the problem of the three methods by which a literary content can be expressed by pictorial means, and that he introduced a terminology which became very familiar to the student of late classical and mediaeval art. Our reasons for not adopting Wickhoff's terms are given here:

For the first method, which we called *simultaneous*, Wickhoff introduced the term *complementary*[1] and he chose for illustration the same Troilus scene (fig. 2) which Robert had already analysed as a paradigm for the same purpose. The identical choice must be considered as accidental, since Wickhoff gives no indication that he knew of Robert's basic study in which the latter, fourteen years before Wickhoff's book on the Vienna Genesis appeared, had made fundamentally the same distinctions. With the term *complementary* (= the German "completirend") Wickhoff characterizes a method which complements the representation of one action by features of other actions, which precede or follow it, without repeating any of its participants. However, the general meaning of the word *complementary* does not necessarily

---

[57] Rosenberg, *op. cit.*, pp. 640-641.—H. Buchthal, *The Miniatures of the Paris Psalter*, London 1938, pl. xxi, fig. 44.

[58] H. Omont, *Miniatures des plus anciens manuscrits grecs de la Bibliothèque Nationale*, 2nd ed. Paris 1929, pl. iv.—Buchthal, *op. cit.*, pl. iv.

[1] Fr. Wickhoff, *Die Wiener Genesis*, Vienna 1895, p. 9.

carry with it the connotation that the features completing the nucleus of a scene must be taken from different actions. Any figure added to the nucleus, whether a personification or a god or a servant or other figures of similar categories, can, with good reason, be called complementary. In this broader sense Robert speaks of a "kompletives Verfahren"[2]—a term which means actually the same as complementary method—wherever a figure not called for in the text can be shown as an addition to the original composition. Thus one is confronted with a twofold and conflicting usage of the word complementary, Robert's application of it being broader, Wickhoff's more limited. To avoid ambiguity and at the same time to find a term which implies as its chief characteristics the coincidence of various actions, we have chosen the word *simultaneous*.

The second method which we named *monoscenic*, but which Wickhoff called "distinguirend," is defined by him as "die Art, die ausgezeichnete Scenen einzeln bringt." He wanted his term to have a double connotation, first that the artist had chosen the distinguishing or, as he says elsewhere, "den entscheidenden, prägnanten oder epochemachenden" moment, and secondly that he represented this moment as a single composition of its own without relation to other scenes. Obviously the painter of the classical period who wanted to represent an epic or dramatic episode by one single composition, usually selected the most decisive moment, but so did the archaic artist in his way, only with the difference that he grouped additional features around a nucleus representing the decisive moment. The term *isolated* which was used in the English translation for "distinguirend" leans closer to the second connotation, that a picture in the new method is supposed to depict one single action and is an artistic unit in itself. At the same time the term *isolating* conveys Wickhoff's notion of the origin of the new method. He assumed a process by which a picture of the earlier archaic manner becomes dissolved into single scenes, the most significant of which was then chosen by the artist of the new method.[3] Theoretically speaking, such isolation from a more complicated archaic model can be accomplished in two ways. Either the copyist strips off all the complementary elements that conflict with the new principle of unity of time and place, thus abbreviating his model, or he may dissolve it by painting as many independent units as there are actions conflated in the model. For instance, if the actions in the Spartan cup (fig. 1) were to be dissolved, there would remain a series of three separated pictures. Both types may, of course, have occurred, but if so they were not very

[2] *Hermeneutik*, p. 142 and *passim*.
[3] *Ibid.*, p. 9: "Es ist leicht einzusehen, wie jenes Vielerlei der Handlung, das uns die completirende Erzählungsweise in einem Rahmen bringt, bei weiterer Ausbildung der Kunst in einzelne Scenen auseinander fällt, von denen nur die ausgezeichneten Momente weiter zur Darstellung kommen. . . ."

34

common, and the historical evidence is against this evolutionary theory. The century of Polygnotus invented mostly new compositions which have no iconographic or formal forerunners in archaic art, except, perhaps, for single figure types which were taken over and used for new compositional arrangements. The connotation of distinguishing an important moment is, in our opinion, not a sufficient differentiation from the first method and, at the same time, the idea of isolating suggests an evolution which does not seem to be supported by historical evidence. Therefore we have chosen the term *monoscenic* as coming closer to Robert's notion of the essential quality of the second method.

The third way of representing a literary text by pictorial means was called by Wickhoff the *continuous method* (= "continuirende Darstellungsweise") by which he meant an uninterrupted sequence of scenes in frieze form. This term, which is very suitable indeed for a certain kind of rendering of consecutive scenes coherently, is, however, in our opinion not comprehensive enough to circumscribe the innovation which had taken place in the Hellenistic period with regard to the transformation of a text into pictorial form. Within the limits of what we call the *cyclic method*, the continuous one, as we tried to make clear, is only one out of several different formal possibilities in the arrangement of pictures of a cycle. Therefore the term *cyclic* is not meant to be a substitution for *continuous*, but a wider and more general term, to which the latter is subordinated as a special case.

According to Wickhoff the most characteristic examples of what he called the continuous method are the Roman sarcophagi. He demonstrates the new principle with an Endymion-Selene sarcophagus and with the first miniature of the Vienna Genesis, showing the expulsion of Adam and Eve from paradise, where three scenes are fused with each other by a common landscape. Later in his book when he deals with the Trajan Column,[4] he makes it a preliminary condition of his *continuous* method that consecutive scenes should be connected by common landscape features. Thus he narrows his term once more by applying it only to one of the three possibilities of frieze arrangement mentioned above, namely the one with intersection motifs for which we cited the Telephus Frieze as the earliest existing example (fig. 23).

Moreover, Wickhoff tried to prove that his continuous method is a Roman invention, the earliest existing examples of which are, in his opinion, the sarcophagi of the second century A.D., and he goes so far as to state that this method would have been impossible at the time of Alexander and still in the period of Augustus.[5] Though knowing the Homeric bowls, the Telephus Frieze and other classical monuments preceding in date the sarcophagi, Wickhoff simply classified them as pseudo-continuous.[6] That the new method

[4] *Ibid.*, pp. 59ff.   [5] *Ibid.*, p. 89.   [6] *Ibid.*, p. 9 and also 81.

did actually start in the period of Alexander and not as late as the Roman sarcophagi had already been fully realized by Robert, and it remains once more to be regretted that his *Bild und Lied* escaped the attention of the Viennese scholar. Wickhoff's belief in the later origin of his continuous method arose from two preconceived ideas: first, the purely emotional argument that after all the Romans also were a creative people and therefore something must be left to their inventiveness; and secondly, the assumption that the continuous method is inseparable from the illusionistic style and that neither of these two elements, which are essential for the origin and the development of the Roman empire style, could have been started without the other. Without going here into an investigation of the origin of illusionism it must be pointed out that, from the mere methodological point of view, the formal arrangements of the scenes, on the one hand, and the stylistic treatment of a picture, on the other, belong to different categories that, though related, are not necessarily so dependent on each other that the origin of the one must be tied up with that of the other.

Robert, as usual not using fixed terms, occasionally applied to a connected sequence of pictures the phrase *Chroniken-Stil* (= the chronicle method).[7] This is an apparent adaptation of the title of Otto Jahn's book *Griechische Bilderchroniken*, the basic study of the picture cycles of the Tabulae Iliacae. We have not adopted Robert's phrase because the word "chronicle" is generally confined to books of strictly historical writings, while the term "cyclic" includes picture cycles of any illustrated text, not only an epos or a drama, but also a novel, a didactic poem or a scientific treatise.

Though Robert places the beginning of the cyclic method, as far as Greek art is concerned, in the early Hellenistic period, he nevertheless does not consider the method, as such, to be a Greek invention. He recognizes it already in ancient Oriental art, as e.g. in a Phoenician silver plate of the seventh century B.C. found in Praeneste,[8] where on the outermost frieze the adventures of a king are told in a method in principle like that applied in the Homeric bowls. So it is apparently not fortuitous that the cyclic method appears in Greek art at the very moment when the latter expanded at the time of Alexander and entered a new and fruitful exchange of cultural relations with the countries of the ancient Orient.

[7] *Bild und Lied*, p. 17 note 12, p. 47 and elsewhere.
[8] *Monumenti inediti*, vol. x, Rome 1874-78, pl. 31, no. 1.—Robert, *Bild und Lied*, p. 17, notes 12, 47; *Hermeneutik*, p. 101 and fig. 84.—Wickhoff, *op. cit.*, p. 9, note 1.—For a replica in the Metropolitan Museum, New York, see A. Marquand, "A Silver Patera from Kourion," *Am. Journ. Arch.*, III, 1887, pp. 322ff. and pl. xxx.—C. D. Curtis, "The Bernardini Tomb," *Mem. Amer. Acad. Rome*, III, 1919, pp. 38ff. and pls. 20-21 (here further bibliography).

36

C. THE MANUSCRIPT AS THE PRIMARY MEDIUM OF THE CYCLIC METHOD

In our analysis of the characteristics and variations of the cyclic method we found no single monument with a complete picture cycle comprising a whole epos or drama in a close sequence of scenes. There were either *sections of a cycle* as in some of the Homeric bowls, or *epitomized cycles* as in the sarcophagi and most of the Iliac tablets. However, in a few cases, some fairly accurate calculations can be made as to the original extent of a full cycle. For this purpose the *sections* of a cycle, where the original density of scenes is intact, at least over a certain length, are more reliable than the *epitomized cycle*, where one cannot be sure about the ratio between the preserved and the dropped scenes.

The best evidence can be obtained from the Homeric bowls. The first of the two Odyssey cups in Berlin (fig. 6) comprises the following three scenes of the twenty-second book as already mentioned (p. 18):

(1) Eumaeus and Philoetius fettering the goatherd Melanthius (v. 161ff.).
(2) Melanthius hanged by Eumaeus and Philoetius (v. 192ff.).
(3) Athena inciting Odysseus and Telemachus (v. 205-235).

The text for these scenes covers about seventy-five verses. The second cup (fig. 7) likewise contains three scenes from the same book, so that we are now in a position to decide whether the spacing in the first cup is arbitrary or can be considered as a norm for an illustrated Odyssey. This second cup illustrates the following scenes (p. 19):

(1) The killing of the seer Leiodes by Odysseus (v. 310ff.).
(2) The pardoning of the minstrel Phemius (v. 330ff.).
(3) The pardoning of the herald Medon (v. 361-*ca.* 380).

Here again three consecutive scenes illustrate altogether about seventy verses, so we may conclude that this is indeed the norm. Further support for this calculation can be seen in the fact that between the two cups there is a lacuna, comprising verses 235-310, i.e. again seventy-five verses which, probably, were also illustrated by three scenes on a cup now lost. If the whole twenty-second book were to be divided up on the same scale, one would have to assume two more cups preceding the one with the Melanthius adventure which would illustrate verses 1-160, and two more after the second cup with the pardoning of Medon illustrating the rest of the book, i.e. verses 380-500. Thus seven cups in all would be needed to illustrate the twenty-second book alone:

Cup I, illustrating verses 1-*ca.* 80 (lost).
Cup II, illustrating verses *ca.* 80-160 (lost).

37

Cup III, illustrating verses 161-235 (preserved).
Cup IV, illustrating verses 236-310 (lost).
Cup V, illustrating verses 311-380 (preserved).
Cup VI, illustrating verses 381-*ca.* 440 (lost).
Cup VII, illustrating verses *ca.* 440-500 (lost).

Naturally one cannot be too sure that each cup had precisely three scenes, since there are cups preserved with only one or two and others with even four or five scenes, though the norm seems to be about three. Therefore a fair estimate of the total number of scenes would be between twenty and twenty-five for one single book of the epos. Moreover, we have good reason to assume also that other books of the Odyssey were illustrated on a similar scale. A fragment of a bowl from Thebes e.g.[1] shows two consecutive Telemachus scenes that again can only be considered as a section out of a large series of illustrations from the first book. On this scale all twenty-four books together would require about 168 cups in order to illustrate the Odyssey by roughly five hundred scenes. Assuming the same amount of scenes for the Iliad, which also was illustrated on the cups as surviving copies prove, one is faced with the astonishing number of about a thousand scenes for the two Homeric poems. This estimate of five hundred pictures for the Iliad seems even conservative since the average number of verses for each book is about six hundred and fifty instead of five hundred in the Odyssey. Whether there actually existed a set of more than three hundred cups on which both Homeric poems were fully illustrated, is quite doubtful. Rather, the impression is that another medium is behind the cups, in which a cycle did not need to be broken up into triads of scenes, but where at least the scenes of a single book were kept united in one and the same monument. This leads to the assumption of models which the terra cotta workers transferred into their own medium, not completely, but by choosing only such sections as seemed most interesting and suitable to them.

If, to the reader, the estimate of five hundred scenes for the illustration of each Homeric poem seems exaggerated, the Tabulae Iliacae may be analysed from the same point of view. The best preserved, though incomplete, is the tablet in the Museo Capitolino[2] which, besides illustrating other epic poems of the Trojan war, gives the greatest amount of space to the Iliad. Organized like a triptych, each wing originally was filled with twelve strips of scenes from the Iliad, but only the right wing with the illustrations to Books

---

[1] Arvanitopoulos, Μεγαρικοὶ σκύφοι Φθιωτίδων Θηβῶν, Ἐφ. Ἀρχ., 1910, pp. 81ff. and pl. II, no. 3.—Robert, *Hermeneutik*, p. 366 and fig. 279.

[2] Jahn, *Griechische Bilderchroniken*, pp. 2ff. and pl. I, no. A.—U. Mancuso, *La "Tabula Iliaca" del Museo Capitolino* (Atti della R. Accad. dei Lincei, Memorie della classe di scienze morali, ser. V, XIV), Rome 1909, pp. 662ff.

XIII-XXIV is preserved. However, the uppermost strip of the lost left wing which contained the beginning of the first book extends across the whole width of the central panel (fig. 31) so that this book is more extensively illustrated than any other and thus particularly fitted for a calculation. For the missing first scene another tablet, now in the Bibliothèque Nationale in Paris, which is a fragment of a repetition of the Museo Capitolino tablet, can be substituted (fig. 30).[3] Altogether there are seven scenes for the first book, as against an average of two or three for each of the others. They represent the following episodes:

(1) Chryses kneeling before Agamemnon, while the Achaeans unload the ransom from the cart (v. 22ff.).

(2) Chryses praying before the temple of Apollo Smintheus (v. 34ff.).

(3) Apollo, revenging Chryses, is killing the Achaeans (v. 43-52).

(4) Calchas speaking in the assembly (v. 74ff.) (Only the figure of the seer is left of this scene).[4]

(5) The meeting of the Achaeans in which Achilles draws his sword against Agamemnon (v. 197ff.).

(6) Odysseus bringing Chryseis to Chryses (v. 497ff.).

(7) Thetis kneeling before Zeus. (v. 500).

It is of particular importance how these seven scenes are spaced: scenes 1, 2, 3 and 4 illustrate at short intervals no more than seventy-five verses altogether, while 5, 6 and 7 are widely scattered over the rest of the book. In other words, while the first half of the frieze is a *section of a cycle*, the other half is an *epitome* of it. This reveals clearly the conditions under which the sculptor worked: he apparently had a full cycle as model, which he started out to copy in its original density, but when he realized that there was not space enough to continue on the same scale, he changed the system and filled the rest of the frieze with selected scenes. So here again a fuller model obviously stands behind the tablet and its full extent can only be judged from the first four scenes, covering the first seventy-five verses. With this as the norm, the whole first book with its more than six hundred verses must have had about thirty scenes. On this scale one would have to assume for the whole Iliad, in which the average number of verses is well above six hundred for each book, a cycle of more than seven hundred scenes, i.e. even more than we calculated for the model behind the Homeric cups. Such calculations have, of course, only a relative value, as hardly needs to be pointed out, as there is no guarantee that the sequence of scenes maintained through-

---

[3] Jahn, *op. cit.*, pp. 4ff. and pl. III, no. c.

[4] The copyist connected him with the preceding scene, to which he does not belong.

out the rest of the poem the same degree of density as at the beginning of the first book.

In other Iliac tablets the sculptor did not even attempt to compress the content of a whole epic book into the frieze, but he confined himself, like the manufacturers of single terra cotta cups, to a mere *section* of one book. The Rondanini tablet e.g. (fig. 8) shows the following three scenes from Book x of the Odyssey:

(1) Hermes gives Odysseus the moly (v. 278ff.).
(2) Odysseus threatens Circe (v. 314ff.).
(3) Odysseus meets the metamorphosed companions (v. 388ff.).

Here the intervals are a little wider than in the previous example. This might suggest that the former estimate was, perhaps, a little too high, though one could also argue vice versa, that the spacing in the Rondanini tablet is the result of an abbreviation and that one or more scenes in between had been dropped. Whatever the number of scenes actually may have been, there can hardly be any doubt that for each of the Homeric poems it went well into the hundreds. It is equally clear that such a stupendous cycle was not invented either by the manufacturers of the Homeric bowls or the makers of the Iliac tablets, not to speak of the sculptors of the sarcophagi, where the cycles are so far epitomized that they no longer provide a basis for similar calculations. What medium, then, actually could comprehend the enormous amount of scenes of a fully illustrated Homer and at the same time easily be available to the copyists of very disparate branches of art? In our opinion the only medium which can fulfill both requirements is the *illustrated papyrus roll.*

In no other medium could the full text and the full picture cycle be brought together in a complete unity. Here a painter could, under the immediate stimulation of the text, most easily transform the content of each consecutive passage into a picture, and place it at the proper place between the lines of writing. Such an arrangement gives the reader the perfect control for appreciating how closely the painter's invention conforms to the text. If, therefore, the papyrus roll can be considered as the ideal medium for the painter to develop his narrative and illustrative talents and at the same time as the only medium which could physically provide the space for the nearly unlimited number of single scenes, then it seems only logical to conclude that the *cyclic method* itself is not only appropriate for the papyrus roll, but actually was invented for it. Consequently we assume that the Homeric bowls, the Tabulae Iliacae, the sarcophagi and all those monuments which show the genuine cyclic method are, as far as their iconography is concerned, derivatives of illustrated papyrus rolls.[5] And from the fact

[5] Pfuhl, *Malerei und Zeichnung*, I, p. 50.

that the cyclic method appears for the first time in the Homeric bowls which date in the third century B.C. we can now draw the further conclusion that the illustration of papyrus rolls must have begun at the beginning of the Hellenistic period.

Besides this internal evidence, other features in the cups and the tablets strongly support their derivation from illustrated rolls. In the two Odyssey cups (figs. 6-7) the artist is not satisfied with adding inscriptions to his figures, a means of identification common since archaic times, but he fills the background with quite a few verses from the poem itself. This goes far beyond a mere hermeneutical necessity and is a most direct indication that the artist had an actual roll before his eyes when he manufactured the cup. It reflects the state of mind of a copyist who has no desire to dissolve the close union of text and picture which he saw in the model.

Where only the names of the acting persons are inscribed, the artist adds sometimes the title of the book, in order to make it plain to the beholder which text he had used. The Iphigenia cup in Berlin (fig. 10) bears the title: ΕΥΡΙΠΙΔΟΥ ΙΦΙΓΕΝΕΙΑΣ; and a damaged inscription of another cup can be restored: ΕΚ ΤΩΝ ΝΟΣΤΩΝ ΑΧΑΙΩΝ ΚΑΤΑ ΤΟΝ ΠΟΙΗΤΗΝ ΑΓΙΑΝ.[6] A similar usage occurs on the Iliac tablets, of which the one in the Museo Capitolino (p. 38) has no less than four book titles:

ΙΛΙΟΥ ΠΕΡΣΙΣ ΚΑΤΑ ΣΤΗΣΙΧΟΡΟΝ ΤΡΩΙΚΟΣ
ΙΛΙΑΣ ΚΑΤΑ ΟΜΗΡΟΝ
ΑΙΘΙΟΠΙΣ ΚΑΤΑ ΑΡΚΤΙΝΟΝ ΤΟΝ ΜΙΛΗΣΙΟΝ
ΙΛΙΑΣ Η ΜΙΚΡΑ ΛΕΓΟΜΕΝΗ ΚΑΤΑ ΛΕΣΧΗΝ ΠΥΡΡΑΙΟΝ

The organization of this tablet by subdividing it into smaller framed areas shows very clearly that the sculptor wanted to make the pictorial cycles coincide with the literary units. This enables the reader of the pictorial narration to re-establish quickly the connection of each cycle with its basic text, of which the sculptor could place only a résumé upon the dividing pilasters.

Shortly after the invention of illustrated papyrus rolls this new branch of painting must have had a widespread influence, judging from the reflections in so many different media. This powerful influence was with all probability not due to the artistic quality of the illustrated papyrus rolls, because the perishableness of the material makes it unlikely that great artists were employed in their illustration, a fact which may also explain why the references in ancient literary sources to book illustration are comparatively meager, though they are by no means lacking. Pliny's remark about the huge portrait cycles in Varro's *Hebdomades* (*N.H.* xxxv, 11) and their wide diffusion fits very well into the concept of book illumination on a large scale in

---

[6] Robert, *Jahrb. d. Inst.*, XXXIV, 1919, p. 72.

classical antiquity. The real importance of the illustrated rolls lies in the vast expansion of iconographic subject matter since the illuminator's primary task was the transformation of an immense number of hitherto unillustrated literary passages into pictorial form. Illustrated rolls became the iconographic storehouse for many other media and this particular role is not only maintained but even greatly expanded in the Middle Ages, notwithstanding the fact that in the classical as well as in the mediaeval period the derived media often surpassed their manuscript models in technical perfection and refinement.

The most direct evidence, however, for the existence of illustrated Homer rolls is provided by their copy in a late classical manuscript. Here we have the advantage of remaining within the limits of the same branch of art, though material and shape had in the meantime changed from papyrus to vellum and from roll to codex. This manuscript, in all probability the earliest illustrated one in existence, is the well-known Iliad codex in Milan, cod. Ambros. F. 205. inf, the date of which vacillates in the mind of scholars between the third and fifth century A.D.[7] This very fragmentary codex contains in its present state fifty-eight miniatures, which are distributed very irregularly among the books of the Iliad. Pictures to Books XVIII, XIX and XX are lacking entirely, while Book I alone is represented by as many as ten pictures. If this is the norm, there must have been 240 pictures in the original codex. Several factors show this estimate, which Ceriani and Ratti made in their facsimile edition,[8] to be too conservative. There are five lacunae in the first book, which the editors[9] assumed to equal one folio each, with the exception of the first larger lacuna for which they assumed two folios as missing. Their reconstruction was based on the calculation that each lacuna contained originally pages filled exclusively with text. But it is also possible that one or another lacuna might have contained pages with an equal distribution of text and pictures which required twice as much space,[10] and therefore the number of framed pictures for Book I may originally have been somewhat larger than at the present. Furthermore, the first miniature (fig. 32) includes four different scenes held together only by a common outer frame, but otherwise as little connected with each other as the scenes on the Megarian bowls and the Iliac tablets. These four scenes represent:

[7] Angelo Mai, *Iliadis Fragmenta Antiquissima cum picturis item Scholia Vetera ad Odysseam*, Milan 1819.—*Idem, Homeri Iliados Picturae Antiquae ex codice Mediolanensi Bibliothecae Ambrosianae*, Rome 1835.—Ant. M. Ceriani et Ach. Ratti, *Homeri Iliadis pictae fragmenta Ambrosiana*, Milan 1905.—Bethe, *Buch und Bild*, p. 75 and fig. 46.

[8] *Ibid.*, p. 8.

[9] *Ibid.*, p. 7.

[10] Fol. 26ʳ and 26ᵛ with the *Picturae* XXVIII and XXIX give an example of such an arrangement.

(1) Chryses praying before the temple of Apollo Smintheus (v. 34ff.).
(2) Apollo, revenging Chryses, is killing the Achaeans (v. 43ff.).
(3) The burning of the pyres of the dead (v. 52ff.).
(4) Calchas speaking in the assembly (v. 74ff.).

However, the crowding of so many scenes into one frame is not maintained throughout the manuscript and is rather an exception. The next picture (fig. 33) has only one scene, in which Achilles, enraged at Agamemnon, draws his sword (v. 197ff.), whereas *Pictura* III shows two or rather three scenes, namely:

(1) Athena flying to heaven (v. 221ff.).
(2) Achilles throwing down the shaft (v. 245ff.).
(3) Achilles departing with Patroclus (v. 306ff.).

Pictura VIII, representing the arrival of Odysseus and his delivery of Chryseis, and *Pictura* IX, showing Thetis kneeling before Zeus and the discourse of the gods (fig. 34), contain at least two individual scenes in each frame. If one takes into account this point as well as the possibility of lost miniatures, one easily arrives at an estimate of about twenty to twenty-five different scenes for Book I of the Milan Iliad. Assuming an equal number for the other books, the calculation for the whole codex coincides fairly well with that based upon the Homeric bowls and the Iliac tablets.

Yet there is a much closer and more direct connection between the Milan codex and the Iliac tablets. It may be observed that the praying Chryses, the revenge of Apollo and the Calchas speaking in the assembly of the first miniature (fig. 32) are also found in the tablet of the Museo Capitolino (fig. 31). This not only suggests identical intervals of the picture cycle in tabula and codex, but also that the two documents are examples of the same pictorial recension since it is hardly likely that identical situations were chosen independently out of the abundance of changing actions in the text from which miniaturist or sculptor might have chosen different moments. Moreover the following scenes of the tabula, the drawing of the sword by Achilles in the assembly, the delivery of Chryseis to Chryses, Thetis kneeling before Zeus, occur likewise in the Milan codex (*Pict.* II = fig. 33; *Pict.* VIII; *Pict.* IX = fig. 34), and some of these in a quite similar iconography. These comparisons suggest that the tabulae and the Milan codex go back to the same archetype which must have been a manuscript earlier than the first century, i.e. prior to the date of the tablets, and hence must have been a papyrus roll, since the codex was not yet invented. In other words, the Milan codex does not mark the beginning of book illumination, as is generally supposed, but is a late link in the history of Homer illustration, which at the time the Milan codex was made looks back already to a past of more

43

than half a millennium. And in all these centuries the extent of the picture cycle seemingly had changed little, while the miniatures were, of course, subjected to considerable stylistic alterations.

To trace the manifold reflections of ancient book illumination which can be seen in contemporary copies of other media and to enumerate and reconstruct on the basis of such documentary evidences the lost miniature cycles of classical antiquity cannot be attempted in the present study, but we should like to give at least some indication of the vastness of miniature cycles which must have existed in Hellenistic and Roman times. The chief groups of texts which were illustrated, as becomes clear from the examples we have chosen so far, were the epic poems and the drama. It was not accidental that among the epic texts we placed the Homeric poems so much in the foreground, because there is every reason to assume that they were the most frequently illustrated texts in all antiquity, taking the position of a classic as later, in the Middle Ages, the Bible. But a great number of other epic poems were also extensively illustrated. On the Megarian bowls there are scenes from the *Aethiopis* of Arctinus of Miletus[11] and of the *Nostoi* of Agias of Troezen,[12] and on the Iliac tablets are preserved episodes from the *Cypria*, the *Iliupersis* of Stesichorus, the *Little Iliad* of Lesches of Mitylene, and again the *Aethiopis* of Arctinus.[13] The sporadic scenes from these poems on the bowls and the Iliac tablets may be considered as mere accidental remains of large miniature cycles, like those of the Iliad and Odyssey. What is left seems clearly to indicate that practically all poems which belong to the so-called κύκλος ἐπικός had been illustrated in the Hellenistic period. Also epic poems of the Theban myths must have existed with illustrations for which Megarian bowls and Iliac tablets alike provide the evidence,[14] and so were numerous other poems the themes of which centered around the life of Theseus,[15] the deeds of Heracles (fig. 12),[16] and so forth.

Among the dramatic texts the most outstanding ones were apparently the dramas of Euripides and, from the relative profusion of scenes from his plays on the Megarian bowls and other groups of monuments, he seems to have been second only to Homer among the illustrated classics of antiquity. Here again an approximate estimate of the number of scenes illustrating a single drama can be made. We have mentioned already the two bowls with scenes from Euripides' *Iphigenia at Aulis*, each of which contains a section of the cycle with apparently the original spacing of the scenes. In the one

[11] Robert, *Homerische Becher*, p. 26 and fig. D.
[12] Robert, *Jahrb. d. Inst.*, XXXIV, 1919, pp. 72ff.   [13] Jahn, *op. cit.*, pp. 9ff., 32ff., 30ff., 27ff.
[14] *Ibid.*, pp. 53ff.—Robert, *Homerische Becher*, p. 83 and fig. d.
[15] Robert, *Homerische Becher*, p. 46.
[16] Jahn, *op. cit.*, pp. 39ff.—Rostovtzeff, *Am. Journ. Arch.*, XLI, 1937, p. 92 and fig. 4.

cup which bears the title of the play (fig. 10) the copyist compressed together as many scenes of his model as the limited space allowed, and succeeded in filling it with the following five items:

(1) Iphigenia, Clytaemnestra and Orestes greet Agamemnon in the camp (v. 621ff.).
(2) The discourse between Clytaemnestra and Achilles (v. 819ff.).
(3) Clytaemnestra informed by her old servant about Agamemnon's intentions (v. 866ff.).
(4) Iphigenia pleads before Agamemnon for her life (v. 1211ff.).
(5) Achilles meets Iphigenia in the presence of Clytaemnestra (v. 1338-1344).

These five scenes illustrate the very center of the drama so that the full picture cycle would require two more cups, one with the beginning and the second with the end of the drama. The cup in the Metropolitan Museum in New York (figs. 9a-e) likewise contains five scenes, the last of which connects immediately with the first on the cup described above:

(1) Agamemnon sends his old servant with a letter to Clytaemnestra (v. 111ff.).
(2) Menelaus takes away the servant's letter (v. 303ff.).
(3) Menelaus reproaches Agamemnon (v. 322ff.).
(4) The messenger announces to Agamemnon the arrival of Iphigenia and Orestes (v. 414ff.).
(5) Iphigenia with Orestes in a cart on the trip to Aulis (v. 416ff.).

Together with the third cup, which is now lacking and illustrated in probably five more scenes the end of the drama, we can be sure that an illustrated *Iphigenia at Aulis* had at least fifteen scenes, and possibly even more if we take into account that the cycle may already have been epitomized.

On other cups there are scenes from the *Phoenissae*,[17] the *Hecuba*,[18] the *Oedipus*,[19] and the satyr play *Sisyphus* or *Autolycus*,[20] and they can likewise be considered as scattered fragments of extensively illustrated Euripidean dramas. On the basis of this evidence we may go even a step further and conclude that there probably existed a complete illustrated edition of all the plays of Euripides of which about seventy-five are known, either complete or fragmentary or at least by their titles. Such an edition, with illustra-

[17] C. Robert, *Jahrb. d. Inst.*, XXIII, 1908, pp. 193ff. and pls. 5-6.—*Idem, Homerische Becher*, p. 59 and fig. M.

[18] Robert, *Homerische Becher*, p. 73 and fig. b.—Kyparissis, Σκύφος Ὁμηρικὸς ἐκ Κεφαλληνίας, Ἐφ. Ἀρχ., 1914, p. 217 and pl. 6.

[19] Robert, *op. cit.*, p. 76 and fig. c.

[20] *Ibid.*, p. 90 and fig. f.—A. von Salis, "Sisyphos," *Corolla, Ludwig Curtius zum 60. Geburtstag*, Stuttgart 1937, p. 161 and pls. 58-60.

tions on the same scale as the *Iphigenia at Aulis*, would contain hundreds and hundreds of pictures. And it is by accident only that unlike Homer, where we possess the Milan codex, not a single drama has come down to us with its illustrations, whether on papyrus or on vellum. But since artists of very different media used an illustrated Euripides as model either directly or indirectly, much of it can be reconstructed (cf. figs. 15-19, 21, etc.).

Furthermore, there were also prose texts, literary as well as scientific, which had been illustrated and which for their iconography were exploited by copyists in other media. But since there is little hope that the soil of Egypt will yield more than occasional fragments of illustrated papyri, the history of ancient book illumination from its beginning in the early Hellenistic period until the time from which the earliest codices are preserved, must be based primarily on derived material in other media. A method of inference will have to be used such as was so successfully applied by classical archaeologists under similar conditions, when they drew conclusions from Roman marble copies as to the lost bronze originals of Polyclitus, or from red-figured vase painting as to lost monumental frescoes of Polygnotus, to quote only two striking examples.

46

II. THE PHYSICAL RELATION BETWEEN THE MINIATURE AND THE TEXT

A. THE SYSTEM OF ILLUSTRATION IN THE CLASSICAL ROLL

BY intrinsic probability certain categories of Hellenistic and Roman monuments, such as the Homeric bowls, the Iliac tablets and the sarcophagi, were considered by us to be derivations from illustrated rolls. Although in a few cases, particularly in the Homeric bowls (figs. 6-7), the copyists took over from their papyrus models a few lines of text, generally the transference of miniatures out of the roll into another medium meant their separation from the text, thus cutting the physical connection between picture and writing and necessitating a rearrangement of the now textless pictures according to new formal requirements. In order to understand fully this process of transference it is necessary first to investigate how, in the papyrus roll, picture and text were physically related to one another before they became separated.

1. *The Existing Greek Roll Fragments*

At once it must be admitted that the existing roll fragments with miniatures are not only pitifully few, but also utterly insignificant from the artistic point of view, a fact easily explained in that all of them are accidental findings from the rubbish piles of Egypt and cannot, therefore, be taken as a norm to judge the artistic standard of book illumination in the Hellenistic and Roman period. Furthermore, they are iconographically too sporadic to permit any conclusions as to the range of literary texts ever illustrated in rolls. But in spite of these shortcomings they are of great importance as primary documents in which at least the formal system of roll illustration can be studied.

Several examples are from scientific fields, especially mathematics and applied mathematics. Such scientific texts are so in need of illustrations by diagrams that they could hardly have existed at any time without them. While previously we considered the beginning of the Hellenistic period as the start of book illumination, we must now make the restriction that this applies only to literary texts and not to scientific ones, which must already have had explanatory drawings considerably earlier. A commentary to Aristotle's *Physica* by the Neoplatonic Simplicius contains excerpts from a treatise about geometry by Hippocrates of Chios, a mathematician of the fifth century B.C.,[1] in which reference is repeatedly made to διαγράμματα; therefore from at least the fifth century on we can actually assume diagrammatic drawings in scientific texts. Such scientific illustrations are much more closely

[1] H. Diels, *Simplicii in Aristotelis Physicorum libros IV priores commentaria*, Berlin 1882, p. 53.

47

related to the text than literary illustrations. They hardly ever are detached to migrate into other media, because in most instances they would immediately lose their meaning and become unintelligible.

No attempt is made to give a complete list of all existing miniature fragments on papyrus. Emphasis is laid upon those of which at least two or more consecutive illustrated writing columns are preserved, so that not only the position of a single miniature but also the relation of several to each other can be examined. The following examples, within the very limited material available, are taken from as many different categories as possible.

(1) Berlin, Staatliche Museen, pap. 11529 (fig. 35).[2] On the verso of a roll fragment, the recto of which contains a deed from A.D. 138, are remnants of two writing columns of a date not much later, belonging likewise to the second century. The text deals with a series of geometrical and stereometrical propositions, each of which is illustrated by a diagram, crudely drawn without ruler and compasses. In the left column, of which only about a third of its width is preserved, are recognizable a parallelogram and a right-angled triangle, and in the right an equilateral triangle, a stone and two concentric circles, standing for a tripod. For these diagrams the writer left free some space at the right side of the writing column so that several lines of the text had to be shortened because of the drawings. By this method the continuity of the writing column remained unimpaired and the diagrams in the reserved spaces were subordinated to the text.

(2) Chicago, Field Columbian Museum, pap. no. 1 (fig. 36).[3] The so-called Ayer Papyrus, bought by Mr. Ayer in Cairo, is supposed to have been found at Hawara in the Fayum and belongs to the first or second century A.D. It contains a part of a practical treatise on mensuration, intended for surveying after inundations farm land of irregular shape, etc. Each of the propositions which ends with the phrase "and the figure will be as follows," is illustrated by a diagram. One such diagram in the first fragmentary writing column is lost, another in the second column below the second line represents a trapezoid, while a third in the middle is again lost. In the third column a parallelogram and a rhombus are visible. For these drawings the writer reserved the space of several full lines of writing, although they are much too small to fill this space and there remains empty ground at both sides. As a result the solidity of the column is broken up, and a greater emphasis is given to the drawing.

[2] W. Schubart, "Mathematische Aufgaben auf Papyrus," *Amtl. Berichte der Berliner Museen*, XXXVII, 1915-16, cols. 161ff. with figure.

[3] E. J. Goodspeed, "The Ayer Papyrus: A Mathematical Fragment," *Am. Journ. Phil.*, XIX, 1898, p. 25 with plate.—*Idem, Chicago Literary Papyri*, Chicago 1908, pp. 19ff.—K. Preisendanz, *Papyrusfunde und Papyrusforschung*, pp. 255 and 265. For the photograph here published we wish to thank the Director of the Field Columbian Museum.

In a similar way geometrical and stereometrical diagrams are inserted in the sixteen, partly destroyed, writing columns of a mathematical roll in the Nationalbibliothek in Vienna, pap. gr. 19996, which belongs to the first century B.C.[4]

(3) Paris, Louvre, pap. no. 1 (fig. 37).[5] A roll of two meters in length, the recto of which contains instructions about the spheres based on Eudoxus, while the verso bears in an acrostic the title Εὐδόξου τέχνη. Besides these propositions taken from the famous fourth century astronomer, those of other authors were also used in the text, which seems to have been a schoolbook. While the earliest letter on the verso of the roll is to be dated between the years 111-97 B.C., thus providing a *terminus ante quem* for the recto, a more precise date was proposed by two scholars on an astronomical basis. Brunet de Presle gives the year 165 B.C., and Böckh limits the time of origin between the years 193-190 B.C. Whichever date is right, we possess in this document the earliest illustrated Greek papyrus roll which has come down to us. The text deals with the eclipse of the sun, the moon, the planets, and a survey of the rotation of the starred heaven. Most of its twenty-three writing columns are interspersed with diagrammatic schemes of the zodiac and drawings of the constellations. Among these diagrams is a simple scheme of the cosmos divided into two hemispheres and twelve sections, which stand for the signs of the zodiac; a drawing of the constellation Orion which, according to Egyptian usage, is symbolized by the god Osiris; the scarab as symbol of the sun; the Claws of the Scorpion and the Scorpion itself. They were made by an inexperienced hand, colored slightly in red and placed in the writing column in such a way that its continuity was broken up by wide gaps left for the purpose of inserting the drawings. At the same time these drawings fill out the space more fully than in the Ayer Papyrus (fig. 36) and occasionally they even transgress slightly the lateral limits of the writing columns which usually are well respected. In one case where the drawing of the zodiac with stars around it is too large to be inserted between the lines of writing, it fills the height of an entire column by itself.[6] Drawings

---

[4] H. Gerstinger, "Eine stereometrische Aufgabensammlung im Pap. Gr. Vindob. 19996," *Mitteilungen aus der Papyrus Sammlung der National Bibliothek in Wien (Papyrus Erzherzog Rainer)*, N.S. fasc. I, 1932, pp. 11ff. and figs. 1-16.

[5] Aug. Böckh, *Über die vierjährigen Sonnenkreise der Alten vorzüglich den Eudoxischen*, Berlin 1863, pp. 196-226.—M. Letronne and W. Brunet de Presle, *Notices et extraits des manuscrits de la Bibliothèque Impériale*, vol. XVIII, pt. 2, 1865, pp. 25ff. Album pls. I-X.—Fr. Blass, *Eudoxi ars astronomica* (Programm zur Kaisergeburtstagsfeier der Universität Kiel), Kiel 1887.—P. Tannery, *Recherches sur l'histoire de l'astronomie ancienne*, Paris 1893, pp. 25, 283-294.—K. Wachsmuth, *Joannis Laurentii Lydi liber de ostentis et calendaria graeca omnia*, Leipzig 1897, pp. 299ff.—Hultsch in Pauly-Wissowa, *R.-E.*, s.v. Eudoxos, VI, 1, cols. 949ff.—Preisendanz, *Papyrusfunde und Papyrusforschung*, p. 83.

[6] Cf. the facsimile pl. I between the cols. IV-V.

of this size, however, seem to have been rare in papyrus rolls and must be considered as exceptions, made necessary by special reasons.

(4) Leyden, Museum van Oudheden, pap. 1.384 (figs. 38a-c).[7] This roll, 3.60 m in length, was found in a tomb in Thebes and contains a collection of magical formulae, which date around 300-350 A.D. They are written on the verso of a much earlier demotic text. Three of these magic formulae are illustrated. The first, an instruction how to deprive a person of his sleep, reads: "take a living bat and paint on its right wing with myrrh the following figure," and is illustrated (fig. 38a) by a seated woman who wears a headdress with a moon between ox-horns and holds in her right hand, stretched forward, a scepter with a bird. Only half the width of the writing column is reserved for the drawing, while the other half is the continuation of the text. The arrangement is similar to that of the mathematical papyrus in Berlin (fig. 35), but with the difference that the writing column of the magical papyrus opens on its left side, while in the mathematical papyrus it is the right which is reserved for diagrams. The second formula with an invocation of Typhon-Seth is illustrated by the figure of Seth with an ass's head, holding a lance in each hand (fig. 38b). Here the writing column is interrupted in order to give ample space to the figure of Seth, which, however, does not fill it entirely but leaves gaps at either side. This scheme is also adopted in the third drawing which stands in a partly destroyed column and represents Anubis with a dog's head in front of a mummy on a bier (fig. 38c).

(5) Oslo, University Library, pap. no. 1 (fig. 39).[8] A magical roll of about two and a half meters in length, acquired by Eitrem in the Fayum and likewise belonging to the fourth century A.D. With seven of its twelve columns illustrated by figures of the invoked demons, it is the most richly illustrated magical papyrus found so far. Since most of the formulae occupy about half or two-thirds of a column, the drawings fill the remaining space at the bottom of the roll. The figure in the first column which, as the text says, the sorcerer has to inscribe on a leaden tablet with a bronze stylus, represents again Typhon-Seth with a head of perhaps a sparrow-hawk, holding a thunderbolt in his right hand. He is placed on the axis of the writing column, with some text at either side, so that he is surrounded by writing on three sides. In the next column which describes how to gain favor and victory at

---

[7] A. Dieterich, "Papyrus magica Musei Lugdunensis Batavi," *Jahrbücher für class. Phil.*, suppl. XVI, 1888, pp. 749-828.—K. Preisendanz, "Die griechischen Zauberpapyri," *Archiv für Papyrusforschung*, VIII, 1927, p. 120 (here the older literature).—*Idem, Papyri Graecae Magicae*, vol. II, Leipzig 1931, p. 27 and pl. II.—*Idem, Papyrusfunde und Papyrusforschung*, p. 195.

[8] S. Eitrem, *Magical Papyri* (Papyri Osloënses, fasc. I), Oslo 1925.—K. Preisendanz, *Archiv für Papyrusforschung*, VIII, 1927, p. 128.—*Idem, Papyri Graecae Magicae*, vol. II, p. 162 and pl. III.— *Idem, Papyrusfunde und Papyrusforschung*, pp. 94, 249.

court, a stethocephalic monster is depicted with eyes upon his breast, holding a snake in the right hand and a key of life in the left. Then there follows in the next writing column underneath the text which deals with a love spell, a demon who drags behind him the very human being to be enticed to love by the invocation, and so on.

There are several more magical rolls preserved with drawings of demons: one in Berlin, Staatl. Mus., pap. 5026 from the fifth century A.D.;[9] another, the so-called Mimant Papyrus, in the Louvre, pap. no. 2391 from the third or fourth centuries;[10] and several in the British Museum, pap. gr. CXXI, CXXII and CXXIII, all of them to be dated between the third and fifth centuries A.D.[11] In the principle of illustration, these are not different from the two examples described above. In this whole category of literature the illustrations are of extreme crudeness and were it not that they are the only major coherent group of illustrated rolls, they would not be worth introducing into the history of art at all.

(6) Paris, Bibliothèque Nationale, cod. suppl. gr. 1294 (fig. 40).[12] This fragment, generally attributed to the second century A.D., contains remnants of three writing columns, the text of which, supposedly an unknown romance, is not yet identified. Each column contains a scene: the first shows two figures in tunics with clavi, one of whom is turning around as if in a hurry to leave the other; the second picture, which is placed one writing line higher up in the column than the first, represents another discussion scene between a man sitting at the left on a throne and two persons standing in front of him; of the third scene, which is about five lines higher up in the column than the second, only a part of a very damaged figure is left, which sits on a piece of brown colored furniture. All figures are outlined by thick. black brush strokes, their garments painted in pink and blue-grey, and their faces in brown, done in a very rough manner with no great skill. Even so, it

[9] G. Parthey, *Zwei Griechische Zauberpapyri des Berliner Museums*, Berlin 1866, pp. 107-180. —Delatte, "Études sur la magie grecque," *Bull. Corr. Hell.*, XXXVIII, 1914, pp. 215ff. and fig. 6.—K. Preisendanz, *Archiv für Papyrusforschung*, VIII, 1927, pp. 106ff.—*Idem, Papyri Graecae Magicae*, vol. I, 1928, pp. 18ff. and pl. I, figs. 1-2.

[10] Delatte, *op. cit.*, pp. 221-32 and fig. 7.—K. Preisendanz, *Archiv für Papyrusforschung*, VIII, 1927, p. 108.—*Idem, Papyri Graecae Magicae*, vol. I, pp. 30ff.

[11] Kenyon, *Greek Papyri in the British Museum*, vol. I, London 1893, pp. 83, 115 and pls. 54, 59, 64, 67.—Delatte, *Bull. Corr. Hell.*, XXXVIII, 1914, p. 204 and fig. 3.—Preisendanz, *Archiv für Papyrusforschung*, VIII, 1927, pp. 117, 119.—*Idem, Papyri Graecae Magicae*, vol. II, p. 1, 45, 50 and pl. I, *figs.* 1-4, 6 and 7.

[12] Strzygowski, *Alexandrinische Weltchronik*, p. 174.—Birt, *Die Buchrolle in der Kunst*, p. 286.— O. Wulff, *Altchristliche und Byzantinische Kunst*, vol. I, Potsdam 1914, p. 280.—H. Gerstinger, *Griechische Buchmalerei*, p. 10.—Gasiorowski, *Malarstwo Minjaturowe Grecko-Rzymskie*, p. 17, p. v and fig. 2.

is clear from the attitudes and the gestures of the figures that a Greek-Hellenistic model stands behind them.

Though the fragments discussed thus far are very heterogeneous and extend in time from the early second century B.C. until the fourth and fifth centuries A.D. there are certain features of the placing of the illustrations in the text which all have in common, no matter whether they are simple diagrams or scenic compositions. These features therefore can be considered as general principles of roll illustration in classical antiquity.

(a) The place of a miniature in a writing column is determined by the text which it illustrates and the picture is subordinated to the writing. Usually the illustration follows at the end of the particular passage to which it belongs, but there are also cases where a miniature precedes.

(b) Each diagram or scene is placed within the lateral limits of a writing column, and hardly ever extends beyond its width. These limits are not actually marked by bordering lines, but determined by the width of the column above and below the miniature. Since the width of the column varies considerably in the papyrus rolls, the space available for the painter differs accordingly. As Schubart has shown[13] there was a preference to write prose texts with narrow text columns, while in poetical texts the width is determined by the length of a verse and is therefore usually greater. Consequently the hexameter, with its considerable length, provides space for a greater number of figures in one scene than columns of prose texts ordinarily do. The height of the miniatures may vary within the same picture cycle according to practical needs.

When a miniature does not fill the whole width of a column, there are two alternatives: either to leave free the space at both sides of it (figs. 36, 38b), or to fill the empty space by continuing with the writing. In the latter case the miniature can be placed either near the left side of the column, so that the writing can continue at the right (fig. 38a), or vice versa (fig. 35).

(c) From the particular placing of each miniature results a lack of formal connection of the diagrams or scenes with each other. In each consecutive writing column the scenes may be—and in most cases they are—placed at a different height. If, as in the Oslo papyrus (fig. 39), they are all at the bottom, this is the result of textual rather than artistic considerations and because each figure is surrounded by text no formal connection is, even in this case, achieved by the illustrator. In other words, no decorative system prevails in the arrangement of the miniatures.

(d) There is no instance known in which the miniature in a roll is framed by a border or, in case of a scene, enriched by a landscape. The diagrams or

[13] W. Schubart, *Das Buch bei den Griechen und Römern*, pp. 63ff.

the figures in a scene are treated just like characters of writing and share with the letters the same neutral ground, thus creating a unity between the physical aspect of text and picture. Framing would, to some extent, have isolated the picture from the text, and most likely for this reason it was avoided. This is all the more remarkable since we are dealing with the very centuries in which the illusionistic style with rich backgrounds was highly developed in contemporary frescoes. Whatever the reason may have been, either aesthetic for the sake of greater unity between the writing and the miniatures as mentioned above, or technical, because papyrus is less suitable for an elaborate picturesque style with layers of gouache, or both, certain stylistic peculiarities are bound up with the medium of papyrus. One might, therefore, speak of a *papyrus style*, in connection with a cycle of compositions that lack frame and background.

Having thus established the general principles of roll illustration we should like to cite a few more papyrus fragments which, being too small to furnish new evidence for the problem of the physical relationship between text and picture, nevertheless throw light on other aspects of the history of roll illustration. They enrich our knowledge about the variety of texts illustrated in classical times and, in artistic quality, are incomparably better than any fragment described so far. Knowing the physical structure of an illustrated roll one can easily imagine how these fragments, all of them devoid of frame and background, were originally placed in the writing columns.

The Johnson Collection in Oxford possesses a fragment from Antinoë with the representation of six charioteers, which are only a part of an originally larger scene. Gasiorowski, who first published this fragment (fig. 41),[14] considers it to be a part of a leaf of a papyrus book, by which he seems to mean a folio of a codex. However, the fact that the back of the fragment does not contain any writing makes it more likely a part of a roll, since in a codex, at least normally, both sides of a leaf are written upon. Above the heads of the charioteers are the ends of three lines of writing, indicating that the column, and consequently also the scene, extended originally further towards the left. The two charioteers on the right may have extended into the free space between two writing columns, but since the lines often differ greatly in length—primarily in poetical texts—it may very well be that other lines above the three preserved extended more to the right and thus may have kept the miniature within the usual limits of the width of a writing column. The fragment belongs to about the fourth or fifth century A.D.[15]

[14] S. J. Gasiorowski, "A fragment of a Greek illustrated papyrus from Antinoë," *Journ. Egypt. Arch.*, XVII, 1931, pp. 1ff. with colorplate.
[15] Gasiorowski's date of around 500 seems somewhat too late.

and is of a quite remarkable quality in design and color. The charioteers, as Gasiorowski recognized, represent the various *factiones* of the Roman chariot race, but since the few letters above the scene are not sufficient for an identification of the text and since the scene seems to be without a precise iconographic parallel, an interpretation of it can hardly be attempted at the present time. In spite of the fact that quite similar types occur in the Milan Iliad in the representation of the race in honor of Patroclus,[16] it is not likely that the papyrus is an illustration of this scene of the twenty-third book of the Iliad, because there are six charioteers whereas in the Iliad only five are enumerated.

In another instance we are more confident of dealing with a fragment from the Iliad. The Staatsbibliothek in Munich possesses a shred of papyrus, gr. mon. 128, from about the fourth century A.D. with a drawing which, like the Oxford one, forms only the right half of a larger composition (fig. 42).[17] The verso was, at least originally, left empty and only later, in the sixth century, used for a letter, a fact which again points to a roll rather than a codex. What is left of the uncolored line drawing depicts a woman with a headdress like a Phrygian cap, who is gently led away by two men, a younger one in front and an older one behind her. A part of a fourth figure from the hips down to the knees is now wrongly attached at the lower left corner, and should be placed much higher, so that, if fully restored, he could stand at the same level as the others. The scene illustrates, in our opinion, the leading away of Briseis from Achilles by the two heralds Talthybius and Eurybates (Iliad I, 347ff.), an identification that is based upon the similarity with the corresponding miniature of the Milan Iliad.[18] The pose of Briseis, the turning of her head toward Achilles, who in the papyrus must have occupied the left half of the miniature now lost, the position of both her arms and other details agree to a large extent. Also the outlines of the heralds are sufficiently similar to justify the proposed identification. In the Milan miniature the younger herald at the right is inscribed Talthybius and the older at the left Eurybates. If we want to trust these inscriptions which date from the Middle Byzantine period, then we might name the two heralds in the papyrus correspondingly. The remnant of the fourth figure would fit very well for Patroclus, who in the Milan miniature, clad in a tunic, stands behind the half nude Achilles. Hartmann, who first published this fragment, makes a number of proposals for the identification of the woman led away, such as Polyxena, Cassandra, Andromache, Andromeda, Hesione, and also Briseis.

[16] Ceriani-Ratti, *Homeri Iliadis pictae fragmenta Ambrosiana*, Pict. LV.

[17] A. Hartmann, "Eine Federzeichnung auf einem Münchener Papyrus," *Festschrift für Georg Leidinger*, Munich 1930, p. 103 and pl. XVII.

[18] Ceriani-Ratti, *op. cit.*, Pict. VI.

But then he specifically rejects the identification of Briseis on the ground that she wears the Phrygian cap which he thinks unsuitable for Briseis. Aside from the fact that slight changes in the costume are not rare in late classical monuments remote from their Hellenistic models, we actually do possess a monument of about the same period, i.e. the fourth or fifth century A.D., which represents Briseis with a Phrygian cap, namely an incised situla of bronze in the Galleria Doria in Rome.[19] In this scene, which is more complete and includes the mourning Achilles, Briseis, led away by Talthybius who roughly grasps her arm, wears the same Phrygian cap with a veil over it as in the papyrus. It seems quite certain, then, that the drawing is a fragment —the only one known so far—of an illustrated Iliad roll.

With an average height of about 11cm. for each figure, the scene seems rather large for a text illustration. This and the fact that no letters of writing are left, may have induced Hartmann to consider the Munich drawing a sketch of a pattern book rather than a miniature from a text roll. However, Hector and Achilles before the Porta Scaea in the Milan manuscript[20] are just as tall as the figures of the Munich papyrus, and if we consider that only about half of the original papyrus scene is preserved, the original width still would not exceed that of the miniatures of the Milan codex, which is about 22 cm. It is true that we possess papyrus fragments which point to the existence of pattern books. Such is the Vienna pap. gr. 30509, which comprises sketches of a nude, a satyr-mask and two other heads in different scales.[21] This kind of sketching of single objects or figures is based on an older Egyptian tradition, as is indicated by a number of papyrus fragments in Berlin and elsewhere, where animals and human beings are sketched in a network of rectangular lines, a grid for transfer,[22] but sketches of this sort are quite different from those of complete compositions like that of the Munich papyrus.

There is another papyrus drawing extant of a narrative representation with figures about twice as large as those of the Munich papyrus and here a doubt seems to be more justified as to whether or not it ever constituted a part of a miniature within a text column. This fragment, found in Oxy-

[19] H. Brunn, "Secchia di bronzo esistente nella Galleria Doria," *Ann. dell' Ist.*, XXXII, 1860, pp. 494ff.; *Monumenti inediti*, VI, Rome 1857-63, pl. 48; *Kleine Schriften*, I, Leipzig 1898, pp. 125ff. and fig. 36.—K. Bulas, *Les illustrations antiques de l'Iliade*, p. 82 and fig. 37.

[20] Ceriani-Ratti, *op. cit., Pict.* LIV.

[21] Karabacek-Wessely, *Papyrus Erzherzog Rainer, Führer durch die Ausstellung*, Vienna 1894, p. 130.—Strzygowski, *Alexandrinische Weltchronik*, p. 177.—H. Gerstinger, *Griechische Buchmalerei*, pl. I.

[22] Erman, "Zeichnungen ägyptischer Künstler Griechischer Zeit," *Amtliche Berichte der Berliner Museen*, XXX, 1908-09, cols. 197ff. and figs. 119-25.

rhynchus, is now in the R. Museo Archeologico in Florence (fig. 43)[23] and represents a scene from the story of Amor and Psyche. Amor reclines leisurely on a couch and turns his head away from Psyche who offers him an object which Vitelli, the first editor of the papyrus, considered to be a mirror. It is a fine and sensitive line drawing with a good understanding of the human body and is so close to a good classical model that Vitelli's dating in the second century A.D. seems rather conservative, though up to the present too few papyrus drawings are known to make a more precise dating possible. Again, the verso has no writing or painting and on the recto the miniature is broken off around all sides, so that it is impossible to ascertain whether there were lines of writing above and below. The composition seems to be preserved to its full width of about 25 cm., a width which can be found among the writing columns in papyri, so that in spite of the comparatively huge size of the figures it is not entirely impossible that the scene was in a text column. Already before the Florentine fragment was discovered, Reitzenstein had assumed an illustrated Greek version of Apuleius' charming novel of Amor and Psyche on the basis of Egyptian terra cotta figurines.[24] This theory, though not uncriticized,[25] is now strengthened by the papyrus fragment which may actually have been part of a Greek illustrated novel of Amor and Psyche.

Some more pen drawings on papyrus are known which might be remnants of larger miniature cycles in rolls, although, because of the lack of writing around them, their former textual association cannot any longer be determined. A few of them may at least be mentioned briefly. A fragment in Vienna, pap. gr. 30507, represents Pegasus[26] and, in front of him, a nude figure holding what looks like a globe. This attribute seems to exclude Bellerophon who most likely would hold either a spear or the reins in his hand. A fresco from the tomb of the Nasonii, now destroyed and known only in an engraving,[27] depicts three nymphs attending Pegasus and one of them holds a vessel, without a handle, of a quite circular shape, so that the papyrus may, perhaps, represent Pegasus attended by the nymphs. Two papyrus drawings in Berlin, the one (pap. 9927) rendering a nude male figure with

---

[23] *Papiri greci e latini* (Pubblicazioni della società italiana per la ricerca dei papiri greci e latini in Egitto, VIII), 1927, pp. 85ff., no. 919 and plate.—A. Minto, *Boll. d'arte*, 1925-26, pp. 190ff. and figs. 1-2.—Bethe, *Buch und Bild*, pp. 5, 80 and fig. 1.

[24] R. Reitzenstein, *Eros und Psyche in der ägyptisch-griechischen Kleinkunst* (Sitzungsber. Heidelb. Akad. Phil.-hist. Kl., V), 1914, no. 12.

[25] Robert, *Hermeneutik*, p. 232.

[26] H. Gerstinger, *Griechische Buchmalerei*, pl. I.

[27] P. S. Bartoli-J. P. Bellori, *Le pitture antiche del sepolcro de' Nasonii nella via Flaminia*, Rome 1680, pl. XX.

a thyrsus and accompanied by a panther[28] and the other (pap. 5004) a Dionysiac warrior fighting against a panther,[29] may originally have belonged to a
poem with Dionysus as the title hero.

All these examples of single miniatures on papyrus, with the exception of
the Iliad scene from Munich, contain unsolved problems of ancient book
illumination. Nevertheless they are mentioned in order to call attention to
what papyrology, if more systematically searched, may eventually contrib-
ute to the earliest phase of book illumination. In this respect the art historian has to follow the lead of the classical philologist who during the last
decades has learned more and more to incorporate papyri into the reconstruction of texts which up to then were almost exclusively based upon later
codices.

2. *The Relation between Greek and Egyptian Roll Illustration*

It is well known that the Greeks were not the first people in the world to
illuminate papyrus rolls. Centuries before them the Egyptians, the inhabitants of the country where papyrus was manufactured and of which it had
more or less a monopoly, used to place illustrated rolls as offerings in the
tombs of the deceased. The question must therefore be raised whether the
Egyptian system of illustrating the rolls shows a similarity with that of the
Greeks, and if so, whether it is likely that the Greeks began their book illumination under Egyptian influence. The answer requires a brief excursion
into the development of the Egyptian roll with regard to the formal relationship between the pictures and the text. Kurt Sethe's essay,[30] as a fairly
recent treatment from the literary and iconographic point of view, has been
taken as basis for our discussions, and a considerable number of dated and
datable rolls, published in facsimile, can be integrated into his outline.

The oldest illustrated roll known today, found in the Ramesseum near
Thebes and therefore called the Ramesseum Papyrus (fig. 44), belongs to
the Middle Empire and contains a ceremonial play in dramatic form written
for the festival of the accession to the throne of Sesostris I, second king of
the XII Dynasty, and thus can be dated around 1980 B.C. This roll, the interpretation of which we owe to Kurt Sethe,[31] is so organized that the text,

[28] W. Schubart, *Das Buch bei den Griechen und Römern*, fig. 29.

[29] Strzygowski, *Alexandrinische Weltchronik*, p. 175 and fig. 25.—Arnold-Grohmann, *The Islamic
Book*, 1929, p. 101, note 21.

[30] K. Sethe, *Die Totenliteratur der alten Ägypter. Die Geschichte einer Sitte* (Sitzungsber. Preuss.
Akad. Phil.-hist. Kl.), Berlin 1931, pp. 520ff.

[31] K. Sethe, *Der Dramatische Ramesseumpapyrus, Ein Spiel zur Thronbesteigung des Königs* (Dramatische Texte zu altaegyptischen Mysterienspielen, Untersuchungen zur Geschichte und Altertumskunde Ägyptens, vol. x, fasc. 2), Leipzig 1928.—Max Pieper, "Die Ägyptische Buchmalerei ver-
glichen mit der Griechischen und Frühmittelalterlichen," *Jahrb. d. Inst.*, XLVIII, 1933, p. 42 and fig. 2.

written in linear hieroglyphs in narrow vertical columns, fills about four-fifths of its height, while the illustrations, about thirty in number, run along its bottom and occupy only the remaining fifth. Clearly the text is the predominant feature and the illustration is subordinated to it. The text was apparently written first and the sketchy scenes were placed underneath afterwards. The illustrator tried to keep pace with the text above, but crowded the figure compositions so much that, toward the end, the text is well ahead of the pictures, and so in the last two scenes empty space is left around the figures. From time to time there are vertical lines drawn which separate the scenes from each other and impede the effect of an uninterrupted continuous picture frieze. These dividing lines, which at least in the earlier part of the roll coincide with the end and the beginning of textual sections, are intended to remind the beholder where to pause and read the text before going on to look at the next picture. The style of the drawings is very simple, so simple indeed that the figures are hardly more than enlarged hieroglyphs. The chief actor, the king in the role of Horus, is repeated again and again, standing inside a little chapel, which is placed on a boat. In several instances the royal figure is dropped and only the empty chapel remains, thus creating the effect of an hieroglyphic sign. This *hieroglyphic figure style*, as one might call it, suggests that we are not too far away in time from the beginning of papyrus roll illustration as a new branch of art, although it must be remembered that this roll is unique both as to its text and as to the period in which it was made.

Not until the New Empire do the next illustrated rolls appear, and by the XVIII Dynasty they exist in considerable numbers and in a nearly uninterrupted sequence until the Roman period. By far the most frequently illustrated text is the so-called Book of the Dead.[32] Already in the Middle Empire this book exists on papyrus but without illustrations,[33] and in other media it occurs even as far back as the Old Empire. In the time of Onnos, last king of the V Dynasty, the Book of the Dead was sculptured in beautiful monumental hieroglyphs on the wall of his tomb chamber at Saqqara, and the conclusion is justified that already by that time it also must have existed on papyrus in order to be read by the high priest during the funeral service. However, these so-called *Pyramid texts* of the Old Empire, as well as the so-called *coffin texts* which in the Middle Empire frequently decorate the sarcophagi on either their inner or their outer sides, are without pictorial decoration save that in the latter the offerings for the deceased are repre-

[32] Ed. Naville, *Das Aegyptische Todtenbuch der XVIII.-XX. Dynastie*, 3 vols., Berlin 1886.

[33] H. Grapow, *Über einen ägyptischen Totenpapyrus aus dem frühen mittleren Reich* (Sitzungsber. Preuss. Akad. Phil.-hist. Kl.), Berlin 1915, pp. 376ff.

sented on the rim of the sarcophagi.[34] Therefore, the XVIII Dynasty copies of the Book of the Dead which are illustrated with ceremonial and mythological miniatures, usually called *vignettes* by the Egyptologists, must be very nearly the earliest so enriched.

One of the earliest and finest illustrated papyri is the Book of the Dead written for Iouiya (fig. 45), chancellor in the time of Amenophis III about 1400 B.C.[35] Like the Ramesseum Papyrus it is written in linear hieroglyphic script in narrow vertical columns which follow regularly from left to right, but its illustration is less homogeneous. This is partly explained by the very nature of the text of the Book of the Dead, which is merely a collection of various chapters of different origin, the number and sequence of which change with practically each copy we possess. The vignettes entered the text early in some chapters and not until sometime later in others. The first chapter of the Iouiya Papyrus, which deals with the day of burial, shows a funeral procession in a short frieze, occupying about a quarter of the height of the roll (fig. 45a), whereas the following seventeenth chapter is still without decoration. It is noteworthy that the funeral procession, which depicts the mummy on a sledge drawn by two men and two oxen toward the tomb before which the outer coffin stands, runs along the top of the roll, instead of the bottom as in the Ramesseum Papyrus, so that the beholder's attention is attracted first to the picture instead of to the text at the bottom, and it is not without significance that from now on this is the preferred arrangement.

Smaller vignettes such as the pylons or cells in the house of Osiris with a genius sitting in each of them (fig. 45b) are also lined up at the top of the roll, but they are separated by double lines which interrupt the continuity of the picture frieze and relate each single vignette to the corresponding text passages underneath, which are likewise separated from each other by double lines. At the same time the placing of the frieze at the bottom is not completely abandoned, as can be seen by the vignette of the Psychostasia, where Iouiya's soul is weighed with Osiris at one side of the balance and the deceased, Thoth in the form of a cynocephalus, and the goddess Maat on the other. The larger size of this vignette, which occupies nearly half the height of the roll, is an indication of the increasing importance of the pictures as against the text. From here it is only one step further to fill the whole height of the roll with vignettes, which then become quite independent units.

[34] R. Lepsius, *Aelteste Texte des Todtenbuchs nach Sarkophagen des altaegyptischen Reichs im Berliner Museum*, Berlin 1867.—P. Lacau, *Sarcophages antérieurs au nouvel empire; Catalogue général des antiquités égyptiennes du Musée du Caire*, 1904-06.

[35] Ed. Naville, *The Funeral Papyrus of Iouiya* (facsimile), London 1908.—M. Pieper, *op. cit.*, p. 47 and fig. 4.

Such full-size vignettes may interrupt the text of the roll at any point,[36] the most favored place being at the very beginning of the roll, where usually the portrait figure of the deceased is represented before Osiris—in the present instance Iouiya and his wife. Here we have a feature which in a certain way corresponds to the dedication picture in the front of later manuscripts.

A complete predominance of the vignettes over the text is reached in the XIX Dynasty, the period of the most beautifully designed and brightly colored copies of the Book of the Dead in existence. One of the finest is the Hunefer Papyrus in the British Museum (fig. 46)[37] written in linear hieroglyphs for Hunefer, the overseer of the palace, superintendent of the royal cattle and royal scribe in the service of Seti I, King of Egypt about 1300 B.C. The increase of space reserved for illustration can be clearly demonstrated by comparing the vignette of the funeral procession (fig. 46a)[38] with that of the Iouiya Papyrus (fig. 45a). Mourners, wailing women and the reader who recites the funeral service lead the way, and where one expects merely the outer coffin before the tomb at the end of the frieze, an enlarged composition with Anubis holding the outer coffin in front of the celebrating family of Hunefer fills nearly the full height of the roll. Such an elaborate composition surely must have been made before the text was written, and the hieroglyphs above the heads are so written as to fit the picture. Another example of the enlargement of the vignette is the representation of the Psychostasia (fig. 46b),[39] in which not only the size of the figures has increased, but also the action has been expanded. Three distinct moments follow each other quickly, one forming a transition to the next. In the first, Anubis leads Hunefer into the Judgment Hall; in the second, Anubis tests the tongue of the balance, while Thoth, the scribe of the gods, notes the result; and in the third, Hunefer is brought by Horus before Osiris enthroned. Here we have an early example of the *cyclic method* in frieze form analogous to the Phoenician silver bowl, which Robert had introduced as proof for the derivation of this method from the ancient orient (p. 36). Another sign of the steady increase of pictorial decoration is the illustration of the important seventeenth chapter (fig. 46a at the right),[40] which in the Iouiya Papyrus was still without a vignette. A long frieze runs all along the top of this extensive chapter, being interrupted only in the middle by Hunefer and his wife Nasha who occupy nearly the full height of an intersection. Hunefer is repeated again and again in this frieze, recalling once more the cyclic method.

[36] Naville, *op. cit.*, pls. XVIII and XXVIII.

[37] E. A. W. Budge, *The Book of the Dead, Facsimiles of the Papyri of Hunefer, Anhai, Kerasher and Netchemet*, London 1899.—M. Pieper, *op. cit.*, p. 48 and fig. 5.

[38] Budge, *op. cit.*, pls. 6-7. Our figure reproduces only the end of the procession.

[39] *Ibid.*, pl. 4. For the Osiris at the right end of the composition, *ibid.*, pl. 5.

[40] Our reproduction gives only the very beginning. For the whole frieze, *ibid.*, pls. 8-11.

In the XXI Dynasty a major change occurred in the illustration of the Book of the Dead when the linear *hieroglyphic* script was replaced by the *hieratic*.[41] Hieratic script, in contrast to the hieroglyphic, is written in horizontal lines of a limited length and under each line follow others of equal length until a *writing column* is formed. This way of writing is similar to the Greek and Latin and differs from both only in so far as it reads from right to left, a feature which applies not only to the single column, but to the whole roll as well, which starts then at the right end. Within each column the lines of writing are tangent to a vertical line (either actually drawn or imaginary) at the side where the writing starts. This may be called the *closed side* of the column, which in hieratic script is at the right, and the left side, which shows a greater irregularity, may be called the *open side*. In Greek and Latin writing the closed side is at the left and the open one at the right. Obviously, the solid columns of hieratic writing lack the versatility of the narrow strips of linear hieroglyphs and cannot nestle so closely to the pictures as in the Hunefer Papyrus (fig. 46a). With the introduction of the hieratic script new formal problems arose in the relationship between picture and text, for which two different solutions were found.

One is represented in the so-called Greenfield Papyrus in the British Museum (fig. 47),[42] one of the richest and most extensive rolls of the XXI Dynasty, which was written for the princess Nesitanebtashru, priestess of Amen-Ra at Thebes during the second quarter of the tenth century B.C., and illustrated with outline drawings of remarkable sensitivity. The artist confines himself to two principles of illustration: either he lets a frieze run along the top of the roll, or he intersects the text with full-size vignettes. In both cases the solidity of the hieratic column remains unimpaired. This means a very marked separation of picture and text, and in this respect the illuminator seems to revert to the older and simpler system of the Iouiya Papyrus rather than to continue the tradition of the Hunefer Papyrus. The separation is so strict that even in instances where the end of a chapter does not fill the space provided for a column, the writer leaves a blank area rather than start a new chapter or fill in a vignette. After a frontispiece vignette with Nesitanebtashru before Osiris, the roll begins with the representation of the familiar funeral procession and the text of the first chapter occupies hardly one and a half writing columns, whereas the picture frieze, being much too long, had to be cut in two halves and to be superimposed (fig. 47a). At the same time the artist reduced the height of the figures so that the proportion between the decoration and the text, which varies between one-fourth and one-fifth throughout the roll, is not much changed compared with the rest in which a

[41] Sethe, *Die Totenliteratur*, p. 535.
[42] E. A. W. Budge, *The Greenfield Papyrus in the British Museum* (facsimile), London 1912.

single frieze runs at the top. An example for the latter is the illustration of the seventeenth chapter (fig. 47b), in which the deceased priestess appears repeatedly in adoration of various gods.

While the system of illustration in the Greenfield Papyrus constitutes an attempt to continue the tradition of the hieroglyphic rolls, another and more progressive solution appears in the nearly contemporary Book of the Dead of the priestess Nesikhonsu, the mother of Nesitanebtashru, a papyrus which was found together with that of her mother and is now preserved in the Museum of Cairo (fig. 48).[48] There is no longer a continuous frieze at the top and the writing columns occupy the whole height of the roll. Only at the beginning and at the end do we find a full-size vignette, an introductory one, in which Nesikhonsu faces Osiris, and a final one, in which she stands before the Elysian fields. Those representations which formerly constituted a frieze are now broken up and each vignette is inserted separately within the lateral limits of a writing column. Recalling our distinction between the *closed* and the *open* side of a writing column, it seems only natural that the illustrator should place the vignettes at the open side, i.e. the left, of the column, which normally has a certain amount of empty space as a matter of course. The painter employs this manner of illustration with such exclusiveness that it seems to be a general and well established principle. Only in one case, where Nesikhonsu stands with Isis, Thoth and two more gods in the barge of Ra, does the vignette occupy the whole width of the writing column, being too large to allow any text beside it. From the mere formal viewpoint this new principle has its disadvantage because it disperses the vignettes irregularly throughout the text and cuts off all formal relationship between them. But on the positive side stands the fact that it brings each single vignette into a much closer physical connection with the particular passage it illustrates. In the hieroglyphic papyri there was, of course, also a desire to place the sections of the top frieze as near as possible to the related passage underneath, and it was owing only to negligence resulting from continued copying if text and vignettes did not keep pace with each other. But now the relationship can be made far more accurate, because the scribe can reserve the necessary space for the vignettes at any height in the writing column where he wishes to have a picture inserted. This may be either the beginning of a chapter, as in chapter 136, where alongside the first lines is the vignette with the hawk's head of the sun-god Ra in a barge (fig. 48, 2nd column from the right); or it may be the middle as in chapter 99, where the vignette with the deceased rowing the barge in the lower world is inserted after five full-length lines

---

[48] Ed. Naville, *Le papyrus hiéroglyphique de Kamara et le papyrus hiératique de Nesikhonsou au Musée du Caire* (*Papyrus funéraires de la XXIᵉ dynastie*, vol. ɪ) (facsimile), Paris 1912, pls. xɪ-xxx.

of writing (fig. 48, 3rd column from the right) ; or the end as in chapter 65, where one line above the beginning of the next chapter is the vignette of the deceased piercing the head of a dragon (fig. 48, 1st column from the right). Since, however, text and pictures are apparently done by two different persons and the text was written first, as indicated by the often inadequate size of the space provided for the vignettes, mistakes could creep into this system also, as Naville has shown for the present papyrus, where in several instances the artist placed a wrong vignette in the provided space. But these are only natural shortcomings resulting from the process of copying and they do not contradict the general fact of a closer relationship between text and picture in this type of hieratic roll.

The two systems of illustration in hieratic rolls, the one with the *top frieze*, as seen in the Greenfield Papyrus, and the other with the *column picture*, as demonstrated by the Cairo papyrus, are not always kept separate. Sometimes they are mixed in one and the same roll, as in a Book of the Dead in the Louvre, no. 3079 (fig. 51), which is written for a Theban priest by the name of Taho apparently not earlier than the XXVI Dynasty, perhaps even as late as the Ptolemaic period.[44] In parts of this roll, the top frieze runs above a considerable number of hieratic writing columns without paying any attention to their division, particularly in the seventeenth chapter which contains the various adoration scenes of the deceased. Most vignettes, however, are distributed singly within writing columns which vary greatly in their width. This means that the system of the Cairo papyrus, by which the vignette is placed in a reserved space at the left side of a column, could be applied only in the wider columns while often the column is so narrow that the writer could not keep the continuity of writing by placing some part of the text alongside the vignette. In such cases he simply interrupted the text in order to provide sufficient space for the vignette. But that the writer was very hesitant to break up the continuity of the column can be seen in those instances where even in a comparatively narrow column he tried to have at least a few letters alongside the vignette.

In the Book of the Dead of the Saitic period, after the XXVI Dynasty, there was a revival of the linear hieroglyphic script, which was considered by the Egyptians to be more sacrosanct than the hieratic because it was Thoth himself who had written the Book of the Dead in hieroglyphs under divine inspiration. It is the script used in the Book of the Dead in Turin from the

[44] M. E. de Rougé, *Rituel funéraire des anciens égyptiens, publié d'après le papyrus du Louvre*, Paris 1861.—Ch. H. S. Davis, *The Egyptian Book of the Dead*, New York 1895, pls. v-xx.—F. Th. Devéria, *Catalogue des manuscrits égyptiens au Musée Égyptien du Louvre*, Paris 1874, p. 123.— Rougé, *op. cit.*, p. xxx. "Son style n'est pas ancien, tout à plus pourrait-on le faire remonter à l'époque de la domination persane, il est probable qu'il a été écrit vers le commencement de l'époque ptolémaïque."

Ptolemaic period,[45] the one by which Lepsius established the division into chapters which became generally accepted. All its vignettes, short scenes as well as longer friezes, are placed at the top of the roll in a manner similar to that of the Iouiya Papyrus. Thus not only the script, but also the system of illustration, is archaistic.

Yet, along with the archaistic hieroglyphic papyri the hieratic ones continue, as can be demonstrated by a fragmentary Book of the Dead of the Ptolemaic period which was given by Robert Garrett of Baltimore to the Princeton University Library (fig. 52).[46] Its system of illustration is similar to that of the Paris papyrus, having a top frieze as well as single vignettes in the midst of writing columns. However, in these column pictures the illustrator adheres exclusively to that type of vignette which completely interrupts the writing column. So in spite of the revival of the hieroglyphic Book of the Dead there seems to have existed a continuity, from the XXI Dynasty down to the Hellenistic period, not only of the hieratic script but also of the peculiar system of illustration connected with it.

While the revival of hieroglyphic script concerns apparently only the Book of the Dead proper, other apocryphal and less sacred funeral texts, such as the *Book of Breathings*, the *Book of Traversing Eternity*, and others[47] are written in hieratic script. Examples of these apocryphal texts, belonging already to the Roman period, are two funeral papyri in Edinburgh, the so-called Rhind Papyri, named after their finder.[48] One of them (fig. 49) is written for a man by the name of Menthesuphis and the other (fig. 50) for his wife Tanue, both of whom died in the same year, 9 B.C. In both rolls, written in hieratic and demotic script, the text columns are separated from each other by double lines which run up to the top and thus separate also the vignettes from each other, all of which are placed at the top of the rolls. At the beginning of the first papyrus (fig. 49), the vignette, where the deceased lies between Anubis and Thoth and underneath the four sons of Horus, occupies a width nearly equal to that of the writing column, but the subsequent one, where the mummy lies between two figures of Anubis, is centered on the axis of the column and leaves empty space at both sides. The same is true for the vignettes of the second papyrus; in one, the deceased wife

[45] R. Lepsius, *Das Todtenbuch der Ägypter nach dem hieroglyphischen Papyrus in Turin*, Leipzig 1842.

[46] *The Development of the Book*, fasc. 1: "*Writing Materials*" (Bulletin 1 of the Princeton University Library), Princeton 1938. Our figure is published with the kind permission of the Librarian of the Princeton University Library.

[47] Sethe, *op. cit.*, p. 537.

[48] A. H. Rhind, *Thebes, Its Tombs and Their Tenants*, London 1862, pp. 118ff.—A. H. Rhind and S. Birch, *Facsimiles of Two Papyri Found in a Tomb at Thebes*, London 1863.—G. Möller, *Die beiden Totenpapyrus Rhind des Museums zu Edinburg*, Leipzig 1913.

64

stands in front of Thoth, and in another, Anubis in front of her mummy (fig. 50). Clearly the painter considered the connection between the vignette and the text more obligatory than that between two pictures, and did not intend to create any impression of a continuous frieze. The vignettes of the Rhind Papyri are primarily not frieze pictures, but column pictures, and, as such, they stand in the tradition of the later hieratic Books of the Dead in spite of their being lined up at the top of the roll. Stylistically they are somewhat different from all preceding examples. While in the papyri of Cairo, Paris and Princeton (figs. 48, 51, 52) the vignettes are drawn with thin, sensitive outlines, the two Rhind Papyri are painted in a thicker brush technique that loses a good deal of the sensitivity of earlier rolls, but at the same time creates, in spite of a certain roughness, a coloristic effect which is lacking in the earlier rolls. This technique resembles somewhat the one used in the Greek fragment in Paris (fig. 40) and points to a mutual influence between the Egyptian and the Greek style in the Hellenistic period.

With the last example we have reached the period to which some of the preserved Greek papyrus fragments belong and can now answer the question previously raised, whether or not there is a connection between the Egyptian and the Greek system of roll illustration. From what has been said above about the difference between the hieroglyphic and the hieratic writing, it is obvious that only the hieratic provides a basis for a comparison with the Greek, because of its similar organization in solid writing columns.[49] The two possibilities for adorning a hieratic text with pictures were, as may be recalled, the top frieze and the column picture. There is no direct evidence that the former had entered the Greek rolls, but with so few Greek examples, this may be accidental; as far as the column picture is concerned, a marked similarity between the Egyptian and the Greek system can indeed be observed. Generally the Greek preference was for miniatures which break off the solidity of the column, regardless of whether they fill the whole width provided for them or not (cf. figs. 36, 37, 38b-c and 40). This variation was used in the early Cairo roll (fig. 48, 2nd column from the right) only as an exception, but became predominant in the later Paris roll (fig. 51) and finally was used exclusively in the Princeton fragment (fig. 52). But the older Egyptian system, in which a scene was placed in the side of a writing column, also entered the Greek roll; in the magical papyrus in Leyden (fig. 38a), as we have seen, the miniature stands, as in all Egyptian rolls, at the left side of the column. But here, with the Greek script replacing the hier-

---

[49] This explains why Pieper in his study, *op. cit.*, did not find a connecting point between Egyptian and Greek illumination—because all Egyptian examples he chose for comparison are hieroglyphic.

atic writing column, the right is the open and hence more suitable side for the insertion of a miniature. This slight incongruity of the Leyden papyrus is most easily explained by a mechanical adaptation of the Egyptian system of illustration, and it was to be expected that in the course of time the Greeks would adjust the location of the illustrations to conform to their custom of writing from left to right; in the mathematical papyrus of Berlin (fig. 35) the picture has been shifted to the right side of the column.

There are still other features which Egyptian and Greek miniatures have in common. It will be recalled that the Greek miniatures have neither frame nor background, sharing with the script the same neutral ground. This is typical also for the hieratic papyri of Cairo, Paris and Princeton (figs. 48, 51, 52), and although lines surround the pictures of the Rhind Papyri (figs. 49, 50) they are not frames in the proper sense of the word, but constituent parts of a larger net of lines coordinated with the writing columns. From all this evidence it can be concluded that the so-called *papyrus style* already had originated in pre-Hellenistic Egypt and was only adapted and further developed by the Greeks.

The most natural place for Egyptian roll illustration to have exerted its influence upon the Greek is, of course, Alexandria, where the two cultures came into close contact after the conquest of Egypt by Alexander the Great. In this great city a new hybrid culture had grown up as a result of a mutual influence. It hardly can be considered merely fortuitous that the sudden appearance of huge miniature cycles of the great epic poems and dramas coincides with the very moment when Alexandria had rapidly become the greatest book center of the Greek world and a center of learning around its famous and fabulously rich library as well as a manufacturing and trade center for papyrus rolls. Indeed, Alexandria was probably the actual center which provided the facilities for the development of roll illustration as a new branch of Greek art. There the Greeks had a chance to see an abundance of illustrated Egyptian rolls from which the system and technique of illustration could be learned and adapted for embellishing their own classic literature, the chief editions of which were made at precisely that time in Alexandria.

The Greeks wrote on papyrus long before they came to Alexandria, but the material had to be imported from Egypt, since papyrus did not grow in Greece. It is possible, then, that, by way of trade, the Greeks may occasionally have seen Egyptian rolls already before the Hellenistic period, and perhaps even illustrated ones. The conquest of Egypt did not necessarily mean the first contact of the Greeks with Egyptian roll illustration, but it was the stimulus for a great expansion in the production of Greek papyrus rolls and for their artistic embellishment.

The Egyptian models which the Greeks had before their eyes at the time they embarked on an extensive illustration of the epic poems of Homer and the dramas of Euripides were not necessarily, of course, Books of the Dead. This funeral text is so much in the focus of Egyptological studies simply because it is the only text to have survived in any considerable number of copies. Most of these were buried in the tombs so it is not even likely that the Greeks, on coming to Alexandria, could have seen much of this kind of illustration. But there existed also profane texts in Egyptian literature of which, just because they were not buried in the tombs, only a few fragments have survived, and it was probably this category of texts which exerted the direct influence upon the Greek illuminators. The influence of the Egyptian rolls upon the Greek was not confined to the adaptation of formal principles. Egyptian subject matter, at least to some extent, also found its way into Greek rolls. Naturally, epic and dramatic illustrations with their highly dramatic actions had no equivalent anywhere in Egyptian iconography, so that not even compositional schemes could be borrowed and made suitable for a new iconographic meaning. Nevertheless, there are quite a few indications of direct iconographic influence in other text recensions.

First of all, one would expect that the Greek magical rolls, like those in Leyden and Oslo (figs. 38-39), were translations and copies from Egyptian texts. The exact models of them seem not to have been preserved, but we do possess at least one illustrated Egyptian example of this category of literature to make sure of its existence in pre-Hellenistic times. There is a magical text from the time of the XXVI Dynasty, written in hieratic and now preserved in the British Museum, pap. no. 10051 (fig. 53),[50] which depicts, among other subjects, the house of Osiris in full size and in front of it four tanks of fire with Seth and a fiend in each of them. These four tanks are placed at the bottom of the writing columns, like the various demons in the Oslo papyrus (fig. 39), and it can be surmised that these demons originally had in an hieratic text a place similar to that which they now occupy in the Greek translation.

It will be recalled that the oldest Greek papyrus with illustrations, the Eudoxus Roll in the Louvre (fig. 37), contains Egyptian symbols for certain constellations, such as Osiris for Orion, although the text does not require the insertion of these symbols into the otherwise simple diagrammatic schemes of constellations. The Louvre roll is unique today, but if we had more illustrated rolls of Greek astronomy we should not be surprised to find in them a similarly strong influence of Egyptian iconography.

The Egyptians provided further models for the Greeks through the illustrated texts of erotic literature. The library in Turin possesses a papyrus

[50] E. A. W. Budge, *Facsimiles of Egyptian Hieratic Papyri*, 2nd ser., London 1923, p. 19 and pls. XXXI-XL.

from the XIX or XX Dynasty with the illustrations of twelve different schemata of symplegma.[51] We also know from literary records,[52] that the hetaera Elephantis wrote, presumably in Alexandria, a book about cohabitation which was illustrated by such schemata, and it seems likely that this treatise harks back to an older Egyptian tradition like the one preserved in the Turin papyrus. Though there is no Greek papyrus fragment known hitherto with representations of those schemata, they can be found in other media, primarily the relief pottery of the Graeco-Roman period.[53] Since, as previously demonstrated in the relief bowls with scenes from Homer and Euripides, this group of documents was widely dependent on roll illustrations for its subject matter, there is every reason to believe that also the cups with representations of the schemata were copied from books like that of Elephantis. Once they were copied by the Greeks from the ancient Egyptians, illustrated erotic texts continued as a literary branch for centuries afterward and spread into other cultures, as can be shown by an Arabic paper fragment of the ninth or tenth century in Vienna,[54] found supposedly in the Fayum, which represents a symplegma without frame and background within the writing column, thus preserving all the formal aspects of Hellenistic roll illustration.

On the same Turin papyrus containing the erotic scenes is depicted a procession of animals which belongs to an illustration of satirical fables.[55] In a humorous way the rule in the animal kingdom is reversed, and the superior animals devotedly serve the very ones whom in actual life they pursue. Other fragments with similar animal fables are preserved in the British Museum (fig. 54)[56] and in Cairo,[57] but only the Turin one possesses remnants of hieratic script above the procession, which prove that these miniatures originally constituted a frieze at the bottom of the roll underneath the explanatory text. A similar animal frieze on a Hellenistic relief vase in Berlin (fig. 55), which was found by the Sieglin expedition in Alexan-

[51] W. Pleyte and F. Rossi, *Papyrus de Turin*, Leyden 1869-76, pp. 203ff. and pl. cxlv.

[52] Suetonius, *Tiber.* 43; *Martial* xii, 43. Cf. Crusius in Pauly-Wissowa, *R.-E.*, *s.v.* Elephantis, vol. v, 2, col. 2324, no. 3.

[53] To quote only a few examples: P. Perdrizet, *Fouilles de Delphes*, vol. v, Paris 1908, p. 179, no. 455.—S. Loeschke, "Sigillata Töpfereien in Tschandarli," *Athen. Mitt.*, xxxvii, 1912, pp. 385ff., fig. 8 and pl. xxx, no. 4.—A. Conze, *Stadt und Landschaft* (Altertümer von Pergamon, vol. i, pt. 2), Berlin 1913, p. 277 and Beiblatt 44, no. 4.—Aug. Oxé, *Arretinische Reliefgefässe vom Rhein*, Frankfurt a. M. 1933, p. 76, no. 121 and pls. xxix-xxx.

[54] Th. Arnold and A. Grohmann, *The Islamic Book*, p. 3 and pl. 2.

[55] Lepsius, *Auswahl der wichtigsten Urkunden des ägyptischen Altertums*, Leipzig 1842, pl. xxiii.

[56] Lepsius, *op. cit.*, pl. xxiii.—*Guide to the Egyptian Collections in the British Museum*, London 1909, figs. pp. 27-30.—H. Ranke, *The Art of Ancient Egypt*, Vienna 1936, figs. 272-273.

[57] E. Brugsch-Bey, "Ein neuer satyrischer Papyrus," *Zeitschr. für ägypt. Sprache*, xxxv, 1897, p. 140 and pl. i.—Th. Birt, *Die Buchrolle in der Kunst*, p. 305 and fig. 179.—M. Pieper, *op. cit.*, p. 41 and fig. i.

dria,[58] represents an eagle with a scepter, and in front of him cats and mice playing, peacefully side by side, a flute, harp and cymbals. Obviously these animals belong to the same genre of satirical fables as those illustrated in the older Egyptian rolls. The technique of this fragmentary relief is closely related to that of the Megarian bowls, which are so particularly dependent on illustrated rolls, and this supports the belief that its scenes are copies from an illustrated Greek text which formed the intermediary step between the Egyptian rolls and the terra cotta relief.

3. *The Continuation of the Roll System in the Codex*

The most fundamental change in the whole history of the book was that from roll to codex, and it is to be expected that an alteration of such importance would, in the course of time, have its effect upon the system of illustration. But one must reckon with the very conservative attitude of the scribes who, judging from the earliest extant codices, did not make changes immediately, but merely transferred the writing columns just as they were in the roll with as little alteration as possible. For the codex they preferred a rather square format which allowed them to fill a page with several columns of writing, and usually just as many as the roll had in a portion of equal width. We have mentioned already in connection with the roll (p. 52) that in prose texts narrow columns are preferred and in poetry wider ones, and consequently in a codex prose texts have normally more columns on a page than poems. In the Codex Sinaiticus, from the fourth century A.D., the Old Testament from Genesis to the Prophets as well as the New Testament are written in four writing columns, while the poetical books from the Psalter to the Book of Job have only two columns on a page.[59]

There is no unanimous opinion about the date when the codex was invented and revolutionized the production of books. Practically every handbook to date has placed the transformation from roll to codex in the fourth century A.D. and the same date has generally been assumed as a point of departure for the illustration of texts. The theory of a fourth century origin of the codex was maintained even in the presence of the fact that for some time two actual fragments of parchment codices had been found which, according to the most prominent palaeographers, are to be dated in the second century A.D. One of these fragments in the Museum in Berlin, pap. no. 217,

[58] R. Pagenstecher, in: *Die Griechisch-Ägyptische Sammlung Ernst von Sieglin* (Expedition E. v. Sieglin, vol. II, pt. 3), Leipzig 1913, pp. 72, 199 and pl. XXIV, no. 2.—F. Courby, *Les vases grecs à reliefs*, p. 532 and fig. 116.—W. Weber, "Die Ägyptisch-Griechischen Terrakotten," *Mitteilungen aus der Ägyptischen Sammlung Berlin*, vol. II, Berlin 1914, TEXT, p. 207 and fig. 106.—Rubensohn, *Arch. Anz.*, XLIV, 1929, col. 215 and fig. 11.
[59] Kirsopp Lake, *Codex Sinaiticus* (facsimile in 2 vols.), Oxford 1922 and 1911.

contains a fragment of the *Cretans* of Euripides[60] and its first editors, Schubart and Wilamowitz, attributed it even to the first century, though Schubart later revised his opinion and dated it in the second century, as did all papyrologists after him. This fragment belonged to a fairly small book and is written in a single wide writing column. The other example, found supposedly in the Fayum, and now in the British Museum, add. 34473,[61] contains a fragment of Demosthenes' *De falsa legatione*. Though very much damaged, one of its two leaves is well enough preserved to indicate that the prose text was written in two fairly narrow columns, and that the format of the codex was again nearly square. These two documents prove sufficiently that the origin of the codex must be placed at least two centuries earlier than hitherto assumed. A literary source supports this evidence. Martial, in one of his epigrams,[62] written at the end of the first century A.D., mentions a text of Virgil, comprised in one single small-sized book of parchment. This epigram can only be understood as referring to a codex and not a roll.[63] Martial speaks so admiringly of the "brevis membrana" that we can be sure he had before him a rather recent innovation. Thus the epigram seems to indicate that one does not need to go back much further than the period of the two extant documents for the invention of the codex. In view of all this evidence we can safely place the origin of the codex about 100 A.D. Though the use of the roll still continued for centuries side by side with the codex, one must always consider, in dealing with later manuscripts, at least the possibility of a codex archetype as far back as the beginning of the second century A.D.

If, as we saw above, the transference of writing columns from a roll into a codex did not require any immediate changes, one would expect the same to be true for the illustration. The typical column picture of the Greek roll was well incorporated in the writing column and formed with it an inseparable unit which did not need to be disturbed when the shift from roll to codex took place. Consequently the principles of roll illustration survive

[60] Schubart and von Wilamowitz-Moellendorf, *Lyrische und Dramatische Fragmente* (Berliner Klassikertexte, fasc. v), Berlin 1907, p. 73, no. 217 and pl. iv.—Schubart, *Papyri Graecae Berolinenses* (Tabulae in usum scholarum, vol. 2), Bonn 1911, pl. 30a.—A. S. Hunt, *Fragmenta Tragica Papyracea*, Oxford 1912, frag. v.—*New Pal. Soc.*, ser. ii, pt. ii, London 1914, pl. 28.—Schubart, *Das Buch bei den Griechen und Römern*, p. 117 and fig. 24.—F. G. Kenyon, *Books and Readers in Ancient Greece and Rome*, Oxford 1932, p. 92.

[61] F. G. Kenyon, "Two New Mss. in the British Museum," *Journal of Philology*, xxii, 1894, pp. 247-261.—*New Pal. Soc.*, ser. i, pt. i, 1903-12, pl. 2.—Kenyon, *Ancient Books and Modern Discoveries*, Chicago 1927, p. 56, and pl. 18.—*Idem, Books and Readers*, p. 92.

[62] *Quam brevis immensum cepit membrana Maronem!*
Ipsius vultus prima tabella gerit. (xiv, 186).

[63] A more explicit interpretation of it will be given by Friend in his forthcoming study about the portraits of the evangelists.

in many mediaeval codices which go back to an archetype of a period before the codex was invented. All three variations of the column picture, as distinguished above—the first, in which the miniature is placed in the left side of a writing column; the second, in which it is shifted over to the right; and the third, in which the column is interrupted in order to provide the space for a miniature of equal width—have survived in later codices and in some cases as late as the eleventh and twelfth centuries.

The first variation may be exemplified by the *Physiologus* manuscript in the Stadtbibliothek of Berne, cod. 318, a Carolingian codex of the ninth century, which goes back to an archetype of probably the fourth century A.D.[64] On the page which contains the paragraph "De quarta natura serpentis" (fig. 56) several lines of writing are shortened at the left side to make room for a miniature of a man piercing a serpent with a lance. This group without frame and background is in true *papyrus style*, and has its parallel in the Book of the Dead, where not only the same system occurs, but even the same subject matter (cf. fig. 48). Another picture on the same page, illustrating the paragraph, "De natura formicae secunda" depicts ants which collect wheat and flee barley. These two vignettes are the only ones of this type in the Berne manuscript, and indicate that at the time of the present copy and perhaps already in that of its late antique model, this manner of placing the miniatures was no longer the usual one. It is not without bearing on the problem of the origin of these miniatures that Max Wellmann[65] places the archetype of the *Physiologus*, or at least its scientific sources, in Alexandria.

The second variation, in which the miniature is placed at the right, has survived in a Dioscurides manuscript from the ninth century in Paris, cod. gr. 2179 (fig. 57).[66] Scientific treatises in general are well suited to our investigation, since they must have been illustrated from the very beginning. Often the text could not be understood without miniatures, and particularly in the case of an herbal, pictures are absolutely required. Dioscurides wrote in the age of Nero, a period in which the codex in all likelihood was

[64] G. Swarzenski, "Die Karolingische Malerei und Plastik in Reims," *Jahrb. d. Preuss. Kunstslg.* XXIII, 1902, p. 87.—G. Loumeyer, "Étude sur les peintures d'un manuscrit du IXe siècle à la Bibliothèque de Berne," *Blätter für Bernische Geschichte, Kunst und Altertumskunde*, VIII, 4, 1912, p. 325. —H. Woodruff, "The Physiologus of Bern," *Art Bull.*, XII, 1930, pp. 226ff.

[65] M. Wellmann, "Der Physiologus, Eine religionsgeschichtlich-naturwissenschaftliche Untersuchung," *Philologus*, suppl. vol. XXII, fasc. 1, 1930.

[66] Omont, *Facsimilés de manuscrits grecs, latins et français du Ve au XIVe siècle exposés dans la Galérie Mazarine*, Paris (Bibl. Nat.), n.d., pl. VI.—Ch. Singer, "The Herbal in Antiquity," *Journ. of Hell. Stud.*, XLVII, 1927, p. 27 and figs. 23 and 25-26.—K. Weitzmann, *Die Byzantinische Buchmalerei des 9. und 10. Jahrhunderts*, Berlin 1935, p. 82 (here further literature) and pl. LXXXVIII, figs. 555-556.

not yet invented, and therefore the earliest Dioscurides text, from which the copy in Paris descends, must have been in roll format.

These two variations of placing the miniatures in either side of the column, are comparatively rare in codices. The norm is the *column picture*, a picture which interrupts the continuity of the column of writing and is found in the majority of those illustrated codices whose archetype existed back in the period when the roll was still the prevailing form. Some of the most striking examples are preserved among the astronomical manuscripts which go under the general name of "Aratea." Whether the *Phaenomena* of Aratus of Soli (310-ca. 245 B.C.) were actually illustrated with pictures of the constellations is not certain,[67] but with greater likelihood there were already pictures in the *Katasterismoi* of Eratosthenes of Cyrene (ca. 275-195 B.C.)[68] which were later taken over into the commentaries and translations of Latin writers such as Germanicus, Cicero, Hyginus and others.

Among the illustrated Latin Aratus manuscripts extant today, the earliest of which belong to the Carolingian period, there is a considerable number in which constellation pictures, without frame and background in the manner of the papyrus style, are placed within the writing columns. Typical are two manuscripts from Salzburg, one in the Staatsbibliothek in Munich, cod. 210 from the year 818 (fig. 58),[69] and the other in the Nationalbibliothek in Vienna, cod. 387 from the same period,[70] which were copied from the same model and show an identical arrangement of their pictorial decoration. The short descriptions are written in two narrow columns and the pictures of the constellations, which in spite of their crudeness are still close to the ancient archetype, are inserted ahead of the paragraphs which they illustrate. Usually two, but sometimes even three, of the constellation pictures are placed in a single column, and if all the pages of these manuscripts were placed side by side, the result would resemble ancient illustrated rolls, not unlike the early Eudoxus Roll from the second century B.C. (fig. 37).

While in these two Aratus manuscripts the pictures precede the text, in others, as e.g. a codex in St. Gall, Stiftsbibliothek no. 902, from the ninth century, the miniatures are placed *after* the passage they illustrate.[71] There

[67] E. Bethe, "Aratillustrationen," *Rhein. Mus. für Phil.*, XLVIII, 1893, pp. 91ff.—G. Thiele, *De Antiquorum Libris Pictis*, chap. I.—*Idem, Antike Himmelsbilder*, Berlin 1898.

[68] Carl Robert, *Eratosthenis catasterismorum reliquiae*, Berlin 1878.

[69] Thiele, *Himmelsbilder*, p. 158.—G. Swarzenski, *Die Salzburger Malerei*, Leipzig 1913, p. 13 and pl. IX, fig. 25.—A. Goldschmidt, *Die Karolingische Buchmalerei*, Munich 1928, p. 19 and pls. 14-15 (here further bibliography).

[70] H. J. Hermann, *Die frühmittelalterlichen Handschriften des Abendlandes: Beschreibendes Verzeichnis der illuminierten Handschriften in Österreich*, vol. VIII, Leipzig 1923, p. 145, pls. XXXIV-XXXV and figs. 101-104 (here further bibliography).

72

is no way of telling which of the two arrangements is more ancient. Perhaps classical rolls had already used both methods side by side.

Among the literary texts from classical antiquity the most frequently illustrated are the comedies of Terence. About a dozen manuscripts are preserved, dating between the ninth and the twelfth century,[72] and the earliest among them, which at the same time is stylistically the closest to the archetype, is a manuscript in the Vatican Library, col. lat. 3868, written and painted by the monk Adelricus of Corvey under the abbot Adelardus (822-826).[73] The illuminator followed in every respect the principles we considered characteristic for roll illustration: the scenes are irregularly placed in the columns and at varying heights, according to the changes of the participants in the dialogue. There are pages without any miniature, some have one, as the page from the fourth act of the *Adelphoe* (fig. 59) at the bottom of which Demea is upbraiding the drunken slave Syrus, and others have two, like the immediately preceding page, in which the old country fellow Demea is represented, first alone and, after a few lines, a second time, meeting his brother Micio. There is no remnant of the *scenae frons* behind the actors, as one might expect from a theater scene of the Roman period, or any other piece of stage scenery save for a little door beside the figure who has just entered; nor is there any frame or even a groundline on which the actors can stand, omissions which all conform to the *papyrus style*.

The period in which the codex is predominant and the roll abandoned, at least for general usage, lies between the fourth and fifth centuries, and from this time on a constant stream of codices has been preserved. Hence manuscripts whose archetype can with good reason be placed in this period or later, were in all likelihood conceived in codex format from the very beginning. But there is a transitional period which extends over the second and the third centuries and perhaps partly over the fourth, in which roll and codex were employed side by side. Therefore, there remains doubt as to whether manuscript archetypes originating in just this period started as rolls or as codices.

One such example is a collection of medical treatises in the Laurentian Library in Florence, cod. Plut. LXXIV, 7, from the tenth century, two of which are accompanied by pictures for instructive purposes. One, written by

[71] Thiele, *Himmelsbilder*, p. 160.—A. Merton, *Die Buchmalerei in St. Gallen*, Leipzig 1912, pp. 56f. and pls. XLIX-LI.—A. Goldschmidt, *Karolingische Buchmalerei*, p. 23 and pl. 80.—A. Bruckner, *Scriptoria Medii Aevi Helvetica*, vol. III, Geneva 1938, p. 122 and pl. XXXVIII.

[72] L. W. Jones and Ch. R. Morey, *The Miniatures of the Manuscripts of Terence*, 2 vols., Princeton 1931 (here further bibliography).

[73] G. Jachmann, *Terentius Cod. Vat. Lat. 3868* (Codices e Vaticanis selecti, vol. XVIII) (facsimile), Leipzig 1929.

Apollonius of Citium, is about the dislocation of bones (fig. 94)[74] and the other by Soranus of Ephesus, concerns bandaging (περὶ ἐπιδέσμων) (fig. 60).[75] Soranus lived first in Alexandria and later in Rome under Trajan and Hadrian and the archetype together with its pictures can thus be dated in the second century. The text is written in two columns and each paragraph is followed by a complete male or female figure, a hand, a leg, a foot, or a head in a medallion, all in their proper bandages. In this Middle Byzantine manuscript the system of roll illustration again has survived thoroughly unchanged, but because of the second century date of the archetype, it cannot be determined whether this treatise was originally written as a roll or already as a codex.

Other examples are the technical treatises on applied mathematics, ballistics, poliorcetics, automatics and so on, which were written by such famous engineers as Apollodorus of Damascus, who built for Trajan and Hadrian, and, most important, Heron of Alexandria, who lived between A.D. 150 and 250. In all these manuscripts, the best copies of which were written between the tenth and thirteenth centuries—Paris suppl. gr. 607[76] and Paris gr. 2442[77] are two of the best examples—the drawings of engines for siege and other purposes, of various mechanisms, of automatic playthings, and many other explanatory diagrams of a technical nature are inserted into the writing columns without frame, wherever the text needs them, in the usual manner of papyrus rolls. In all these treatises, for which a second or third century archetype must be assumed, there again is no way of determining whether the original was written and illuminated in a roll or a codex.

The same uncertainty prevails in the case of the didactic poem of the *Cynegetica* by Oppian of Apamea, usually called Pseudo-Oppian. This poem was written around 200 A.D. and dedicated to the Emperor Caracalla, and it seems more than likely that the third century archetype already possessed most of those miniatures which now enrich the eleventh century manuscript in Venice, cod. Marc. gr. 479, the earliest and by far the best copy among

[74] H. Schöne, *Apollonius von Kitium*, Leipzig 1896.

[75] J. Ilberg, "Die Erforschung der griechischen Heilkunde," *Neue Jahrb. für das klass. Altertum*, XXI, 1908, p. 596.—K. Sudhoff, *Beiträge zur Geschichte der Chirurgie im Mittelalter* (Studien zur Geschichte der Medizin, fasc. 10), Leipzig 1914, p. 5 and figs. 1-4.—J. Ilberg, *Soranus* (Corpus Medicorum Graecorum, vol. IV), Leipzig 1927 (here complete reproduction of the miniatures).—Bethe, *Buch und Bild*, p. 26 and fig. 7 (here further bibliography).

[76] C. Wescher, *Poliorcétique des grecs*, Paris 1867—R. Schneider, "Herons Cheiroballistra," *Röm. Mitt.*, XXI, 1906, p. 142, and figs. pp. 146, 150, 154, 162.—H. Diels and E. Schramm, *Herons und Philons Belopoüka* (Abhandl. Preuss. Akad. Phil.-hist. Kl., 1918, Abh. 2 and 16), Berlin 1918-19.—A. Rehm and E. Schramm, *Bitons Bau von Belagerungsmaschinen und Geschützen* (Abhandl. Bayr. Akad. Phil.-hist. Kl., N.F. 2), Munich 1929, *passim*.

[77] Wescher, *op. cit.*, *passim*.—R. Schneider, *op. cit.*, p. 147 and figs. pp. 147, 151, 155, 159, 163.

the three known today.[78] The majority of the very lively miniatures illustrate either the various types of hunting, as hunting with dogs (fig. 61) "impetuous and of steadfast valour, who attack even bearded bulls and rush upon monstrous boars and destroy them and tremble not even at their lords the lions" (1,414ff.),[78a] or depict certain groups of animals which are explicitly described in the text with zoological accuracy. All these pictures show the now familiar arrangement in the text.

In the fifth century, a period in which, according to general opinion, the codex had definitely acquired predominance, the system of roll illustration was still employed by illustrators who had to invent a picture cycle for new texts such as the *Psychomachia* of Prudentius, written at the beginning of the fifth century and apparently illustrated shortly afterward. One of the earliest copies, the codex Paris lat. 8085 from the ninth century,[79] has preserved most faithfully the system of illustration of the archetype. It is written in two columns, each of which contains, at the proper place, one or two miniatures as can be seen in the example (fig. 62) where Fides tramples Idolatria under her foot and crowns the martyrs and where Pudicitia is attacked by Libido and then disarms the latter. Sometimes there are even three miniatures in a single column. The figures stand on a wavy groundline, which perhaps is already a later addition, since other copies, in conformity with the papyrus style, do not have it, but other than this there is no background or frame.

Another group of illustrated texts, harking back to an archetype of the same period, consists of historical chronicles. A papyrus leaf of a codex from the end of the fourth or the beginning of the fifth century, now in the Museum in Berlin, pap. no. 13296,[80] is written in two columns and enriched by frameless miniatures, which represent the passion of Laurentius and Cyprianus, the destruction of churches by Diocletian, the passion of Timothy, the translation of the relics of Andrew and Luke, etc. Though these compositions are very damaged, their system of distribution is still clearly recognizable, and thoroughly conforms to the older roll tradition. The same is

[78] A. W. Byvanck, "De geïllustreerde Handschriften van Oppianus' Cynegetica," *Mededeelingen van het Nederlandsch Historisch Instituut te Rome*, v, 1925, pp. 34ff.—Ch. Diehl, *Manuel d'art byzantin*, vol. II, Paris 1926, p. 602 and figs. 283-284.—Gasiorowski, *op. cit.*, p. 162 and figs. 77-79.—W. Lameere, "Apamée de Syrie et les Cynégétiques du Pseudo-Oppien dans la miniature byzantine," *Bull. de l'Inst. hist. Belge de Rome*, XIX, 1938, pp. 1ff.—Bethe, *Buch und Bild*, p. 24 and fig. 3.

[78a] This and other quotations of the *Cynegetica* are taken from the translation of A. W. Mair (Loeb Class. Lib., 1928).

[79] R. Stettiner, *Die illustrierten Prudentiushandschriften*, TEXT, Berlin 1895, p. 38; PLATES, 1905, pls. 75ff.—H. Woodruff, "Illustrated Manuscripts of Prudentius," *Art Studies*, VII, 1929, p. 40.

[80] H. Lietzmann, "Ein Blatt aus einer antiken Weltchronik," *Quantulacumque, Studies Presented to Kirsopp Lake*, London 1937, pp. 339ff. and plate.

true for the fifth century Ravennate *Annales*, of which an eleventh century fragment in the Domkapitel of Merseburg was recently published.[81] Only half of a single leaf is left from a codex which was written in three narrow columns on a page. Its frameless illustrations of historical events from the years 412 to 454, which seem to be much abbreviated in the narrow columns, are inserted at irregular intervals in the exact passages they illustrate. Also the third fragment, the famous Alexandrian World Chronicle which formerly belonged to the Goleniscev Collection and is now preserved in the Museum of Fine Arts in Moscow, employs the same system of unframed column pictures,[82] though not exclusively. Some of the very mutilated pages show the rarer type of the miniature placed at the indented side of a solid column,[83] a proof that also this variation was still applicable for an illustrator of the late classical period.

Even when Hrabanus Maurus' encyclopedia *De rerum naturis* was illustrated for the first time, probably in Fulda in the ninth century, the illustrator still used the traditional papyrus system, as can be seen in the manuscript in Montecassino, cod. 132 from *ca.* 1023 (fig. 63),[84] where e.g. the pruning of branches and the ploughing and hoeing of the earth is depicted in two superimposed and frameless miniatures in the two-column text.

Finally the same system is also applied in Christian texts such as the Spanish Bible in St. Isidoro in Leon from the year 960 (fig. 64).[85] This clearly points to the fact that Bible illustration likewise had started out with frameless column pictures. But since we do not know the date of the beginning of the Old Testament illustration, we are not in a position at the present time to make any suggestion as to whether it could actually have started in a papyrus roll, or whether a codex which had adapted the roll system must be assumed as archetype.

These examples may suffice to prove the general and widespread usage of the roll system, of which only very few fragments have come down to us in the original medium of papyrus, and, at the same time, its persistence for centuries after papyrus itself had been abandoned. This means that it remained an appropriate system of illustration even after richer and more splendid systems had developed in the meantime. The tenacious adherence

---

[81] B. Bischoff und W. Koehler, "Eine illustrierte Ausgabe der spätantiken Ravennater Annalen," *Medieval Studies in Memory of A. K. Porter*, vol. I, Cambridge, Mass., 1939, pp. 125ff. and figs. 1-2.

[82] Strzygowski, *Alexandrinische Weltchronik*, pl. III recto and verso.

[83] *Ibid.*, pl. VI recto.

[84] A. M. Amelli, *Miniature sacre e profane dell' anno 1023 illustranti l'enciclopedia medioevale di Rabano Mauro*, Montecassino 1896.—E. A. Lowe, *Scriptura Beneventana*, vol. II, Oxford 1929, pl. LIX (here further bibliography).

[85] W. Neuss, *Die katalanische Bibelillustration um die Wende des ersten Jahrtausends und die altspanische Buchmalerei*, Bonn 1922, figs. 67-78.

to the old system is easily explained by the fact that it connects picture and text with each other in a more intimate way than the later more elaborate systems. It never went completely out of fashion and can even be found still unaltered in countless Gothic manuscripts.

4. *The Reconstruction of Classical Rolls*

With the analysis of the system of illustration in the existing roll fragments as well as in many codices of classical ancestry, we have secured the basis on which a reconstruction of lost rolls can now be attempted with the help of those monuments which we have already shown to be derivations from such papyrus models.

Figure A is an attempt to suggest the particular roll which served—directly or indirectly—as model for the manufacturer of the terra cotta cup in Berlin (fig. 6). The average number of writing lines in a roll is, according to Schubart, between twenty and thirty,[86] though occasionally rolls may have even more than sixty. We have chosen twenty-eight lines for this and the following sketches because this number occurs quite frequently in some of the finest papyri of the Graeco-Roman period. The roll, of which Figure A is supposed to represent the middle section, contained probably no more than the twenty-second book of the Odyssey, since on the basis of the normal length of ancient papyri it can be assumed that each book of the poem was written on a separate roll. For the writing we have used a script resembling the characters of the third century B.C.[87] and placed the miniatures within the columns at the particular passage they illustrate. After arbitrarily starting a column with verse 170, we inserted the miniature of the fettering of the goatherd Melanthius between verses 177 and 178, reserving for this and the following miniatures a space equal to seven writing lines. The Hanging of Melanthius is associated with the proper passage between verses 194 and 195, thus following the preceding miniature at a distance of only seventeen verses and the third scene, in which Athena incites Odysseus and Telemachus, is placed between verses 225 and 226, thus separated by a somewhat larger distance from the second scene than the second is from the first. In this way we have tried to suggest the physical appearance of an early Hellenistic illustrated papyrus roll which is in compliance with the principles we established for the roll illustration of this period. The terra cotta worker or perhaps the metal worker, whoever first transformed the miniatures into reliefs, had to condense the scenes in width in order to assemble as many as possible on the rather limited space of the surface of a cup, on which,

[86] Schubart, *Das Buch bei den Griechen und Römern*, p. 60.
[87] E. M. Thompson, *An Introduction to Greek and Latin Palaeography*, Oxford 1912, p. 144.

Figure A. Reconstruction of an Odyssey Roll of the Third Century B.C.

furthermore, because of its hemispherical shape, the groundline is shorter than the rim line. This accounts for the many overlappings of the figures in the relief, particularly of their legs, for which there was no necessity in the roll. Therefore, some details were apparently visible in the model which were lost in the cup: in the first scene the back leg of Philoetius, who brings the twisted rope for the fettering; in the center of the second scene the lower part of the standing warrior, who is either Eumeus or Philoetius; and finally in the third scene practically the whole of the bodies of the wooers below their shoulders. The clarity of each single composition, as we now see, was greatly impaired by the condensation in the cup.

Quite similar, as far as the distribution of scenes is concerned, must have been the appearance of a Euripides roll of the same period. Figure B shows an open roll which illustrates verses 827-868 of the *Iphigenia at Aulis*, written in characters which are again an imitation of an alphabet of the third century B.C. As is to be expected in a dramatic roll of this period, the change of the actor is not indicated by his name, but merely by a short stroke between the lines, the so-called paragraphus. Verse 830 is followed by the representation of the discourse between Clytaemnestra and Achilles, who is about to leave the stage, and verse 866 by the subsequent scene, in which the old servant reveals to Clytaemnestra the intention of her husband Agamemnon to sacrifice her daughter, both compositions being based upon the Megarian bowl in Berlin (fig. 10). This bowl, which contains five scenes instead of the average three, is even more condensed than the Odyssey bowl, and hence we must reckon not only with overlappings but even with omissions of complete figures which are required by the text. We may therefore be allowed to insert in the second scene of our sketch a figure of Achilles which is not on the bowl but, according to the text, ought to be present during the discourse between Clytaemnestra and the old servant. Robert, too, assumed that Achilles was dropped in this scene, but he explained this omission by the artist's desire to avoid a repetition.[88] The one reason does not contradict the other, and it seems quite possible that both played their part in the decision of the copyist to eliminate the figure of Achilles. As far as the distribution of the scenes is concerned, the section of an Iphigenia roll resembles the two pages facing each other in the opened Terence codex of the Vatican (fig. 59), and in agreement with the latter manuscript we need not assume any frame or stage scenery around the actors. The reconstructed Euripides roll from the third century B.C. and the Terence manuscript mark the beginning and the end of a long history of the illustration of the classical drama, which must have been one of the most important branches of early

[88] Robert, *Homerische Becher*, pp. 55-56.

Figure B. Reconstruction of an Iphigenia Roll of the Third Century B.C.

book illumination, extending over a period of far more than a millennium and maintaining throughout the centuries an inclination to exaggerated actions and motions as one of its chief characteristics.

In the same manner reconstructions of lost rolls can be made from any monument of the Hellenistic-Roman period which contains a section of a cycle with the original density of scenes and of which we know the basic text. It may be recalled, for instance, that in the Tabula Iliaca of the Museo Capitolino the illustrations of Book I of the Iliad followed each other in the first half of the frieze in the original sequence (figs. 30-31), which, however, could not be kept up in the second half. On this evidence we attempted in Figure C a reconstruction of the beginning of an Iliad roll using for its text an alphabet of an Odyssey papyrus from about 1 A.D.[89] The first scene, which is made up from the two reliefs Jahn B and C, represents Chryses kneeling before Agamemnon and the unloading of the ransom he had brought with him. It follows verse 16 as its most suitable place. Verse 36 is followed by the second scene in which Chryses, after having been rebuffed by Agamemnon, prays in front of the temple of Apollo Smintheus. For this scene the relief Jahn A was used as model, but having a wider space available than the sculptor, the composition could be spread out, thus making the temple more fully visible. The Revenge of Apollo, inserted between verses 52 and 53, is likewise based upon the relief Jahn A, but somewhat corrected: while in the tablet, as a result of condensation, Apollo stands upright and shoots his arrow over the heads of his victims at Calchas who does not belong to this scene, we drew Apollo in an oblique position as if flying down from heaven and directing his arrow against the victims on the ground. This correction is all the more justified since Apollo is depicted in the same oblique position in the corresponding miniature of the Milan Iliad (fig. 32), the manuscript we considered as belonging to the same pictorial recension as the Iliac tablet. Thus our reconstruction of the beginning of the first book of the Iliad contains one miniature in each writing column and though this density may not, perhaps, have been maintained throughout this and the following books of the Iliad, the number of scenes must nevertheless have been very great.

B. THE GRADUAL CHANGES IN THE CODEX

When the parchment codex was introduced at the beginning of the second century, the new material seems not to have been valued as highly as good papyrus,[1] but gradually it must have been welcomed as a great achievement, particularly by the miniaturists. Parchment is more durable than papyrus,

[89] E. M. Thompson, *op. cit.*, pp. 122, 145.
[1] F. G. Kenyon, *The Palaeography of Greek Papyri*, Oxford 1899, p. 113.—Birt, *Die Buchrolle in der Kunst*, pp. 27 ff.

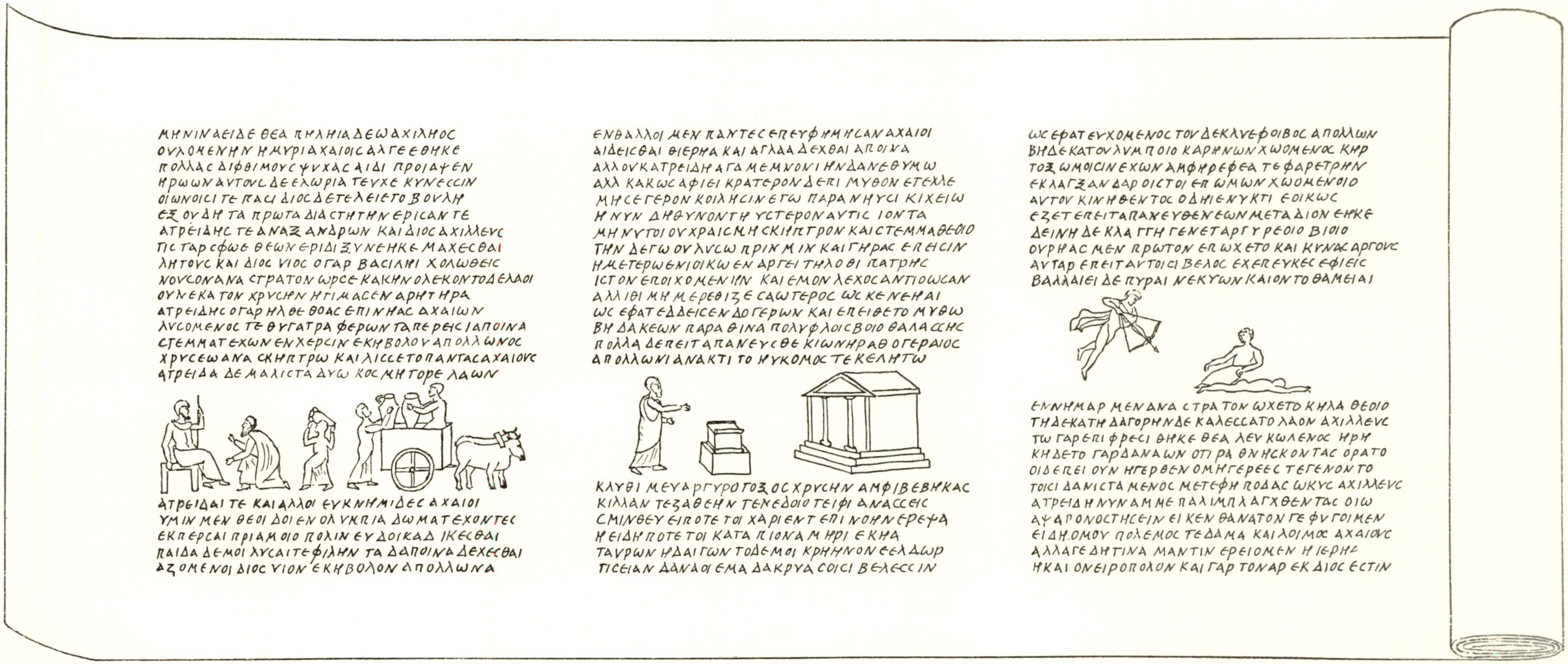

FIGURE C. Reconstruction of an Iliad Roll of the First Century B.C.

which under normal conditions rarely outlasts three generations, and this aspect must have been inviting to painters. At the same time it provided a surface more suitable for delicate techniques. While papyrus, according to our present knowledge, was used only for line drawing and water coloring, parchment allowed the application of thick layers of gouache. Moreover, the flat leaves of a codex prevented the gouache from flaking off as would inevitably have been the result of using this technique for rolls whose surface is subject to bending and cracking, whenever the roll is read. The instances in later Byzantine times in which gouache was nevertheless used for liturgical rolls are ample proof of the unsuitability of this technique for a roll, since their pictures are nearly always badly flaked, leaving only the preliminary drawing visible. With the invention of the parchment codex great possibilities were provided, from the technical viewpoint, for raising book illumination to a higher artistic level, though, as we will see, the illuminator often took advantage of them only hesitatingly and belatedly.

Besides the innovation of a new technique, the new format of the codex had a decisive influence upon the formal development of miniature painting. The proportions of a single page induced the painter gradually to adjust the format of the picture. The column picture, after it was taken over from the roll, developed step by step in size and splendor of execution and became more and more independent of the text until it reached perfection as a picture which occupies the entire page. Though within the limits of a certain recension the various changes follow each other in an organic development, it must be emphasized that they do not occur in each recension at the same period. As already demonstrated, there are certain recensions, particularly among the scientific treatises, whose miniatures do not change at all and maintain the primitive system of frameless column pictures until the late Middle Ages. Other recensions may advance one or two steps towards enriching their miniatures and still never exploit all the available possibilities. Furthermore the final stage of development, i.e. the full-page picture, is reached in different recensions at different times: one recension performs a series of changes in quick succession shortly after the introduction of the codex, while another only reluctantly makes similar changes. We shall have to use chiefly mediaeval manuscripts for demonstration, and thus often cannot be sure whether the changes we observe in them took place at the time when the copy was made or perhaps already considerably earlier, in the late classic or Early Christian period. The full-page framed picture which stands at the end of the formal development occurs already in the Vatican Virgil, cod. lat. 3225 (fig. 91), which may be dated roughly about 400 A.D.[2]

[2] *Fragmenta et picturae Vergiliana Codicis Vatic. lat. 3225* (Codices e Vaticanis selecti, vol. I), 2nd ed., Rome 1930, *Pict.* 2, 10, 17, 18 and 26.—Bethe, *Buch und Bild*, p. 73 and fig. 45.

This means that the painter of the Virgil and most likely also other minia-turists of the same period had already at that time exploited all possibilities and gone through various intermediary stages. The three centuries, from the second to the fourth, of which, unfortunately, so little is left, were appar-ently the most decisive ones for the formal development of the art of book illumination, and it must be realized that the alterations we will observe in manuscripts of later centuries had precedents in manuscripts before the fourth century.

1. *The Extension of the Writing Column and the Miniature*

The number of writing columns on a codex page varies, in the early period, from one to four, the prose texts preferring more and narrower columns, the poetical texts fewer and wider ones. Partly on account of the change from a square format to one which is higher than it is wide, the use of three and four columns becomes less frequent although it does not disappear en-tirely, and one- and two-column texts become more or less the norm. In certain texts which had begun as a codex with two columns there is a tend-ency to fuse the columns into one for the sake of greater unity, creating, in the case of illustrated texts, a formal problem which could be solved in different ways.

Among the illustrated Aratea (fig. 58) there was, to judge from the numerous copies preserved, a strong tradition for two columns on a page, but, as a result of their fusion, a considerable number of one-column texts also exist. In a manuscript of the Staatsbibliothek at Berlin, cod. Phillipps 1832, which comes from Metz and belongs to the tenth century (fig. 65),[3] the constellation pictures are inserted into the text with its extended lines of writing, while the same intervals are maintained as in the text of the two-column model. Consequently the miniatures had to be copied in the same scale as in the model, so that they fill only half the width of the space avail-able between the elongated lines of the single-column text. The constella-tions of Gemini and of Leo in our example are a good illustration; they would fit much better into a two-column text like that of the Munich manu-script (fig. 58).[4]

As an alternative the space provided for the picture could be heightened

---

[3] V. Rose, *Die Meerman-Handschriften: Verzeichnis der lateinischen Handschriften der Kgl. Bib-liothek zu Berlin*, vol. 1, Berlin 1893, p. 289.—G. Thiele, *Himmelsbilder*, p. 157, figs. 67 and 72.— J. Kirchner, *Die Phillipps-Handschriften: Beschreibendes Verzeichnis der Miniaturen-Handschriften der Preuss. Staatsbibliothek zu Berlin*, vol. 1, Berlin 1926, p. 30 and fig. 37.—Bethe, *Buch und Bild*, p. 45 and fig. 27.

[4] As Cancer and Asini are pictures of the same constellation, the model of the Berlin manuscript very likely had only one of them in its narrower columns, since usually one *or* the other are represented in the Aratus manuscripts.

and the miniature itself enlarged so as to fit better in the broadened column. This method can be demonstrated by two Aratus manuscripts, both of which were written in the same scriptorium, one being an exact copy of the other. Made in St. Gall, they are still preserved in the Stiftsbibliothek of that monastery under nos. 902 and 250 and may be dated in the ninth and tenth centuries. The former is written in two columns, and distributes the drawings of the constellations in the traditional manner of the roll, as e.g. on the page where Eridanus and Piscis are placed in the left column, and Ara in the right.[5] The illustrator of codex 250[6] fused the two columns of the model into one, reducing the size of the whole codex, and at the same time widening the one column so that e.g. in the corresponding page the passage about Piscis, which in codex 902 needed ten lines, is now written in only seven. Correspondingly the constellation pictures are enlarged in about the same proportion as the text is widened: the head of Eridanus is bigger, the waves of the sea help to fill the empty space, and though the Piscis is taller and more extended horizontally, it does not even then fill the whole space provided for it.

While a mediocre draughtsman may now and then have difficulty in enlarging the pictures of his model, for a skillful artist it must, on the contrary, have offered a welcome chance to bring the miniature into greater prominence, as e.g. for the able illustrator of an Anglo-Saxon Aratus manuscript in London, cod. Cotton Tiberius B.V., from the turn of the tenth to the eleventh century.[7] The Aquila (fig. 66), which occupies a large area between the descriptive prose lines at the top and the Ciceronian poem at the bottom, is artistically well balanced, spreading with ease its wings across the entire page. The Ciceronian verses occupy only half the width of the page. The writer, who could not change the fixed length of a verse, might either have enlarged the letters or placed the poem on the axis of the whole page; but as it is placed now it suggests a left writing column of a two-column model.

A third solution to the problem of filling the enlarged area provided for illustration by the reduction of the text from two columns to one was found by placing two or even more items side by side. In an Aratus manuscript in the Universitätsbibliothek of Basel, cod. A. N. IV. 18, which belongs to the

---

[5] Merton, *Die Buchmalerei in St. Gallen*, pl. L, no. I (for further bibliography cf. p. 73, note 71).

[6] Thiele, *op. cit.*, p. 160, where this codex is considered earlier than cod. 902. This point is corrected by A. Merton, *op. cit.*, p. 66 and pls. LXII-LXIV.—A. Bruckner, *Scriptoria Media Aevi Helvetica*, vol. III, p. 86 and pl. XXXVIII.

[7] W. Y. Ottley, "On a Ms. of Cicero's Translation of Aratus," *Archaeologia*, XXVI, 1836, pp. 47-214 and pls. IX, X, XI, XIII, XV, XX and XXI.—G. Kauffmann, *De Hygini memoria scholiis in Ciceronis Aratum Harleianis servata* (Breslauer philol. Abhandl. III, fasc. 4), Breslau 1888.—Thiele, *op. cit.*, p. 152.—Gasiorowski, *Malarstwo Minjaturowe Grecko-Rzymskie*, p. 94 and fig. 34.

tenth century and was, perhaps, written and illuminated in Fulda,[8] the constellations Aquarius and Capricornus (fig. 67) share the same pictorial area, while in an earlier stage of the development they would have been one below the other, separated by a paragraph of text.

Though in the Basel manuscript the joining of two constellations is still an exception, there are manuscripts in which the new principle is used throughout the whole picture cycle. An herbal of Dioscurides in Lavra on Mount Athos, cod. Ω. 75 from the eleventh or perhaps the twelfth century,[9] places regularly two or, in most instances, even three plants side by side, whereas in most of the earlier manuscripts, such as the famous Julia Anicia codex in Vienna from the sixth century,[10] or the codex M. 652 in the Morgan Library in New York from the tenth century,[11] each plant is connected with the proper passage separately in accordance with the principles of roll illustration. In the example chosen from the Lavra codex (fig. 68) three plants inscribed ἐλαιοσέλινον, ἐφήμερον and ἔρινον are lined up in a row but since there is only enough space within the limits of the writing column for two plants, the third had to be pushed over into the margin. This suggests that the model was with all probability a two- and not a three-column manuscript, similar to the Latin herbal in Munich, cod. 337, from the tenth century (fig. 116). The placing of a third plant into the margin is the result of an increased economy on the part of the illustrator who in this manner cuts down the number of interstices of the model to about one-third. This economy has a far-reaching consequence. In the older system the column picture immediately follows or precedes the text which it illustrates, but in the new system only one illustration can maintain this close connection, while the others in the same row are separated from their respective passages. In the case of the Lavra Dioscurides—this applies also to other manuscripts illustrated in the same fashion—it is always the first picture at the left which maintains the original connection, while the picture at the extreme right is the most distant from the passage which it illustrates. In the present instance, the description of the plant ἐλαιοσέλινον is directly underneath the picture, then follows, at a distance of three lines, the description of the ἐφήμερον and the top of the following recto-page contains the passage about the ἔρινον. We have here

[8] K. Escher, *Die Miniaturen in den Basler Bibliotheken, Museen und Archiven*, Basel 1917, p. 32 and figs. 5-6 (here the older literature).—Gasiorowski, *op. cit.*, p. 90.

[9] H. Brockhaus, *Die Kunst in den Athosklöstern*, Leipzig 1891, pp. 168, 232, note 1.—Spyridon and Eustratiades, *Catalogue of the Greek Mss. in the Library of the Laura on Mount Athos*, Cambridge, Mass. 1925, p. 343.

[10] A. v. Premerstein, K. Wessely and J. Mantuani, *Dioscurides, Codex Aniciae Julianae picturis illustratus, nunc Vindob. Med. gr. 1* (Codices Graeci et Latini photogr. depicti, vol. x) (facsimile), Leyden 1906.

[11] *Pedanii Dioscuridis Anazarbaei de Materia Medica*, 2 vols. (facsimile), Paris 1935.

the first step of a long process of dislodging the miniatures from their original position in the text. One needs only to compare the analogous plants in the Dioscurides of the Morgan Library in order to understand easily the change described above: here each of the same three plants heads separately the respective passage (fols. 47ʳ-48ʳ). The Lavra manuscript is a rather late example of this new system, which can be seen already in a Dioscurides manuscript in Naples (*olim* Vienna, Nationalbibliothek, suppl. gr. 28) from the seventh century, where likewise as many as three plants occur side by side on one page,[12] and it may very well be that the system is still older.

A similar process can be observed in the illustrations of literary texts, where whole scenes are sometimes placed side by side in wide writing columns. In a miniature of the third act of *Hecyra* in the Vatican Terence manuscript (fig. 69)[13] the left half represents a dispute between the two slaves Parmeno and Sosia, while at the right the same Parmeno is sent by his master Pamphilus to the Acropolis. Again the text which immediately follows is related to the left scene, while that referring to the right is further removed. However, cases where two scenes join each other in the same interstice are exceptions in the Terence manuscripts where normally one scene fills the whole width of the writing column, and consequently there is no reason to assume an archetype written in two columns. Apparently it just happened that two subsequent scenes were sufficiently narrow so that the illustrator could place them side by side without taking more space than was usually required by one single scene, and it is by no means impossible that this junction was made already by the first painter who ever illustrated Terence.

In other recensions the joining of scenes is the rule and not the exception, as e.g. in some profusely illustrated Greek Gospel books, the richest of which, in number of scenes, is the codex Laurent. Plut. vi, 23 from the eleventh century.[14] Heading the third chapter of John is a miniature consisting of two different scenes (fig. 70); on the left Christ and Nicodemus are in conversation with each other and on the right Christ baptizes in Judaea and addresses John the Baptist. While the text to the first scene is directly underneath, not until the second following page does the proper passage for the other scene (John iii, 22) occur. Although this second scene involves many more persons than the first, both occupy about an equal half of the wide writ-

[12] Ch. Singer, *Journ. of Hell. Stud.*, XLVII, 1927, p. 23 and fig. 16.

[13] Jachmann, *Terentius Cod. Vat. Lat. 3868* (facsimile), pl. fol. 70ᵛ.—Robert, *Hermeneutik*, p. 189 and fig. 145 (from cod. Paris. lat. 7899).

[14] A. M. Bandini, *Catalogus Codicum Manuscriptorum Bibliothecae Mediceae Laurentianae*, vol. I, Florence 1764, pp. 147, 163 and pl. III, no. 9.—N. Kondakoff, *Histoire de l'art byzantin considéré principalement dans les miniatures*, vol. II, Paris 1891 p. 143.—O. M. Dalton, *Byzantine Art and Archaeology*, Oxford 1911, fig. 411.—G. Millet, *Recherches sur l'iconographie de l'évangile*, Paris 1916, *passim* (cf. Index, p. 739).

ing column and could conveniently be re-installed into a two-column text. Quite often the illustrator is so economical that he places three or even four scenes into a single row, as in the miniature heading the eleventh chapter of John (fig. 71); in its first scene two men report the sickness of Lazarus to Christ (v. 3); then Martha goes out to meet Christ (v. 20); in the third scene Martha returns home and speaks with Mary, her sister (v. 28); and finally Mary, too, approaches Christ and falls down at his feet, thus being represented twice in the same scene (v. 32). As usual, only the first of these scenes is immediately connected with the text, while the passages for the other three cover the following two pages. One may ask, then, whether the ultimate model was not written, perhaps, in more than two writing columns; in one of the earliest existing Bibles, the Codex Sinaiticus, the New Testament is actually written in four columns. However, some of the polyscenic rows of the Florentine manuscript look rather compressed and abbreviated, so that a four- or even three-column text as model does not seem very likely, and a two-column text still remains the most reasonable suggestion.

The scenes of the Florentine Gospel book are frequently separated from each other by rather schematic buildings. In the miniature last described the roofed building with Mary standing in its doorway is to be understood as the house in which Lazarus lives with his sisters and therefore it is motivated by the text, but the other schematized buildings have no iconographic function, and neither has the house between the Nicodemus and the baptism scene in the preceding miniature. Obviously the painter introduced them as artistic devices in order to allow the beholder a quick orientation as to where one scene ends and the next begins. So they can be considered as *insertion motifs*, resulting from the lining up of several scenes in a frieze-like composition. These insertion motifs, used extensively in the Florentine Gospel book, are by no means confined to this manuscript, but are quite a common device wherever two or more scenes follow each other in a friezelike manner. They fulfill a purpose similar to the insertion motifs found as early as the Telephus Frieze in Pergamon (fig. 23).

There are, however, exceptions where the joining of scenes in a row cannot be explained as above, but is part of the original conception of the illustrator. In the Venetian manuscript of the *Cynegetica* (fig. 72) Pseudo-Oppian speaks of Jealousy in the following words (III, 244-248): "He also in former times arrayed against their own children heroes themselves and noble hero-ines—Theseus, son of Aegeus, and Athamas, son of Aeolus, and Attic Procne and Thracian Philomela and Colchian Medea and glorious Themisto." This short passage is illustrated, in two superimposed rows, by several episodes which represent the personification of Jealousy, Theseus, Athamas, Themisto (wrongly inscribed Philomela), Medea cutting Pelias to pieces and her infanticide.[15] Naturally, these various scenes never existed separately in an earlier Oppian text, since all of them refer to only a few lines of text that could not be split in as many parts as there are scenes mentioned in it.

2. *The Emancipation of the Miniature from its Text*

Once the immediate physical connection between a miniature and the text passage it illustrates began to dissolve, step followed step until a final separation was achieved. While in the preceding examples the first scene in a row remained anchored to the text passage proper, the next step was to dislocate the whole row of scenes, including the first one, and to place them in the text, wherever for mere formal reasons it seemed desirable. This stage of development is best represented by the well-known Genesis in the National Library of Vienna, cod. theol. gr. 31, a Bible fragment from the beginning of the sixth century. Its illustrators, instead of placing the strips of miniatures irregularly in the text, reserved the lower half of each page for the pictorial decoration and the upper half for the writing, thus arriving, artistically speaking, at a more systematic and unified distribution of the pictures than had been known hitherto. Equal space was here provided for both pictures and text, where formerly—as a glance at codices where the roll system is particularly well preserved will show—the area occupied by the miniatures had been on an average smaller than that used by the scribe. This artistic unification of the page in the Vienna Genesis could be achieved only through sacrificing some of the space allotted to the text, which therefore had to be abbreviated or excerpted, to the expansion of the picture area.

One page, with pictures belonging to the group attributed by Wickhoff to the so-called "miniaturist," may be analyzed from this point of view. Of the two scenes in the upper row (fig. 73),[16] the first represents Abraham standing devoutly before the angel who promises him prosperity (Gen. XXII, 15-18), and the second, his return to the young men who had waited for him during the sacrifice (v. 19). As these two scenes of nearly equal width stand side by side without being related by formal means, one easily recognizes in them column pictures which formerly had stood in writing columns of half the width of the present page. The assumption of a two-column model is supported by the third scene, in the lower row of the same miniature, in

[15] For a more detailed explanation of this miniature, cf. K. Weitzmann, "Euripides Scenes in Byzantine Art," in the forthcoming volume of *Hesperia*.

[16] Wickhoff, *Die Wiener Genesis*, p. 149 and pl. XI.—H. Gerstinger, *Die Wiener Genesis*, Vienna 1931, p. 84 and pl. XI (here the older bibliography).—P. Buberl, *Die Byzantinischen Handschriften*, vol. 1 (Beschreibendes Verzeichnis der illuminierten Handschriften in Österreich, vol. VIII, pt. 4), Leipzig 1937, p. 94 and pl. XXVI, no. 11.

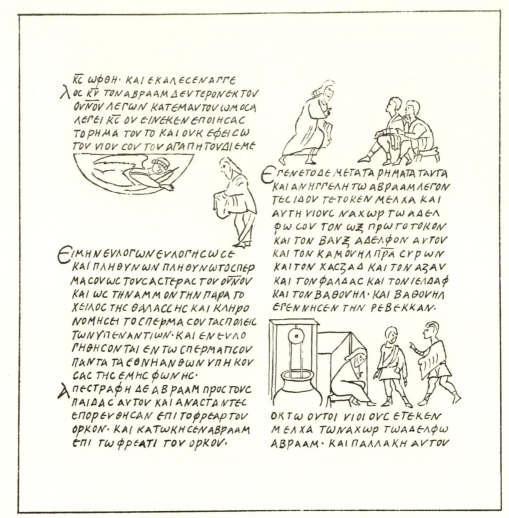

FIGURE D. Reconstruction of the Model of the Vienna Genesis

which one of two servants announces to Abraham the posterity of his brother Nahor (v. 20-24). All that belongs to it as an iconographic unit—the well of Beer-sheba (mentioned XXI, 30-31), Abraham sitting before his tent, and the two servants—occupies only the left half of the second row, and the right half is taken up by a rocky mountain, which is not an integral part of the scene. This clearly reveals the working process of the artist, who reserved in the lower half of the page the space for four scenes, two in each row, but having only three available, filled the area of the fourth quarter with a feature of mere decorative value. At the same time the text had to be shortened. The fourteen lines above the miniature contain verses 15-19, to which only the first two scenes can be related, while for the third, illustrating verses 20-24, the explanatory text was lost in the process of its abbreviation.

Figure D is an attempt to reconstruct the model on the basis of these observations: the height of the writing columns is calculated as equal to twenty-eight lines of writing, as many as the Vienna Genesis would have had if a single page were completely filled with writing, and their width is determined both by the single scenes and on the basis of the corresponding text passage of the Codex Alexandrinus of the fifth century, which actually is written in two columns.[17] Each scene is placed close to the verse it illustrates and in this manner also the third scene could be attached to the proper passage, which was lost in the Vienna manuscript. The general appearance, as far as the distribution of scenes in the text is concerned, is quite similar to our reconstructed Homer and Euripides rolls (Figures A-C) as well as to those codices which followed the system of roll illustration, including Christian manuscripts like the Bible of St. Isidoro (fig. 64).

The illustrators of the Vienna Genesis solved the problem of arranging a variable number of scenes over a predetermined area in many different ways. A second miniature (fig. 74),[18] illustrates Lot's Drunkenness (Gen. XIX, 29-35) in three scenes: in the first, the two daughters offer wine to their father before the older one is to lie with him; in the second, the older daughter persuades the younger to approach their father the next night; and in the third, the young daughter embraces her father. Instead of placing two scenes comfortably in an upper row and the third in a lower, as in the previous case, the miniaturist lined up all three of them in one single row, diagonally from the lower left to the upper right corner. This arrangement created two triangles, the upper left one remaining empty, while the lower right was filled by rocky mountains. At the same time the three scenes seem to have been abbreviated and therefore we have tried, in Figure E, not only to place each scene in its proper place in a two-column text, but also to re-establish the original width of each scene by adding those features which we believe to have been lost by the later condensation. Beside the daughters in the first scene is a column crowned by a capital which we consider as the remnant of the interior in which the scene takes place.[19] It is the same type of column which occurs tripled and with an architrave in the dream of Pharaoh (Pict. 35) and doubled and connected by a curtain in the dream of Abraham (Pict.

[17] F. G. Kenyon, *The Codex Alexandrinus* (facsimile), London 1915. Old Testament, pt. 1, fol. 12^{v}.

[18] Wickoff, *op. cit.*, p. 149 and pl. x.—Gerstinger, *op. cit.*, p. 83 and pl. x.—P. Buberl, *op. cit.*, p. 93 and pl. xxv, no. 10.

[19] Wickoff's interpretation as "Ruinenlandschaft" is just as incompatible with the common usage of architectural formulae in the Vienna Genesis, which tend to render distinct localities in abbreviated form, as is Gerstinger's suggestion of mere "Staffage" (i.e. accessories). Buberl follows Springer in explaining the column as remnant of the city Segor, but according to the formulae used in this manuscript, one would expect to see a city represented by a circular wall. Beside the point is Birt's attempt (Buchrolle, p. 278 note 4) to identify the column with Lot's wife transformed into a column of salt.

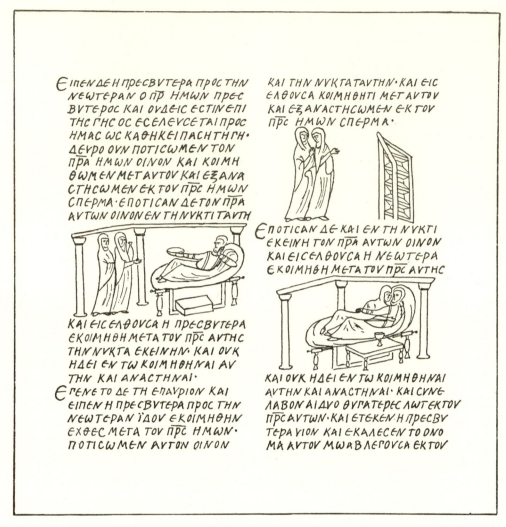

FIGURE E. Reconstruction of the Model of the Vienna Genesis

8). It is true that according to the Bible text, this scene takes place in a cave and not in a building, but it may be inferred from the Octateuchs[20] that the mediaeval illustrators actually did depict a house instead of a cave to indicate the locality of Lot's drunkenness. Furthermore, the mattress on which Lot lies is placed too high to suggest the same floor level on which the sisters stand. If we place a couch underneath the mattress similar to that in the Abraham and Pharaoh pictures (*Pict.* 8 and 35), the spatial relationship becomes quite plausible, and hence we assume that some of the cubes of rocks, which fill the lower right triangle, actually replace a couch. In the second scene the older sister points with her right hand to the place where the younger is going to meet her father, but the entrance itself, whether to the

[20] D. C. Hesseling, *Miniatures de l'octateuque grec de Smyrne* (Codices Graeci et Latini photogr. depicti, suppl. VI) (facsimile), Leyden 1909, pl. 24, no. 69.

cave or, more likely, again to a building, is omitted, so that the gesture of invitation in the present abbreviation of the scene can only be understood as pointing either into a void or into the following scene. In order to give this gesture a more precise meaning, we inserted in our sketch an open door, which is another of those frequently used formulae in the Viennese fragments (*Pict.* 8). The third scene takes place in the same interior as the first and therefore we added once more in our drawing three columns with an architrave, as well as a couch underneath the mattress and, under the table-top, which bears a chalice, we placed the necessary four legs which, like those of the couch, were submerged in the rocky landscape. In a similar way most miniatures of the Vienna Genesis can be divided into smaller iconographic units, which originally were separately placed in a two-column text, though in some cases the fusion of scenes within the reserved area has gone so far that the original stage cannot so easily be reconstructed as in the two preceding examples.

As the next step in the expansion of the picture area, the illustrator covers the whole page exclusively with pictures as may be illustrated by a St. Gall manuscript of the tenth century which is now in the University Library of Leyden, cod. Perizoni 17, and contains the First Book of the Maccabees. It is a narrative cycle which covers twenty-eight full pages;[21] two scenes are usually superimposed, as can be seen in the page (fig. 75)[22] where King Antiochus on his sick-bed and his friends (VI, 10) are depicted in the upper half, while the burial of Antiochus (VI, 16) is in the lower. In the archetype these two scenes in all probability stood separated from each other by several lines of writing, either within the same or in two successive columns. Furthermore, two pages with pictures usually confront each other in the Leyden manuscript, so that the reader, instead of finding the explanatory text on the page opposite the picture, must turn either to the preceding or to the following page in order to find the corresponding passages with which, in the archetype, the scenes had been physically connected—another clear sign of the progressive emancipation of the pictures from the text.

Finally the illustrators collect all the miniatures of a coherent cycle into a unit of its own and place them in the front of the whole text in one or more gatherings so that the picture story could be read in a sequence without any consultation of or interruption by the text. A typical example is the well-known Gospel book in the Cathedral of Rossano from the sixth century,[23]

---

[21] Merton, *op. cit.*, pp. 64ff. and pls. LV-LXI.—Goldschmidt, *Karolingische Buchmalerei*, pp. 22, 58 and pls. 72-73.—A. W. Byvanck, "Les principaux manuscrits dans les collections publiques du Royaume des Pays-Bas," *Bull. de la soc. franç. de reprod. de mss. à peint.*, XV, 1931, p. 68.

[22] Merton, *op. cit.*, pl. LVII, no. 1.

[23] A. Haseloff, *Codex Purpureus Rossanensis*, Berlin-Leipzig 1898.—A. Muñoz, *Il codice purpureo di Rossano e il frammento Sinopense*, Rome 1907.

in which the scenes from the life of Christ, most of them supplemented by figures of prophets who point to the New Testament events above their heads, form a unit which is placed in front of the text of the four Gospels. Some of the miniatures depict the story in two scenes side by side like the one with the Healing of the Man Born Blind (fig. 76),[24] in which Christ puts his hand upon the eye of the blind man (John IX, 6) and the latter washes his eyes in the pool of Siloam (John IX, 7). This suggests that, just like the Rossano codex itself (fig. 77), the archetype must have been a two-column text, and that in it these two scenes were attached separately to their proper text passages in fairly narrow columns. The general appearance of the model must have been very similar to the model of the Vienna Genesis (Figures D and E).[25] In general, the separation of the picture section from the text section offered a great advantage in the process of manufacturing, since scribe and painter could work independently on different gatherings of the same codex at the same time.

Whereas in the codex of Rossano the collecting of the miniatures in a separate section gave to the painter a greater freedom of arrangement and a chance of expansion, in other manuscripts a similar collection was made for just the opposite reason, namely greater economy. An example is a miniature which adorns the paraphrase of the *Ornithiaca* of Dionysius of Philadelphia, a treatise which forms a part of the famous Dioscurides manuscript in Vienna, cod. med. gr. 1.[26] Whereas in Books I and II each bird is placed in the text in its proper place according to the tradition of classical roll illustration, in Book III all birds, twenty-four in number, are taken out of the text and placed together on a single page (fig. 78) which for greater clarity is divided in a net of crossing lines, so that each bird is framed and separated from the next. Since in the first two books a bird normally does not occupy the whole width of the space provided for it, the new pattern saved much empty space, and at the same time the illustrator gave to the collective picture a decorative appearance, which must have appealed to artists in other media who wanted to use birds for an ornamental purpose. A mosaic floor found recently in Antioch[27] of about the fifth century, i.e. in date not far removed from the Vienna manuscript, fills the reticulated ground with a great variety of birds in a manner not unlike that of the miniaturist. The birds are represented with a zoological accuracy which, to use Morey's

---

[24] Haseloff, *op. cit.*, pl. IX.—Muñoz, *op. cit.*, pl. XI.

[25] However, not all scenes of the Rossano Gospels could originally have been situated in narrow columns of writing. The two full-page miniatures with Christ before Pilate and the Communion of the Apostles were, in all probability, copied from monumental paintings.

[26] Premerstein, Wessely and Mantuani, *Dioscurides*, vol. II, fols. 474-485.—Buberl, *Die Byzantinischen Handschriften*, vol. I, p. 56 and pls. XVII-XX.—Bethe, *Buch und Bild*, p. 25 and fig. 4.

[27] *Antioch-on-the-Orontes* II, *The Excavations of 1933 to 1936*, Princeton 1938, p. 189 and pl. 47, no. 62.—C. R. Morey, *The Mosaics of Antioch*, London-New York 1938, p. 42 and pl. XXII.

phrase, "Audubon himself would not have disdained," but which was not required by the purely ornamental character of the mosaics and can be most easily explained by presupposing the use of a scientific treatise with collective miniature pages like the one in Vienna. Thus the very type of full-page illustration, which results from the accumulation of former column pictures, becomes—unintentionally, perhaps, to begin with—a pattern book which could comfortably be used by artists in other media.

In the same way whole cycles of narrative scenes were occasionally condensed on a few consecutive pages. In a miscellaneous manuscript in the University Library of Leyden, cod. Voss. lat. oct. 15, from the beginning of the eleventh century, there is, among other illuminated texts, a complete set of illustrations belonging to and preceding the *Psychomachia* of Prudentius.[28] By superimposing four or even five rows, and filling each with as many scenes as the space permitted, the whole cycle of more than seventy scenes was condensed on ten pages. On one of them (fig. 79)[29] the first row depicts two scenes side by side: Sobrietas throwing a stone at Luxuria, and Sobrietas inveighing against Luxuria, scenes which originally stood separated in a two-column text, like that of the earlier manuscript in Paris (fig. 62). So in this instance we actually possess the earlier stage of the development within the same recension, which in the case of the Vienna Genesis and the Codex Rossanensis is lost. The second row presses even four scenes into a row: Jocus throwing away the cymbals, Amor fleeing after having abandoned quiver and bow, Pompa throwing away ornaments and Voluptas fleeing. The other rows are similarly crowded.

The isolation of the Prudentius scenes from the text may have been prompted, in part, by the miniaturist's desire to provide more easily accessible iconographic models for artists working in other media. The *Psychomachia* was often copied in the Middle Ages in stone, bronze, and ivory sculpture, in mosaics, enamels and other media,[30] and the short inscriptions attached to the scenes of the Leyden drawings were sufficient to make them usable for any mediaeval artist who had a general knowledge of this extremely popular text. In a sense, then, this collection of drawings is a *pattern book*, but transmitting only iconographic content rather than artistic forms, as was characteristic of such later ones as the sketch book of Wolfenbüttel[31] or the drawings of Villard de Honnecourt in the Bibliothèque Nationale of Paris.[32]

[28] R. Stettiner, *Die illustr. Prudentiushandschriften*, p. 11 and pls. 19-23.

[29] *Ibid.*, pl. 22, no. 4.

[30] Ad. Katzenellenbogen, *Allegories of the Virtues and Vices in Mediaeval Art*, London 1939.

[31] Fr. Rücker and H. R. Hahnloser, "Das Musterbuch von Wolfenbüttel," *Mitteilungen der Gesellschaft für vervielfältigende Kunst, Beilage der "Graphischen Künste,"* LII, Vienna 1929, pp. 1ff.

[32] H. R. Hahnloser, *Villard de Honnecourt, Kritische Gesamtausgabe des Bauhüttenbuches ms. fr. 19093 der Pariser Nationalbibliothek*, Vienna 1935.

In the Leyden manuscript the Prudentius text follows the emancipated miniature cycle, but elsewhere the initial gathering with pictures has been divorced from the text so that the basic text from which the dislocated miniatures were originally made up is not easily identified. The Vatican Library possesses a Greek manuscript of the fifteenth century, cod. gr. 1087, which contains a set of constellation pictures together with the zodiac, the planisphere and two hemispheres, all of which are in wash drawing and condensed on ten folios.[33] As many as four or five constellations fill one page, with only short inscriptions for identification purposes, as in the example which depicts the Cygnus, the Aquarius, the Capricornus and one of the two Ursae (fig. 80). No text follows these drawings, and since no other Greek manuscript with constellation pictures is known—in contrast to the Latin West where we possess in considerable number illustrated Aratus commentaries by Hyginus, Cicero, Germanicus, and others—we are unable to determine the precise text with which they were originally connected. It may have been the *Katasterismoi* of Eratosthenes of Cyrene or one of the many Greek commentators on Aratus such as Hipparchus of Nicaea, Diodorus of Alexandria, Sporus of Nicaea and others.

Extractions of miniatures from their basic text are comparatively numerous in medical manuscripts. Here the explanatory drawings were apparently considered so much more essential than the text that the latter was either reduced to short explanatory phrases or dropped entirely. The most frequently copied set of illustrations demonstrates the various applications of the cautery, and Sudhoff, whose studies are fundamental in the field of illustrated medical manuscripts, counts twenty copies of it.[34] The basic text which once must have described each treatment at some length is lost, though in some manuscripts there are short explanatory remarks. Sudhoff is inclined to assume for the lost text an Alexandrian origin from the beginning of our era, though cauterizing as such was known already much earlier by Hippocrates. In the pictures of an English manuscript in the cathedral of Durham, cod. Hunter 100 (fig. 81), even the short directions are lacking.[35] The upper row of one of its miniatures, which date in the beginning of the twelfth century, represents a physician who holds the branding iron in his hand and stands behind a patient who points to his head, where two spots indicate the points to be cauterized. A second patient, with similar spots on his forehead,

[33] fols. 300ᵛ-310ᵛ. Boll-Gundel, "Die Sternbilder der Griechen und Römer," in Roscher, *Mythol. Lexikon*, vol. VI, Suppl., cols. 869ff. and figs. 1-13, 15-19.

[34] Sudhoff, *Beiträge zur Geschichte der Chirurgie*, p. 75 and pls. XV-XXXVI.

[35] This codex is not in Sudhoff's list.—*New Pal. Soc.*, ser. II, parts VI-VII, 1923, pl. 125.—Ch. Singer, *From Magic to Science*, London 1928, p. 137 and fig. 50.—R. A. B. Mynors, *Durham Cathedral Manuscripts*, Oxford 1939, p. 49 and pl. 37.

sits at the right, and below, in the second row, stand no less than three patients with spots at various locations on the body. In earlier copies, such as the Florentine one in the Laurentian Library, cod. Plut. LXXIII, 41, from the ninth century,[36] a physician is each time associated with a patient, but in the Durham manuscript, as the result of collecting as many examples of cautery treatments as possible on one page, all physicians are omitted except the one of the first treatment, who is supposed to be related by the beholder to each individual patient. The marking of the spots on the body of the patients is considered as sufficient for the understanding of the medical treatment.

Known through three English copies of the twelfth century—to quote another example in the medical field—is a set of three operation pictures, representing the cutting of hemorrhoids, the removal of the polypus from the nose and the operation for cataract, and once more for these scenes the explanatory text is lost.[37] Brief mentions of these operations by Aëtius and Paulus of Aegina are the only hints that we are actually dealing with ancient treatments and therefore permitted to assume a classical archetype in which each operation picture was imbedded in a text.

We have followed, thus far, step by step the gradual emancipation of the column pictures from the text to which, in the roll and earliest codices, they had been subordinated. We have seen that the impetus for this development was provided by the invention of the codex, and that its various stages could be traced in the codex from the initial lining up of several scenes in a row, through the superposition of several rows, to the final isolation of the pictures from, and their full equality with, the text.

3. *The Addition of Frame and Background*

The desire of the illustrator to increase the importance of the miniature expressed itself in still other forms. He started to draw a simple borderline around a miniature, with the result that now the beholder's eye no longer conceives text and illustration as homogeneous, as in a papyrus roll, but tends to see a framed picture isolated from the text, as if it were on a different plane. Frames must have been introduced very soon after the invention of the codex, since they occur already in the miniatures of the Milan Iliad, the earliest existing codex fragment with pictures (cf. p. 42 and figs. 32-34). In other manuscripts the scenes are not framed until considerably later, if at all, and of particular interest are those instances where the treat-

---

[36] Sudhoff's date (*op. cit.*, p. 90) in the eleventh century is apparently too late. Cf. E. A. Lowe, *Scriptura Beneventana*, vol. I, Oxford 1929, pl. XI.

[37] K. Sudhoff, *op. cit.*, pp. 11ff. and pls. I and XVII. Two of the manuscripts are in London, Brit. Mus., cod. Sloane 1975 and Harley 1585, and the third is in Oxford, Bodl. Libr., cod. Ashmole 1462.

ment is not consistent throughout a larger cycle and miniatures with and without a frame are intermingled.

The Pseudo-Oppian manuscript in Venice, whose frameless miniatures we have introduced already as illustrating the survival of the *papyrus style* (fig. 61), has other miniatures which are surrounded by simple borderlines, like the two (fig. 82) illustrating "Polydeuces arraying saw-toothed dogs for battle with wild beasts" (II, 18-19), and "both slaying baleful men in battle of the fists and overcoming spotted wild beasts with swift hounds" (II, 20-21). Normally, if an artist starts out with a frame, he takes care to balance the composition within the self-imposed limits, but in these miniatures the legs of the hunted doe, the antlers of a stag and the fist of fighting Polydeuces protrude beyond the borderlines, and the frame is obviously a later addition to a scene which was originally conceived frameless. Most likely the border was drawn at the same period in which the actual copy was made. Though in a materialistic sense the background inside and outside the frame is the same uncolored parchment, in our imagination the frame creates space and depth around the figures, establishing a contrast between the miniature and the two-dimensional writing column.

The illustration of Prudentius also was begun in the papyrus style (fig. 62), but in the tenth century copyists began to frame the miniatures of the *Psychomachia*. A transitional stage can be seen in the Paris manuscript, cod. lat. 8318 (fig. 83),[38] whose illustrator drew, in many cases, simple or double lines hesitatingly around only two or three sides of the pictures. He was anxious to keep the frame within the limits of the width of the writing column, but met an obstacle in figures whose arms, legs and attributes often stick out into the margin. In the scene where Avaritia casts men into flames (v. 490), the artist apparently felt himself blocked by the flames, which spread too far into the margin, and therefore did not continue the frame, while in other cases he solved the difficulty by allowing the frame to cut through the protruding parts as the illustrator of the Pseudo-Oppian had done.

Like the frameless pictures, scenes with frames were also lined up two or more in a frieze, and with several variations in method, each of which may be illustrated by some miniatures from the *Octateuchs*. In the codex of the Seraglio in Istanbul (fig. 84)[39] two consecutive scenes, one representing the discourse of Moses with the Lord in the presence of Aaron and Miriam (Num. II, 4), and the other, Moses sending men to search for the land of Canaan (Num. III, 2), are treated side by side as independent compositions,

[38] Stettiner, *op. cit.*, pp. 3ff. and pls. 1-12, 15-16.
[39] Th. Ouspensky, *L'octateuque de la Bibliothèque du Sérail à Constantinople*, Sofia 1907, p. 153 and pl. XXVII, no. 165.

each with its own frame and separated from the other by about the same distance as usually lies between two writing columns. Here the distinction between two iconographic units is respected, but in another Octateuch in Smyrna[40] the two scenes are joined in such a way that the neighboring sides of the frames coincide. From here it is only a short step to eliminate the dividing line entirely, as is done in the corresponding scenes of the Octateuch in the Vatican Library, cod. gr. 747, so that two different compositions are now united by a common frame.[41] However, the logical development from step to step to be observed in these examples from the Octateuchs of the eleventh and twelfth centuries cannot be assumed for every miniature cycle. It is quite likely that other illustrators omitted one or another intermediary step in order to reach more quickly the final stage in which several scenes become spatially united by a common frame. Furthermore, this final stage was reached in other manuscript recensions much earlier than the Octateuchs. As a matter of fact, in the earliest illustrated codex in existence, the Milan Iliad, there are already instances of several scenes combined in a common frame (figs. 32 and 34). Hence, all those changes which we have demonstrated in the later Octateuchs must already have taken place in the first two or three centuries after the invention of the codex.

In the course of time illustrators realized the artistic possibilities of the borderlines and turned them into massive decorative frames, as e.g. in most miniatures of the Carolingian *Physiologus* in Berne, cod. 318 (fig. 85), the same manuscript which also preserved the earlier type of frameless miniatures (fig. 56). The next step is the filling of the area inside the frame with landscape and sky. In the miniature which illustrates the "prima natura leonis" we can quite accurately determine the amount of additional background features. In the late classical model the lion was apparently walking on a strip of ground between trees, elements which occur similarly in the animal miniatures of the Pseudo-Oppian (fig. 82). To these original elements the illustrator added a high mountain range with one peak encompassing the left tree and another the lion and the right tree. This formation is painted in a grisaille-like manner, quite different from the more substantial ground on which the lion walks, and if the outline of the mountain were not studded with little trees, likewise in grisaille, there might even be some doubt as to whether a cloud bank was perhaps intended instead of a mountain. Moreover the corners are filled with the sky, and thus the whole surface inside the frame is completely covered with paint. Again it must be emphasized that the addition of landscape occurs already at a much earlier date than the Carolingian period in the miniatures of the Itala fragments

[40] Hesseling, *op. cit.*, pl. 69, no. 227.
[41] Fol. 163ʳ. Photo in the Department of Art and Archaeology of Princeton University.

from Quedlinburg[42] and of the Virgil in the Vatican Library, cod. lat. 3225,[43] in which a pink strip of the sky at the hour of sunset turns gradually into a cool blue. Thus at least at the beginning of the fifth century, perhaps even somewhat earlier, we can expect cases analogous to the *Physiologus* of Berne, but since we do not know earlier illustrations of the Book of Kings or of the Aeneid, we cannot be sure whether there existed earlier models of the Quedlinburg Itala or the Vatican Virgil in which the miniatures had no landscape background. The assumption of such models, especially in the case of the Book of Kings, is by no means unfounded, since we know from the majority of the miniatures of the Vienna Genesis (figs. 73-74) that Old Testament cycles actually did exist in the frameless papyrus manner.

Like the frameless pictures again, scenes enriched by frame and background were occasionally placed side by side and above each other, occupying the whole page. The fragments of the Quedlinburg Itala are so organized that always four scenes in a square fill one page, and similarly the first miniature of the Vatican Virgil combines six framed scenes taken from various books (Eclogues, Georgics and Aeneid). In the course of time the illustrators began to eliminate the inner frames and more often the vertical ones, as in quite a number of pages of the Gregory manuscript in Paris, cod. gr. 510.[44] Elimination of the horizontal frames is rarer since it is naturally more difficult spatially to unite superimposed scenes than those alongside each other, but an example exists in the same Gregory manuscript in the illustration, in two rows, of the story of Jonah.[45]

The illuminators who first introduced landscape backgrounds in miniature painting after the parchment codex was well established probably used models from a medium, other than their own, in which landscape painting had existed for a long time. These models were most likely fresco paintings which already in the first centuries B.C. and A.D. had fully elaborated the landscape, as e.g. the Odyssey landscapes from the Esquiline, and perhaps also encaustic panels of which, however, too few are left to support this hypothesis. On the other hand, once landscape features had entered book illumination, which is one of the most conservative fields in all the fine arts, they persisted in it much longer than in fresco and other branches of painting

---

[42] V. Schultze, *Die Quedlinburger Itala-Miniaturen der Kgl. Bibliothek in Berlin*, Munich 1898.— H. Degering and A. Boeckler, *Die Quedlinburger Italafragmente*, Berlin 1932.

[43] *Fragmenta et Picturae Vergiliana Cod. Vat. lat. 3225* (Codices e Vaticanis selecti, vol. I, editio altera) (facsimile), Rome 1930.

[44] H. Omont, *Miniatures des plus anciens manuscrits grecs*, pl. XXIV (fol. 52ᵛ: scenes from Genesis); pl. XXVI (fol. 69ᵛ: story of Joseph); pl. XXX (fol. 87ᵛ: scenes from Gospels and the life of Gregory) and others.

[45] *Ibid.*, pl. XX (fol. 3ʳ).

where, after the late classical period, a more abstract treatment of the background became common.

When miniaturists started to add landscape backgrounds to figural compositions which originally were conceived without them, they frequently did it in a rather mechanical manner and with no regard for iconographic requirements. In the scene of the Vienna Genesis, in which Jacob blesses Ephraim and Manasseh in the presence of Joseph and his wife (fig. 86) [46] the figures occupy only half the width of the area reserved for the pictorial decoration, i.e. precisely as much as was required for a narrow column in a two-column text (fig. 73), and the remaining space at both sides is filled with an atmospheric mountainous landscape. Iconographically the blessing scene takes place inside a house and not in the open air, and this discrepancy can be used as a strong argument for considering the landscape a later addition. It is true that an ancient or mediaeval illustrator was not always capable of designing convincingly an interior, but he usually solved the difficulty by placing a house behind the scene in order to indicate the locality inside of which the action is supposed to take place. This actually was the solution which the illustrators of the Octateuchs had found for the same scene. [47]

Still more incongruous is the situation in the miniature where two scenes representing Jacob's Death are placed before a common background (fig. 87). [48] One depicts Jacob already deceased on a couch while Joseph and the other sons stand around him weeping and mourning; the other shows the entombment of Jacob's mummy in the cave of Mamre. When in the model, as we assume, these two scenes were still separated in different writing columns—more or less as in sketches D and E—only the entombment could have had any landscape elements, whereas the couch with the deceased must have stood either in an interior or in front of a house, as is the case in the Octateuch, Vat. gr. 747. [49] While the illustrators of the earlier part of the Vienna Genesis, whom Wickhoff calls the *miniaturist* and the *colorist*, followed the older tradition of placing two different scenes simply on a common groundline, the *illusionist*, Wickhoff's third master, unites them by a rather stereotyped background formula which is typical for all his pictures, i.e. by atmospheric mountains, and a pink and blue sky. By doing so he eliminated sometimes, as in the scene of Jacob's death, the distinction of the

[46] Wickhoff, *op. cit.*, p. 161 and pl. XLV.—Gerstinger, *op. cit.*, p. 109 and pl. 45.—Buberl, *op. cit.*, p. 125 and pl. XLIII, no. 45.

[47] Hesseling, *op. cit.*, pl. 47, no. 144.

[48] Wickhoff, *op. cit.*, p. 162 and pl. XLVIII.—Gerstinger, *op. cit.*, p. 110 and pl. 48.—Buberl, *op. cit.*, p. 127 and pl. XLIV, no. 48.

[49] On fol. 70ᵛ. Photo in the Department of Art and Archaeology of Princeton University.

locality, but created a spatial continuity for the scenes on the basis of which Wickhoff derived his principle of continuous method. It is no accident that in the Vienna Genesis the atmospheric background and continuous method are regularly employed only by the latest artist, who at the same time is artistically the weakest, while the better artists at the beginning of the manuscript still work without background in the traditional *papyrus style*, in which the archetype of the Vienna Genesis was apparently conceived.

In agreement with the general tendencies of mediaeval art, in the course of time a more ornamental background was used instead of a landscape. The three-dimensional element, which together with the landscape had entered the early codex miniatures, was eliminated again, while a two-dimensional ornamental pattern brought the miniature back to the same projection as the writing. Sometimes a gradual shift from one form of background to the other can be observed, the pink and blue stripes of the sky, for example, becoming geometrical bands;[50] but in other cases, as some English herbals, a patterned background is placed behind miniatures which in the immediate model had no background at all. Whereas the Pseudo-Apuleius manuscripts in London, Brit. Mus., cod. Cotton Vitellius C. III from the eleventh century[51] and Oxford, Bodl. Lib., cod. Bodley 130 from the beginning of the twelfth century,[52] retained the classical tradition of painting the plants as silhouettes on the plain surface of the parchment, the English miniaturists of the end of the twelfth century placed behind the plants an abstract multicolored background as can be seen in the miniatures of the herbal London, Brit. Mus., cod. Sloane 1975 (fig. 88).[53] The scene in which a man kills a snake stands against a violet ground, covered with a pattern of white dots and surrounded by a frame in blue and white, and the miniature of the camelia on the same page is similarly ornamentalized. The three stems of the plant serve at the same time to divide the dotted ground into areas of color: the area between the stems is blue, outside of them red, and between the blossoms violet. Similar ornamental backgrounds with a variety of patterns are found in a great number of Romanesque manuscripts, bestiaries, surgical

[50] E.g. the praying Job in the cod. Vat. gr. 749 from the ninth century. Weitzmann, *Byzantinische Buchmalerei*, p. 79 and pl. LXXXV; no. 532 (fol. 21ᵛ).

[51] G. Swarzenski, "Mittelalterliche Kopien einer antiken medizinischen Bilderhandschrift," *Jahrb. d. Inst.*, XVII, 1902, p. 48.—Ch. Singer, *Studies in the History and Method of Science*, vol. II, Oxford 1921, pls. IV, XVI, XXV;—*Idem, Journ. of Hell. Stud.*, XLVII, 1927, fig. 37 and pls. III-IV;—*Idem, From Magic to Science*, fig. 64, pls. III-V.

[52] Ch. Singer, *Studies*, vol. II, colorplate V, pls. XV, XXIII;—*Idem, Journ. of Hell. Stud.*, XLVII, 1927, pls. VII-VIII;—*Idem, From Magic to Science*, pls. VI-VIII.

[53] Ch. Singer, *Studies*, vol. II, fig. 32 and pls. XV, XXV;—*Idem, Journ. of Hell. Stud.*, XLVII, 1927, pl. X.—Th. Meyer-Steineg and K. Sudhoff, *Geschichte der Medicin im Überblick*, Jena 1921, p. 196 and figs. 91-92. For the surgical miniature of the same ms. cf. K. Sudhoff, *Beiträge zur Geschichte der Chirurgie*, p. 11, pl. I, no. 1 and pl. XIX.—Bethe, *Buch und Bild*, pp. 35, 37 and fig. 15.

treatises, literary texts, etc. For some of them the earlier stages with frame-less and groundless miniatures are still preserved, while in others they can be assumed only by analogy.

Besides frame and background there are still other methods by which the mediaeval artist could display his decorative inclinations. Especially when two or more scenes are lined up in a row, a very common device for relating them is the application of an arcade in such a manner that each scene is placed under a separate arch. In a miniature from the codex A. II. 15 of the Casanatense Library in Rome, a medical manuscript from the thirteenth century (fig. 89),[54] a number of scenes of cauterizing are lined up in superimposed rows as in the earlier Anglo-Saxon manuscript of Durham (fig. 81), but, while in the latter the patients are unrelated to each other on the plain parchment, the illustrator of the Casanatense manuscript organized the scenes under arches. Only in the first scene, again as in the Durham minia-ture, is the physician depicted beside the patient; in all the others the phy-sician's hand, which sticks out from behind the column of the arch, is all that is left of him as a result of the condensation of originally fuller composi-tions. The impression is that the physicians are standing behind the archi-tecture, hidden by the columns, so that a spatial value is implied along with the decorative one.[55]

There are great variations in the structure of the architectural frame. Let us take one more example from the medical field. In a treatise on midwifery in Copenhagen, Royal Lib., Thottske Saml. no. 190 from the twelfth cen-tury,[56] the pictures of the position of the embryo in the uterus are placed in a decorative setting, in which each single picture is under a separate arch of a two-story arcade the spandrels of which are richly filled with ornaments. In an earlier Carolingian copy of the same treatise in Brussels, Royal Lib. cod. 3701-3715 (fig. 118), the pictures are still without a frame and dis-tributed in the text in the papyrus style. The decorative use of the arcade as frame is not, however, an innovation of the mediaeval illuminators; they merely followed the custom of classical artists, who sometimes, as in the Tensa Capitolina (fig. 22), arranged narrative scenes under similar archi-tectural structures after having extracted them from the rolls and trans-ferred them into a new medium.

[54] K. Sudhoff, op. cit., p. 100 and pl. xxv.—P. Giacosa, Magistri Salernitani nondum editi, Turin 1901, pl. 23.

[55] It may be mentioned that in the Durham manuscript along with the miniature reproduced in fig. 81 there are other cauterizing scenes which, too, are already placed under an arcade. Cf. Ch. Singer, From Magic to Science, p. 137 and fig. 50.—Mynors, op. cit., pl. 37a.

[56] K. Sudhoff, Tradition und Naturbeobachtung (Studien zur Geschichte der Medizin, fasc. 1), Leipzig 1907, p. 71 and pl. XVIII.

4. *The Full-page Miniature*

The ultimate exploitation of artistic possibilities in a codex was the creation of a single picture which filled a full page. This occurred very soon after the invention of the codex but, at first, for a very special case only, namely the frontispiece which contained either portraits of authors, singly or in groups, dedication pictures in which an author, scribe or donor dedicates the book to a dignitary or divinity, title saints of the locality for which the manuscript was made, or other personalities of a similar rank. Such pictures may sometimes be based on specific passages in the text, but they are not text illustrations in the proper sense of the word; they had never been incorporated within the writing columns nor had so close a physical connection with them as the narrative scenes. They always precede, as an isolated unit, either the whole codex, or, if the codex is subdivided in several books, they head single books. In the miniatures of narrative cycles, as far as we have dealt with them, the figure scale was not essentially altered, even after they were grouped together in short friezes or on a whole page, or enriched by frame and background; but the frontispiece, from the very beginning, adopted a scale which far surpasses that normally used in scenic compositions. Friend, in his forthcoming study of the evangelist-portraits, will make clear that as early as the second century A.D. the existence of framed full-page miniatures can be assumed for the authors of the Gospels, shown sitting in front of a rich architecture or a landscape background, and he will show that these miniatures depended on monumental art, i.e. on sculpture for the seated authors, on architecture for the theater-background and perhaps on frescoes for the landscape elements. Thus these frontispieces obviously contained from the very beginning all those features whose gradual infiltration into the narrative scenes we observed in the preceding chapter, and we can, therefore, conclude that the frontispieces stimulated the addition of frame and background to the scenic compositions. However, the different types of backgrounds available in the frontispieces could hardly suffice for the great variety we find in narrative scenes of all kinds, and there is evidence that the illustrators of large and extensive cycles consulted monumental painting directly for new landscape and other background motifs.

Most frontispieces have a monumental character which contributes largely to the impressiveness and the dignity of the title miniature, and in this point they resemble panel paintings. It is this quality which in a final stage of development the illustrators try to imitate in the narrative scenes as well. Instead of filling a page with several strips of joined scenes (cf. figs. 78-81), they now reserve the whole area for one single scene and, though impairing somewhat the continuity of the narrative cycle, they give to each scene a greater formal independence and individuality. This process had far-reaching consequences. Since in very extensive cycles with often hundreds of scenes the illustrator probably never even attempted to enlarge each single scene to a full-size picture, the monumentalization of a picture cycle is accompanied by a reduction in the number of its scenes. Only the more prominent ones are chosen for the enlargement, and the comparatively insignificant are dropped. The full-size Aeneid miniatures of the Virgilius Romanus, Vat. lat. 3867,[57] are fewer in number than the illustrations of the earlier Virgil cod. Vat. lat. 3225, which, on an average, are smaller. Similarly Greek Gospels and lectionaries with full-size miniatures contain only a fraction of scenes compared with the narrative cycles of the Gospel books in Florence, Laurent. Lib. cod. Plut. VI, 23 (figs. 70-71) and Paris, Bibl. Nat. cod. gr. 74,[58] and the same phenomenon could be demonstrated in many other picture recensions.

Cycles were thus abbreviated, as we have seen, already in classical antiquity whenever artists used illustrated rolls as models for a copy in another medium where space did not permit the rendering of a complete miniature cycle. Now we may use the term *selective cycle* in connection with book illumination too, to indicate that a copyist makes a selection from a more extensive model. This is such common practice in mediaeval manuscripts that the selective cycle by far outnumbers in examples the full cycle of the archetype.

A composition which originally stood within a writing column can be enlarged to fill the whole page in various ways. The easiest and simplest is to place a former column picture in a frame which fills a full page or, if there was already a frame before the picture left the writing column, to increase its height correspondingly. The result can be seen in a miniature of the Carolingian Aratus manuscript in Leyden, Univ. Lib., Voss. lat. quart. 79,[59] in which the constellation of Aquila (fig. 90)[60] is surrounded by a frame higher than it is wide, so that the eagle's wings which push hard against the lateral border had to be shortened while much empty ground is left above the eagle. A comparison with the same constellation in the Anglo-Saxon manuscript in London (fig. 66), where the eagle is placed in the midst of a writing column and spreads out its wings unhampered by decorative limitations, rep-

[57] *Picturae Ornamenta complura scripturae specimina cod. Vat. 3867* (Codices e Vaticanis selecti, vol. II) (facsimile), Rome 1902.

[58] H. Omont, *Évangiles avec peintures byzantines du XIᵉ siècle*, 2 vols., Paris (n.d.).

[59] G. Thiele, *Himmelsbilder* (here the older bibliography).—Gasiorowski, *op. cit.*, pp. 78, 81 and figs. 27-30.—A. W. Byvanck, *Bull. de la soc. franç. de reprod. de mss. à peint.*, XV, 1931, p. 65 and pl. XIX.—Bethe, *Buch und Bild*, pp. 50, 54 and fig. 30.

[60] Thiele, *op. cit.*, p. 118 and fig. 43.

resents obviously the more original stage in the development of the constellation pictures.

A new formal problem arises when narrative scenes with a landscape background are turned into full-page pictures. Among the miniatures of the Vatican Virgil, cod. lat. 3225, most of which are placed within the text, there are a few which originally must likewise have been broader than tall, but were heightened later, probably in the present copy. How this was achieved can be seen in the miniature which represents the sacrifice of the shining white bull in the country of the Thracians and Aeneas' discourse with the voice of Polydorus in front of the latter's tumulus near the bleeding tree (fig. 91).[61] The copyist has apparently not changed the scale of the figures or of the temple, and an imaginary line can be drawn unimpeded from the ridge of the temple toward the top of the tumulus, a line which in the model supposedly marked the upper frame. The area below this line contains everything necessary to explain the action of the scene, while the added upper area is occupied by superfluous fillings. The tree, which for iconographic reasons does not need to be higher than the temple, has grown up and branches off so as to fill decoratively nearly half the upper area, the other half of which is occupied by a row of elongated barrack-like buildings seen in bird's-eye view and surrounded by a wall. This complex of houses, usually considered to be the city of Aeneadae, the first of many founded by Aeneas, does not correspond to the traditional representational formula for a walled city which had been in use in Greek and Roman art since the Hellenistic period,[62] and which occurs also in this same manuscript for the city of Carthage.[63] The incongruity can now easily be explained by the process of expansion described above: while the city of Carthage lies in a zone which belongs to the original picture cycle and goes back to an archetype of the earlier Roman period in which this type of walled city was generally used, the city of Aeneadae is an invention of the period when the upper zone was added, i.e. a period which had lost the understanding of perspective and organic grouping of buildings inside a towered wall.

A column picture could be enlarged to a full page also by cutting a scene in two halves and placing one part above the other, for which the illustration of the Crossing of the Red Sea in the Paris Psalter, gr. 139 (fig. 92),[64]

[61] Facsimile, *op. cit.*, *Pict.* 18.

[62] Fr. M. Biebel, "The Walled Cities of the Gerasa Mosaics," *Gerasa, City of the Decapolis*, New Haven 1938, pp. 341ff.

[63] Facsimile, *op. cit.*, *Pict.* 23.

[64] H. Omont, *Miniatures des plus anciens manuscrits grecs*, pl. IX.—H. Buchthal, *The Miniatures of the Paris Psalter*, London 1938, pl. IX. The date of this manuscript is much disputed. While one school with C. R. Morey as its champion dates it in the eighth century, other students of Byzantine art, including the present writer, attribute it to the tenth century.

is a typical example. This composition, which did not originate in a Psalter but in the Book of Exodus (cf. p. 132), is organized in the form of a frieze in all copies of the Octateuchs[65] and reads from left to right, while in the Psalter the right part of the composition with Moses and the Israelites is placed above the drowning of Pharaoh's army. Consequently the gaze of the pursuing Egyptians and of the escaping Israelites no longer meets, and Moses does not close the Red Sea in *front* of the Egyptians, but *over* their heads, a mistake which reveals the original relationship between the two groups. In redistributing the compositional elements the artist increased the scale of the figures since he had now to fill a picture area at least twice as large as a column picture of equal width and in doing so he advanced considerably toward the monumentalization of the composition at the expense of its narrative distinctness.

But even solutions of this kind did not satisfy the ambition of illustrators who wanted to give to narrative scenes the monumentality of frontispieces. Finally, they adopted the same figure scale, and as a result the figures came to occupy nearly the full height of the page. In many cases this meant an enlargement by more than twice the original figure size and at the same time a reduction of the original width of the composition by condensation or even by abbreviation. In the miniature of the same Paris Psalter which represents David's Repentance (fig. 93)[66] we are able to follow this process of enlargement in detail, since we possess the earlier stage of the same composition in the Vatican Book of Kings, cod. gr. 333,[67] where it is still connected with the very text in which the composition originated (cf. p. 132) and at the same time has kept its original shape of a column picture, although the manuscript is of the eleventh century and hence later than the Paris Psalter. A comparison of these two miniatures reveals that the angel, who in the Psalter was placed above David's head and is now cut out, stood originally in full length behind the king's throne. The kneeling David in the Paris miniature is so close to the seated one that Nathan could no longer, as in the Vatican miniature, stand on the same groundline between the two, but had to be moved slightly upward; and, finally, the hand of God, to which the kneeling David of the Vatican miniature is praying, is dropped entirely so that the meaning of the proskynesis is now lost. Thus the regrouping of figures for mere compositional reasons was at the expense of iconographic distinctness, a by no means isolated case in mediaeval book illumination, particularly in de luxe manuscripts, where quite often minia-

---

[65] Hesseling, *L'octateuque de Smyrne*, pl. 59, no. 179.

[66] Omont, *op. cit.*, pl. VIII.—Buchthal, *op. cit.*, pl. VIII.

[67] J. Lassus, "Les miniatures byzantines du Livre des Rois," *Mélanges d'archéologie et d'histoire*, XLV, 1928, pp. 38ff. and pl. V, fig. 9.

tures are painted with the intention of appealing rather to the artistic and aesthetic sense of the patron than of satisfying the demands of iconographic meaning and accuracy.

Another way of converting a column miniature into a full-page one is by filling the increased area with ornamental features. The most common device is the application of a framing arch, which fulfills a function similar to that of the arcades mentioned previously (fig. 89). It is used, for instance, throughout the treatise on the dislocation of bones (περὶ ἄρθρων) by Apollonius of Citium in a manuscript of the tenth century in the Laurentian Library in Florence, cod. Plut. LXXIV, 7.[68] In the scene (fig. 94)[69] in which a patient with a dislocated vertebra is bound on a wooden board, while two assistants stretch his body with a windlass, and a physician applies pressure by sitting on the victim's back, we observe that the two kneeling men overlap the columns, and do not fit the space within the arch. Clearly picture and frame were not conceived together, and the framing elements were added some time later. If we free the figural composition from the arch and reinsert it into a writing column as indicated in Figure F, it will be realized how well it fits spatially into the text and how it complies with the principles of roll illustration. The similarity in arrangement should be noticed between this purified archetype of the Apollonius and the illustrated treatise on bandaging by Soranus of Ephesus (fig. 60), which is a part of the same Florentine manuscript and illustrated apparently by the same artist. Apollonius lived in the first century B.C. and if his writings, as seems extremely likely for scientific treatises of this kind, were illustrated during or shortly after his lifetime, they could have existed only in the form of rolls, whereas the addition of the arch presupposes the transformation from roll into codex. However the arch was not necessarily introduced in the first copy in codex form. The addition may have been made in any intermediary copy, not excluding the Florentine manuscript itself. The structure and the ornament of the arches are very similar to those of the canon tables and the letter of Eusebius in the Gospel books.[70] Other features also favor a derivation from this decorative system, as the curtains, which are taken to the sides and fastened to the columns with either plain or jewel-studded metal bands. Such curtains occur in the canon tables of Eastern Gospel books, like the Greek one in the Walters Art Gallery in Baltimore, no. 532,[71] as well as of

[68] H. Schöne, *Apollonius von Kitium*, Leipzig 1896.—Gasiorowski, *op. cit.*, p. 153 and figs. 72-73.—Weitzmann, *Byzantinische Buchmalerei*, p. 33 and pl. XLI, no. 227 (here more complete bibliography).—Bethe, *Buch und Bild*, p. 26 and fig. 6.

[69] Schöne, *op. cit.*, pl. XVII.

[70] Carl Nordenfalk, *Die spätantiken Kanontafeln*, Göteborg 1938, pls. 13, 25, 32.

[71] S. de Ricci and W. J. Wilson, *Census of Medieval and Renaissance Manuscripts in the U.S. and Canada*, vol. 1, New York 1935, p. 759, no. 5.

ΜΕΤΑ ΔΕΤΑ ΠΡΟΚΕΜΕΝΑ ΟΥΤWϹ ΕΠΙΛΕΓΕΙ ΚΑΙ
ΑϹΙΝΕϹΤΑΤΗ ΜΕΝ ΑΥΤΗ ΗΑΝΑΓΚΗ ΑϹΙΝ ΗϹΑΘ
ΚΑΙ ΚΑΘΕΖΕϹΘΑΙ ΤΙΝΑ ΕΠΙ ΤΟ ΚΥΦ WΜΑ ΑΥΤΟΥ
ΑΜΑ ΚΑΤΑΤΕΙΝΟΜΕΝΟΥ ΚΑΙ ΕΠΕΝϹΕΙϹΑΙ ΜΕΤ
ΕWΡΙϹΘΕΝΤΑ WϹΤΕ ΤΗϹ ΑΥΤΗϹ ΚΑΤΑΤΑϹΕWϹ
Η ΚΑΙ ΤΗϹ ΔΙΟΝΙϹΚWΝ ΓΙΝΟΜΕΝΗϹ ΑΝΤΙ ΤΟΥ
ΤΑΙϹ ΧΕΡϹΙ ΠΙΕΖΕΙΝ ΔΙΑ ΤΗϹ ΚΑΘΕΔΡΑϹ ΕΠΕ
ΡΕΙΔΟΝΤΑϹ Η ΚΑΙ ΕΝϹΕΙΟΝΤΑϹ ΑΝΑΓΚΑΖΕΙΝ
ΤΟ ΥΠΕΡΕΧΟΝ ΤWΝ ϹΦΟΝΔΥΛWΝ ΕΙϹ ΤΟ ΚΑΤΑ
ΦΥϹΙΝ ΑΠΟΧWΡΕΙΝ ΟΝ ΤΡΟΠΟΝ ΔΕ ΔΕΙ ΤΟΝ ΚΑΤ
ΑΡΤΙϹΜΟΝ ΠΟΙΕΙϹΘΑΙ ΟΥΤWϹ ΥΠΟΤΕΤΑΚΤΑΙ

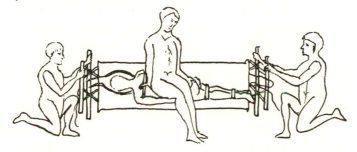

ΕΠΟΜΕΝWϹ ΔΕ ΤΑΥΤΑ ΚΑΤΑ ΚΕΧWΡΙΚΕΝ ΑΤΑΡ
ΚΑΙ ΕΠΙΒΗΝΑΙ ΤW ΠΟΔΙ ΚΑΙ ΟΧΗΘΗΝΑΙ ΤΟ ϹW
ΜΑ ΚΑΙ ΗϹΥΧWϹ ΕΠΙϹΕΙϹΑΙ ΟΥΔΕΝ ΚWΛΥΕΙ
ΤΟΙΟΥΤΟΝ ΔΕ ΠΟΙΗϹΑΙ ΜΕΤΡΙWϹ ΕΠΙΤΗΔΕΙΟϹ
ΑΝ ΤΙϹ ΕΙΗ ΤWΝ ΑΜΦΙ ΠΑΛΑΙϹΤΡΗΝ ΕΙΘΙϹΜΕ
ΝWΝ ΚΑΙ ΟΥΤΟϹ ΔΕ Ο ΤΡΟΠΟϹ ΟΥΤWϹ ΑΝ ΕΠΙΤΕ

FIGURE F. Reconstruction of the Model of the Apollonius of Citium

Western ones. The fourth century A.D., the earliest possible date for the invention of the canon tables, would be a *terminus post quem*, then, for their adaptation in the Apollonius manuscript.

Of particular interest in this connection are the mediaeval Terence manuscripts, where, at the beginning of each drama, the so-called σκευή, the implements of the theater, which include not only the masks, but also attributes like fillet, torch and others, are enclosed in a somewhat similar architectural structure. In the picture of the Vatican Terence, cod. lat. 3868, representing the masks of the *Andria* (fig. 95)[72] the structure consists of a pair of col-

[72] Jones and Morey, *op. cit.*, fig. 7.—G. Jachmann, *Terentius*, fol. 3ʳ and colorplate III.

umns connected by an architrave and gable and forms an aedicula; as a whole as well as in the details, such as the rings which subdivide the columns into three sections, it resembles the canon table decoration of certain Carolingian Gospels from the school of Rheims,[73] which on its part represents the earliest and most structural stage in the development of the canon tables, to judge from the extant material. Our interpretation of the aedicula as a mere decorative frame is in contradistinction to the opinion of many scholars[74] who see in it a *scrinium* or *armarium*. But the aedicula has neither a wall behind the shelves with the masks, nor doors in the front as one would expect from an armarium, and among the numerous representations of groups of masks in frescoes, mosaics and reliefs in classical antiquity, there is no instance, to our knowledge, in which the masks were placed either in an aedicula similar to those in the Terence manuscripts or in any structure which might be considered an armarium. Typical for the arrangement of the σκευή in classical antiquity is the example of a Pompeian fresco from a peristyle of a house at the Stabian road, whose masks, joined by other implements like the harp of Perseus, were identified by Carl Robert as belonging to Euripides' *Andromeda*.[75] Robert conjectured that such fresco compositions of masks, which are neither in a scrinium nor in a decorative setting of any sort, originally formed headpieces of illustrated dramatic editions[76] which at that period, of course, could only have been papyrus rolls. There was apparently a century-old tradition for a picture with masks at the beginning of a drama long before a painter introduced an architectural frame under the influence of canon tables in a late classical Terence codex. The purpose of this addition is obvious, namely to give the first page to each drama the character of a frontispiece and thus greater distinction and prominence.

There are certain centers of book production, as the Alemannic monasteries, which show a distinct predilection for the arches of canon tables as decorative frames for all kinds of pictures. The martyrology of Wandelbert, Vatican cod. Reg. lat. 438, probably written in St. Gall,[77] surrounds each

---

[73] Nordenfalk, *op. cit.*, pp. 195, 201 and pl. 168.—A. Boinet, *La miniature carolingienne*, Paris 1913, pl. LXXIII.

[74] E. Bethe, *Terentius Cod. Ambrosianus H. 75 inf.* (Codices Graeci et Latini, vol. VIII) (facsimile), Leyden 1903, col. 53.—M. Bieber, *Die Denkmäler zum Theaterwesen im Altertum*, Berlin-Leipzig 1920, p. 171 and fig. 137.—C. Robert, *Die Masken der neueren attischen Komoedie* (25. Hallisches Winckelmannsprogramm), Halle 1911, p. 103, is more cautious in the interpretation of the decorative frame of the masks.

[75] C. Robert, "Maskengruppen," *Arch. Zeit.*, XXXVI, 1878, p. 14 and pl. 3.

[76] *Ibid.*, p. 24.—*Idem*, *Masken der neueren attischen Komoedie*, p. 86.

[77] A. Riegl, "Die mittelalterliche Kalender-Illustration," *Mitt. d. Inst. für österr. Geschichtsforschung*, X, 1889, pp. 40ff. and pls. I-II.—A. Goldschmidt, *Karolingische Buchmalerei*, pp. 23, 59 and pl. 76.—J. C. Webster, *The Labors of the Month in Antique and Mediaeval Art*, Princeton 1938, pp. 41, 130 and pl. XI.

single personification of the months by an arch, whose derivation from the canon tables is apparent from the use of peacocks as filling motifs for the spandrels and similar features. In several instances, just as in the Apollonius of Citium manuscript, the personifications overlap the arch, thus indicating that scene and frame were originally not conceived together. Treated with great splendor is the adaptation of the canon table decoration in the Gospels and lectionaries of the school of Reichenau. In the Annunciation of the Virgin of the Liuthar Gospels in the Cathedral of Aachen (fig. 96)[78] the framing architecture is even doubled: one gabled structure which surrounds the scene proper is then again enclosed by a second structure. In both, as is characteristic for canon tables, the spandrels are filled with birds, the inner one with peacocks, which generally were used as decoration of the first canon or of the arch around the Eusebius letter. The model of this scene was apparently not a full-page picture, but a horizontal composition, which stood in the midst of a writing column as we see it in the corresponding scene of the Egbert codex in the Stadtbibliothek at Trier, no. 24,[79] which represents the more original stage of the Gospel illustration. The painter of the Aachen Gospels kept more or less the original figure size of the angel and the Virgin, but filled the area above and alongside them by richly orna-mented canon table structures, an addition which he could make only at the expense of dropping the city of Nazareth in order to gain space for the two sets of columns. As in David's Repentance of the Paris Psalter (fig. 93), iconographic explicitness was sacrificed in behalf of a splendid frontispiece effect.

At the same time it should not be overlooked that quite frequently in mediaeval book illumination full-page miniatures were, in later copies, again reduced in scale. In a Greek Psalter on Mount Athos, Pantokratoros cod. 49, which belongs to the same recension as the Paris Psalter, gr. 139, the miniatures fill only about three fourths of a page (fig. 157),[80] while the other quarter is occupied by several lines of writing and an historiated ini-tial. However the proportions remained the same in spite of the reduction in scale, a fact which distinguishes miniatures of this kind from the more friezelike compositions of the earlier stage of development.

[78] St. Beissel, *Die Bilder der Handschrift des Kaisers Otto im Münster zu Aachen*, Aachen 1886, pl. xx.

[79] Fr. X. Kraus, *Die Miniaturen des Codex Egberti in der Stadtbibliothek zu Trier*, Freiburg 1884, pl. ix.

[80] G. Millet, "Quelques représentations byzantines de la salutation angélique," *Bull. Corr. Hell.*, xviii, 1894, p. 453 and pl. xv.—O. M. Dalton, *Byzantine Art and Archaeology*, figs. 277 and 278. —G. Millet and S. Der Nersessian, "Le psautier arménien illustré," *Revue des études arméniennes*, ix, 1929, p. 165 and pl. ix.—In the fragmentary Paris Psalter the Habakkuk picture is unfortunately lost.

The reduction in size may go even so far as to allow the superimposition of two or more miniatures which had originally occupied a full page of their own. In a tenth century Aratus manuscript in the Bibliothèque Municipale at Boulogne-sur-mer, cod. 188,[81] there are, as a rule, two framed constellation pictures above one another, whereas in the Leyden manuscript (p. 105), the model of the Boulogne codex, each occupies a full page of its own. In the example where the Engonasin and the Corona are arranged in the way described (fig. 156) each picture preserved its original proportions and even its own frame,[82] but in most cases the two miniatures share the inner frames with each other. This superimposition of two miniatures resulted in a very elongated picture area, equalling roughly the space of one writing column in a two-column text. Consequently the explanatory text, which in the Leyden manuscript was on a separate page opposite the picture, in the Boulogne codex is written on the same page like a second column. In this economizing way no less than four pages of the Leyden manuscript, two with pictures and two with text, were condensed on a single page. In one case the Boulogne manuscript superimposes even three miniatures (fig. 97) with Serpens, Cratera and Corvus forming the first, Canis minor the second, and the five planets the third. Here, and in this instance only, the copyist was compelled to change the proportions of his model and to turn the first and second miniatures into horizontal compositions.

C. MARGINAL AND COMMENTARY ILLUSTRATION

Three methods of placing an illustration alongside the writing column may be distinguished: (1) the casual addition of miniatures which were not planned for in the layout; (2) the systematic filling of the margins by cyclic illustrations; and (3) the commentary illustration, either in conjunction with a commentary text or without it.

Just as a scribe uses any available space between, above or below a writing column, be it in a roll or a codex, in order to supply an omitted verse or text passage which he may have passed over in the process of copying, so a painter may be forced to seek a place for a miniature outside the writing column, if the scribe forgot to provide the necessary space for it. In the Vatican manuscript of the *Christian Topography* of Cosmas Indicopleustes, cod. gr. 699 from the ninth century,[1] which in most parts is illustrated by unframed column pictures, the scribe forgot to provide the necessary space in

[81] Thiele, *Himmelsbilder*, p. 82 and figs. 53, 58-59.

[82] Cf. the corresponding miniatures in the Leyden codex on fol. 6ᵛ and 8ᵛ. Thiele, *op. cit.*, figs. 19 and 20.

[1] C. Stornajolo, *Le miniature della Topografia Cristiana di Cosma Indicopleuste Codice Vaticano greco 699* (Codices e Vaticanis selecti, vol. x) (facsimile), Milan 1908.

the column for the figure of Luke (fig. 98)[2] so that the illuminator was forced to reduce its size and to squeeze it between two columns. There can be no doubt that the original intention was to have him standing inside the column and that his present position is the result of mere neglect on the part of the scribe.

In some instances the decision to add a set of illustrations to a text was not made until after the manuscript was already completed, and then naturally no other place except the margin was available. In some cases this may have been immediately after the writing was finished, so that the scribe himself or a painter colleague from the same scriptorium added the illustrations. In a lectionary on Patmos, cod. 70, from the tenth century,[3] a few scenes from the life of Christ, painted in a style and technique so close to that of the original ornamentation that they must have been executed at about the same time, were placed in the lower margin in such a way that some of the figures could raise their heads only between the columns, as Christ in the Healing of the Blind Man (fig. 99). Even so the painter was not able to find space for all figures involved in each composition, and he had to abbreviate the scene to a minimum of its participants. All these are clear indications that a systematic illustration of this lectionary had not been contemplated when the text was written.

In other cases the marginal illustrations were added considerably later, as can be seen in the Armenian Gospels in Etschmiadzin, cod. 229,[4] whose full-page illustrations at the beginning of the codex are contemporary with the text from the year 989. One of the added illustrations, the Adoration of the Magi,[5] is arranged on the lower margin similarly as the miniatures in Patmos 70, with the Virgin enthroned intruding into the zone between the two writing columns. In a representation of the Holy Women at the Tomb, the two Marys between the writing columns are reduced to busts, while the tomb is at the outer margin,[6] and in a repetition of the same scene (fig. 100)[7] the number of the Marys is reduced to one and the tomb on the margin is omitted altogether. In this manuscript as well as in the Patmos lectionary

---

[2] *Ibid.*, pl. 44.

[3] Weitzmann, *Byzantinische Buchmalerei*, pp. 66, 67 and pl. LXXIII (here further bibliography).

[4] J. Strzygowski, *Das Etschmiadzin-Evangeliar* (Byzantinische Denkmäler, vol. 1), Vienna 1891. According to him the initial miniatures were Syrian products of the sixth century and the marginal ones were contemporary, but this opinion is not maintained by the following authors.—Fr. Macler, *L'évangile arménien, Edition phototypique du Ms. No. 229 de la Bibl. d'Etschmiadzin*, Paris 1920.—K. Weitzmann, *Die armenische Buchmalerei des 10. und beginnenden 11. Jahrhunderts*, Bamberg 1933, p. 8 and *passim*.—S. Der Nersessian, "The Date of the Initial Miniatures of the Etschmiadzin Gospel," *Art Bull.*, XV, 1933, p. 333.

[5] Macler, *op. cit.*, fol. 10ʳ.—Der Nersessian, *op. cit.*, fig. 2.

[6] Macler, *op. cit.*, fol. 110ʳ.—Weitzmann, *op. cit.*, pl. IV, no. 10.

[7] Macler, *op. cit.*, fol. 222ᵛ.

the miniatures do not even constitute a *selective cycle* in the sense that out of a formerly richer cycle the most important scenes were selected; but their choice is quite casual, which is typical for this kind of added marginal illustration.

Of greater importance is the marginal illustration planned in advance, in which an extensive cycle of scenes accompanies the text alongside the writing column at fairly regular intervals. To understand this formal principle we have to go back into the classical period. The normal papyrus roll provides no space for marginal illustration because its writing columns are on an average no more than about one inch apart, an interval too small for any organized illustration. Only under very peculiar circumstances was there possible an arrangement of miniatures in a roll which resembles marginal illustration at least superficially if not in a technical sense. Not enough fragments of papyrus rolls are preserved in which these conditions can be demonstrated, but they occur in a similar manner in one of the papyrus fragments of the Alexandrian World Chronicle from about the fifth century (fig. 101).[8] Here three miniatures—depicting, at the top, the Emperor Theodosius with Honorius, the Bishop Theophilus in the middle, and the abbreviated representation of the Serapeion at the bottom—follow each other with no space for a single line of writing left between them so that the column of writing could nowhere reach its normal width. These three miniatures, then, resemble a marginal illustration, but in appearance only, for in reality they are not placed on a margin but alongside a writing column of curtailed width. Such rare cases of what we might call the *pseudo-marginal method* go far back to the hieratic Book of the Dead. Already as early as the XXI Dynasty in the papyrus of Katseshni[9] four vignettes of equal width have the appearance of a marginal picture strip in spite of the fact that one single line of writing between each vignette acts as a reminder of the full width of the original writing column.

A system of marginal illustration did not and could not develop before the invention of the codex. After having placed one or more writing columns on a single page of a codex, a formal relationship was established between the shape of the sheet and the writing columns which provided a margin of approximately equal width all around the script, thus creating what in printed books is called a *type page*. Whereas the inner margin partly disappeared in the process of binding, the outer margin added new free space which did not exist in rolls, because their columns followed each other too closely, with only narrow intervals in between. Already in the earliest

[8] Strzygowski, *op. cit.*, fol. VI verso.

[9] Ed. Naville, *Le papyrus hiératique de Katseshni au Musée du Caire* (Papyrus funéraires de la XXIe dynastie, vol. II), Paris 1914, pl. XXVIII.

codices in existence, such as the Sinaiticus, this outer margin is of a considerable width, giving the illuminator a chance to fill it with narrow scenes or diagrams if he wanted to do so. Thus, after the invention of the codex in the second century A.D., conditions were immediately present for the development of a marginal illustration proper. How soon the illuminators took advantage of this opportunity we do not know because of the scantiness of documents in the earliest period of codex illustration.

However, all evidence points to the fact that the miniature cycles which are found on the margins of existing manuscripts were not created for this location, but go back to an archetype in which they had been placed inside the writing column. In other words, we are dealing with a *derived method of illustration* which arose from pushing scenes out of the columns into the margin, whether in the model they had occupied the indented side or the whole width of a column. In most instances this shift resulted in an abbreviation of scenes, since a margin is normally considerably narrower than a writing column. This can be clearly demonstrated in the richly and coherently illustrated Gospel book in Paris, Bibl. Nat., cod. gr. 115, from the tenth century,[10] by a page on which two scenes from St. Matthew's Gospel are represented (fig. 102) ; one shows Christ healing a leper (VIII, 1-4), and the other, badly rubbed, the centurion from Capernaum kneeling before Christ and asking his help (VIII, 5-13). In the existing parallels, in which the corresponding miniatures are placed within the text column, the scenes are spread out in width and contain additional figures which are iconographically necessary, but which had to be dropped when the scenes were shifted over into the margin. In the Gospel book in Paris, cod. gr. 74, Christ is accompanied by two of his disciples when he meets the leper, and the latter is followed by a large crowd of Jews. In the same manuscript, when Christ is confronted with the centurion and the inhabitants of Capernaum, he is joined by several disciples,[11] while in the marginal Gospels of Paris neither disciples nor Jews are present.

The necessity to condense is apparent wherever the illustrations are marginal, and it becomes especially clear in the hundreds of scenes of the *Sacra Parallela* of St. John of Damascus in Paris, cod. gr. 923[12] from the ninth century. Again in an example from the New Testament (fig. 103) two

[10] Bordier, *Description des peintures et autres ornements contenus dans les manuscrits grecs de la Bibliothèque Nationale*, Paris 1883, p. 137.—G. Millet, *Recherches*, figs. 240, 269 and *passim*.—H. R. Willoughby, *The Rockefeller McCormick New Testament*, vol. III, Chicago 1932, pls. XX, XXXV.—*Idem, The Four Gospels of Karahissar*, vol. II, Chicago 1936, pls. XLVI, XCIX.

[11] H. Omont, *Évangiles avec peintures byzantines*, vol. I, pl. 14, no. 2 and pl. 15, no. 1.—Cf. also the Gospels Florence, Laurent. Libr. cod. Plut. VI, 23, fol. 14ᵛ.

[12] J. Rendel Harris, *Fragments of Philo Judaeus*, Cambridge 1886.—Weitzmann, *Byzantinische Buchmalerei*, p. 80 and pl. LXXXVI (here further bibliography).

phases of the Healing of the Man Born Blind (John IX, 1ff.) are conflated and the disciples as well as the bystanders eliminated;[13] and in the next scene with the Woman of the Issue of Blood (Luke VIII, 41ff.), where the artist tried to copy Christ's disciples from his larger model, he had to condense them until little more than the tops of their heads are seen.[14] No wonder that, in most instances, the illuminator preferred to omit completely the secondary participants rather than to repeat this unsatisfactory solution; thus in the scenes of the Healing of the Bent Woman (Luke XIII, 11) and of the Man with an Unclean Spirit (Mark I, 23ff.) he refrained from again depicting the disciples or a crowd.[15] It may be noticed that the miniatures of the *Sacra Parallela* are not placed alongside each of the two columns, but are joined together on the outer margin of the whole page, since the space at the inner margin and between the columns is too narrow. This means that only those scenes which are related to the outer writing column are anchored near their passages, while those illustrating a passage from the inner writing column are physically separated from it, so that the reader has to study the text of both columns in order to ascertain the precise relationship between text and picture.

Just as the pictures in the column, after they began to be loosed from their ties to the text, were occasionally disassociated from the whole body of writing and placed in front of it (cf. the Rossano Gospels, figs. 76-77), so the marginal illustrations were sometimes collected out of the text pages and taken over into a preceding gathering. Such is the case in the well-known Syriac Gospels in Florence, Laurent. Lib. cod. Plut. I, 56, which was written in 586 by a monk Rabula.[16] The canon tables of this manuscript are accompanied on both sides of the supporting columns by scenes from the life of Christ, which are just as much abbreviated as those of the manuscripts Paris gr. 115 and Paris gr. 923. In the examples representing the Healing of the Bent Woman and the Discourse with the Woman of Samaria (fig. 104), the disciples are again omitted, while in other cases, where the space was too narrow for even an abbreviated composition, the artist split the scene and placed half on the left of the canon table and the other half

---

[13] Cf. again the fuller composition in the codex Paris gr. 74. Omont, *op. cit.*, vol. II, pl. 159, no. 2 and pl. 160, no. 1.

[14] Cf. Paris gr. 74, Omont, *op. cit.*, vol. II, pl. 111, no. 1, where also a crowd following Jairus is represented.

[15] Cf. Paris gr. 74. Omont, *op. cit.*, vol. II, pl. 121, no. 2 and vol. I, pl. 60, no. 2.

[16] S. E. Assemanus, *Bibliothecae Mediceae Laurentianae et Palatinae Codicum Mss. orientalium Catalogus*, Florence 1742, pp. 1ff. and pls. I-XXVI.—R. Garrucci, *Storia della arte cristiana*, vol. III, Prato 1876, pls. 129-138.—C. Nordenfalk, *Die spätantiken Kanontafeln*, pp. 239ff. and pls. 130-148.

on the right side.[17] As in the Rossano Gospels, we can assume also in the Rabula Gospels a *selective cycle* which is derived from a fuller illustrated Gospel book with column pictures.[18] In assuming such an evolutionary theory in the shifting of New Testament scenes first from within the text into the margins and later to the front of the whole codex, we must conclude that by the sixth century, the date of the Rabula Gospels, the marginal text illustration must have existed for some time before it reached this advanced stage. Moreover, although the Rabula Gospels is a product of Syriac art, we have no reason to assume that the method of marginal illustration was invented in Syriac book illumination. Perhaps the association of marginal scenes with the canon tables is a Syriac peculiarity, since it occurs in a second Syriac Gospel book from the sixth century, Paris cod. syr. 33,[19] and is not found in Greek canon tables. On the other hand, the widespread use of marginal text illustrations in Greek manuscripts leaves hardly any doubt that the method as such originated in Greek book illumination. Judging from the scarce remnants of early mediaeval manuscripts, marginal illustrations seem to have been particularly popular in the Greek manuscripts of Syria and Palestine. This region is indicated by the provenance not only of the Rabula Gospels, but also of the model of the richly illustrated *Sacra Parallela* and most likely of the impressive group of the so-called monastic Psalters with which we have to deal later on.

The scenes at the sides of the canon tables of the Rabula Gospels are not confined to subjects of the New Testament. In the spandrels formed by the arches, there are author figures and scenes which are taken mostly from the Prophets, such as Micah standing frontally and Jonah asleep under the gourd above the city of Nineveh on the page described above. Furthermore, the New Testament and the books of the Prophets are not the only sources for the painter of the Rabula Gospels: Moses Receiving the Law, Aaron and Joshua[20] involve an Octateuch as a model; and the figures of Samuel, Solomon and David[21] either a Book of Kings or a Psalter. Still greater is the number of cycles from which scenes are selected for the *Sacra Parallela* manuscript in Paris. They comprise all major books of the Bible as well as patristic literature, such as the homilies of Basil, Gregory of Nazianzus, John

[17] E.g. the Annunciation to the Virgin; the Miracle of Cana; the Healing of the Son of the Widow of Nain; the Healing of the Possessed; Christ, Peter and the Tribute Money; Healing of Blind and Cripples; Christ before Pilate. Nordenfalk, *op. cit.*, pls. 131, 133, 136, 140, 141, 145, 148.

[18] A different viewpoint is taken by Nordenfalk (*op. cit.*, p. 247), who assumes that the New Testament scenes involved in the Syrian canon tables were invented for their present position and thus constitute a rather short cycle of their own from the very beginning.

[19] Nordenfalk, *op. cit.*, pp. 239ff. and pls. 114-128.

[20] fol. 3ᵛ and 4ʳ. Nordenfalk, *op. cit.*, pls. 130-131.

[21] fol. 4ʳ and 4ᵛ. Nordenfalk, *op. cit.*, pls. 131-132.

Chrysostom and others. It thus seems that marginal illustrations, because of their abbreviated nature and their convenient placing, were much favored in cases where a great number of scenes from different sources had to be combined in one single book.

Typical for this kind of accumulation of marginal miniatures from different sources is also the ninth century codex E. 49-50 inf. of the Ambrosian Library in Milan, which contains illustrations to all forty-five homilies of Gregory of Nazianzus.[22] Medallion portraits as well as scenes are placed all over the margins of this voluminous manuscript, even making use of the narrow inner margin, as can be seen on the page (fig. 105) where the medallion busts of Joseph, Abraham and Moses are placed near the seam of the book, while a somewhat larger medallion with John the Baptist adorns the outer margin. Two scenes, the Anointing of Saul and the Anointing of David, are situated above the text, and Elijah and Elisha on Mount Carmel are placed below. The three scenic compositions mentioned are all from the Books of Kings, but on other pages scenes were chosen from other biblical books as well. The models the copyist used may have been quite different in their system of illustration, but he unified them by applying exclusively the marginal method in order to give the manuscript a homogeneous character.

Though the so-called monastic Psalters are usually considered as the examples of marginal illustrations par excellence, we prefer not to classify them together with manuscripts like the *Sacra Parallela* and the Milan Gregory, but in a separate group of manuscripts whose illustrations are connected with a commentary instead of with a basic text. However, in order to understand the conditions which led to the creation of what might be called the *commentary illustration*, we have first to make a few general remarks about the relationship of a text and its commentary.

In the Hellenistic period and particularly in Alexandria, the center of learned and scholarly writing, commentaries to poetical and scientific literature were written on separate rolls. This custom was never entirely abandoned, even after the codex was introduced, and in the Middle Ages many commentaries, not only on pagan but also on Christian writers, were still written as separate books not physically connected with the basic text of which they are the commentary. At the same time one finds occasionally, between the text columns of a manuscript of the basic text itself, critical notes, word explanations and the like, wherever the writer could squeeze them in. The earliest roll fragments with such annotations belong in the first century A.D. or perhaps as early as the first century B.C. Very soon these

[22] Weitzmann, *Byzantinische Buchmalerei*, p. 81 (here further bibliography) and pl. LXXXVII.— A. Grabar, *Les miniatures du Grégoire de Nazianze de l'Ambrosienne*, Paris 1943.

annotations increase and already in the fragment of a partheneum of Alcman in Paris from the first century A.D.[23] the interval between the columns is not sufficient for them so that the upper and lower margins had to be used for further annotations. In this connection the invention of the codex at the turn from the first to the second century must have been felt to be very timely, because the margin at the outer side of a codex page provided considerably more space for the annotations than the interval between two writing columns of a roll. In cases where the writer knew in advance the ratio between the annotations and the text proper, he easily could balance the space of a page by narrowing the writing column of the basic text and by widening the margin, or vice versa. There is no early annotated codex known at the present time, but we do possess two fragments of papyrus rolls, one from Oxyrhynchus, containing a paean of Pindar[24] and the other of a lost comedy, perhaps from Aristophanes (fig. 106),[25] in which the interval between the writing columns is so wide that the annotations form narrow intermittent columns of their own. This means that the scribe already took the addition of annotations into account when he made the layout of the text. The scholars who published these fragments date the former in the second and the latter in the third century A.D., i.e. in a period *after* the invention of the codex, and it seems therefore possible that annotations on wide margins of codex pages had influenced the scribes of papyrus rolls to leave free space after each column equal to that of a fairly broad margin.[26]

Meanwhile the writers of codices did not stop with adding shorter or lengthier annotations on the margins, but they began, after a while, to write full commentaries alongside the basic text, thus joining physically in one and the same document what in the classical period was divided between two separate rolls. This was an important achievement, which facilitated a

[23] E. Egger, *Notices et extraits des manuscrits de la Bibliothèque Impériale*, vol. XVIII, pt. II, 1865, TEXT, p. 416, no. 71, PLATES, pl. L (here wrongly numbered 70).

[24] Frag. no. 841. Grenfell and Hunt, *The Oxyrhynchus Papyri*, vol. V, London 1908, p. 11 and pls. I-III.—W. Schubart, *Das Buch bei den Griechen und Römern*, p. 96 and fig. 20.—*Idem*, "Das antike Buch," *Die Antike*, XIV, 1938, p. 185 and fig. 6.

[25] Grenfell and Hunt, *The Amherst Papyri*, vol. II, London 1901, p. 4, no. XIII and pl. V.

[26] G. Zuntz, "Die Aristophanes-Scholien der Papyri," *Byzantion*, XIV, 1939, p. 559, explains the wide spacing of the columns as the result of mere aesthetic considerations and he denies that it was intended from the very beginning for the reception of scholia as Grenfell and Hunt had assumed. However, this objection to the interpretation of the two English papyrologists seems not too convincing. It is true that in very ambitious rolls a somewhat wider interval is preferred, but in such cases it hardly ever exceeds half the width of a narrow writing column, and from the aesthetic viewpoint this seems to be already the limit in wide spacing without disrupting the rhythm of the roll as a whole. Cf. e.g. the commentary to Plato's Theaetetus in Berlin, as an example for wide spacing. H. Diels, W. Schubart and J. L. Heiberg, *Anonymer Kommentar zu Platons Theaetet* (Berliner Klassiker-texte, fasc. 2), Berlin 1905.

comparative reading of the text and its commentary. We do not know exactly when this junction of text and commentary took place for the first time, but if classical philologists like White[27] are right in that the present Aristophanes manuscripts with their extensive scholia all around the four margins copy truthfully not only the readings of the text but also its formal arrangement from an archetype of the fourth century A.D., then we would have to assume that at this time the system was not only merely existent, but already very elaborate. The evidence points, then, to the innovations having been introduced somewhere between the invention of the codex in the second century and the Aristophanes archetype in the fourth century. The system was taken over from classical texts by Christian writers and the earliest existing codices combining text and commentary are actually Christian ones. One of them is a Job in Patmos, cod. 171,[28] in which the biblical text, written in beautiful large uncials, is surrounded on three sides by a commentary which is written in small characters and is several times as long as the basic text. This manuscript belongs in the seventh or the beginning of the eighth century and the perfect balance between the two parts of writing points to an old and well-established tradition.[29]

Particularly in scientific treatises, scholia and commentaries sometimes need explanatory drawings just as much as the basic text itself, so commentary illustration is probably just as old as this kind of literature itself and may have existed already in papyrus rolls. Illustrated scientific scholia are preserved, for instance, in a manuscript of Euclid's *Elements* in the Bodleian Library in Oxford, cod. d'Orville 301, from the year 888, in which the Euclid text proper is enriched by explanatory diagrams throughout the manuscript, while only a few are found in the scholia which themselves fill the margins quite irregularly (fig. 107).[30] The diagrams in the commentary

[27] J. W. White, *The Scholia on the Aves of Aristophanes*, Boston-London 1914, pp. LXVIIIff.

[28] Weitzmann, *Byzantinische Buchmalerei*, p. 49 (here fuller bibliography) and pls. LV-LVI.

[29] G. Zuntz (*op. cit.*, p. 582), who presents a new theory according to which the commentary did not join the text before ca. 700 A.D., tries to get rid of the Patmos codex by maintaining Wattenbach's date in the tenth century (Wattenbach-v. Velsen, *Exempla codicum Graecorum litteris minusculis scriptorum*, Heidelberg 1878, pl. 4). But so late a date, particularly in view of the miniatures, is untenable and Tischendorf's and Sakkelion's date in the seventh to eighth centuries is undoubtedly nearer the truth. Recently W. H. P. Hatch (*Quantulacumque, Studies Presented to Kirsopp Lake*, London 1937, p. 333; and *The Principal Uncial Manuscripts of the New Testament*, Chicago 1939, pl. XXV) dated the Codex Zacynthius, a New Testament manuscript with marginal scholia, in the sixth instead of the eighth century as was generally assumed. If this is true we would have a commented text even earlier than the Patmos codex.

[30] *Pal. Soc.*, vol. I, 1873-83, pls. 65-66.—N. Bees, *Revue des études grecques*, XXVI, 1913, p. 65. —K. Lake, *Dated Greek Minuscule Manuscripts to the Year 1200*, vol. II, Boston 1934, pls. 94 and 104.

are of considerably smaller size than those in the basic text, just as the scholia themselves are written with smaller characters.

Commentaries usually require more space than scholia and occupy often what amounts to a second writing column, differentiated from the basic column only by the use of smaller characters and a greater density of lines. This means that a picture in such a column can be just as large and elaborate as a normal column picture. The text of the Vatican Psalter, cod. gr. 752, written about 1059,[31] is accompanied by the commentaries of Hesychius, Theodoret, Athanasius, John Chrysostom and others which are richly illustrated by framed miniatures similar to those one finds in any basic text, as may be exemplified by the representation of Christ addressing Asaph and Korah (fig. 108).[32] Just as commentaries are distinguished from scholia by a greater coherence and more steady distribution of the text, so do the commentary miniatures constitute a more coherent and more regularly spaced picture cycle than the more sporadically distributed diagrams or scenes in the scholia.

In the same category with the codex Vat. gr. 752 belongs the group of the so-called *monastic Psalters*, the earliest of which are a fragment in the Bibliothèque Nationale of Paris, cod. gr. 20, the Chloudoff Psalter in the Historic Museum of Moscow and the Athos manuscript Pantokratoros no. 61, all from the ninth century.[33] Here, too, as can be seen in an example from the Pantokratoros codex (fig. 109), the Psalter text proper occupies only the inner half of the page, while the outer half is reserved for the commentary and in this respect the formal structure of the page is fundamentally the same as in the Vatican Psalter described above. However, in the area provided for the commentary the relationship between the text and the pictures is reversed insofar as the miniatures occupy most of the space while the text is confined to short quotations. One might even say that the miniatures do not accompany the commentary, but are themselves the commentary. The representation of the discourse between Christ and the Woman of Samaria, related to verse 10 of Psalm XXXV: "For with thee is the fountain of life: in thy light shall we see light," is without any text and thus the picture itself can be understood as a replacement for the corresponding passage from the fourth chapter of St. John. In other instances, as in the second scene of the

[31] E. T. DeWald, *Vaticanus Graecus 752. The Illustrations in the Manuscripts of the Septuagint*, vol. III, pt. 2, Princeton 1942.

[32] Reproduced after K. Lake, *op. cit.*, vol. VIII, 1937, pl. 526. Cf. DeWald, *op. cit.*, pl. XXXIX, fol. 261ʳ.

[33] J. J. Tikkanen, *Die Psalterillustrationen im Mittelalter (Acta Societatis Scientiarum Fennicae*, vol. XXXI, no. 5), Helsingfors 1903, pp. 11ff.—Weitzmann, *Byzantinische Buchmalerei*, pp. 53ff. (here more complete bibliography) and pls. LIX-LXII.

same page representing the Arrest of Christ, at least one verse of the commenting text is written alongside the picture (John XVIII, 6) in order to facilitate for the reader the finding of the precise literary connection between the New Testament scene and verse 13 of the same Psalm: "There are the workers of iniquity fallen: they are cast down, and shall not be able to rise." Sometimes, where a considerable number of scenes are grouped on a single page, each scene is marked with a sign which refers to a corresponding one in the text and helps the reader to establish the proper connection between the commentary picture and the Psalter text. Such signs are a very common device in manuscripts with extensive scholia like those containing the comedies of Aristophanes, to quote an arbitrary example,[34] and the illustrators of the Psalters apparently adapted this usage from older classical texts. Furthermore, with an area greater than that of the text itself provided for illustrations, they did not need to be so abbreviated and squeezed as the typical marginal scenes in the *Sacra Parallela* in Paris or the Gregory in Milan (fig. 103 and 105). An explanation for the predominance of the pictures over the commenting text may be sought in the fact that most of the scenes are not illustrations of patristic tests as in the codex Vat. gr. 752, but of well-known passages from the Bible. The familiarity of the iconography of a biblical scene, aided now and then by a title or a short verse, was obviously a sufficient clue for a mediaeval man of general learning to find by himself the complete Bible passage involved, so that there was no need to write out the commentary text in its full length.[35] On the basis of these observations we propose for the pictures just discussed the term *commentary illustrations*, differentiating them from the *marginal illustrations* proper.

This brings to an end our survey of the various methods of connecting physically a miniature with a text, methods which in their primitive stage are all rooted in ancient papyrus rolls. The postclassical centuries have not contributed much to this formal development that could be considered fundamentally new. The chief enrichment of mediaeval book illumination lies in the field of ornamental decoration, which in papyrus rolls apparently did not exist at all.[36] Even in late classical and Early Christian codices the application of ornamental decoration is very scanty and confined to canon

---

[34] J. W. White and Th. W. Allen, Ἀριστοφάνους Κωμωιδίαι, *Facsimile of the Codex Venetus Marcianus 474*, London and Boston 1902.

[35] At the same time it must be admitted that this explanation is not so satisfactory with regard to those scenes alluding to historical events of the iconoclastic controversy which presuppose a text which hardly could have been popular in the sense the Bible was.

[36] The ornamental patterns one finds occasionally on papyri (Schubart, "Miniaturen auf Papyrus," *Amtl. Berichte der Berliner Museen*, XXX, 1908-09, col. 294 and elsewhere) cannot be considered as an ornamentation of the text. They are nothing else than patterns on scraps of papyrus made to serve as models for other media, notably textiles.

tables, ornamented frontispieces and the like. Not before the Irish started to develop their highly ornamentalized book art do certain forms of ornaments like headpieces, initials and the like, spread into the writing column proper and mingle with it, while in the Greek East such forms appear hardly before the ninth century and even then are never as sumptuous and complex as in Western manuscripts. In the course of the development the general process of ornamentalizing the art of illumination affects also the scenic illustration. Now and then scenes are enclosed in initials, or human figures themselves form the stems of initials, but this particular form of illustration reaches far beyond the period and the material which have a bearing on the roll and codex problem and therefore is excluded from the present investigation.

D. THE PROBLEM OF THE CONTINUOUS FRIEZE IN ROLLS

In the preceding chapters we have followed the development of the miniature from a rather simple and artistically unpretentious column picture in the rolls, the purpose of which was merely to illustrate with the greatest possible terseness the content of a certain passage, to an independent full-page picture. Beginning with the examination of a few extant illustrated papyrus fragments (figs. 35-40) and a number of codices which were illustrated in the same method as the papyri (figs. 56-64), we have observed how gradual and organic this development was, and we have seen that it was not until after the invention of the codex, with the addition of scenes in rows, their enrichment by frame and background, and their enlargement, that the final transformation into full-page miniatures took place. It must be pointed out, however, that this concept of the evolution of early book illumination is not the currently accepted one. It is, in fact, in full disagreement with Birt's theory as published in a chapter entitled "Die Trajanssäule und das Bilderbuch,"[1] a theory which has been followed by most scholars.

According to Birt, the most faithful and immediate copy of an illustrated classical roll is to be seen in the Column of Trajan, whose long relief band he believed to be conceived in a roll and then transferred into monumental sculpture. Even technical details such as the wavy edges of the spiral reliefs were explained by him as reflections of the unevenness of the edges in a papyrus roll. From this Birt drew the general conclusion that classical illumination consisted primarily of picture rolls composed as friezes in continuous method and without any accompanying text, which for its part existed in separate rolls. Birt cited as strong support of his theory the well-known

[1] Birt, *Die Buchrolle in der Kunst*, pp. 269-315.

Joshua Rotulus in the Vatican Library, cod. Pal. gr. 431 (fig. 111),[2] a parchment roll of more than ten meters in length with illustrations of chapters II-X of the Book of Joshua, which he considered to be an exact copy of a late classical model. In trying to trace this method of illustration back to its origin Birt pointed to the Egyptian satirical papyri like the one in London (fig. 54) as proof for the very early existence of continuous picture friezes in rolls without accompanying text. Hence the chief documents on which his theory rests are the Trajan Column, the Joshua Roll and the Egyptian satirical papyri.

In dealing with the latter we have already pointed out that the one in Turin has preserved above the animal frieze several lines of writing which are damaged all along the upper border so that we do not know the original height of the writing columns, nor, consequently, how the total surface was proportionally divided between the text and the picture frieze. The fragments in London (fig. 54) and Cairo are similarly damaged immediately above the picture frieze, and the assumption is thoroughly justified that they likewise possessed writing columns in the same place. The script in the Turin fragment is hieratic, so that the roll in its original layout must have looked in its arrangement somewhat like the Greenfield Papyrus (fig. 47), except that the frieze ran, not along the top, but at the bottom of the roll, as is the case in the Ramesseum Papyrus, the oldest of all (fig. 44). Thus it becomes clear that the existence of a picture roll *without text* cannot be proved by these satirical papyri. The date of the latter is controversial: most Egyptologists date them at the beginning of the New Kingdom,[3] i.e. about the same period to which the Greenfield Papyrus belongs, namely the XXI Dynasty. We have tried to show that the Egyptian roll from the beginning of the New Kingdom down to the Hellenistic period, when the Greeks came in touch with the Egyptians, had undergone considerable changes; therefore the satirical papyri are not a good basis for a comparison with Greek ones from which they are separated by more than half a millennium.

More fundamental is the issue raised by associating the Column of Trajan[4] with book illumination. The chief task of the miniaturist has always been—except in the case of frontispieces—to translate the content of a specific text into visual form as literally as possible. It is primarily this quality which relates the scenes of the Megarian bowls so convincingly to

[2] *Il Rotulo di Giosuè* (Codices e Vaticanis selecti, vol. v) (facsimile) Milan 1905.

[3] Pleyte-Rossi (cf. p. 68, note 51) date the Turin papyrus in the XX Dynasty, Brugsch-Bey (cf. p. 68, note 57) the Cairo one in the XXII, while Ranke (cf. p. 68, note 56) speaks of the London papyrus in only general terms as of the late period.

[4] C. Cichorius, *Die Reliefs der Trajanssäule*, Berlin 1896-1900.—K. Lehmann-Hartleben, *Die Trajanssäule*, Berlin 1926.

book illustration, because the beholder is enabled in practically every single scene to point to a special verse of a poem or drama. This is not true of the Trajan Column. The fact that no text is known, on which the reliefs of the column could be based, would, of course, not be a sufficient counter-argument, because the text might be lost. It is known that Trajan himself wrote two books, *Bella Dacica*, which have not come down to us, and, as is to be expected, Birt assumed them to be the source for the column reliefs. However, Lehmann-Hartleben has presented impressive arguments not only against Trajan's *Bella Dacica*, but against any specific historical writing as the source of the column reliefs. First of all, judging by the records we have of the Dacian wars such as Cassius Dio, some of the relief scenes are not in the chronological order we would expect. Although at least the great battles follow in the right order,[5] conventional scenes, like the *adlocutio*, sometimes appear in places not historically justified.[6] Important missions are passed over, other events are distorted, and there are marching bodies of troops apparently with no point of departure and no aim which would identify them as representing specific historical events.[7] Moreover conventional compositions are repeated at certain intervals for purely artistic considerations and there is, as Lehmann-Hartleben has demonstrated, a formal arrangement of scenes with regard to their location on the column. Thus all marching scenes are orientated along the Western axis of the column and furthermore the scenes of each turn form a unit as regards their content. It is quite obvious, then, that the monumental frieze was from the beginning conceived for the shape of the column and not for any other medium, such as papyrus rolls, where the distribution described above would be without motivation. The unevenness of the edges of the frieze, a small detail of which Birt makes such an important point, may be simply explained as wavy groundlines.

Further intrinsic probabilities speak against a roll as model for the gigantic relief monument. As an artistic creation of the Trajanic period the column reliefs rank very high and apparently some of the best artists were employed to make the layout for the reliefs. This was at a time when the parchment codex had just been invented and when its miniatures still followed closely the terse column pictures of the roll and were void of frame and background. Quite different are the column reliefs with their accumulations of large troop formations, placed in a rich surrounding of landscape and architecture, features which entered miniature painting only sometime thereafter. It seems more reasonable to assume, with Lehmann-Hartleben, that the source of the column reliefs is to be sought within the same iconographic realm, i.e. in triumphal paintings,[8] rather than in rolls.

[5] Lehmann-Hartleben, *op. cit.*, p. 88.   [6] *Ibid.*, p. 11.
[7] *Ibid.*, pp. 116, 56, 89, 63ff.   [8] *Ibid.*, pp. 79, 86, 118 and elsewhere.

The key document which Birt associated so closely with Trajan's Column in order to prove the existence of textless picture rolls in classical antiquity, is the Joshua Roll. But, in the first place, are the systems of arranging narrative scenes in frieze form in Trajan's Column and in the Joshua Rotulus really so similar as Birt claimed them to be? And, secondly, is the assumption justified that the Joshua Rotulus, being a mediaeval product, copies unchanged and faithfully a late antique roll? As known to students of Byzantine art, the actual date of the pictures of the Joshua Rotulus is one of the most controversial issues in the field and varies between the fifth and tenth centuries,[9] while the date of the text written underneath points unquestionably to the tenth century. It is important to notice that the pictorial part fills the inner side of the parchment scroll in such a way that the highest points in each scene, whether the summit of a mountain, the tip of a head or a spear point, are—to be quite precise—on an average one centimeter distant from the upper edge of the roll,[10] while the distance from the feet to the lower edge varies between 4.5 and 6.5 m.[11] Therefore the picture frieze was not centered on the parchment, but the illustrator had calculated already in the layout the space for text underneath.[12] Consequently the theory that the pictures were made earlier than the text would have to presuppose that the space provided for several lines of writing remained empty for several hundred years until a writer was found who was able to fill in the text in precisely the same way as it was originally planned, since it now corresponds fairly well with the pictures.[13] The actual date of the Vatican Rotulus has no immediate bearing on the present problem; the fact that text and pictures were thought of as corresponding parts in the layout makes the Joshua Roll an essentially different type of frieze from that of the Trajan Column, which fills the full height of the spiral band.

[9] Kondakoff (*Histoire de l'art byzantin*, I, Paris 1886, p. 95), the editors of the facsimile edition (*op. cit.*, p. 7), Gerstinger (*Griechische Buchmalerei*, p. 11), Wulff (*Altchristliche und Byzantinische Kunst*, I, p. 281) and Morey ("Notes on East Christian Miniatures," *Art Bull.*, XI, 1929, p. 46) are the chief champions of an early date, while Bond and Thompson (*Pal. Soc.*, ser. I, 1873-78, pl. 108), Venturi (*Storia dell' arte italiana*, vol. I, Milan 1901, p. 380), Lietzmann ("Zur Datierung der Josuarolle," *Festgabe zum 60. Geburtstage von H. Degering*, Leipzig 1926, p. 181) and the present writer (*Byzantinische Buchmalerei*, p. 44) assumed a tenth century date.

[10] Only in 3 of the 15 sheets (facs. pls. XII, XIV, XV) is the highest point 2-2.5 cm. distant.

[11] With only one exception (facs. pl. II), where the distance is less, namely 4.2 cm.

[12] For a different opinion on this point cf. Morey, *op. cit.*—*Idem*, "The 'Byzantine Renaissance,'" *Speculum*, XIV, 1939, p. 141.

[13] The situation is similar to that of the Etschmiadzin Gospels, where Strzygowski had argued that the arches of the canon tables had been left empty for several centuries, because he believed their decoration to belong to the sixth century, while the script in the tables unmistakably points to the tenth century. As to the objection against Strzygowski's view, cf. Der Nersessian and Weitzmann, in the bibliography quoted p. 113, note 4.

126

The other question is whether the method of frieze composition in the Joshua Roll is indeed the same as that of Trajan's Column and therefore could justifiably be considered as a derivation from classical antiquity. Let us compare a section from the column frieze with a section from the rotulus. In the example chosen from the column (fig. 110)[14] one recognizes first a short scene with seven legionaries cutting trees and then there follows a much larger battle scene which takes place under the eyes of the emperor himself.[15] These two scenes are so interlocked that the one legionary cutting a tree at the lower right corner is placed underneath a marching soldier of the second scene. This artistic device of interlocking scenes is used throughout the column, and we see it also at the left side of the tree-cutting scene where a space is hollowed out for a young officer who leads a group of soldiers belonging to the preceding composition.[16] Similarly at the right end of the battle scene above the wounded Dacian in the lower right corner stands Trajan with two accompanying officers from the next scene where he inspects some buildings.[17] As a glance at the plates in Lehmann-Hartleben's publication in which the divisions of the frieze coincide with iconographic units will show, in the majority of cases it is not possible to draw a straight vertical line between the end of the one and the beginning of the next unit. This interlocking of scenes undoubtedly results from the artistic intention of the sculptor to obscure purposely the scenic divisions and to create an uninterrupted flow of events, one leading immediately over into the next. The beholder is made to believe that the whole war is like a great triumphal procession and nowhere can the eye rest until it sees the Nike between two tropaea in the middle of the column, i.e. at the end of the first war. Here is the only real caesura, after which the frieze again runs uninterruptedly until the end of the whole column.

In contrast to Trajan's Column, each iconographic unit of the Joshua Rotulus is spaced from the next by a wide and very marked caesura. The four scenes (fig. 111) which represent Joshua receiving two messengers (Joshua VII, 3), the three thousand Israelites marching against the men of Ai (VII, 4), the Israelites defeated by the men of Ai (VII, 5) and Joshua with the Elders falling down before the Lord (VII, 6), are so markedly separated from each other—by 5 cm. on an average—that the beholder is compelled to pause after each scene, thus made conscious where one scene ends and the next begins.

[14] Cichorius, *op. cit.*, vol. II, p. 109 and pl. XVII.—Lehmann-Hartleben, *op. cit.*, pl. 14.

[15] Cichorius, *op. cit.*, vol. II, p. 111 and pls. XVIII-XIX, explains it as the battle of Tapae, the first great engagement of the first Dacian war.

[16] Cichorius, *op. cit.*, vol. II, p. 105 and pl. XVII.—Lehmann-Hartleben, *op. cit.*, pl. 13, no. XXII.

[17] Cichorius, *op. cit.*, vol. II, p. 122 and pl. XX.—Lehmann-Hartleben, *op. cit.*, pl. 15, no. XXV.

Moreover, each scene has its own text passage underneath, which consists of wide but low writing columns separated from each other by the same intervals as the scenes above them. Thus each scene of the rotulus is related to and actually stands within the limits of a writing column. From a normal ancient papyrus roll with column pictures the rotulus differs essentially in that the ratio between text and pictures is reversed: while in the papyrus roll the picture is subordinated to the text, in the Joshua Roll the picture is predominant and the text abbreviated. The principle of enlarging the picture area at the expense of the text is by no means unique in the Vatican Rotulus. It is apparent in a preliminary stage in the Vienna Genesis, where, too, the text is abbreviated, but only to the extent that text and picture have an equal share of the total area, while in the Joshua Roll the pictures occupy far more than half of it. This gain could only be achieved by a considerable increase in the scale of the figures, comparable and nearly identical with that of the Paris Psalter (figs. 92-93), the very manuscript with which the Joshua Rotulus is most closely connected in style. It may be recalled that we considered the pictures of the Paris Psalter as the result of a transformation from friezelike column pictures, such as in the Book of Kings, into full-page miniatures, which increased the height of the compositions and more than doubled the scale of the figures (cf. p. 107). An analogous development can be assumed for the Joshua Roll, and we expect a model behind it with miniatures of a much smaller scale. Such a model must have been very similar to the Octateuchs of the eleventh and twelfth centuries which include the very same picture cycle[18] and therefore go back to the same archetype as the Vatican Rotulus. In all Octateuchs the size of the figures is hardly half that of the Rotulus and follows more closely the normal scale of Early Christian manuscripts like the Vienna Genesis and others. It follows that the archetype of the Joshua Rotulus was probably either a roll with column pictures of a smaller size irregularly distributed in the full biblical text, or a codex like the Octateuchs which adheres to the same method. The Rotulus must, then, be regarded as an individual solution of a later period rather than a typical representative of the earliest period of book illustration. This individual solution, as we see it now, was the result of an elaborate process by which the Septuagint text became excerpted, the pictures lined up in a frieze and the scale of the figures considerably enlarged.

In the lining-up of scenes in frieze form, the Rotulus must be considered as the last step of a development which had started in early codices within the limits of a single page, where two or up to three and four scenes were

---

[18] These are: Vat. gr. 747, Vat. gr. 746, Istanbul Seraglio cod. 8, Mount Athos Vatopedi cod. 602 and Smyrna cod. A. I (which burned during the destruction of that city in 1923).

joined in short friezes as in the Vienna Genesis (figs. 73-74), the Gospels of Florence, Plut. VI, 23 (figs. 70-71), and other manuscripts. But while in the Vienna Genesis two consecutive scenes were usually separated by empty space, the illustrator of the Florentine Gospels placed between them what we called *insertion motifs* (cf. p. 88), which consist mostly of rather schematic, towerlike buildings. The painter of the Joshua Roll used very similar artistic devices to fill the gaps between the formerly separate column pictures, but being a greater artist he used a greater variety of insertion motifs, like the sculptor of the Telephus Frieze centuries before him. In our example from the Joshua Roll we see between scenes 1 and 2 a structure resembling an altar and a tree, between 2 and 3 a group of three blocklike houses and a tree, between 3 and 4 again an altarlike structure against the city wall with which it is not organically connected, and elsewhere in the rotulus there are still other insertion motifs.[19]

The physical relationship between text and picture is of course only one aspect of the problem of the Joshua Rotulus. Its iconography would have to be considered also if a new position for this key document of Byzantine book illumination is to be justified. We shall have occasion, in a later chapter, to discuss the iconography of the Rotulus in at least two instances (p. 171 and figs. 167 and 171), both of which will demonstrate that the Joshua Rotulus is, from this point of view also, far removed from the archetype, showing more changes, errors and re-interpretations than the corresponding pictures in the Octateuchs.

The Joshua Roll, so interpreted, can no longer be used as evidence for Birt's theory of ancient picture rolls with continuous friezes. Likewise, Wickhoff's idea that the continuous method as such is characteristic and especially suitable for manuscript painting, based primarily on the Joshua Roll, becomes untenable. A more appropriate medium for the continuous method in classical antiquity would seem to be the friezes in sculpture or fresco which ran around the inside or outside wall of a temple or house or, as in the special case of Trajan's favored monument, around a column. Nevertheless in spite of all our arguments in favor of illustration by isolated column pictures as the most common method in ancient rolls, the possibility that some ancient illuminator may have used the continuous method in a papyrus roll for a special purpose, should not entirely be excluded, although we have, at the present, no direct evidence for it.

[19] A full discussion of the problems connected with the Joshua Rotulus will be published by the author in the near future as a monograph.

III. THE RELATION BETWEEN THE MINIATURE AND THE TEXT WITH REGARD TO CONTENT

A. THE ASSOCIATION OF A MINIATURE WITH VARIOUS TEXTS

NO discussion of the iconographic relationship between a miniature and its accompanying text passage is possible without first considering whether or not text and picture have been connected with each other from the very beginning. It is by no means as common as one might expect that they retain in the process of repeated copying the junction which they had had in the archetype, and there are many instances in which a miniature has been taken over from what might be called its *basic text* into a new one. When the new text is only a revision of the basic one, the latter can easily be determined, but when, on occasion, the new text is entirely different, the task of identifying the basic text is much more difficult. In the latter case the new text must be used with great caution, or even disregarded entirely in the interpretation of the iconography of the miniatures. And if the basic text has not been preserved at all, then there is no means of controlling the degree of faithfulness, change, error, and so on, in a transplanted miniature. It will be seen that such a *migration of miniatures* from one text into another took place on a considerable scale, and in the following examples we wish to demonstrate the various kinds of migrations and to try to establish in each case the basic text for which the miniatures were originally conceived.

1. *A Miniature Connected with its Basic Text*

When the Homeric poems or the various books of the Bible—two of the most important illustrated basic texts—were first decorated with miniatures, the illuminators had to create hundreds of new scenes. Certainly representations based on Homer's poems existed long before the text was illustrated in papyrus rolls at the beginning of the Hellenistic period, but they were few in number, compared with the many scenes needed to accompany the text in a more or less regular spacing. Likewise in the various books of the Old Testament, as can be inferred from the earliest documents, i.e. the Cotton Bible and the Vienna Genesis, the number of scenes was extremely large, and the demands on the creativeness of the first illustrators of the Septuagint were, perhaps, even greater than in the case of Homer, since it is not likely that many Biblical representations existed previously in any other medium which could be used and incorporated into the miniature cycle. But once the scenes were created, later generations of illustrators copied, whenever it was possible, from the established pictorial archetype, and comparatively seldom was a new cycle of miniatures invented for a text which existed already with pictures. This explains why all Septuagint representations in manuscripts as well as in other media which depend on manuscripts can be reduced to very few archetypes.

A new problem arose when, for a special purpose, a basic text was divided into sections, and these sections became rearranged in a new order, or when a text was excerpted and these excerpts combined with ones from other texts. Now when an illustrated text was so treated, did the illustrator invent a new picture cycle for the rearranged text, or did he rather try to copy from the cycle of the basic text as much as he could, and satisfy himself with the rearrangement of the miniatures according to altered circumstances? For instance, the Greek Psalter is usually followed by a series of Odes or Canticles which are excerpts from other books of the Septuagint. Ode I consists of a part of the fifteenth chapter of Exodus, Ode II of the thirty-second chapter of Deuteronomy, Ode III of the second chapter of the First Book of Kings and several others repeat passages from the Prophets. In many Psalters these Odes are illustrated. Did the painter invent new miniatures for the Odes, or did he take them over from those illustrated books of the Septuagint from which the passages of the Odes were excerpted? The second Ode of a Psalter manuscript in the Athos monastery Vatopedi, cod. 760, which belongs to the so-called aristocratic group and is to be dated in the eleventh or twelfth century,[1] represents Moses sitting on a mountain and reciting the song before Joshua and two groups of Israelites (fig. 113). In the various Octateuchs the same subject is used as an illustration of the thirty-second chapter of Deuteronomy: in the Vat. cod. gr. 747 (fig. 112) Moses in the left scene sits on a mountain and speaks to a group of Israelites, and in the right he stands and addresses Joshua and again a group of Israelites, illustrating verse 44: "And Moses wrote this song in that day and taught it to the children of Israel; and Moses went in and spoke all the words of this law in the ears of the people, he and Joshua the son of Nun." Moses with a book in his hand represents the Writing of the Ode and refers to the first half of the verse, while the second scene is related to the other half. In both manuscripts, Vatopedi Psalter and Octateuch, the figure of Joshua in particular is so strikingly similar that a common archetype must be assumed. The Psalter picture, then, must be understood as a conflation of the two Octateuch pictures, carried out in such a way that the seated Moses of the first Octateuch scene was placed in the upper zone, and Joshua and the two groups of Israelites in the lower, while the standing Moses, in order to avoid a repetition, is

---

[1] Tikkanen, *Die Psalterillustration im Mittelalter*, p. 141.—Н. П. КОНДАКОВЪ, Памятники Христіанскаго Искусства на Афонѣ, S. Petersburg 1902, p. 286 and fig. 99.—G. Millet and S. Der Nersessian, *Revue des études arméniennes*, IX, 1929, p. 165 and pls. XIII-XIV.—Buchthal, *op. cit.*, pl. XXVI, nos. 80-81.

dropped entirely. As already mentioned, both scenes are based upon verse 44 of the thirty-second chapter of Deuteronomy. However, the text of the Ode proper ends with verse 43 so that the miniature, especially in the case of Joshua, who is not cited in the Ode proper, cannot be explained on the basis of the Ode text alone, but only on the fuller Octateuch text. This makes it all the more certain that the picture was actually invented for the Octateuch which is then its basic text, and sometime later was taken over and re-adjusted as title picture of the Ode.

A similar migration can be shown for the other Ode pictures: the representation of the Crossing of the Red Sea, which precedes the first Ode, is iconographically very closely related to the corresponding picture in the Book of Exodus and consequently we can conclude that this Ode picture was taken over from the latter source. Furthermore, the praying Hannah of the third Ode is identical with the corresponding miniature in the First Book of Kings in the Vatican codex gr. 333 and therefore is derived from an earlier copy of this historical book of the Bible, and we would expect that similarly most of the remaining Ode pictures were taken over from an illustrated Prophet book. As to the illustrations from the life of David which usually precede the first Psalm we have already called attention to parallels in the Book of Kings which must be their source (fig. 93). On this evidence it may be concluded that the whole cycle of full-page miniatures of this Psalter group was not created for the Psalter but excerpted and compiled from various illustrated books of the Septuagint. In other words, text recension and picture recension do not coincide, and the invention of the Psalter with the addition of the Odes as a liturgical book cannot be regarded as a *terminus post quem* for its miniatures. Nevertheless the first illustrator of the aristocratic Psalter made some formal and iconographic changes and therefore any future study of this group of manuscripts will have to take into consideration how much has survived in them from the original compositions in the Octateuch, the Book of Kings and the Prophets, and how much has been altered with regard to the new textual affiliation.

Identical problems of migration of miniatures from a basic text into a compiled one occur also in the illustration of the New Testament. When the text of the Gospels was divided up into lessons and these were rearranged in the lectionary, miniatures invented for the Gospels were taken over into the new liturgical book. Again slight changes were occasionally necessary in regrouping the picture cycle, but by far the majority of miniatures remained iconographically unchanged. To cite one example: the illustration of the healing of the blind man (John IX, 1-7) in the Gospels of Rossano (fig. 76) sufficiently corresponds, from the iconographic viewpoint, with the same scene in the lectionary from Patmos, cod. 70 (fig. 99), as to justify the assumption of a common pictorial archetype, which naturally was invented for the Gospels as the basic text and subsequently taken over into a lectionary. Once more the date of composing the lectionary as a liturgical book cannot be taken as a *terminus post quem* for the pictures.

Besides liturgical books there are other compiled texts in which passages are gathered together not only from various parts of the Bible, but from patristic and profane literature as well, as e.g. the *Sacra Parallela* of John of Damascus in Paris, cod. gr. 923, which we have mentioned already in connection with marginal illustration. This manuscript is a florilegium, where passages are arranged alphabetically according to their catchwords, and in the chapter of the letter Iota the first paragraph entitled περὶ ἰαμάτων ὑπὸ κυρίου is illustrated by placing the healing of the blind man and the washing of his eyes in the pool of Siloam (fig. 103) alongside the respective passage from the Gospel of St. John. Here again the iconographic connection of these two scenes with the corresponding ones from the Rossano Gospels (fig. 76) is close enough to suggest that the illustrator of the *Sacra Parallela* used a Gospel book as a model and did not make up the scenes for an illustrated edition of the *Sacra Parallela*, and the same is true for the other scenes on this page: Christ with Jairus and the Woman with the Issue of Blood, the Healing of the Bent Woman and the Healing of the Demoniacs.

The same manuscript also contains many scenes from the Old Testament. Those from the Octateuch or the Book of Kings or Job can be compared with existing illustrated manuscripts of the Septuagint, and one will easily detect that also in these cases the illustrator of the florilegium exploited as models the relative books of the Bible and confined himself to readjusting the miniatures he took over to the limited space in the margin. Moreover, there are quite a number of illustrations from other books of the Septuagint, of which no illustrated copy has come down to us. As a matter of analogy we can assume that, also in their case, we are dealing with copies from the books of the Septuagint, which only by accident are not preserved or are not yet found. There are, for example, several passages from Chronicles enriched by miniatures. In one of them (fig. 114) David rides out of the city of Rabbah, which he had destroyed and spoiled as the accompanying passage (I Chron. xx, 2-3) narrates. From the existence of these miniatures it can be concluded that also the text of Chronicles was originally illustrated in a manner similar to the Book of Kings of which we have the one remaining copy in the Vatican Library, cod. gr. 333. Furthermore, on the same page of the *Sacra Parallela* are depicted two scenes from the Book of Jeremiah, one in which the King of Babylon gives the order to slay the sons of Zedekiah (Jer. LII, 10) and the other where Zedekiah himself, lying on his back, is blinded by two men (LII, 11). All extant Greek illustrated books of the

Prophets confine themselves more or less to the author portraits, but now, on the basis of the *Sacra Parallela*, in which narrative scenes are also preserved from the Book of Jonah as well as quite a few from the Book of Daniel, we can conclude that the books of the Prophets, major and minor as well, existed with extensive miniature cycles.

The Paris *Sacra Parallela* is one of the richest iconographic indices, and it provides the evidence for many more miniature cycles which in their original form have been lost and are now preserved only in this manuscript in an excerpted fragmentary form. This applies not only to excerpts from the Bible, but also to those from patristic and profane literature. From a series of illustrations alongside a text passage of the *Bellum Judaicum* of Flavius Josephus we learn with certainty that also this historical text once existed richly illustrated. On one page (fig. 115) several scenes follow each other from the episode of a mother, named Mary, who during the siege of Jerusalem devoured her own child (VI, 205-212): first she nourishes the babe at her breast, then she kills it, roasts it on a fire and finally offers the remains of the meat to some rebel soldiers. The quick succession of various phases of the same episode in this one instance leads one to suspect that the illustration of a full Josephus text must have been extremely extensive in its number of scenes. Furthermore, since the *Sacra Parallela* (on fol. 192ᵛ) contains an illustration from Book IX of the *Antiquitates Judaicae* of the same author, we can be certain also that this work existed with a cycle of miniatures.

From these examples it is apparent that illustrators had the tendency to leave miniatures, wherever possible, united with the basic text, even when the latter was broken up and portions of it were reorganized in new textual combinations. Not that it necessarily must be so in every case. The possibility remains that a painter may have conceived a new miniature cycle for a new text arrangement, but such cases must be considered as exceptions rather than as the rule, and it will be more difficult to prove the originality of a miniature cycle in a rearranged text than to assume its dependence upon an illustrated basic text. This means that the history of the illustrations of a certain text must take into consideration not only the manuscripts in which the original connection between the pictures and the basic text has been preserved, but also those rearranged texts which contain scattered scenes of the original cycle.

2. *A Miniature Carried over into a New Text Recension*

A new situation arises in the relationship between text and picture when a text undergoes actual changes, whether by translation, revision, paraphrase or by similar alterations. If an artist has to illustrate a revised text, which very often goes under a new author's name, does he, under normal circumstances, start out with a new miniature cycle, or does he rather search for the same source which the writer of the new text consulted and copy from it the miniatures, if it had any? Where the writer mentions his literary source, there is no difficulty in finding a proper model, but if the writer conceals his source, some literary knowledge on the part of the painter is required to locate a model with the desired prototypes.

When Dioscurides states that he took over quite a number of plant descriptions from Crateuas' herbal, we can suspect that the illustrator of the Dioscurides herbal likewise copied the corresponding pictures from an illustrated Crateuas, and this is all the more probable, since Pliny tells us (*N.H.* xxv, 8) that Crateuas himself *did* make the pictures of plants for his herbal. This would mean that some plant pictures in the archetype of the Dioscurides were not made for his text, and that consequently the text does not furnish a *terminus post quem* for all its illustrations.

The text of Dioscurides was translated into Latin and with it the illustrations migrated from Greek into Latin codices like that in Munich, Staatsbibliothek cod. lat. 337, a South Italian manuscript from the tenth century with plant pictures which surely stand in the Greek tradition (fig. 116).[2] In about the fifth century a new herbal was written in Latin which goes under the name of Pseudo-Apuleius, the best copies of which are now in the University Library in Leyden, cod. Voss. lat. quart. 9, from the seventh century,[3] and in the Landesbibliothek in Cassel, cod. phys. fol. 10, written in the tenth century perhaps in Fulda.[4] Its text is chiefly based upon the Dioscurides herbal, and if we compare the representations of the *salvia* and *coriandrum* in the Cassel manuscript (fig. 117)[5] with the corresponding plants in the Greek Dioscurides manuscripts,[6] we will realize that the Western illustrator did not draw on new observation of nature, but that he depended on the very tradition of plant pictures which goes back to Dioscurides. He and his followers only increased the stylization and thus deviated more and

[2] Lowe, *Scriptura Beneventana*, vol. I, pl. XLII (here further bibliography).

[3] E. Howald and H. E. Sigerist, *Pseudoapulei Herbarius* (Corpus Medicorum Latinorum, vol. IV), Leipzig, 1927, pp. 13-225.—A. W. Byvanck, *Bull. de la Soc. franç. de reprod. de Mss. à peint.*, XV, 1931, p. 58 and pl. XVII (here fuller bibliography).—Gasiorowski, *Malarstwo Minjaturowe Grecko-Rzymskie*, p. 68 and figs. 19-22.

[4] Howald-Sigerist, *op. cit.*, p. XIII.—Ch. Singer, *Journ. of Hell. Stud.*, XLVII, 1927, pp. 43ff. and figs. 29, 40, 45.—Ad. Goldschmidt, *Karolingische Buchmalerei*, p. 20 and pls. 19-20.—Bethe, *Buch und Bild*, pp. 35, 37 and fig. 11.

[5] After Goldschmidt, *op. cit.*, pl. 19.—Howald-Sigerist, *op. cit.*, figs. pp. 184-185.

[6] Cf. the Julia Anicia Codex in Vienna. Premerstein, Wessely and Mantuani, *Dioscurides*, vol. I, fols. 121[r] and 155[v]. Also the Morgan Manuscript in New York: *Pedanii Dioscuridis Anazarbaei Materia Medica* (facsimile), Paris 1935, fols. 50[r] and 88[v], and especially fol. 312[r], where the coriandrum is repeated more simplified and without blossoms just as in the Cassel manuscript.

more from the natural appearance of the plants which they had possessed in the Hellenistic-Roman period. To the scholars of the history of botany it is a well-known fact that herbals from the classical period down to the late Middle Ages did not invent any new plant pictures, but that the classical herbal, chiefly that of Dioscurides, was the sole source for the pictorial tradition. Charles Singer, who in his various writings has given ample proof for this, demonstrated in a well-chosen example that the pictorial type of the *mandragora* in the Dioscurides of the Morgan Library in New York is the same as that in an Anglo-Saxon Pseudo-Apuleius of the eleventh century and also in a copy of the fifteenth century in London and that it still had not changed in a woodcut edition printed in Rome *ca.* 1481.[7] Therefore the pictures of the Dioscurides herbal whose text was translated, rewritten and attached to a new author's name, remained essentially the same through many centuries, save for the stylistic changes. The same is true, to quote another example, for the various Aratus manuscripts. Often revised, edited and commented on by Germanicus, Cicero, Hyginus, Bede and others, the edition of a new version of the text did not result in a newly invented set of constellation pictures.

The conservative attitude observed in the herbal illustration can be expected also in other scientific treatises, though in many cases the migration from one text to another cannot be so clearly demonstrated with the existing documents. There is a gynaecological treatise of the Carolingian period in the Bibliothèque Royale in Brussels, cod. 3701-15, which is accompanied by a number of schemata illustrating the various positions of the embryo in the uterus (fig. 118).[8] This treatise is written by a physician Muscio or Mustio, who lived about the sixth century in North Africa.[9] Is the conclusion justified from this textual evidence that the pictures were invented at this time? Valentin Rose[10] first discovered that the treatise of Mustio is only a translation and revision of a gynaecological treatise by the famous physician Soranus of Ephesus, who first worked and wrote in Alexandria and later, in the

---

[7] Ch. Singer, *Jour. of Hell. Stud.*, XLVII, 1927, p. 40 and figs. 34-37.

[8] K. Sudhoff, *Weitere Serien von Kindslagenbildern* (Studien zur Geschichte der Medizin, fasc. 4), Leipzig 1908, pp. 73ff. and pls. XIX-XXIII.—Joh. Ilberg, *Die Überlieferung der Gynäkologie des Soranos von Ephesos* (Abhandl. der Sächsischen Gesellsch. der Wissenschaften, vol. XXVIII, no. II), 1910, pp. 11ff. and pls. III-VI.—W. Koehler, "Die Denkmäler der karolingischen Kunst in Belgien," *Belgische Kunstdenkmäler*, vol. I, Munich 1923, p. 7 and fig. 7.—C. Gaspar and F. Lyna, *Les principaux manuscrits à peintures de la Bibliothèque Royale de Belgique*, Paris 1937, p. 15 and pl. IV.—Bethe, *Buch und Bild*, p. 26 and fig. 5 (here further bibliography).

[9] A Greek text under the name Moschion is not by the Greek physician of this name, who lived in the first century B.C. (Deichgräber, in Pauly-Wiss., *R.-E.*, *s.v.* Moschion, vol. XVI, pt. I, col. 349), but according to Ilberg, *op. cit.*, it is only a Byzantine retranslation of the Latin Mustio treatise back into the Greek.

[10] V. Rose, *Sorani Gynaeciorum vetus translatio latina*, Leipzig 1882.

time of Trajan and Hadrian, in Rome. Two points favor the assumption that the Soranus treatise was already adorned with pictures and that the first illustrator of the Mustio translation, knowing the literary source of the Latin text, copied the pictures from a Greek model. First there exist other treatises by the same Soranus, and one of them, dealing with bandaging, has actually preserved its pictures (fig. 60), thus providing the evidence that some of Soranus' writings did in fact have illustrations. Secondly, the figures in the Brussels miniatures are very slender, what seems to be particularly inappropriate for an embryo. With their small feet and narrow ankles they resemble the patients in the bandaging treatise of Soranus (fig. 60) and also those in the Apollonius of Citium (fig. 94) and thus seem to reflect the style of an Eastern model. The Mustio treatise with its pictures was often copied between the twelfth and fifteenth centuries,[11] and again in the woodcuts of the *Rosengarten* by Eucharius Rösslin of Worms of the year 1513 the same set of traditional pictures is used without any influence from a renewed observation of nature.[12] The history of these medical pictures bears a striking analogy to that of the herbal pictures, insofar as we deal with a set of miniatures invented in the classical period, copied throughout the centuries until the end of the Middle Ages, and connected with a text which has changed, in the meantime, both its language and the name of its author.

From scientific treatises we may turn to literary writing. There is an illustrated text known from three English copies of the eleventh and twelfth centuries to which the title "Marvels of the East"[13] was given by Montague James, who recognized as one of its chief sources the so-called Letter of Fermes of the fourth or fifth centuries A.D., which in turn goes back to a Greek source. Were the miniatures in the extant copies of the *Marvels* invented by English artists of the Middle Ages or did the Fermes Letter or perhaps already its Greek source possess illustrations of which those in the *Marvels* are only late copies transmitted by migration from one text version into another? In the earliest of the three extant copies, London, Brit. Mus., cod. Cotton Vitellius A. xv, there is mentioned a cynocephalus whom the Fermes Letter[14] and its Greek source, which in all probability was the Alexander Romance of Pseudo-Callisthenes (III, 28),[15] describe in very similar

[11] K. Sudhoff, *Kindslagen in Miniaturen, Schnitten und Stichen vom 12. bis ins 18. Jahrh.* (Studien zur Geschichte der Medizin, fasc. 1), Leipzig 1907, pp. 69ff. and pls. XVI-XVIII.

[12] *Ibid.*, p. 72 and figs. 25-26.

[13] M. R. James, *Marvels of the East*, Oxford 1929, where the pictures of the three Mss. are published complete. No title has come down in any of these copies, so James (p. 10) supposes that the model was mutilated at the beginning.   [14] James, *op. cit.*, p. 43, par. 15.

[15] Ad. Ausfeld, *Der griechische Alexanderroman*, Leipzig 1907, pp. 106 and 197.—W. Kroll, *Historia Alexandri Magni*, Berlin 1926, p. 129.

terms. Therefore we may ask whether the miniature of this monster (fig. 119)[16] also goes all the way back to an illustrated Pseudo-Callisthenes Romance. The existence of an illustrated Pseudo-Callisthenes could hardly be assumed from this evidence alone, but some miniatures of the Pseudo-Oppian provide other and more conclusive evidence that the Pseudo-Callisthenes Romance was illustrated at an early period (cf. p. 145 and figs. 133-134),[17] and it becomes increasingly likely that this popular and often translated romance did indeed possess, among other miniatures, also those of the strange monsters which descended from it through various texts to the English *Marvels of the East*.

A situation in many regards similar to that of the *Marvels of the East* occurs in the *Bestiarium*, a collection of moralizing animal descriptions which in the twelfth and thirteenth centuries was one of the most often illustrated books in England. It is well known that a great many of its animal stories go back to the *Physiologus*, the Latin text of which is only a translation from the Greek, and therefore it is not surprising to find the models of some of the animal pictures of the bestiary in illustrated *Physiologus* manuscripts. For instance, the paragraph about the deer which tells us that it is the enemy of snakes and kills the snake coming out of a rocky cleft, is accompanied in a bestiary in Oxford, cod. Bodl. 764, from the end of the twelfth century, by a miniature with two animals of this species (fig. 120), one drinking water and the other eating a snake.[18] The second of these types agrees well with the corresponding picture of the Greek *Physiologus* in Smyrna, which today is destroyed but of which we possess a sufficiently accurate description to allow an iconographic comparison.[19] The *Physiologus* was written in the third, or, more likely, in the fourth century[20] and in all likelihood was already illustrated at that time. But can we be sure that the deer picture was indeed invented by the first illustrator of the *Physiologus*, or are there indications that it may go back to a still earlier source and then have been taken over

[16] James, *op. cit.*, pl. II, fol. 100a. For the subject of the cynocephalus cf. Strzygowski, "Das Byzantinische Relief aus Tusla," *Jahrb. der Preuss. Kunstsammlungen*, XIX, 1898, pp. 57ff.

[17] So far illustrations of the Alexander Romance had been known only from a fourteenth century Greek copy in S. Giorgio dei Greci in Venice (cf. Kondakoff, *Histoire de l'art byzantin*, vol. II, p. 174), from still later Armenian manuscripts (F. Macler, *L'enluminure arménienne profane*, Paris 1928), and from a Serbian manuscript of the fifteenth century (A. Grabar, *Recherches sur les influences orientales dans l'art balkanique*, Paris 1928, p. 108 and pls. XII-XVI), not to mention, of course, the numerous Latin copies with illustrations.

[18] M. R. James, *The Bestiary*, Oxford 1928, suppl. pl. 14.

[19] Strzygowski, *Der Bilderkreis des griechischen Physiologus* (Byzantinisches Archiv, fasc. 2), Leipzig 1899, p. 37: "Die Miniatur stellt den Hirsch dar, welchen die Schlange scheinbar ins Maul beisst, besser, der sie heraufgezogen hat und einschlürft."

[20] For a more recent discussion of the date of the archetype, see Max Wellman, "Der Physiologus," *Philologus*, suppl. XXII, fasc. 1, 1930.

into the *Physiologus* text which itself is a compilation? The story of the enmity between the deer and the snake is told in various texts which are older than the *Physiologus*, such as Aelian (II, 9; IX, 20), Pliny (*N.H.* VIII, 118), Pseudo-Oppian (*Cyn.* II, 233ff.), and others. Of the Pseudo-Oppian there is an illustrated copy in Venice, to which we have referred on several occasions, where the representation of the deer eating a snake (fig. 122) is in the same pictorial tradition as the two examples described above. Since the *Cynegetica* of Pseudo-Oppian were written and most probably illustrated in the time of Caracalla, we have an indication that animal treatises with illustrations did exist prior to the *Physiologus*. We cannot be sure however that the first illustrator of the *Physiologus* used a Pseudo-Oppian manuscript as model; other texts like Aelian and still earlier ones may just as well have possessed the same miniature, so that the pictures in both the bestiary and the Pseudo-Oppian may depend upon a common older source.

Other bestiaries have a different composition preceding the same paragraph on the deer. In a manuscript in the University Library in Cambridge, cod. K. k. IV. 25, from the thirteenth century, a group of four deer is depicted swimming through the sea (fig. 121),[21] a miniature which illustrates another passage in the same paragraph of the bestiary, stating that deer cross the sea only in company, always following the leadership of one of them. This passage does not exist in the *Physiologus*, but it can be traced to other sources, namely to Isidore's *Etymologiae* (XII, I, 18-19), to Solinus (XIX, 12) and so on back to the same Greek sources mentioned already in connection with the previous scene: Aelian (V, 56) and Pseudo-Oppian (*Cyn.* II, 217ff). In the Venetian copy of Pseudo-Oppian we do find a miniature with four deer swimming in a row (fig. 123) immediately preceding the picture with the deer eating snakes, and the composition is similar enough to that of the Cambridge manuscript to permit the assumption that the second deer picture of the bestiary also is derived ultimately from a classical source, though in this instance it is not the *Physiologus* but another illustrated text which formed the intermediary link. Like the illustrations of the herbals and medical treatises, it is apparent that a certain group of animal pictures was invented in the Hellenistic-Roman period and then passed through various texts down to the English bestiaries.

Biblical illustrations undergo similar migrations, leaving the canonical text and entering new texts which tell the biblical stories in their own way. An example of a vernacular version of the Bible is a rhymed poem in Middle High German in which an Austrian poet of the end of the eleventh century told the stories of Genesis and Exodus in a language understandable to a

---

[21] James, *The Bestiary*, suppl. pl. 22a.

larger public. He chose only those episodes which were suitable for his purpose, interweaving them with parallels and hints from the New Testament and with moralizing remarks of his own. A twelfth century copy of this poem, which was written apparently in Millstatt, in Carinthia, and is now preserved in the Museum Rudolfinum in Klagenfurt, is illustrated with a fairly extensive miniature cycle (figs. 124 and 125) but of Genesis only.[22] Was this miniature cycle made up from the text of the poem or did the miniaturist who first illustrated the poem use an older Genesis cycle from an Old Testament manuscript? The very fact that the miniatures contain only features which can be explained by the canonical Bible text, and no new elements based upon some of the poet's own remarks, points to the latter alternative. But we can be even more precise and determine the very Genesis recension on which the cycle is based. It is the same as that of the so-called Cotton Genesis in London, Brit. Mus., cod. Cotton Otho B. VI, a manuscript of the fifth century,[23] which, save for a number of carbonized fragments, was nearly completely destroyed by fire, but whose picture cycle can partly be reconstructed with the help of the mosaics from S. Marco in Venice[24] and the Genesis pictures of the Carolingian Bibles from Tours.[25] In the Creation of Adam in the Millstatt Genesis (fig. 124)[26] the outstanding iconographic features are the full-length figure of Christ as Creator standing behind Adam—other recensions represent merely the hand of the Lord—and the addition of an angel in front of Adam. Both features occur similarly in the Turonian Bible in London, Brit. Mus., cod. add. 10546 (fig. 178),[27] and, from what has been said above, can also be assumed to have existed among the now lost miniatures of the Cotton Bible. Or, to strengthen the connection of the Millstatt miniatures with the Cotton Bible recension, we may point to the scene in which Isaac blesses Jacob in the presence of Rebecca (fig. 125).[28] The interior is indicated by a pair of columns with open curtains slung around them, a formula which is so common in the

[22] Jos. Diemer, *Genesis und Exodus nach der Milstäter Handschrift*, Vienna 1862.—R. Eisler, *Die illuminierten Handschriften in Kärnten* (Beschreibendes Verzeichnis der illum. Handschriften in Oesterreich, vol. III), Leipzig 1907, p. 50 and pls. V-VI.

[23] *Vetusta Monumenta Rerum Britannicarum*, vol. I, London 1747, pls. LXVII-LXVIII.—O. M. Dalton, *Byzantine Art and Archaeology*, p. 446 and figs. 263-264.—Lethaby, "The Painted Book of Genesis in the British Museum," *Arch. Journal*, LXIX, 1912, pp. 88ff.; LXX, 1913, p. 162.

[24] F. Ongania, *La basilica di San Marco in Venezia*, Venice 1880-93.—J. J. Tikkanen, *Die Genesismosaiken von S. Marco in Venedig und ihr Verhältnis zu den Miniaturen der Cottonbibel* (Acta Societatis Scientiarum Fennicae, vol. XVII), Helsingfors 1889. This scholar was the first to establish beyond doubt the connection between the Cotton Bible and the Venetian mosaics.—O. Demus, *Die Mosaiken von San Marco in Venedig 1100-1300*, Baden bei Wien 1935, pp. 53ff.

[25] W. Köhler, *Die Schule von Tours*, vol. I, pt. 2, Berlin 1933, pp. 186ff., clearly recognized the dependence of the Turonian Genesis cycle upon a model related to the Cotton Bible recension.

[26] Diemer, *op. cit.*, fig. p. 4.   [27] Köhler, *op. cit.*, pl. 50.   [28] Diemer, *op. cit.*, fig. p. 49.

mosaics of S. Marco, as e.g. the Birth of Cain and Abel,[29] that it can be considered also as typical for the Cotton Bible recension. Thus the ultimate source for the miniatures of the Millstatt manuscript was obviously a Greek Genesis of the Early Christian period, which through Latin intermediaries became known to the artist who illustrated the Austrian poem.

The Biblical stories were used and incorporated into texts of very different kinds. There is the well-known and once very popular *Christian Topography* of Cosmas Indicopleustes where, in the fifth book, patriarchs, prophets, evangelists and other representatives of the Old and New Testament are quoted as witnesses for Cosmas' theory that God had divided the whole world into two states. These witnesses reach from Adam to Paul, following more or less the sequence of the Biblical books. In most cases the painter of the Vatican copy, cod. gr. 699, satisfied himself with the portrait figure of the witness (fig. 98) but occasionally, as in the paragraph about Abraham, he added a full-page miniature in which several scenes are combined (fig. 129) :[30] first two young men lead an ass, then Isaac carries on his shoulders the wood for the burnt offering, and finally the sacrifice of Isaac himself is represented. The Cosmas text says in the paragraph about Abraham:[31] "Now the journey which Abraham made for three days until he reached the place which God showed him as that where he should offer up his son as a sacrifice on one of the mountains, as is written, and his showing the father a ram which he might offer instead of his son who was born to him in wedlock and in the course of nature . . . ," and then in the following paragraph it says that Isaac "on his own shoulders carried the wood for his own sacrifice as also the Lord Christ carried his own cross on the shoulder." Nowhere in this text is anything said about the two young men driving an ass, and this raises at once the question whether the miniature could have been made up from the Cosmas text proper. A fuller text is to be expected as the ultimate source of the ass-driving scene, and it must have been the Septuagint. But again we can be even more precise and relate the Cosmas scenes to a specific Genesis cycle, namely the one found in the Byzantine Octateuchs. Not only do the details correspond closely enough, but by comparing the Cosmas and the Octateuchs we find that in the latter the corresponding scenes are fuller and that consequently the miniature of the Cosmas is an abbreviation. In the first scene of the Octateuch in the Seraglio (fig. 126) the two ass drivers are followed by Isaac and Abraham, who are

[29] Ongania, *op. cit.*, Album vol. II, pl. XVII.—Tikkanen, *op. cit.*, pl. XII, fig. 88.—Demus, *op. cit.*, fig. 29.

[30] Stornajolo, *Miniature della topografia cristiana*, pl. 22.

[31] Migne, *P.G.*, 88, col. 240.—transl. by J. W. McCrindle, *The Christian Topography of Cosmas*, London 1897, p. 177.

omitted in the Cosmas although they are required for the correct understanding of the story (Gen. XXII, 3). From the second scene (fig. 127) in which the two young men wait, while Abraham lays the wood for the burnt offering upon Isaac's shoulder (Gen. XXII, 5-6), only Isaac carrying the wood is taken over in the Cosmas, and only the Sacrifice as the most important scene (Gen. XXII, 12) is completely copied (fig. 128). As the result of this transformation from one text into another the Cosmas miniature is on the one hand too comprehensive to fit the Cosmas text, and on the other much condensed in comparison to the Octateuch cycle.

Among the several witnesses of the New Testament Cosmas devotes one paragraph to Paul, emphasizing him as the writer of the Epistles. Therefore the illustrator chose, as the center of the full-page miniature, an author portrait of Paul standing frontally and pointing to a codex in his arm (fig. 130),[32] a type most probably borrowed from the title picture in front of the Pauline Epistles. This figure of Paul is surrounded by three scenes in a smaller figure scale illustrating his Conversion, to which Cosmas alludes in the following words: ". . . since the choice of him at first was made by Jesus calling to him from heaven, and when he was instructed, he was not disobedient to the heavenly vision?"[33] The passage is clearly insufficient to justify the scenes, and once more a fuller text must be sought to explain the details of the picture. This text is of course the Acts of the Apostles, where it is explicitly narrated how Paul was struck by a light from heaven (IX, 3), how he fell down to earth (IX, 4), and how he was led away to Damascus (IX, 8). The Cosmas miniature, therefore, copied and combined three scenes from an illustrated copy of the Acts of the Apostles. But unlike the Octateuchs, to which the Abraham and Isaac scenes could be related, no fully illustrated Acts in Greek has been preserved from the Early or Middle Byzantine period.[34] Therefore this miniature and a second one with the Stoning of Stephen are extremely valuable as *disiecta membra* of a lost illustrated manuscript of the Acts with a more or less extensive narrative cycle.

This theory of the migration of miniatures from a basic Biblical text into the *Christian Topography* has far-reaching implications. Ainaloff, in his study *The Hellenistic Origins of Byzantine Art*,[35] made the Vatican Cosmas

---

[32] Stornajolo, *op. cit.*, pl. 48.

[33] Migne, *P.G.*, 88, col. 301.—McCrindle, *op. cit.*, p. 228.

[34] Only the third scene, i.e. the leading away to Damascus, occurs in a thirteenth century copy of the Acts in Chicago, the only New Testament manuscript with at least a fragmentary cycle of the Acts. H. R. Willoughby, *The Rockefeller McCormick New Testament*, vol. III, p. 254 and vol. I, fol. 115ʳ.

[35] Д. В. АЙНАЛОВЪ, "Эллинистическія Основы Византійскаго Искусства," Записки Императорскаго Русскаго Археологическаго Общества, new ser., vol. XI, pts. 3-4, S. Petersburg 1901, pp. 1ff.—Summary of this study by O. Wulff, *Repert. f. Kunstwissenschaft*, XXVI, 1903, pp. 35ff.

a chief witness for Alexandrian book illumination, since he took it for granted that the miniatures had all originated at the same time and in the same place where Cosmas wrote his *Topography*, i.e. Alexandria. If, however, all the Biblical pictures are taken over from an illustrated Octateuch, a New Testament and other Biblical Books, then they might very well be considerably older than the period in which the Cosmas text was composed. In this case a contemporary origin of text and miniatures can be assumed only for Cosmas' geometrical schemes of the universe, from which, however, little can be learned about Alexandrian art. Moreover, the transfer of the Biblical miniatures from a Bible into the Cosmas need not have taken place in Alexandria, but at any other locality and also at any time between the sixth and the ninth centuries, i.e. between the archetype of the Cosmas and the Vatican copy, where and whenever an art lover asked an illuminator to manufacture a particularly splendid copy. Secondly, even if the transformation took place in Alexandria, the Biblical models need not have been products of the Alexandrian school, though it is, of course, possible that one or the other of the models involved did go back to an Alexandrian archetype. Therefore the arguments in favor of or against an Alexandrian origin of most of the Cosmas miniatures cannot be based upon the history of the Cosmas text, but only upon the history of the Septuagint and the New Testament illustration.

From the preceding examples it appears that the average classical, Byzantine or Western illuminator up to the Romanesque period, was extremely conservative and tried to copy wherever he could find a model, avoiding as far as possible the invention of new iconographic subjects. On the other hand, we have deliberately chosen only examples in which a new text recension does not coincide with a new picture recension, but where the miniatures have an ancestry in earlier texts. There was always a chance to invent a new miniature cycle for new text recensions, but apparently advantage was seldom taken of it. The general tendency of the illuminator was to exploit other models and, unconcerned as he was about the charge of plagiarism, to content himself with few changes and to show his artistic skill within the limits of an established iconography.

3. *A Miniature Transplanted into a Heterogeneous Text*

So far it has been fairly easy to determine the basic text from which a miniature was taken over into a new recension. Pseudo-Apuleius and Mustio are translations and revisions of Dioscurides and Soranus of Ephesus; for the English bestiaries and the *Marvels of the East*, there were earlier animal treatises of the same kind; in the case of the Millstatt Genesis and the Cosmas Indicopleustes the nature of the text suggested immediately an illustrated Septuagint and New Testament as source. In these instances either whole cycles or at least larger sections of them were involved in the shift from one recension into another. There are, however, other texts which merely allude to a story or a single event which is outside the line of the main subject, such as a mythological allusion in a scientific text. When an illustrator picks up such an allusion and illustrates it by a mythological scene, the latter is iconographically unrelated to the rest of the scientific illustrations. The finding of the prototype of a miniature thus inserted is often complicated by the fact that the present text does not reveal the source which the painter may have used.

The Bibliothèque Nationale in Paris preserves a tenth century manuscript of the *Theriaca* of Nicander, cod. suppl. gr. 247, which in addition to the numerous pictures of snakes, scorpions and the plants which heal the bites of those animals contains also a few mythological scenes.[36] Verses 13-20[37] describe the scorpion as follows: "As to the scorpion which has a sting with which it paralyzes the body, it is the creation of the Titanide [=Artemis, the daughter of Coeus, the Titan], when she in her wrath desired the death of Orion of Boeotia, who had dared to put his hands upon the virginal peplos of the goddess. The deadly scorpion, hidden under a rock, stung the heel of the criminal, whose image in the position of a hunter was put among the stars and stays there forever visible." The accompanying miniature (fig. 131)[38] depicts a scorpion as one pictorial unit and—quite unrelated to it—Orion as another. One might have expected from the text a more narrative illustration depicting Orion being stung in the heel by the scorpion. However, as already observed by Lenormant and reiterated by Thiele,[39] the figure of Orion, with the lagobolon as the attribute of the hare hunter, is not made up from the text of Nicander, but corresponds to the constellation type of Orion to which the text refers and whose attitude is determined astrologically. The only Greek Aratus miniatures we possess today are in the Vatican codex gr. 1087, of the fifteenth century, and among them is a striding Orion in quite the same posture (fig. 132), though his weapon is a sword instead of the lagobolon. The illustrator of the Nicander must have copied the figure of Orion from an Aratus manuscript similar to the Vatican one but earlier, and hence the lack of formal relationship between Orion and the scorpion. The intrusion of this and other mythological scenes in the Nicander was not

[36] H. Omont, *Miniatures des plus anciens manuscrits grecs*, p. 34 and pls. LXV-LXXII.—Weitzmann, *Byzantinische Buchmalerei*, p. 33 (here fuller bibliography) and pl. XLI, no. 228.

[37] O. Schneider, *Nicandrea, Theriaca et Alexipharmaca*, Leipzig 1856, p. 219.

[38] Chanot et Lenormant, "Peintures d'un manuscrit de Nicandre," *Gaz. Arch.*, I, 1875, p. 125 and pl. 32, no. 3.—Omont, *op. cit.*, pl. LXV, no. 1.—Bethe, *Buch und Bild*, pp. 24, 70 and figs. 2 and 42.

[39] Thiele, *Himmelsbilder*, p. 120.

necessarily effected in the illustrated archetype of Nicander, but could have been at any time before the present copy in Paris. There are even indications that it did not happen too soon after the first illustration with purely scientific miniatures. When a certain Eutecnius, whose date is unknown, wrote a paraphrase of Nicander's *Theriaca*, the illustrator took over the miniatures of an illustrated Nicander, as can be seen in the two extant copies of this paraphrase, one in Vienna[40] and the other in the Morgan Library in New York,[41] each of them bound together with the Dioscurides herbal. But their decoration consists exclusively of snakes, scorpions and plants, and it at least seems likely that at the time the paraphrase was written and illustrated the Nicander, which was used as model, contained only those pictures which were scientifically indispensable and formed an integral part with the didactic poem probably from the very beginning when the first copy was dedicated to Attalos III (138-133 B.C.).

A similar intrusion of mythological scenes can be observed in the *Cynegetica* of Pseudo-Oppian, the source of which can be inferred only from a formal analysis of the pictures themselves. Where the text reads (I, 229-230): "Bucephalas, the horse of the warrior king of Macedon, fought against armed men,"[42] a miniature is added in which a horse inscribed "Bucephalas" constitutes an essential part of the composition (fig. 133). This miniature, in which the famous horse is brought by a groom before King Philip enthroned, does not correspond to the account in Pseudo-Oppian's poem, and there must have been another text from which the picture was derived. This text is undoubtedly the Alexander Romance, which goes under the name of Pseudo-Callisthenes. Here we read (I, 13): "And once the chiefs of the horse keepers from Cappadocia brought as a gift to Philip a horse, immensely large and secured by many bonds, and it was said of it, that it ate men."[43] This passage unquestionably fits the miniature better and is evidence that the Alexander Romance was illustrated at an early time and served as a model for the illustrator of the Pseudo-Oppian.

Moreover, the illustrator of the *Cynegetica* took over two more pictures from the same source and placed them without textual interruption on the verso of the same page (fig. 134), though the Pseudo-Oppian text has no more to say about the whole Bucephalas story than what is told in the two verses cited above. One of the two added miniatures depicts Bucephalas in a cage behind an iron grating. But the same paragraph of the Pseudo-Callisthenes, confirming this as indeed the basic text, continues: "Philip saw that he

[40] Cod. med. gr. 1, fols. 393-437ᵛ. Premerstein, Wessely and Mantuani, *op. cit.*
[41] Cod. M. 652, fols. 338ʳ-360ᵛ. Cf. facsimile, *op. cit.*
[42] Transl. by A. W. Mair, *Oppian* (Loeb Class. Libr.) p. 29.
[43] Ausfeld, *op. cit.*, p. 37.—Kroll, *op. cit.*, p. 14.

145

was beautiful and he said: '. . . since you have hurried to bring him, take him and enclose him unbridled behind an iron grating, so that we may throw to him those who under the law are caught for piracy or murder.' And quickly there was carried out what the king had said." Even such details as the ox head on the thigh of Bucephalas is thoroughly explained by the Pseudo-Callisthenes text (I, 15) : "The horse was called Bucephalas because it had upon its thigh as a brand the head of an ox." There seems to be no other reason for adding this scene than the desire for enrichment of the miniature cycle. The third miniature, depicting the pursuit of Darius by Alexander, can likewise be explained by the Alexander Romance in which the battle of Arbela is described in the following words (II, 16) : "The Macedonians were led forward by Alexander, who was riding upon his horse Bucephalas. And nobody could approach the horse because of its divine nature. . . . After many Persians had come to their deaths, Darius swung around the reins of his own chariot and the whole crowd of the Persians took to flight." The miniature agrees in its essential features with this description, though it appears to be an abbreviation of a once richer composition. These three miniatures of the Pseudo-Oppian provide the proof for the existence of an illustrated Pseudo-Callisthenes for the Middle Byzantine period, i.e. several centuries earlier than the actually preserved Alexander Romances with pictures known hitherto,[44] and the chances are that the first illustration was done as early as the late classical period, very shortly after the text itself was composed.

The search for more *disiecta membra* from picture cycles of classical texts must consult not only the profane, but also ecclesiastical literature, wherever it contains allusions to Greek mythology. One of the homilies of Gregory of Nazianzus, entitled *In Sancta Lumina* is rich in allusions to classical myths, which in several copies are accompanied by miniatures. One such passage reads: "Our interest is not in the births and thefts of Zeus, the tyrant of the Cretans, nor in the noises of the Curetes and their clanging and dancing with weapons, which drowned out the wailing of a weeping god so that he might escape his child-hating father. For it was disgraceful to make him weep as a child, who was to be swallowed as a stone."[45] An eleventh century manuscript in the Panteleimon monastery on Mount Athos, cod. 6, contains two miniatures for this passage (figs. 135-136) : the first depicts Rhea as she gives to Chronos a stone to swallow wrapped in swaddling clothes and the second represents the Curetes making a noise around the cradle in which the Zeus child lies.[46] It should be noticed that Rhea does not figure at all in the passage quoted above. This means that the painter had a more precise

[44] Cf. the manuscripts quoted on p. 138, note 17.   [45] Migne, *P. G.*, 36, col. 337.

[46] Brockhaus, *Die Kunst in den Athosklöstern*, p. 194.—E. Panofsky, *Studies in Iconology*, New York 1939, p. 76 and pl. XXIV, no. 42.

knowledge of the details than the Gregory text could have provided, and we must again seek a more fitting text. There exists a commentary by Pseudo-Nonnus, which explains, in a series of paragraphs, the various mythological subjects mentioned in four of Gregory's homilies and which is generally assumed to have been written in the sixth century.[47] Here we read about the birth of Zeus: "Chronos, who was wedded to Rhea, used to take all the children, to whom she gave birth, and eat them. And since this happened over a long time, Rhea remained without children. When Rhea gave birth to Zeus she was afraid that this newborn babe might also perish the same way. Therefore she gave to Chronos a stone wrapped in swaddling clothes to swallow as if it were the newborn babe. But Zeus she carried to Crete and she placed the Curetes and Corybantes round the babe so that they might dance and rattle and make their weapons resound and thus produce the greatest possible noise in order to conceal and drown the crying of the child so that Chronos might not learn the hiding place of the infant and take and swallow it."[48] Fortunately there is an illustrated copy of the Pseudo-Nonnus commentary preserved in the Patriarchal Library in Jerusalem, cod. Τάφου 14, from the eleventh century,[49] which has, attached to this very passage, a composition nearly identical with that of the Panteleimon manuscript. This leaves no doubt that an illustrated Pseudo-Nonnus was the immediate source for the Gregory painter, although it does not necessarily mean that for this composition Pseudo-Nonnus is the basic text. Just as the Pseudo-Nonnus text derived its information from mythological handbooks of the Roman period, so the miniatures too may go back ultimately to a classical text.[50]

As the mythological miniatures in scientific and patristic texts, so Old and New Testament scenes can be found scattered in other texts whose title or general content would not immediately suggest their inclusion. Wherever a text, either ecclesiastical or profane, contained an allusion to an Old or New Testament scene, there was always the possibility that a miniaturist consulted an illustrated Septuagint or Gospels and copied the miniature he needed. In a homily about the Virgin by the monk Jacobus Kokkinobaphus there are interspersed among the scenes from the life of the Virgin also a

[47] A. Westermann, Μυθόγραφοι, Brunswick 1843, pp. 359ff.—Migne, P.G., 36, cols. 985ff.— E. Patzig, De Nonnianis in IV orationes Gregorii Nazianzeni commentariis (Jahresbericht der Thomasschule in Leipzig), Leipzig 1890.—Thad. Sinko, "De expositione Pseudo-Nonniana historiarum," Charisteria Casimiro de Morawski, Cracow 1922, pp. 124ff.

[48] Migne, P.G., 36, col. 1065.

[49] Papadopoulos-Kerameus, Ἱεροσολυμιτικὴ Βιβλιοθήκη, vol. I, S. Petersburg 1891, p. 45.— Ch. Diehl, Manuel d'art byzantin, vol. II, Paris 1926, p. 626 and figs. 300-303.—W. H. P. Hatch, Greek and Syrian Miniatures in Jerusalem, Cambridge, Mass. 1931, p. 58 and pls. I-XVIII.

[50] A more detailed analysis of the Pseudo-Nonnus miniatures in the Jerusalem manuscript will be given in a forthcoming study "Illustrated Greek Mythographers."

few miniatures from various books of the Old Testament, from Genesis, Judges and Prophets, the presence of which, in view of the general content of the homily, seems unexpected. In the chapter on the Annunciation to the Virgin, Jacobus speaks about angels and seraphim, and this brings to his mind the Vision of Isaiah, of which he quotes verses 6 and 7 of Chapter VI: "Then flew one of the seraphim unto me, having a live coal in his hand, which he had taken with the tongs from off the altar: And he laid it upon my mouth, and said, Lo this hath touched thy lips; and thine iniquity is taken away, and thy sin purged."[51] The two extant manuscripts of the homily, the one in the Vatican, cod. gr. 1162,[52] and the other in the Bibliothèque Nationale in Paris, cod. gr. 1208 (fig. 138),[53] both from about the beginning of the twelfth century, contain nearly identical illustrations for this passage, consisting of two successive scenes, one representing the Vision proper with the prophet gazing at the Lord, who is surrounded by angels and seraphim, and the other depicting the prophet as he receives the coal from a seraph. Only for the latter scene does the quotation in the homily text provide a sufficient basis: for the former the full biblical text is needed—proof that an illustrated Prophet book was used by the painter of the homily. As previously mentioned no Greek Prophet book with a narrative cycle of miniatures has come down to us, save for a number of illustrated passages incorporated in the *Sacra Parallela* of John of Damascus, Paris, cod. gr. 923, which fortunately contains at least the passage Isaiah VI, 1-3 and alongside it on the margin (fol. 39ᵛ) Isaiah's Vision with Christ enthroned, though here the composition is reduced to but two seraphim because of lack of space. This proves sufficiently the existence of an illustrated Prophet book whose narrative cycle included the Vision.

Another recension into which pictures from the major Prophets migrated is the Psalter with the Odes. The same manuscript in Vatopedi, cod. 760, whose picture of the Deuteronomy Ode (fig. 113) could be traced back to the Octateuchs (fig. 112), contains as the title picture of the Ode of Isaiah the same two scenes which were taken over in the homily of Jacobus Kokkinobaphus, i.e. the Vision and the Receiving of the Coal (fig. 139). The position of this miniature in front of the Ode is all the more surprising, since the text of the Ode is taken from the twenty-sixth chapter of Isaiah, where nothing is said about the vision at all, while the picture refers to the sixth chapter. Apparently the painter had an illustrated Prophet book before him,

[51] Migne, *P.G.*, 127, col. 641.

[52] C. Stornajolo, *Miniature delle omilie di Giacomo Monaco* (Codices e Vaticanis selecti, series minor, vol. 1), Rome 1910, pl. 52 (fol. 119ᵛ).

[53] H. Omont, "Miniatures des homélies sur la Vierge du moine Jacques," *Bull. de la soc. franç. de reprod. de mss. à peint.*, XI, 1927, pl. XXI (fol. 162ʳ).

out of which he chose what he must have considered the most prominent and characteristic scenes of the whole book, and he abbreviated them considerably: the Isaiah of the Vision is conflated with that of the scene of the coal, and the illustrator apparently made the mistake of letting an angel instead of a seraph give the coal to the prophet.

Miniatures may migrate not only once but twice, and then we can speak of a *double migration*. This process can be demonstrated by a miniature of the well-known Gregory manuscript in Paris, Bibl. Nat., cod. gr. 510, written between 880 and 886 for Basil I (fig. 137),[54] which is divided into the following four scenes: (1) Habakkuk, who is carried through the air and brings food to Daniel in the lion's den; (2) the three Hebrews in the fiery furnace; (3) the prayer of Manasseh; and (4) Isaiah prophesying to Hezekiah, the sick king. This miniature precedes the letter to the monk Euagrius,[55] the authorship of which is still a matter of dispute, being attributed by some to Gregory of Nazianzus, by others to Gregory of Nyssa or Gregory Thaumaturgos.[56] The letter, about the Divinity, contains nothing that would explain or even give a hint about any of the four scenes. The miniature must, then, have been intended originally for another place in the Gregory—where, it is not easy to determine for not one homily among the forty-five combines references to all four scenes.[57] Whatever their original position in the Gregory text, as the four scenes stand now on one page they appear to be a set of miniatures all of which go back to one and the same source. This source is undoubtedly a Psalter of the so-called aristocratic recension in which each one of the four scenes was attached to an Ode. A Psalter in the Athos monastery Pantokratoros, cod. 49, from the eleventh century, which is closely related to the Psalter in Paris, gr. 139, depicts in a similar fashion the angel flying with Habakkuk through the air and bringing food to a praying person below, who should be Daniel, but by some mistake, to be explained later, is again Habakkuk (fig. 157). The same Pantokratoros Psalter contains, on a leaf which is now in the Benaki Museum at Athens,[58] an analogous composition of the three Hebrews in the fiery furnace, embraced by the angel above their heads. The praying Manasseh behind a brazen bull occurs similarly in

[54] H. Omont, *Miniatures des plus anciens manuscrits grecs*, pl. LVII (fol. 435^v).

[55] Migne, *P.G.*, 46, cols. 1101-1108.

[56] O. Bardenhewer, *Geschichte der altkirchlichen Literatur*, vol. III, 2nd ed., Freiburg 1923, p. 184.

[57] At least the first two, i.e. Daniel in the lion's den and the three Hebrews, occur jointly in one and the same paragraph of the homily *In laudem Basilii Magni* which reads: "I pass by the rest, the three young men bedewed in the fire . . . the just man in the den restraining the lion's rage" (Migne, *P.G.*, 36, col. 596), while the prayer of Manasseh is mentioned in the 19th homily *Ad Julianum tributorum exaequatorem* (Migne, *P.G.*, 35, col. 1052) and the Hezekiah story in the 18th homily *Funebris in patrem* (Migne, *P.G.*, 35, col. 1021).

[58] Dalton, *Byzantine Art and Archaeology*, fig. 278.

149

a Psalter in the National Library in Athens, cod. 7, from the twelfth century,[59] and finally the best known parallel to the Isaiah addressing Hezekiah is in the Paris Psalter, gr. 139.[60]

Yet we have not found the basic text in which the pictures originated, since the text of the Odes also fails to provide a sufficient basis for them. The Ode of Habakkuk (Hab. III, 2-19) deals with the prophecy of the Lord, which causes the prophet to tremble. The miniature with Habakkuk bringing food to Daniel finds no explanation in this passage, but is based upon the apocryphal book of Bel and the Dragon, which in the Septuagint is the fourteenth chapter of the Book of Daniel (v. 32-38). The text of the Ode of the three Hebrews is from the third chapter of the Book of Daniel (v. 2-19) and consequently we assume that its picture was taken over from the same source as the preceding one. The existence of an illustrated Book of Daniel can again be proved by the *Sacra Parallela*, in which the scene of the three Hebrews in the furnace (fol. 373ᵛ) occurs alongside the passage Daniel III, 16-17, being only one of several scenes from various chapters of the same Prophet book. We search in vain in the prayer of Manasseh for an explanation of the brazen bull in front of the adoring king and we suspect once more that the picture was not invented for this text. The prayer of Manasseh is mentioned, though not given in extenso, in the thirty-third chapter of the Second Book of Chronicles (v. 11-13, 18-19), and from the same chapter we learn that the king, before he repented, was well known as an idolator, who had "set up groves and graven images." The miniaturist may have chosen a brazen bull for a "graven image" in adaptation of the idol of the golden calf, which had caused the wrath of Moses. Thus it seems quite likely that the Manasseh miniature means to visualize the king's former idolatry and that as such it was invented for the Second Book of Chronicles. It may be remembered that the existence of an illustrated Books of Chronicles could likewise be proved out of the *Sacra Parallela* in Paris (cf. fig. 114), though among its sporadic scenes Manasseh's idolatry is not included. Concerning the Hezekiah picture the text of this Ode occurs twice in the Septuagint, once in the book of the prophet Isaiah (XXXVIII, 10-20) and a second time in the Fourth Book of Kings (XX, 1ff.). Probably both books were illustrated so that we cannot be sure about the immediate source for the painter of the Ode. We know only that in most cases he did make

[59] P. Buberl, *Die Miniaturenhandschriften der Nationalbibliothek in Athen* (Denkschriften der Wiener Akademie, Phil.-hist. Kl., vol. 60, Abh. 2), Vienna 1917, p. 15 and pl. XIX, fig. 48. Here wrongly described as Hezekiah.

[60] Omont, *op. cit.*, pl. XIV. In this manuscript the title pictures to the Odes of Habakkuk, the three Hebrews and Manassah are now lost, but they must have been similar to those of the Gregory manuscript.

use of an illustrated Prophet book, while on the other hand the same composition is found in the *Sacra Parallela* alongside the passage from the Book of Kings.[61]

Thus the *double migration* of the four Gregory pictures can fully be reconstructed: having originated in the Prophets, the Chronicles and perhaps the Book of Kings, they were gathered together by a painter of a Psalter as title miniatures of the Odes and from this source the illustrator of the Gregory collected the four and united them on a single page. During all these changes no copyist felt compelled to remodel the scenes or to make them more consistent with a new text, but each carried the pictures over from one text into another so faithfully that the original text connection can still be determined, even after the double shift.

4. *A Miniature without Textual Basis*

After a miniature has once or perhaps more than once changed its textual affiliation it is sometimes impossible to find the basic text, which may be lost. The picture may then become a valuable document for reconstructing a literary story. The Iliac tablet in the Museo Capitolino has two friezes at the bottom of the central part, one with scenes from the *Aethiopis* of Arctinus and the other from the *Little Iliad* of Lesches of Mitylene with episodes which are not told in the *Chrestomathy* of Proclus or anywhere else, and thus are a valuable documentary source for the reconstruction of the lost poems.[62]

However, the question must be raised whether, for each unidentified miniature, the existence of a basic text must necessarily be assumed or whether miniatures exist which never had any basic text. In other words: is it possible that certain conditions prevailed under which an illustrator might invent new narrative miniatures whose literary content he made up himself without relying on the written word? In most cases where one might be tempted to assume the creation of a new scene by an illustrator, we are actually dealing with a migrated picture. Nevertheless, there are definite indications that occasionally miniatures did originate from the desire of an artist to tell his own story or episode by pictorial means. For want of classical material our arguments must be based on Biblical manuscripts only.

Most Psalters of the so-called aristocratic recension have at the very beginning a series of full-page miniatures from the life of David, most of which, like the fight of Goliath or other events of David's youth, were copied from an illustrated Book of Kings where the scenes had originated. Once

---

[61] Weitzmann, *Byzantinische Buchmalerei*, pl. LXXXVI, no. 543.
[62] Jahn, *Griechische Bilderchroniken*, pp. 27ff., 30ff.

this set of miniatures had lost its connection with the basic text and formed a new pictorial cycle in front of the Psalter independent of any text, painters began to add new scenes whose content they made up themselves. The first miniature of the Psalter in the Athos monastery Pantokrators cod. 49 starts the life of David with a representation of his Birth (fig. 140), preceding his Anointing. The sixteenth chapter of the First Book of Kings, which tells the story of David's youth, introduces David for the first time as keeper of the sheep and nothing is said about his earlier childhood, and consequently the Psalter picture could not have been copied from an illustrated Book of Kings. It was apparently the painter's wish to depict a full biographical account of the life of his hero and for this purpose he invented a scene of David's birth. The compositional scheme for such a scene he did not need to invent, but could adapt it from birth scenes in Gospel books or lectionaries or elsewhere and this he obviously did. Because no father is present and there is only one midwife bathing the newborn child, the model seems to have been, not the Birth of Christ, but more likely that of the Virgin.

In another Psalter, cod. Vat. gr. 752, written around 1059,[63] the Birth of David is followed by a scene inscribed ἡ ἀν[ατ]ροφὴ τοῦ δα(υί)δ, i.e. the Education of David. It represents the proud mother in a seated position, holding the child in her lap, while a female attendant stretches her hands out toward the child. This scene likewise is not based upon the Book of Kings nor, as far as we can see, on any other text, and therefore we are inclined to consider also this composition an invention of the miniaturist. Both scenes of this Vatican Psalter are very badly flaked, but they occur similarly, not only more recognizable, but, especially in the second scene, more complete on a tenth century Byzantine ivory casket in the Palazzo di Venezia in Rome (fig. 141),[64] whose friezes with scenes of the life of David are obviously derived from a manuscript of the same recension. Therefore, as far as the iconography is concerned, they can be treated as equivalents of the damaged miniatures, taking into consideration the fact that the height of the scenes was reduced to fit the shape of the casket. In the Birth of David only David's mother lying on a couch and one midwife washing the babe are represented, while the Education of David includes also Jesse who is about to take his son in his arms, a figure lacking in the Vatican miniature. A very similar composition occurs in the picture cycle which is based on an apocryphal Gospel and illustrates the youth of the Virgin. In a mosaic of the Kahrieh Djami in Constantinople, which is inscribed ἡ κολακεία τῆς θεοτόκου,[65] Joachim and

[63] E. DeWald, *Vaticanus graecus 752*, pl. I.

[64] Ad. Goldschmidt and K. Weitzmann, *Die Byzantinischen Elfenbeinskulpturen*, vol. 1, Berlin 1930, p. 64 and pl. LXXI, no. 123b.

[65] Θ. И. ШМИТЪ, Кахріэ-Джами, Sofia 1906, p. 147 and pl. XXIV.

Anna sit together on a bench and caress the Virgin in her mother's lap. An earlier copy of this scene may very well have provided the compositional scheme for the David scene, just as his Birth seems to be influenced by a scene of the Birth of the Virgin.

The desire of a miniaturist to arrange full-page miniatures as antithetic couples seems to have been one of the most frequent causes for the creation of new scenes. The eleventh century lectionary in the Athos monastery Panteleimon cod. 2,[66] for instance, has at the beginning of each of the major feasts two full-page miniatures, one containing the feast proper and another representing a scene preliminary to the feast. In most cases both scenes were copied from a Gospel book as e.g. the Metamorphosis (Luke IX, 29-36) which is preceded by a scene with Christ, Peter, John and James going up into the mountain (Luke IX, 28), or the Birth of John the Baptist (Luke I, 57-58) which has in front of it the Annunciation to Zacharias (Luke I, 5-20). However, a representation preceding the feast proper was not always available in the Gospel cycle, and then the painter had to invent a counterpart, if he wanted to preserve the formal principle of antithetic pairs. This seems to have been the case with the Presentation in the Temple (Luke II, 22-40), where the feast proper is depicted in the conventional compositional scheme (fig. 143), while in the preceding miniature Simeon stands in front of the Virgin and stretches his arms out toward the Christ child sitting in the Virgin's lap (fig. 142). This latter composition has no basis in the Gospel text and does not exist in any of the extensive miniature cycles like those of Paris, cod. gr. 74, or Florence, cod. Plut. VI, 23. The gesture of Simeon can hardly mean the taking of the child into his arms (Luke II, 28), first because this motif is the main theme of the Presentation proper and most likely was not duplicated, and secondly because his hands are not covered. It was, perhaps, the intention of the painter to allude in this picture to the revelation to Simeon that he would see Christ before his death (Luke II, 25-26).

We wish to reiterate that invented scenes of this sort presumably were extremely rare in ancient and mediaeval book illumination, and great caution should be observed before the claim is made that no basic text ever existed for a problematical miniature.

[66] H. Brockhaus, *Die Kunst in den Athosklöstern*, 1891, pp. 190, 227.—Н. ПОКРОВСКІЙ, Евангеліе въ Памятникахъ Иконографіи, S. Petersburg 1892, figs. 2, 3, 24, 46, 81, 93.— Д. АЙНАЛОВЪ, "Византійскіе Памятники Аөона," Византійскій Временикъ, VI, 1899, p. 63 and pl. IX.— Н. В. ПОКРОВСКІЙ, Очерки Памятниковъ Христіанскаго Искусства и Иконографіи, S. Petersburg 1910, p. 145 and figs. 92, 93, 94.—G. Millet, *Recherches*, v. index p. 736, and figs. 81, 132.

B. THE VARIOUS KINDS OF DEPENDENCE OF A MINIATURE
UPON ITS BASIC TEXT

If two miniatures illustrating the same text passage and also belonging to the same pictorial recension show some variations, there is always the question as to which of the two represents the more original and which the more altered version. Usually the more intelligible version is the one closer to the archetype, assuming a priori that the artist who invents a miniature for a certain passage is more faithful to the content of the text than an average copyist who in most cases copies a miniature without re-examining the text with regard to the iconographic accuracy of the picture. The negligent attitude of the copyist thus quite often gives rise to errors. The situation is much like that in textual criticism where of two different readings of a passage the more coherent one can normally be assumed to be closer to the archetype. At the same time, in both texts and pictures there are instances where a later writer or painter successfully improved the archetype, so that occasionally an altered version may be more intelligible than the original one. In miniature painting such cases are even less rare than in the textual field, but as a general rule the picture which corresponds best to the basic text is the closest to the archetype.

Furthermore the miniature which, among the extant copies, can be considered the most faithful to the archetype is not necessarily the earliest one. A later miniature, which may be separated from the archetype by fewer intermediary copies, may very well be more exact in iconography than an earlier one where more repeated copying may have changed considerably the original composition. Neither style nor quality have a direct bearing on the iconographic relation between miniatures, and by no means is a greater artist more faithful to the archetype than a copyist of average capability. On the contrary, the former, though making perhaps fewer gross errors, may be more inclined deliberately to change his model either through formal considerations or through a more independent interpretation of the literary content.

1. *The Use of Conventions in the Creation of the Archetype*

Where only a single copy is preserved of a certain text, textual criticism is left without criteria for the reconstruction of the archetype, since the latter is determined chiefly through the comparison of copy with copy. In picture criticism, too, a single preserved copy, which may have undergone considerable iconographic changes, permits little beyond mere speculation as to what was the original composition of the archetype. The gesture of a figure or the action of a whole composition may not entirely agree with the text, but a pictorial version which would correspond in all particulars cannot be reconstructed on the basis of the text alone. The artist inventing a miniature cycle did not always carry out the requirements for a theoretically perfect illustration of a passage; in every period he made use of certain conventions, i.e. pictorial formulae adaptable to similar situations in different texts. Such conventions, either figures or groups of figures, might or might not coincide in every detail with a specific narrative, and, depending on the intelligence of the artist, they might or might not be modified to suit the particular situation, so that some incongruities between picture and text appear even in the archetype itself.

A few examples of such *conventions* will be discussed here. In the Vatican Virgil, cod. lat. 3225, there is a miniature (fig. 144)[1] in which Neptune and Venus face each other in a dispute (Aeneid v, 779ff.). Venus stretches her right hand out toward Neptune in a gesture of speech which conforms very well to the situation suggested by Virgil. Not so Neptune! He rests his left foot on an elevation of ground and leans with his right arm leisurely on his trident, relaxed and unconcerned with the person addressing him, in an attitude not motivated by the text. This slight incongruity between picture and text is easily explained by the assumption that the figure of the sea-god was conceived originally for another context and adapted by the miniaturist as a convention for Neptune. Its ultimate source is obviously the famous statue whose original presumably stood in the open air at the Isthmus of Corinth, the likeness of which is best preserved in the life-size statue in the Lateran Museum (fig. 145) and on coins of Demetrius Poliorcetes.[2] This statuary type was apparently well known in classical antiquity and the miniaturist must have felt that its adaptation lent greater distinction to the god of the seas than a rather indifferent pose with a gesture of speech would have done, even though less accurate in representing the situation described in the Aeneid.

Another kind of convention grew out of the painter's realization that certain features of a text could not be visualized pictorially, so that some modification of the literary content became necessary. For instance, in the Iliac tablet which was formerly in the Rondanini Collection (fig. 8) Odysseus' companions are depicted as hybrids with human bodies and animal heads, while Homer's text leaves no doubt that Circe's victims were completely

---

[1] *Fragmenta et Picturae Vergiliana Codicis Vaticani Latini 3225* (Codices e Vaticanis selecti, vol. 1, 2nd ed.) (facsimile), Rome 1930, fol. 44ᵛ.—P. de Nolhac, "Le Virgile du Vatican et ses peintures," *Notices et extraits des manuscrits de la Bibliothèque Nationale*, xxxv, pt. 2, 1896, p. 762.

[2] Brunn-Bruckmann, *Denkmäler griechischer und römischer Skulptur*, pl. 243.—Bulle, in Roscher, *Mythol. Lexikon*, s.v. Poseidon, col. 2889.—Helbig, *Führer durch die Öffentl. Samml. Klassischer Altertümer in Rom*, vol. ii, 3rd ed., Leipzig 1913, p. 25 and fig. 32.

transformed into animals. In the case of Odysseus' companions they were swine, but on other occasions Circe transformed human beings into various kinds of animals,[3] which accounts for the fact that in the Rondanini relief various animal heads were used instead of those of swine only. It is obvious that a too literal illustration of the text, which would have meant a rendering of complete animals, was not satisfactory to the representational artist, who wanted to express that the human being was still preserved under the shape of an animal. By using the semi-anthropomorphic shape as an artistic convention, the artist was, perhaps, less accurate as to the letter of the poem, but in a wider sense he interpreted very well its meaning with pictorial means of his own. This artistic convention for the victims of Circe was by no means the invention of the miniaturist who created the model of the Rondanini plaque, but had been the universally accepted form from the time of its first appearance on black-figured vases. Consequently we can be quite sure that no earlier stage of Homer illustration before the time of the Rondanini tablet represented the companions more realistically as complete animals in accordance with the text.

Christian book illuminators, who particularly in the early period aimed at as close a correspondence as possible between picture and text, likewise made wide use of conventions of various kinds similar in principle to those of their pagan ancestors. Whenever a ruler or high dignitary was to be represented, the usual formula employed was that of a Byzantine emperor enthroned with a bodyguard standing on either side, a formula for the visualization of the highest power of the state; thus Joseph in Egypt, or Pharaoh himself,[4] King Saul, King David,[5] or King Solomon[6] all look alike, because the same convention was used for each of them. In the Vatican Octateuch, cod. gr. 746 (fig. 147), for instance, a group of Egyptians is asking for bread (Gen. XLVII, 15-16) in front of Joseph, who is clad in the imperial chlamys, crowned with the pearled diadem of the Byzantine emperors and flanked by two members of the bodyguard. The illustrator of the Bible may have seen this group in an historical chronicle where it occurred repeatedly in court scenes of all kinds. Or, to cite another example, the illustrator of the same Octateuch (fig. 146) used for Noah speaking to his sons and cursing Canaan (Gen. IX, 25) the formula of an ancient philosopher who teaches his pupils

---

[3] F. Müller, *Odyssee-Illustrationen*, p. 51.

[4] Cf. the Octateuch in Smyrna, Hesseling, *L'octateuque de Smyrne*, pls. 45, no. 136; 46, no. 141; 47, no. 142 and elsewhere.

[5] Cf. the Book of Kings, cod. Vat. gr. 333, fol. 24ᵛ: David and Jonathan before Saul (I Reg. XVIII, 13); fol. 50ʳ: Messenger reports to David Uriah's death (II Reg. XI, 22-25). Photos in Princeton, Department of Art and Archaeology.

[6] Paris gr. 510, fol. 215ᵛ. The Judgment of Solomon (Omont, *Miniatures des plus anciens manuscrits grecs*, pl. XXXIX).

and holds a scroll in his left hand, an attribute which is not explained by the Genesis text. This conventional philosopher type was introduced with the apparent intention to evoke in the mind of the beholder the association with a familiar type of teacher.

2. *The Influence of Fashion on the Process of Copying*

Once a pictorial archetype is established, a process of copying begins in which each copy differs from the other to a greater or lesser degree, no matter how accurately a copyist tries to imitate his model. This is caused primarily by the stylistic influences of the period in which the copyist works. The folds of drapery, the distribution of highlights upon them, the treatment of the flesh color and similar features change inevitably with each individual copy. At the same time there are conservative elements—and this applies to other media of the representational arts as well—which remain comparatively unaltered, elements which identify the miniature as belonging to a certain recension. In the case of the human figure the comparatively stable features are the movements and gestures expressing a certain action, and these may become so fixed that the recension to which a figure belongs can be determined by the characteristics of its outline. Furthermore the relationship between the participants of a narrative scene is to some extent fixed and often is a decisive factor for the picture's attribution to a particular recension.

Copies of miniatures in which composition and figure types remained unaltered while only the style changed, may be considered the most normal ones, though they are not as frequent as one might expect. Often the alterations which take place in the process of copying cut deeper into the substance of a composition. A feature which nearly always infiltrates even the most normal copy, if the process of copying extends over a considerable length of time, is *fashion*. In itself a product of the style of a certain period, fashion becomes crystallized into certain forms and patterns, which in themselves can be treated as iconographic features such as certain types of garments or shapes of headdresses or crowns.

Among the constellation pictures in the Aratea, because of their frequent copying from the Hellenistic period to the Middle Ages, are striking examples of alterations due to fashion. The Carolingian Aratus in Leyden depicts Cassiopeia with her arms stretched out as a woman enthroned (fig. 148), whose drapery, consisting of a chiton fastened over one shoulder and leaving one breast free and a himation taken around the hips and legs, clearly reflects a Hellenistic model. In a tenth century copy in St. Gall, cod. 250, Cassiopeia sits in a similar pose though more frontal (fig. 151), but her dress is changed into a long-sleeved tunic and an upper garment with half-length sleeves which falls down to the feet and is richly embroidered around the neck and down the front. The headdress, which in the preceding instance resembles a conical tiara, has turned into a crown with connecting bows. All the attires in the miniature of St. Gall are typical for the period of the copy and, as a comparison with the earlier Leyden copy will confirm, were not invented for this constellation type, but must be understood as *replacements* of more Hellenistic ones, of which not even a trace remained visible in the later copy.

In other instances a garment may not be a replacement for an older one, but an *addition* to a body which in the model was nude. A Greek Ptolemy manuscript in the Vatican Library, cod. gr. 1291, written between the years 813 and 820 and with miniatures close to a Hellenistic source,[7] represents a nude type of Aquarius who turns his head around, holds the vase with streaming water in his arms which are stretched forward, and wears only a chlamys fluttering from his back (fig. 149). The same type of Aquarius occurs in an Anglo-Saxon Aratus in Durham, cod. Hunter 100, but here he is depicted as a youth with shoes, dressed in trousers and in a tunic with long sleeves and wearing an embroidered chlamys (fig. 152),[8] whereby the Anglo-Saxon miniaturist paid tribute to the fashion of his period.

These two examples make it sufficiently clear that fashion is an element which can be imposed upon a fixed type at any period as an attire and can be replaced from time to time in order to modernize a picture without interfering with the composition as a whole or the attitude and gesture of an individual figure in particular. It thus follows that fashion cannot be used to determine the period of a pictorial archetype. In cases where a miniaturist does not change the fashion of his model so that it may appear antiquated in his copy, light may be thrown upon the date of the immediate model, but not necessarily upon the archetype. If one were to try to date the archetype of the Aratus illustration exclusively on the basis of the costumes in the St. Gall and Durham manuscripts, one could not go far behind the period of the present copies.

The same would be true for the mediaeval copies of comedies of Terence. In the Carolingian copy in Paris, cod. lat. 7899, there is at the beginning of the third act of the *Eunuchus* (fig. 150)[9] a representation in which Gnatho, a parasite, flatters the boasting captain Thraso, while Parmeno, the slave,

---

[7] F. Boll, *Beiträge zur Überlieferungsgeschichte der griechischen Astrologie und Astronomie* (Sitzungsber. Bayr. Akad. Phil.-hist. Kl.), Munich 1899, I, pp. 110ff.—Weitzmann, *Byzantinische Buchmalerei*, p. 1 and pl. I, no. 4.—Bethe, *Buch und Bild*, p. 54 and fig. 33.

[8] The photo here reproduced is from the bequest of A. G. Cotton.

[9] Jones and Morey, *Miniatures of the Manuscripts of Terence*, pp. 42ff. and fig. 198.

overhears their conversation. Thraso wears a tunic which is adorned, over the knees, with patches, the so-called *segmenta*, and a military headgear of cylindrical shape. Jones and Morey in their publication of the Terence manuscripts have pointed out that these two details of the costume occur most frequently in the fourth and fifth centuries A.D. and used them as evidence for the dating of the archetype of the Terence illustration in the same period. In view of the now apparent ease with which details of costumes are interchanged, it may be asked whether the segmenta must necessarily have belonged to the archetype or whether they could have been added to an originally undecorated tunic, or whether the cylindrical cap could be a replacement for a Roman helmet. In this case the characteristics in the Paris miniature would only point to an intermediary stage in the development which apparently coincides with the period when Calliopius in the fifth century made a new recension of the text of Terence, while the archetype of the miniatures might very well be older and hark back to the late classical or perhaps even pre-Christian period.[10] Within the later Terence manuscripts ample proof for the change of fashion can be found. The corresponding scene from the *Eunuchus* in the twelfth century copy in Oxford, Bodl. Lib., cod. Auct. F. II. 13 (fig. 153),[11] has preserved the compositional scheme and also the movements and gestures of each single actor, i.e. all those elements which help to determine the redactional affiliation, but now Thraso wears a mediaeval crown with prongs, and his tunic, having lost its patches and clavi, is prolonged down to the feet and adorned with an ornamental border. Moreover the mantle, which in the model is thrown over the left shoulder, is changed into a chlamys held over the right shoulder, and the same form of chlamys is also used for Gnatho, who wore a himation in the Paris miniature. Naturally, with the evidence of earlier manuscripts, nobody would date the archetype of the Oxford miniature on the basis of the costumes, because it would not lead far back beyond the present copy. Similarly one must reckon with the possibility that also a fifth century painter might have taken the liberty to make replacements in the costume, so clearly fashion alone cannot be used as the *terminus post quem* of the pictorial archetype.

The relationship between the miniature and its basic text is not affected by the change in fashion as long as only the mere decorative aspect of a costume is involved, but a discrepancy is created when a new feature of the costume alters the rank of a person. In the example from the Terence in Oxford we observed that Thraso wears a crown, whereas the text of the drama makes it plain that he is just an officer in the army, but not of royal

[10] Leo and Robert placed the archetype in the first century B.C., Bethe in the second century A.D. Cf. Robert, *Masken der neueren attischen Komödie*, pp. 103ff.

[11] Jones and Morey, *op. cit.*, fig. 200.

rank. Thus the change of the headdress must be regarded not only as an item concerning a change in fashion, but at the same time as an *error* offending against the meaning of the text.

3. *Misunderstandings*

Errors and misunderstandings are inevitable in the process of copying, and once an error has crept into a miniature, it is likely to be repeated in each following copy and only in rare cases is it later corrected again and the original better version restored. Misunderstandings and errors are the most helpful means in establishing groups within a certain recension, and in this respect picture criticism resembles most closely textual criticism where corrupt readings are most valuable for the grouping of manuscripts in families. In some cases the mistake might have been prevented if the illustrator had taken the trouble to read the passage with which the miniature is connected. However, we have good reason to assume that quite often the painter confined himself strictly to the pictorial task of repeating a miniature after the model without consulting the text anew, particularly in cases where scribe and painter were two different persons and the latter was concerned only with the filling of the spaces which the scribe had provided for him. The possibilities for errors increased greatly when a miniature was no longer connected with the basic text, but had migrated into another context. If in such a case the painter was not well acquainted with the textual sources of his pictures, he could not easily control the accuracy of his copy.

The various errors and misunderstandings may once more be illustrated by miniatures from Aratus manuscripts. The constellation picture of Andromeda (fig. 154) of the same Anglo-Saxon manuscript at Durham from which the Aquarius was chosen (fig. 152), is represented by a figure which is completely nude in contrast to the Andromeda in the Carolingian Aratus in Leyden[12] where, following the classical tradition, she wears a mantle thrown around hips and legs. In the Anglo-Saxon drawing the body is indistinct and resembles a male rather than a female person, and particularly the short hair suggests that the copyist may have misunderstood the sex. Moreover in the Leyden manuscript, and for that matter in all better copies, Andromeda's hands are fastened to a rock on either side, while in the Durham drawing rocks and bonds are omitted. All these errors reveal clearly that the painter had no knowledge of the mythological meaning of the constellation figure. If the picture had been in connection with Aratus' text of the *Phaenomena* (v. 197ff.), the painter could have read about the bonds which bind Andromeda even in heaven as a constellation, and thus might

[12] Thiele, *Himmelsbilder*, p. 106 and fig. 31.

160

have avoided one or the other of the errors. But the short text about the order and position of the stars, which now accompanies the picture, has dropped
any mention of the myth and so the painter was actually left without control
over the accuracy of his illustration.

A peculiar kind of error can result from the working process by which a
scribe first writes the whole text and leaves space for the pictures to be executed later. Under such circumstances it happens occasionally that the
painter places a wrong picture in the reserved space. An Aratus manuscript
in the Bibliothèque Municipale of Boulogne-sur-mer, cod. 188, from the
tenth century, depicts as illustration of the constellation Engonasin a youth
clad in an exomis and holding a skin and a lagobolon (fig. 156). It corresponds not at all with the text which describes Heracles in a kneeling position as suggested already by the name of the constellation. Other Aratea,
like the codex A.16 in the National Library of Madrid from the twelfth
century,[13] represent, indeed, Engonasin as a nude and bearded Heracles who
kneels before the dragon guarding the apples of the Hesperides and swings
his club against the attacking serpent, and this is undoubtedly the original
constellation type. The picture in the Boulogne manuscript cannot be interpreted as a disintegrated or corrupt type of Heracles, but must have originally represented a different constellation type which by mistake replaced
the original Heracles type. Thiele has convincingly shown that the constellation type which in the Boulogne manuscript goes under the name of Engonasin, is in reality a repetition of the Bootes, for whom exomis, lagobolon
and the striding position are most characteristic.[14] A special group of manuscripts within the recension of illustrated Aratea, and to which in addition
belong the earlier Aratus in Leyden and a later manuscript in the Stadtbibliothek of Berne, cod. 88, from the eleventh century,[15] may be established on the
grounds of having this error in common.

Another cause for errors is *omission*. Not that every omission necessarily
affects the content of a scene. Quite often subordinate figures and accessories
are dropped during the process of copying without changing the nucleus,
and hence the meaning, of an iconographic unit. But sometimes a figure essential for the understanding of a scene is omitted and the content thereby obscured or even falsified. This is particularly true in cases where the miniature has migrated from one text into another and has left the copyist without
the control of the basic text. An example may be seen in the Daniel minia-

[13] Bethe, *Rhein. Mus.*, XLVIII, 1893, p. 91.—Thiele, *op. cit.*, p. 143 and fig. 62. Cf. also fig. 69.—
Bethe, *Buch und Bild*, p. 45 and fig. 25.
[14] Thiele, *op. cit.*, pp. 92-93 and fig. 19.
[15] H. Hagen, *Catalogus codicum Bernensium*, Bern 1875, p. 108.—Thiele, *op. cit.*, p. 83.

ture from the Cosmas manuscript in the Vatican, cod. gr. 699 (fig. 155),[16] for which an illustrated Prophet book must have served as model. The text of the Cosmas containing passages from the ninth, seventh, and second chapters of Daniel[17] explains only the lower part of the miniature which depicts the rulers of the four universal empires riding on monstrous animals as described in chapter 7, while it makes no reference to Daniel in the lion's den, appearing in the upper half of the picture. This story, not even alluded to in the text of Cosmas, is told twice in the Bible, in the sixth and fourteenth chapters of Daniel. The prophet stands in the attitude of an orans, between two lions, while every indication of the den is omitted, and he is approached by a youthful figure flying down on a cloud bank. Only in the second passage from the Bible is a person mentioned flying toward Daniel, namely the prophet Habakkuk who supplies him with food. According to this text he is taken through the air by an angel and carries food in his hands; and in the corresponding scene of the Gregory manuscript in Paris (fig. 137) he is actually represented flying with an angel, and carrying a basket and a pitcher. By the omission of the angel and the food vessels in the Cosmas miniature, the meaning of the flying figure is now obscured and we cannot be sure whether the painter himself still had a clear idea about the identity of this figure as Habakkuk. Stornajolo, the editor of the Vatican Facsimile, calls him the *Son of Man*, an identification which apparently resulted from the desire to connect the picture with the present Cosmas text, where the corresponding passage from Daniel, mentioning the Son of Man (VII, 13), is quoted. However, the Son of Man does not appear to Daniel while the latter is in the lion's den and, furthermore, does not come down to him with a gesture of presenting something, but is himself brought before the Ancient of Days. A Christian painter would invariably have interpreted and represented him as Christ with a crossed nimbus standing alongside the Lord enthroned and most likely surrounded by an aureole. Thus the Daniel miniature is an instructive example for the kind of confusion which results from the omission of essential features, here the angel and the prophet's attributes.

A further source for repeated mistakes is the *conflation* of scenes. Two consecutive miniatures may be fused into one, and the copyist may drop some of the participants and regroup the remaining ones. Naturally he will try to make the conflated composition as coherent as possible, but he may not always succeed. In the miniature from the Psalter in the Athos monastery Pantokratoros, cod. 49, which illustrates the Ode of Habakkuk (fig. 157), the center is occupied by the prophet who raises his hands in a gesture

[16] Stornajolo, *Miniature della Topografia Cristiana*, pl. 40.
[17] Migne, *P.G.*, 88, col. 272.

of prayer and hears the prophecy of the Lord as told in the text of the Ode (Hab. III, 2-19). Above the prophet's head one recognizes an angel guiding and holding the flying Habakkuk, who carries a basket with bread and a pitcher. This upper group was originally created as part of a composition in which Habakkuk brings food to Daniel in the lion's den (cf. fig. 137) and it has just as little to do with the text of the Ode as it had in the previous example with the Cosmas text. The incongruity between the two parts of the Psalter miniature can easily be explained by assuming a model in which the scene with Habakkuk bringing food to Daniel in the lion's den existed on the one page and the praying Habakkuk on the opposite one. When these two miniatures were conflated Daniel in the lion's den was dropped and a new composition came into being, where Habakkuk brings food to Habakkuk —obviously iconographic nonsense.

4. *Decorative Fillings*

Additional features, whether landscape, architecture or human figures, may usually be used to enrich a composition without interfering with its iconography, but sometimes such additions do contradict the meaning of the text. We shall first discuss only decorative fillings such as landscape and architecture, reserving a special paragraph for the addition of various types of human figures.

One of the chief reasons for additions—just as for omissions—is the change in format. While in the miniature of the Vatican Virgil with Aeneas before the tumulus of Polydorus (fig. 91) the features in the added area neither contributed to, nor were at variance with, the essential meaning of the scene, occasionally the enlarged area (usually an upper zone of a heightened miniature) is filled with elements which do not harmonize with the rest. In a miniature from the Milan Iliad, which contains in one frame two consecutive scenes from the sixth book (fig. 159)[18] we recognize at the left Hecuba and three of the aged wives, before Theano, the priestess to whom they present their robes (VI, 297ff.) and at the right Hector is addressing Paris, who sits on a couch together with Helen (VI, 313ff.). It may be recalled that frequently in the Milan manuscript two or even more scenes are united in a common frame (cf. figs. 32 and 34), which in an earlier papyrus roll had been separated in the narrow writing columns. In such a model the open air scene, which takes place in front of the temple of Athena within the precinct of her sanctuary, most likely was of the same height it is now, while the interior scene with Hector, Paris and Helen was presumably lower in format and had its upper border immediately above the three participants

---

[18] Ceriani-Ratti, *Homeri Iliadi pictae fragmenta Ambrosiana*, Pict. XXV.

as is suggested by their strong isocephalic arrangement. To indicate the interior of a palace chamber nothing else was needed than a wall with perhaps a few pilasters and an entrance door, as can be seen in the Feast of the Gods,[19] a setting which would be in close agreement with the normally rather simple scenes in papyrus rolls. But when the two scenes of uneven height were joined by a common frame, the empty space over the originally lower right scene had to be filled and the illustrator did it with architectural features by which he meant to represent the city of Troy. Thus he created a unifying background for the two scenes and amalgamated them into a larger artistic unit at the expense of an accurate rendering of the meaning of the text, for the couch with Paris and Helen now appears to be in the open street.

It may be recalled that also the painter of the Vienna Genesis made ample use of decorative fillings when he added a piece of rocky landscape in the miniature of Abraham's Return from the Sacrifice of Isaac (fig. 73), or an open sky behind Jacob's Death which is supposed to take place in an interior (fig. 87). How far such discrepancies can obscure the original meaning of a scene may be shown by the miniature of a tenth century Bible, the cod. Vat. Reg. gr. 1, which represents the carrying of the ark of the covenant by the priests in the presence of Aaron and Moses (fig. 158).[20] This scene, to begin with, was not invented for its present place at the beginning of Leviticus, because the text of this book does not deal with the carrying of the ark of the covenant. In the Octateuchs the event is represented twice, once as illustration to the passage of the Red Sea (Exod. XIV, 22), and a second time, where the passing through the desert of Mount Sinai is described (Num. X, 33).[21] In the former the setting is a hilly landscape around the group of Israelites who march through the dry ground of the Red Sea; in the other there is no setting at all, and the figures are just silhouettes against a colorless background. In both the composition is friezelike, and some such model as this must have served the illustrator of the Regina Bible when he made up the frontispiece for Leviticus. In transforming a frieze picture into a full-page miniature, he maintained the isocephalic character of the model, but at the same time he not only considerably enlarged the scale of the figures, but also filled an extensive area above the scene proper, an area nearly as high as the figure frieze itself, employing an architectural landscape consisting of two houses, a dome-shaped building—which, because of overlapping, resembles unintentionally an apse—two cubic structures in the corners and a tree. These fillings give to the scene a splendid and rich

[19] *Ibid., Pict.* x.

[20] *Miniature della bibbia cod. Vat. Regin. greco 1 e del salterio cod. Vat. Palat. greco 381* (Collezione paleografica Vaticana, fasc. 1), Milan 1905 (here the older bibliography), pl. 8.

[21] Cf. the Octateuch of Smyrna, Hesseling, *op. cit.*, pl. 58, no. 178 and pl. 68, no. 224.

setting, but from the iconographic viewpoint they contradict the meaning of the basic text according to which the ark was carried through the desert.

5. Complementary Figures not Required by the Text

Just as landscape and architectural features are added around the nucleus of a scene, so are complementary figures, either single or in groups, in order to fill an expanded picture area. Several categories of added figures can be clearly distinguished.

In the first their function is merely to occupy additional space, like the decorative buildings and landscape features, and thus they may simply be called *filling figures*. The beginning of the tenth book of the Iliad is illustrated in the Milan codex by a miniature (fig. 160)[22] in which Nestor, followed by Odysseus and Diomedes, addresses the assembly consisting of Meges, son of Pyleus, the two Ajaxes, Menelaus, Agamemnon and Idomeneus. These figures who correspond closely with the text form the nucleus of the scene to which, however, is added on either side a herald surrounded by hoplites. The presence of the heralds is not only not explained, but is even contrary to the text, which tells explicitly how Agamemnon went to wake up Nestor and how Nestor woke up Odysseus and so on, thus doing themselves the job of heralds. Nor is the presence of soldiers motivated, since according to the text the leaders gathered together alone. It follows that the two groups at the ends of the frieze are fillings, and a caesura is still felt at the left behind the standing Odysseus and at the right behind the seated Idomeneus. At the same time the heralds standing on either side of the assembly are not an invention of the copyist but only an adaptation from other miniatures where they are required and therefore belong to the archetype of the picture, as in an illustration of Book IX, where Agamemnon addresses the assembly summoned by the heralds.[23] The reason for the expansion is, as far as we can see, a formal one, the archetype being a papyrus roll in which the miniatures and writing columns were apparently narrower. In expanding the width of both, the scribe needed only to use more monumental characters, while the extended space for the miniatures could be taken up in one of three ways, all of which were actually employed in the Milan Iliad: either by enlarging the scale of the figures,[24] or by adding scenes side by side (figs. 34 and 159), or, as in the present instance, by patching on figures or groups of figures, even at the expense of iconographic accuracy.

Filling figures occur also in several miniatures of the Vienna Genesis, as for instance in the Temptation of Joseph by Potiphar's Wife (Gen. XXXIX,

[22] Ceriani-Ratti, *op. cit.*, *Pict.* XXXIII. [23] *Ibid.*, *Pict.* XXXI.
[24] Most prominently in the miniature illustrating the battle near the Scaean Gate; *ibid.*, *Pict.* LIV.

9-13) where the seducing wife sits on the couch in the palace chamber while she snatches the garment of the escaping Joseph, and where Joseph is repeated leaving the palace and looking backward toward the open door (fig. 161).[25] So far the miniature agrees with the Septuagint text. But these two Joseph scenes were not sufficient to fill the space reserved for the picture and therefore the painter had to introduce new pictorial elements from the outside in order to fill the remaining space. For this he chose genre figures which have nothing to do with the scene of escape, figures which have already been interpreted by other scholars as additions beyond the requirement of the text.[26] They represent women attending children and spinning, and when the unknown model for these figures was apparently exhausted, the illustrator made up the rest by two trees, somewhat incongruous features here since spinning, in ancient and mediaeval times, was normally a household occupation and should have been represented in an interior. Thus heterogeneous filling elements are here combined which, though intended purely as decoration, give to the whole miniature the appearance of a *garden scene*.

A second category of complementary figures is to be found chiefly, though not exclusively, in scientific treatises, where they are added to a plant or a construction or an engine, or whatever the object may be, in order to explain to the beholder its usefulness, effectiveness, mechanism or other functions. These may be called *explanatory figures*.

In a miniature of the Dioscurides herbal in Lavra on Mount Athos (fig. 68) a woman can be seen by the side of and related to the third plant, inscribed ἔρινον. The text explains that the seed of this plant is used for a healing salve and hence the woman is to be understood as plucking the fruit in order to collect the useful seed. The earlier Dioscurides manuscripts in Vienna, cod. med. gr. 1, and in New York, cod. M. 652, both of which possess more accurately depicted plants and therefore are closer to the archetype, do not have such explanatory human figures, while in the Lavra codex they are quite frequent. Surely they did not exist in the archetype of the classical period, most probably not even in Early Byzantine copies, and when in the Middle Ages an illustrator introduced them he did it with the idea of representing not only the plant as such, but also its usefulness.

Similar figures occur in Western Dioscurides manuscripts as well. In the Latin copy from the tenth century in Munich, cod. 337 (fig. 116), there is a serpent depicted alongside the plant *tripolion* because the herb, as Dioscurides states, was used as remedy against poison, and on the same page the

---

[25] Wickhoff, *Die Wiener Genesis*, p. 156 and pl. XXXI.—Gerstinger, *Die Wiener Genesis*, pl. 31.—Buberl, *Die Byzantinischen Handschriften*, vol. I, pl. XXXVI, no. 31.

[26] Gerstinger, *op. cit.*, p. 101.—Buberl, *op. cit.*, pp. 113-14.

flower of the plant *cemos* is touched by a seductive woman with bare breasts and a feather crown—perhaps a mediaeval version of Venus herself—in order to demonstrate the author's assertion that the plant's root is useful as an amulet for a love spell. In this Munich manuscript the later addition of the explanatory human figures and animals is clear from their position in the margin, while the plants proper are placed as usual within the writing columns.

Similarly in the Paris manuscript of Nicander's *Theriaca* and *Alexipharmaca* the representations of poisonous animals are supplemented by human figures who illustrate the actual or potential effectiveness of the poison. Youths are depicted as they flee attacking serpents or insects,[27] and in one case the victim, already bitten by a poisonous salamander, is creeping on the ground (fig. 162),[28] illustrating the passage (Alex. 550ff.) : "If one has taken a beverage infected by a poisonous lizard . . . called salamander . . . he will be taken with exhaustion and a bad trembling will deprive his limbs of all strength in such a way that falling on the ground he can only drag along on all fours like a little child, that has not yet learned to walk. . . ." This creeping youth must be regarded as a later addition for the same reason as the constellation of Orion (fig. 131), because he is lacking in the illustrated paraphrase of Nicander by Eutecnius in the Dioscurides manuscripts of Vienna and New York. As he is placed, between the two animals, he appears to be an intrusion which has so pushed aside the lizard and the salamander that their tails had to be turned upward in the margins. This points to a model in which the two creatures, before the intrusion of the youth, had more conveniently occupied the space inside the lateral limits of the writing column. It may also be noted that the youth and the poisonous animals do not form a coherent scene, not so much because of their different scale, which might easily be due to a desire to emphasize the animals, but because the lizard and the salamander are seen from above in a projection most common and profitable for scientific analysis, while the youth is depicted as seen from the side. It is exactly the same incongruity we encountered in the miniature with Orion and the scorpion.

In technical treatises male figures become associated with certain instruments, engines or weapons in order to demonstrate their mechanism. The Vatican Library possesses a richly illustrated poliorcetic treatise, cod. gr. 1605, from the eleventh century,[29] the text of which is attributed to Heron

---

[27] Omont, *op. cit.*, pls. LXV, no. 4 and LXVII, nos. 1-3.

[28] *Ibid.*, pl. LXVII, no. 4.

[29] Seroux d'Agincourt, *Histoire de l'art par les monuments*, vol. V, Paris 1823, pl. XLIX, no. 6.—H. Diels, *Antike Technik*, 2nd ed., Leipzig-Berlin 1920, p. 111, pl. VIII.—Gasiorowski, *Malarstwo Minjaturowe Grecko-Rzymskie*, p. 171 and fig. 85.

of Byzantium, who in the tenth century, at the time of the Emperor Constantine VII Porphyrogennetos, excerpted the works of ancient writers on poliorcetics like Heron of Alexandria, Apollodorus of Damascus and others.[30] In one of its miniatures the ἀρίς, i.e. the weapon which is used for boring into a walled city, is represented (fig. 163) once on a large scale piercing the wall and then a second time for the sole purpose of showing its manipulation by two soldiers. The text is based upon the *Poliorcetica* of Apollodorus of Damascus and in copies of this Roman treatise the corresponding miniature[31] depicts the same bow-drill piercing a walled city, but characteristically enough, without its repetition where it is manipulated by soldiers. Evidently the explanatory figures were invented for the Middle Byzantine treatise, while the Roman texts, to judge from their later copies, did not have them.

A further category of complementary figures which plays a very important role in the classical as well as in the Christian texts, consists of *personifications* and *allegories*. Their relationship to the basic text is twofold: they are usually based on the mention of a locality or a human quality or whatever object or idea in the text seemed suitable to be personified, and yet their connection with the text is not so close that their omission would seriously impede the intelligibility of a scene. In other words, if a miniature does contain a personification, the text may help to identify it, but because of the complementary nature of the personifications the text provides no evidence as to whether they were a part of the pictorial archetype or not.

Obviously we can exclude from our discussion those personifications which were introduced in the text by the poet himself as acting and speaking personalities. In a miniature of the Milan Iliad in which Scamander accuses Achilles of his slayings (XXI, 212)[32] the river-god, leaning upon an urn and raising his hand in a gesture of speech towards Achilles (who is now lost through damage), is of course a constituent part of the composition and cannot be considered as complementary.

Complementary personifications have probably been associated with miniatures as long as book illumination itself has existed. In a Megarian bowl with illustrations from Euripides' *Phoenissae* (fig. 172),[33] the personification of the city of Thebes sits on a rock near the fighting brothers, depicted as a woman with a mural crown and a scepter and touching her chin with

[30] Pauly-Wissowa, *R.-E.*, *s.v.* Heron, vol. VIII, pt. 1, col. 1074, no. 53.

[31] C. Wescher, *Poliorcétique des grecs*, Paris 1867, p. 150 and fig. LIII.

[32] Ceriani-Ratti, *op. cit.*, *Pict.* LII.

[33] H. B. Walters, *Catalogue of the Greek and Etruscan Vases in the British Museum*, vol. IV, London 1896, p. 254, no. G. 104 and pl. XVI.—C. Robert, *Jahrb. d. Inst.*, XXIII, 1908, pp. 193ff. and pl. 6.—F. Courby, *Les vases grecs à reliefs*, p. 294, no. 20.

her hand in surprise or sorrow. The general knowledge of the fratricide taking place before the city of Thebes was reason enough for the artist to depict this personification, which, however, is not an integral part of the fighting scene. Therefore it is not impossible that it was added by the worker in relief, and did not yet exist in the illustrated roll upon which the Megarian bowls ultimately depend.

The fact that the earliest extant manuscripts such as the Milan Iliad and the Vatican Virgil contain quite a few personifications makes it clear that they were just as common and widely spread in manuscripts as in any other medium of classical art. It is only natural that also the earliest illustrators of the Bible employed them in much the same way as their classical predecessors, like the artist who depicted a nymph at a spring in two miniatures of the Vienna Genesis[34] which illustrate the Rebecca story.

But, although personifications could have existed in practically every miniature cycle from its very beginning, depending on the personal inclination and the taste of the illustrator, there are definite indications that quite frequently they were not conceived in the archetype, but were added later and sometimes even considerably later, whenever an individual copyist wished to make some enrichment. Since the text is of little help in determining whether or not a personification belonged to the archetype, we have to look for other criteria within the realm of the miniatures themselves. Our judgment as to whether and when a personification was added depends chiefly on three criteria which do not exclude each other, and sometimes come into play simultaneously.

First—and this is true not only for personifications but any complementary feature—an added personification may not be thoroughly amalgamated into the composition, so that the addition reveals itself by formal discrepancy. In the miniature with the Coronation of David in the well-known Paris Psalter (fig. 187),[35] the crowning woman emerges from behind a crowd of onlookers of five to six rows in depth, her spatial relation to David being an impossibility,[36] and she seems to be suspended in the air without any support. Such incongruities make necessary the assumption of a later insertion of this female figure, who fulfills the function of a classical Nike, though the fact of her standing instead of flying and the absence of wings make it doubtful whether the copyist had any knowledge of the classical Nike type.

[34] Wickhoff, op. cit., pls. XIII-XIV.—Gerstinger, op. cit., pls. 13-14.—Buberl, op. cit., pl. XXVII, nos. 13-14.

[35] Omont, op. cit., pl. VI.—H. Buchthal, op. cit., p. 24 and pl. VI.

[36] Weitzmann, "Der Pariser Psalter ms. grec. 139 und die mittelbyzantinische Renaissance," *Jahrbuch für Kunstwissenschaft*, 1929, p. 181 and fig. 9.

A second criterion can be gained from the investigation of the pictorial stemma by determining whether, in an earlier stage of the development, the scene possessed the personification under consideration or not. A miniature from the Psalter, cod. 49, of the Athos monastery Pantokratoros represents Moses receiving the tablets of the law (fig. 164),[37] while some Israelites, half hidden by a mountainous landscape, raise their hands in astonishment at this event. In the lower left corner there can be seen a half-nude figure, seated and turning its back to the beholder, which, by analogy to the corresponding miniature of the Paris Psalter,[38] can be identified as a personification of Mount Sinai. We have pointed out repeatedly that the pictures of the aristocratic Psalter group were not invented for it, but taken over from other Biblical books, and accordingly we may expect to find the earlier stage of development of the Moses scene in an illustrated Book of Exodus. The general arrangement as well as the formal treatment, particularly of the figure of Moses, are indeed very much alike in the corresponding scene of the codex gr. 747 (fig. 165), but neither in this nor in any other Octateuch does the illustration to Exodus XXXI, 18 include the personification of Mount Sinai. We may conclude, therefore, that this personification was added only after the picture had migrated from an Octateuch into the Psalter. The next question, then, would be whether it was inserted already in the archetype of the aristocratic Psalter recension or perhaps in some later copy. The fact that there are Psalter copies of the same recension without the figure of the Oros Sina[39] seems to favor the second alternative. The same criterion may be applied to the so-called Nike in the Coronation of David of the Paris Psalter (fig. 187), in addition to the argument about her incongruous placing. The ultimate source of this scene is to be sought in the Book of Kings, and the only copy of it in existence, the codex Vat. gr. 333, contains characteristically enough the corresponding scene *without* the crowning Nike (fig. 183). Thus we may again conclude that the Nike was added only after the whole composition had been taken over from a Book of Kings into the Psalter.

Finally, there is a third criterion by which the later intrusion of a personification may be recognized. Two miniatures, which iconographically belong

[37] The miniature precedes the Deuteronomy Ode. It was, however, conceived as title picture to Psalm LXXVII, a location which it still maintains in some other psalters of the same recension, while the original composition to the Deuteronomy Ode is preserved e.g. in the Psalter Vatopedi 760 (fig. 113).

[38] Omont, *op. cit.*, pl. x.—Buchthal, *op. cit.*, pl. x.

[39] E.g. in the codex Vatopedi 760, fol. 143ʳ (photo in the Department of Art and Archaeology of Princeton University). The picture cycle of this Psalter has many conservative features indicating that this manuscript, though not earlier than the eleventh or twelfth century, is particularly close to the archetype.

to the same recension, may have a different personification in the same place, of which only one can go back to the archetype, while the other must be a substitute. In the Vatican Joshua Roll there is a scene (fig. 167),[40] in which during an assault at night the Israelites set on fire the evacuated city of Ai after another part of the Israelite army had lured the men of Ai into a trap (Joshua VIII, 19-20). Before the city wall sits a personification of the city of Ai with a mural crown on her head, and balancing a cornucopia with the tip on the ground. The corresponding scene in the Octateuch, cod. Vat. gr. 747 (fig. 166, left half),[41] which belongs to the same recension, has on the same spot a personification of the Nyx holding an inflated veil over her head. Only one of the two personifications can have been in the archetype, either the city of Ai or the Nyx. The text favors the Nyx as being the more essential and therefore the original one. No less than three times particular emphasis is put on the fact that the event takes place during the night (Joshua VIII, 3, 9 and 13). Thus it seems as if the picture in the Vatican Octateuch, though in other respects more condensed, having dropped the pursuing men of Ai, possesses nevertheless the original personification, while the city of Ai in the Vatican roll is but a substitute for the Nyx.

6. *Conscious Deviations from the Text*

Not every deviation of a picture from the text is a pictorial corruption resulting from a misunderstanding of the model. One must also take into account the freedom and originality of an able miniaturist, who, dissatisfied with merely technical copying, likes to assume a writer's competence in narrating a scene in his own way and to deviate consciously from the text in one manner or another. The instances quoted previously in which a miniaturist invented out of his own imagination even entire scenes without any textual basis (p. 152 and figs. 140-142) justify the belief in his ability also to change purposely a traditional composition. However, any attempt to distinguish a corruption from a deliberate change must be supported by convincing suggestions as to the reasons which might have induced the artist to make his alterations. Two instances of what we might call *conscious deviations* may be described.

In the miniature of the Milan Iliad (fig. 168),[42] Hector, meeting Andromache at the Scaean gate (VI, 390ff.), sits upon a couch in the middle of a street instead of in an interior, and before him stands his son Astyanax, who, according to Homer, should be a mere babe whom the handmaid carries in her arms. The Iliac tablet,[43] as is to be expected from a strict illustration of

[40] *Il rotulo di Giosuè* (facsimile), pl. X.   [41] *Ibid.*, TEXT, pl. L, no. 3.
[42] Ceriani-Ratti, *op. cit.*, *Pict.* XXVI.
[43] Jahn, *Griechische Bilderchroniken*, p. 15 and pl. II, no. B.

171

the text, shows Astyanax as a babe which Hector had just laid in Andromache's arms before he departs. The change of the age of Astyanax in the Milan miniature can hardly be explained as an error in the usual sense; it suggests rather a conscious deviation from the text, the explanation for which can be found in the very Homer text which at the first glance it seems to contradict. At the end of the farewell scene Hector kisses his son, fondles the babe in his arms and speaks: "Zeus and ye other gods, grant that this my child may likewise prove, even as I, preeminent amid the Trojans, and as valiant in might, and that he rule mightily over Ilios" (VI, 476ff.). In these words Hector envisages the child as the future ruler, and in order to transform the vision into pictorial form, the illustrator depicted Astyanax as a grown-up boy.

The second example is chosen from Christian illumination. The Octateuch Vat. gr. 747 represents the first mission of the Gibeonites to Joshua (fig. 169) by four ambassadors, who, in order to feign a long journey, show to the Jewish commander-in-chief all the attributes which the text explicitly enumerates, namely old garments, old shoes, dry and mouldy bread, old sacks and wine bottles, or rather skins (Joshua IX, 6-13). Shortly afterwards the Gibeonites send a second mission (Joshua X, 6), and no longer attempting to deceive Joshua, they approach him directly for help against the Amorites. This second approach is depicted in the same manuscript by two ambassadors kneeling in front of Joshua and raising their hands in supplication (fig. 170). Both scenes are faithful to the text and characteristic of the care which a Byzantine illuminator normally pays to the details of the literary source. The corresponding scenes in the Joshua Roll (fig. 171)[44] are, from the iconographic viewpoint, less precise. The fact that in the first scene the number of ambassadors is reduced from four to two has little significance since the text does not mention their number, but more important is the omission of the ambassadors' attributes, which are so essential to the full understanding of the scene. In this respect the Vatican Octateuch represents undoubtedly the truer and more original version and the Joshua Roll the altered one. This only confirms the conclusion drawn from the comparison of the same two monuments on the basis of the personifications, that the Nyx in the Vatican Octateuch (fig. 166) represented the better version as against the city personification in the Joshua Roll (fig. 167). On the other hand, the high artistic quality of the Joshua Roll eliminates the likelihood of negligence or carelessness and it is more reasonable to suppose that its illustrator had a definite purpose when he changed the original composition. It will be observed that in both scenes of the roll the ambassadors approach Joshua

---

[44] *Il rotulo di Giosuè* (facsimile), pl. XII.

with their hands veiled by a mantle.[45] Already the Roman emperors were approached by envoys in this manner, as can be seen on a relief of the Column of Marcus Aurelius,[46] and it was apparently a characteristic imperial court ceremonial. Its introduction into a Byzantine roll, most probably under the influence of a monument like a triumphal column, suggests that the roll was made for a member of the Byzantine court, perhaps the emperor himself, and that the painter therefore tried to make the Triumph of Joshua and the Israelites as ceremonious as possible.

The reasons for deliberate deviations vary, of course, greatly. For instance, in order to emphasize the liturgical character, the painters may turn a narrative scene of a Biblical book into a more hieratic composition with an iconlike quality, especially when they transformed a Gospel cycle into a lectionary cycle, and any study of the history of the lectionary illustration must take account of intentional deviations of this kind. It is apparent that some ancient and mediaeval illuminators were quite aware of the meaning of the subject matter they painted, taking the liberty to reinterpret it not only according to their representational abilities but also according to their own literary conceptions.

7. Adaptation of Compositional Schemes

The use of single conventional figures, changes in the costume, misunderstandings of the model, additions of objects or persons not required by the text or conscious deviations—all the alterations discussed thus far—affected only parts of the original composition invented for the archetype. The nucleus of the composition remained intact, at least to the extent that its iconographic affiliation with other members of the same recension could still be determined. At times, however, the illustrator was not satisfied with a partial alteration, but adapted a whole compositional scheme as a convention. Two categories of such thorough adaptations can be distinguished: first, the creator of the archetype may employ traditional compositional schemes alongside newly invented ones in order to simplify the task of making up a comprehensive cycle; and, secondly, a copyist may, within a given recension, replace one compositional scheme by another whereby an already established iconographic continuity became interrupted. In the first case the artist desired to make convenient use of compositional achievements of the

[45] In the Vatican Octateuch one of the ambassadors of the first scene carries the dry bread in his hands which are covered with a napkin, but here the motif has quite a different meaning.

[46] E. Petersen, A. von Domaszewski, and G. Calderini, *Die Marcus Säule*, Munich 1896, vol. I, pl. 56A. The editor of the facsimile of the Vatican Joshua Roll has already called attention (*op. cit.*, p. 14) to this parallel.

past, while in the second he endeavored to obtain a new expression or effect for a very specific reason.

On the Megarian bowl on which the later part of Euripides' *Phoenissae* is illustrated in several successive scenes (fig. 172), the representation of the initial stage of the fight between Eteocles and Polyneices, when they attacked each other with their lances before drawing their swords (v. 1380-1389), is quite in agreement with the description in the text yet without particularity. It is a scheme for a single combat which would fit descriptions of fights in many epic poems and dramas and since the early archaic period was used time and again for the duels of Greek heroes. Obviously, then, the first illustrator of the *Phoenissae* did not need to invent this group.[47] The adaptation of such formulae in a time when the concept of plagiarism did not exist is not necessarily to be judged as a lack of artistic imagination. The same illustrator's capacity for highly individualized compositions is demonstrated by the next scene in which a messenger has just reported to Jocasta the imminent fight between the two brothers (v. 1264-1282), whereupon she leaves at once for the battlefield to prevent the fratricide, and she calls Antigone to join her. Every moment and gesture is well motivated and the result is a highly dramatic composition, which is created for the specific situation as described by Euripides.

It can be expected that the illuminators who were faced with perhaps the biggest single task in the history of book illumination, namely the illustration of the Septuagint with hundreds and hundreds of scenes, made extensive use of compositional schemes which they saw in classical rolls. We have referred repeatedly to Homer and Euripides as the chief illustrated classics in antiquity, but not until the Hellenistic and Roman monuments, which reflect illustrated Homer and Euripides rolls now lost, are gathered together more systematically, will we be able to give a more satisfactory answer to the question of how extensive the influence of the classical miniature cycles upon the Septuagint illustration actually was. The following discussion of a few examples of classical and related Biblical scenes with regard to their coincidental compositional schemes should be considered only as a first attempt in the direction in which future investigation of the sources of the Septuagint illustration must proceed.

In the Sacrifice of Isaac in the Paris Gregory, cod. gr. 510 (fig. 173),[48] Abraham is depicted in a striding position and so is Isaac, whom he grasps by his head and threatens to kill with a knife by cutting his throat. He appears to have caught the boy when the latter tried to escape. In front of this group is the burning altar, but according to the text (Gen. XXII, 9) Isaac

---

[47] C. Robert, *Hermeneutik*, pp. 201ff.   [48] Omont, *op. cit.*, pl. XXXVII.

174

should be on the top and not in front of it. This slight incongruity with the text can be explained by the assumption that the illuminator adapted the compositional scheme from a model in which the various elements were in a closer agreement with the text. We might, therefore, ask what illustrated classical text contained a similar and at the same time well-known description and illustration of the sacrifice of a boy which the first illustrator of the Septuagint might have remembered and whose scheme he could have adapted for his own purpose. The high moment in the *Telephus* of Euripides is the seizure of the little boy Orestes by Telephus, who flees with the child to the sacred altar and threatens to kill it unless the Achaeans agree to heal his wound with the spear of Achilles. The Achaeans comply with his request, the sacrifice does not take place, and Orestes is saved. Illustrations of this drama are known from Etruscan urns, on which the episode with the attempted killing of the boy Orestes is represented in at least three different successive moments: first Telephus seizes the fleeing boy; secondly, with the captured boy he has reached the altar and kneels with one knee upon it; and third, he sits upon the altar still threatening the boy and arguing with Agamemnon about his own healing.[49] In the first of these three scenes, preserved among other copies on an urn in Florence (fig. 175),[50] the pursuing Telephus turns his head backward and once held in his right hand, now broken, the knife in a menacing attitude close to the throat of the victim who tries to escape. This very scene may have been used as model for the Sacrifice of Isaac and all those features which we considered as minor deviations from the Bible text, such as the placing of Isaac before instead of upon the altar, and the rushing attitude of both participants, are now explained. The changes necessary in order to use this scheme for the Bible were comparatively slight. According to the text Isaac's hands were fettered and so we see in the Gregory miniature his hands bound at his back. Consequently the left hand of the executioner, who grasps the left arm of the prospective victim in the classical scene, holds the head by its hair in the Biblical picture. Beyond this gesture changes were required only in the drapery.

Another example may be taken from the Book of Kings in the Vatican, cod. gr. 333, where in the miniature of David's return from the battle against Goliath the hero holds the giant's head lifted upon the point of the spear and shows it to the jubilant women of Israel (fig. 174). The spear in David's hand can only be the one taken from Goliath, but this contradicts the text, which states explicitly that David put Goliath's armour in his tent (I Reg. XVII, 54), while he is supposed to hold the giant's head in his hands when he brings it back to Jerusalem (I Reg. XVII, 57). The illustrator of the arche-

[49] Brunn, *Urne etrusche*, vol. I, pls. XXVIII; XXIX, 9; XXX, XXVI-XXVII, XXXII-XXXIII; XXXI, 11.
[50] *Ibid.*, pl. XXVIII, 6.

type of the Book of Kings must have seen in another manuscript a man carrying the head of a slain man on the point of the spear, and he adapted this scheme for what appeared to him a similar situation. There is in the Iliad (XIV, 499ff.) an episode in which Peneleos pierces the head of Ilioneus through the eye, and after having smitten off the head he holds it high up upon the spear in order to frighten the fleeing Trojans. This is illustrated in a miniature of the Milan Iliad (fig. 176),[51] where, following closely the text, Peneleos in the advancing frontline of the Achaeans holds Ilioneus' head high up on his lance in a manner not unlike that of David in the Vatican miniature, so that the left half of the Iliad composition could very well have provided the model for the corresponding group in the Biblical picture.

The search for models used by the artists who created the illustrated archetype of the Septuagint need not be limited to the Homer and Euripides rolls. There are good reasons to believe that other sources also, such as general handbooks of mythology with illustrations, served as models for the Bible illustrators, especially for the one who first depicted the creation of Adam in the Cotton Bible recension. Among the fragments of the Cotton Bible itself the illustrations of the Adam creation are lost, but since the mosaics of S. Marco and some miniatures of the Turonian Bibles are quite faithful copies of either the Cotton Bible itself or a manuscript of the same recension (cf. p. 140), we can consider them as substitutes for the lost Greek miniatures. In one of the mosaic panels (fig. 177) we recognize the Lord seated and shaping the right arm of the upright clod of earth which represents Adam; in a miniature of the Grandval Bible in London, Brit. Mus. cod. add. 10546 (fig. 178),[52] Adam is represented lying on the ground completely rigid so as to suggest his lifelessness, while the Lord bows over Adam's head, holding it with both hands as if to give the body the first spark of life. The two concepts are so different that a transformation from one into the other does not seem possible; either both scenes were in the Cotton Bible as successive illustrations of Genesis 1, 26-27, or one of the two examples has infiltrated into the cycle from the outside. Two points favor the former alternative: first, the homogeneity of the two scenes insofar as the Lord is represented as a full-length figure of Christ, a feature typical for this very recension; and secondly, that other recensions like the Octateuchs, though their iconography is very different, likewise illustrate the same passage by two successive acts which might be distinguished as the *shaping* and the *enlivenment*.[53] There is only one classical myth which contains a similar conception of the creation of mankind and which, at the same time, was popular enough in literature

[51] Ceriani-Ratti, *op. cit.*, *Pict.* XLIII.
[52] W. Köhler, *Die Schule von Tours*, vol. I, pt. 2, Berlin 1933, pp. 186ff. and pl. 50.
[53] Cf. the Octateuch of Smyrna, Hesseling, *op. cit.*, pl. 3, no. 9 and pl. 4, no. 10.

ADAPTATION OF COMPOSITIONAL SCHEMES

and fine arts to be remembered and adapted by a Christian artist, namely the creation of the human race by Prometheus. This myth is represented among other monuments in a series of Roman sarcophagi and here again the act of creation is depicted in two different phases which correspond in many ways to those of the Cotton Bible recension. In one of them Prometheus sits and holds the instrument for the modelling of the little human-shaped clay figure, which itself stands on a pedestal; in a variation of the same compositional scheme on a fragment in the Vatican (fig. 180),[54] the clay model is larger in size than in the other sarcophagi and stands directly upon the ground. The second phase is represented by a sarcophagus in the Museo Nazionale at Naples (fig. 181)[55] where the clay model lies stiff on the ground with both arms attached to the body, while Prometheus is seated behind it, touching its head with one hand, and observing the enlivenment of the model by Eros and Psyche. Thus the two phases of the creation on the sarcophagus reliefs accord with the representations of the shaping and enlivenment of Adam in the mosaic and the Carolingian miniature with regard not only to their compositional schemes, but also to their meaning. Compared with the similarities between the Christian and the pagan representations, the differences are of a comparatively minor nature: the Lord in the S. Marco mosaic holds the right arm of the clay model with both hands, while Prometheus uses only one for this purpose and holds the other over the model's head; furthermore, the Lord in the Grandval Bible bows over the model and touches the head with both hands, concentrating completely on the act of enlivenment, in which Prometheus is assisted by Eros and Psyche.

Moreover, a third scene of the creation episode, the *animation* of Adam by the Lord (Gen. II, 7) which too, judging from a S. Marco mosaic (fig. 179),[56] must have existed in the cycle of the Cotton Genesis, also has its counterpart in the Prometheus sarcophagi. The motif of a little Psyche whom the Lord, in the mosaic, holds by her wings, represents the same idea as a butterfly on a Prometheus sarcophagus in the Museo Capitolino in Rome (fig. 182)[57] which Athena holds in her extended right hand over the newly created man in order to introduce the living soul into his body. The implications are that the Christian artist who illustrated the archetype of the Cotton Bible with three scenes relating to the creation of Adam, used an ancient text with illustrations of the Prometheus story as model, in which the creation of the human race was depicted in the same three phases, i.e. the *shaping*, the *en-*

[54] C. Robert, *Die antiken Sarcophag-Reliefs*, vol. III, 3, pp. 436ff. and pls. CXVI-CXVII, nos. 351-352, 354-356.
[55] Robert, *op. cit.*, p. 448 text-figure and pl. CXVIII, no. 357.
[56] Tikkanen, *Die Genesismosaiken von S. Marco*, pl. I, no. 3.
[57] Robert, *op. cit.*, p. 441 and pl. CXVI, no. 355.—H. v. Schoenebeck, *Röm. Mitt.*, LI, 1936, pp. 264ff. and pls. 35-36.

livenment and the *animation*. This model might have been a mythological handbook similar to that of the *Bibliotheke* which goes under the name of Apollodorus of Athens,[58] although in the present case it hardly could have been this particular handbook, because the Prometheus story is told too briefly therein (Lib. I, VII. 1), and one would expect a more detailed literary source which today seems lost.

The other type of adaptation of a complete compositional scheme, which takes place as a *substitution* within a certain recension, can be demonstrated in a miniature from the Book of Kings in the Vatican, cod. gr. 333, where David is raised upon a shield and acclaimed by the men of Israel (fig. 183). The accompanying text (II Reg. v, 3) mentions only David's anointing when he was made king at Hebron, but says nothing about his being raised upon a shield. We know from historical sources that in the Early Byzantine period emperors were raised upon shields. Julian the Apostate seems to have been the first proclaimed in this manner, and the event is narrated by Ammianus Marcellinus (XX, 4, 17) and, among the Greek historians, by Zosimos (III, 9),[59] who describes it with the following words: "And after they had risen up from the drinking bout with great tumult they rushed, with the wine cups still in their hands, to the praetorium, and breaking through the doors without any order, they brought down the Caesar by public consent, raised him, unsupported, on a kind of a shield, pronounced him as Imperator Augustus, and forcibly placed the diadem upon his head." The pictorial scheme of the raising upon the shield fits the Zosimos text much better than the tale of David's anointing at Hebron and consequently we assume that it originated in an historical chronicle. It is not impossible that the source for the Vatican miniature was actually an illustrated chronicle of Zosimos, the pagan historian who glorified Julian, but it might just as well have been another chronicle which contained a similar passage with the same composition. The scheme of an emperor raised upon a shield was apparently very popular in Byzantine chronicles and in the chronicle of John Scylitzes in Madrid, Bibl. Nat. cod. 5-3N-2, a fourteenth century manuscript,[60] we see it still used for the coronation of Leo Tornikios (fig. 185), an Armenian general, who in 1047 made an unsuccessful uprising against Constantine Monomachus. Clad in the imperial loros, the general is raised on a shield and surrounded by onlookers in a compositional arrangement which is quite sim-

[58] *Idem, De Apollodori Bibliotheca*, Berlin 1873.—J. G. Frazer, *Apollodorus, The Library* (Loeb Class. Lib.) 2 vols., 1921.

[59] Imm. Bekker, *Zosimus* (Corpus script. hist. Byzant.), Bonn 1837, p. 136.

[60] G. Millet, *La collection chrétienne et byzantine des Hautes Études*, Paris 1903, p. 26, nos. B.369-375; p. 54, nos. c.869-1277.—Schlumberger, *L'épopée byzantine à la fin du dixième siècle*, vols. II and III, Paris 1900 and 1905, *passim*.

ilar to that in the Book of Kings. Moreover, in the Vatican Book of Kings the same scheme is used for the coronation of several other Jewish kings, namely Saul (I Reg. XI, 15) (fig. 186), Rehoboam (III Reg. XI, 1 = fol. 89ᵛ), and Abijam (III Reg. XV, 1 = fol. 95ʳ).

If this coronation scheme were already introduced into the archetype of the Book of Kings, the picture cycle of this part of the Septuagint could not be older than the end of the fourth century, i.e. after Julian as the first emperor was raised upon the shield. But if the scheme replaces an older one, then the miniature cycle might well be more ancient and have undergone only compositional changes in the fourth century or later. The representation of the raising on the shield of Saul as king (fig. 186) differs from the other examples in the Book of Kings insofar as it is combined with his anointing by Samuel, who stands with him upon the shield. In reality these two distinctly different actions cannot have taken place simultaneously and therefore can only be understood as a pictorial conflation of two originally separate scenes. Consequently only one of them can be original and the other must be a later supplement. Since the act of anointing is closer to the meaning of the Biblical text it can be considered as the more original part of the composition, an idea supported by the fact that in the scene of the first proclamation of Saul as king (fig. 184) the anointing alone is represented. Also the election of Solomon as king (fol. 71ᵛ), to quote another example, is depicted merely as his anointing by Zadok, the priest. All this leads to the conclusion that the compositional schemes in which Jewish kings are raised upon the shield are substitutions for older anointing scenes, made under the influence of historical chronicles.

A miniature like that of the Vatican Book of Kings (fig. 183), in which David stands alone upon the shield with nobody to crown him, must have been the model for the illustrator of the Paris Psalter, cod. gr. 139 (fig. 187), who, as we concluded already from formal incongruity (cf. p. 169), added a crowning Nike. However, the Nike is not the only type of complementary figure which was added within the limits of the aristocratic Psalter recension in order to place the crown on David's head. In the corresponding miniature of an eleventh century aristocratic Psalter in Vatopedi on Mount Athos, cod. 761 (fig. 188),[61] we see an emperor fulfilling the same function. This motif is without textual foundation in the Book of Kings and apparently never existed in a miniature of this text, but was, like the Nike, added to the composition only after the picture had left the Book of Kings and entered the Psalter recension. The crowning emperor shows the same formal incongruity as the Nike, being suspended in the air without a platform under

[61] G. Millet and S. Der Nersessian, *Revue des études arméniennes*, IX, 1929, p. 173 and pl. X, no. 2.

his feet, and his addition is probably the result of the renewed influence of a chronicle picture. In the same Scylitzes manuscript in Madrid mentioned above, Michael Rhangabes also stands on the shield when he crowns Leo the Armenian[62] and it seems to have been a model of this kind which influenced the coronation picture of the Vatopedi Psalter.

To sum up, four phases in the development of the scheme of the raising on the shield can be distinguished: (1) its invention in an historical chronicle; (2) its adaptation in the Book of Kings, either by substituting it for or by conflating it with the traditional scheme of the anointing; (3) its migration from the Book of Kings into the aristocratic Psalter recension; (4) the addition of a crowning king or Nike.

For quite a different reason was the substitution of a compositional scheme made in the first miniature of the menologion of Basil II in the Vatican library, cod. gr. 1613.[63] At the head of the lesson for September first (Luke IV, 16-20) Christ is depicted standing in full frontality on a footstool and holding an open book, while the listening Jews on either side bow in devotion (fig. 189). The composition is more hieratic than seems fitting for the narrative text passage, which describes how Christ comes to Nazareth, takes the book of the prophet Isaiah presented to him, opens and reads it and then sits down to explain it. In such a narrative manner is the passage actually illustrated in the Gospel book, cod. gr. 74, of the Bibliothèque Nationale in Paris,[64] where Christ reads from a lectern and addresses a crowd of people from Nazareth, and in the lectionary, cod. gr. 21, of the Public Library in Leningrad (fig. 191),[65] where Christ sits in front of the city or its synagogue. With neither of these miniatures has the picture in the menologion anything in common as far as the compositional scheme is concerned.

In the Gospels the episode of Christ reading in the synagogue of Nazareth is of no particular prominence and therefore its illustration is just one of many in an extensive cycle; in the lectionary, however, it has a very important position, illustrating the very first lesson of the calendar year, starting with September first. Moreover, the last lesson of the preceding first part (Matt. XXVIII, 1-20), read on the Sabbath of the Holy Week, deals with the Mission of the Apostles, and in the lectionary of Leningrad, on the recto of the same folio on which the preaching in the synagogue is depicted on the verso, this scene is represented with Christ standing frontally upon a footstool and blessing the two groups of apostles who approach him with veiled

---

[62] Millet, *Collection des Hautes Études*, p. 54, no. c.869 (= fol. 10ᵛ).

[63] *Il menologio di Basilio II* (Codices e Vaticanis selecti, vol. VIII) (facsimile), Turin 1907, pl. 1.

[64] Omont, *Évangiles avec peintures byzantines*, vol. II, pl. 101.

[65] C. R. Morey (*Art Bull.*, XI, 1929, pp. 53ff.) dates this manuscript in the eighth century, while the present writer (*Byzantinische Buchmalerei*, p. 59) dates it in the tenth century.

hands (fig. 190). It is obviously this very compositional scheme of the Mission of the Apostles which the Vatican menologion painter used for the scene of Christ reading in the synagogue, and therefore his model must have been a lectionary, since only in this service book were the two scenes involved so closely connected. In order to make the scheme fit the new text, he only needed to put the open Book of Isaiah into Christ's hands and to change the apostles into Jews by increasing the number of the listeners to more than twelve. The reason for the substitution of the whole compositional scheme was very probably the desire to place at the very beginning of the menologion a hieratic composition with a strong symmetrical arrangement which is much more effective than the casual grouping of the figures in the narrative synagogue scene would have been.

IV. THE RELATION BETWEEN TEXT CRITICISM AND PICTURE CRITICISM

IN our investigation of the relation between picture and text we repeatedly pointed out the similarities in method between picture criticism and text criticism so that the reader must already have become aware that both methods are closely related to each other. But there are also essential differences between them, and we wish here to supplement our remarks, emphasizing the differences as much as the correspondences.

Text criticism is concerned primarily with readings and their interpretation. Other features such as the physical appearance of the documents, particularly the style of writing or what generally is called palaeography, are only of secondary interest, although they help to establish the genealogy of the manuscripts involved; they have no direct bearing on the interpretation of readings and so can be treated as independent evidence. In miniatures, on the other hand, the content, or what is called the iconography and which is the equivalent of the readings of the text, is fused with the style, i.e. the element corresponding with palaeography, to form such a close artistic unit that the one cannot be considered apart from the other. To do so for methodical purposes always involves some act of violence. The intrusion of style leads to an inevitable alteration of some of the iconographic details in later copies of the archetype. As a result, certain features of the archetype can no longer be established by critical methods. In textual criticism it is possible to reconstruct a text in its purity so nearly completely that disputed and unclear readings remain a negligible portion of the whole text. Hort, for instance, in his introduction to the New Testament,[1] estimated that of the New Testament, which is one of the most accurately transmitted texts, seven-eighths are virtually accepted as correctly restored; furthermore, that in the remaining eighth part, many differences in the readings are comparatively trivial, so that the proportion of variations which are really subject to doubt amount to one-sixtieth. In pictorial criticism, however, the penetration of style into iconography prevents the reconstruction of even a single picture of a large cycle in its absolute purity. One can only try to extract iconographic features from stylistic ones with varying degrees of accuracy.

This situation in picture criticism is at the same time a very positive asset. In textual criticism each deviation from the autograph text, apart from helping in the discovery of the original reading, is in itself of a negative value.

[1] B. F. Westcott and F. J. A. Hort, *The New Testament in the Original Greek, Introduction*, New York 1882. The chapter by Hort, "Methods of Textual Criticism," is used by the present writer as the main basis for his statements on textual criticism.

We assume that, at least as a rule, no later writer can improve by correction the original text though he himself may think so, and therefore every alteration is to be judged only by its relationship to the archetype, which determines the better reading. The study of the transmission of miniatures has exactly the same aim, namely, to find the iconographically purest version of the archetype, but this is not necessarily the most satisfactory version with regard to the visualization of the content. Miniatures in the course of copying can be altered and enriched in iconography as well as in style, and these changes and additions, though in a technical sense errors with respect to the archetype, may quite often improve the content of a miniature. Paradoxical as it may sound, iconographic corruption and artistic improvement can coincide in one and the same miniature, depending on the scale of values for different periods. A decrease in iconographic agreement with the archetype may be counterbalanced by a new inventive spirit of the copyist, who by following less literally an earlier text-bound illustration, may, by changing it, even intensify its meaning. Some examples of this were discussed in the paragraph on *conscious deviations*.

Because of the penetration of style into iconography and the ever-changing nature of the former, the differences between copies of miniatures have a much wider range than those between copies of texts, and therefore each illuminated manuscript has a greater individuality than a mere text. Whereas a text critic, in dealing with a late text, tries to sift it from later alterations in order to comprehend the spirit of the time of the author in its greatest possible purity, a picture critic has to judge a miniature cycle from two angles, namely, to reveal the spirit of the time of its origin as well as that of the period in which the actual copy was made, evaluating the two on a more equal basis. It follows that with regard to the historical problem of how a certain literary content was understood by a later period, miniatures often give a clearer insight than texts. It is this interplay of two overlapping time factors which gives to the study of miniatures its peculiar richness and variety and makes the history of a miniature recension appear as a process of organic growth rather than a process of gradual fading as in text transmission.

An error in text criticism, negative as it is in itself, is an absolute quantity and it depends exclusively on the critic whether or not he is able to detect it. In picture criticism the limits between iconographically accurate compositions and their alterations are often fluid in cases where the changes involved are comparatively minute. Whether a slight change, in e.g. a gesture, alters the interpretation of the action and therefore should be called an iconographic error, or whether the change remains within the limits of mere stylistic development which must ensue even in the most faithful and accurate copying and hence would not justify the application of the term *error*, is a problem which will sometimes have to be resolved by the personal judgment of the picture critic. Therefore an error in pictures is a less precise determinant than an error in texts.

Another important difference between a text and a cycle of miniatures lies in the relation to what might be called the *basic unit*. A text is a fairly stable unit. Additions and omissions usually amount only to phrases and sentences, seldom to whole paragraphs and chapters, and where in a copy large sections are missing, it is, in most cases, due to external damage of a codex in a later period and not to the intention of the copyist to excerpt the model. Instances like the Vienna Genesis, where the Septuagint text is purposely condensed, are comparatively rare. In book illumination instances where a miniature cycle consists of a definite number of scenes and where this number is kept fairly stable in later copies do of course occur, as in the Terence and the Prudentius manuscripts, but they are exceptions rather than the rule in the history of the transmission of miniature cycles. In the Biblical books, on the other hand, which were copied much more frequently, the selection of scenes from the larger cycle of the archetype takes place in varying extents. If we examine, from this point of view, the Gospels as one of the most frequently copied books with illustrations, there are hardly two miniature cycles which have the same number of scenes. Between extremely rich cycles like that of the Florentine Gospels, cod. Plut. vi, 23 (cf. figs. 70-71), with hundreds of scenes, and those which confine themselves to a very few pictures of the main feasts any variation is possible and the principle of selection is often quite arbitrary and depends on exterior circumstances. Because of his dependence upon the text as the more stable unit the illustrator is in a position to make a free choice of scenes, since the text supplies the necessary information for every gap in the miniature cycle, and thus the miniature cycle, thinned out as it may be by continuous omissions of scenes, still maintains a coherence as long as it keeps its connection with the text.

At the same time a change in the number of miniatures cannot be used for chronological evidence. Wherever in a scriptorium a venerated old codex with a rich miniature cycle was available, a later copyist might easily make fuller use of it than an earlier one (though in the stylistic transformation he may be even further removed from the original). The eleventh century Cosmas in the Sinai monastery, cod. 1186, to cite one of many similar examples (fig. 192),[2] has a fuller miniature cycle than the famous Vatican copy,

---

[2] Weitzmann, *Byzantinische Buchmalerei*, p. 58 and pl. LXV (here further bibliography).

cod. gr. 699 (fig. 130), which is about two centuries earlier. But while the number of scenes is greater, the iconographic value of the individual miniature may at the same time decrease. Thus a miniature cycle will have to be judged both from the extent of the cycle and the faithfulness of the individual pictures. The results from these two lines of evidence need not necessarily coincide. On the contrary the restriction of the cycle in the number of scenes is quite often accompanied by a greater care for the individual picture. The high quality of many lectionaries, illustrated by a cycle of the feasts only, compared with a more average level of the extensive miniature cycles in Gospel manuscripts elucidates this point.

Concerning the methods of textual criticism Hort distinguishes in the main three kinds of evidence, the first of which he calls the *Internal Evidence of Readings*. Every method of textual criticism is comparative, i.e. at least two variants of readings are needed in order to detect and to reject an error and the more variants we have the more promising is the outlook for arriving at a sure result. In some instances, in what Hort calls *Intrinsic Probability*, mere intuitive judgment as to which reading makes better sense can decide the issue of a better reading either by an immediate judgment or by weighing cautiously various elements like conformity to grammar, congruity to the purport of the rest of the sentence, congruity to the usual style of the author, etc. Similar categories of intrinsic probability can be used in picture criticism such as congruity to the iconography or congruity to form and style. In the miniature illustrating the Ode of Habakkuk in the Psalter of Pantokratoros, where the prophet brings food to another Habakkuk (fig. 157), the iconographic nonsense can be determined by an immediate judgment. In the miniature of the Paris Psalter (fig. 187), where the relation of the crowning woman to David is conflicting, the judgment is based upon lack of formal congruity. In reality, evidences from intrinsic probability rarely stand alone and are usually supplemented by other evidence. In textual as well as in picture criticism one has to guard oneself against too stringent a method: just as in a text the best words are not always those which the author actually employed, but those which a later scribe substituted, so in the pictorial tradition the archetype may start out with certain conventions of types or compositions (cf. p. 154) which a later copyist may be able to make more specific and closer to the words of the basic text or to its meaning than the first painter was able or willing to do.

A second form of the internal evidence of readings is concerned with what Hort calls *Transcriptional Probability*. It is based on the assumption that wherever we have two rival readings the variations have to be accounted for in such a way that one can be seen to be related to the other. It is not so much the question of the excellence of one reading compared with the other, but also of its fitness for casting light on the existence of the other. Transcriptional probability does not rest on common sense like intrinsic probability, but on an acquaintance with the general nature of the causes of corruptions. Picture criticism depends to an even greater extent upon this method. As a matter of fact, wherever two pictures of the same iconography are to be compared, there is necessarily the problem of transcriptional probability involved, since two pictures are never perfectly alike, whereas long stretches in two comparative texts may show hardly any variation at all. Often variations between two miniatures are, of course, a mere trifle and not worth a detailed analysis, but, in principle, transcriptional changes are inherent in every example of picture copying. The generalizations, the knowledge of which helps to establish the actual dependence of documents upon each other, can, as in textual criticism, be quite manifold. An example of transcriptional probability in pictures can be seen in the two representations of the Canticle of Moses (figs. 112-113). Their difference in arrangement cannot be judged by intrinsic probability, since both versions are in themselves coherent and make sense. Nevertheless, one is a variation of the other and the variation must be explained. On the basis of the general development of picture format as outlined in the present study we can be sure that the strip miniature gradually turned into the full-page miniature higher than wide and therefore, on the basis of this generalization, we can determine the version in the Octateuch (fig. 112) as the more original and that in the Psalter (fig. 113) as the more derivative. Among the manifold generalizations the change of format is one of the most essential ones, though other generalizations, based on iconographic grounds, are of equal importance.

Before the text critic passes final judgment upon readings a knowledge of the documents should precede, and this leads to the second method, which Hort calls the *Internal Evidence of Documents*. It deals with the fixing of the date of the document and, if possible, of its locality. The chief instruments for doing so are first the colophon, which may contain the year of origin, the place of manufacture, the name of the scribe or other information, and secondly the style of writing, i.e. palaeography. In the history of miniatures the direct evidence comparable with a colophon is very rare. The Vatican menologion, cod. gr. 1613, where every miniature is signed by an artist, is an exception (cf. p. 200) and there are very few miniatures on which a date is inscribed. Occasionally a miniature can be dated by the representation of a contemporary historical personality, who may be identified by an inscription or by his portrait. As far as stylistic evidence is concerned, the style of the miniatures and also that of the ornamental decoration of a manuscript are very often a more precise instrument for dating and localization than palaeography. It stands to reason that the more complex an object is, the more various and accumulating the evidence must be. When single letters become enlarged and form richly ornamented initials, the variations among them are much greater and more manifold than those between ordinary letters of the script. As an example we refer to a group of Greek manuscripts which are written in so-called Slavonic uncials, a hieratic script which changed very little over a fairly long period. Thus the dating of a manuscript, written in this script, merely on the basis of the style of letters, can vary often between the seventh and the tenth centuries. A study of ornament as well as of miniatures frequently limits the possibilities to a few decades and at the same time helps to establish local groups,[3] which hardly could have been determined on palaeographical grounds alone.

In text criticism the older text can usually be considered the better one, but its superiority must be sustained by other factors as well, the early date alone not being sufficient. The possibility that a later text may be better must always be considered. Similarly in miniatures the earlier cycle is generally assumed to be the better one, but at the same time we expect this initial assumption of superiority to be strengthened by other evidence since not infrequently a later cycle provides more evidence for the reconstruction of an archetype than an earlier one. The Cosmas manuscript in the St. Catharine's monastery on Mount Sinai, for instance, represents the episode of Paul's conversion in a miniature (fig. 192) which agrees in iconography with the corresponding one in the Vatican Cosmas manuscript (fig. 130), save that the former contains an additional scene where Paul receives the letter to Damascus from the high priests (Acts IX, 1-2). The Sinai picture from the eleventh century, then, is more complete and from the iconographic viewpoint, therefore, a better witness to the original cycle than the Vatican one, which dates in the ninth century.

Moreover, the greater or lesser purity of an early document has to be proved by a plurality of cases, not only as concerns texts but for miniature cycles as well. A copyist may feel inclined to make iconographic changes only in a certain number of miniatures of a certain cycle, while others remain closer to the archetype and therefore purer. The analysis of a whole cycle, picture by picture, is required for a clear idea of the distribution of more progressive and more antiquated miniatures in it, a distinction which parallels that between "good" and "bad" readings in texts. Such inconsistencies make it difficult to reach a general judgment as to the degree of purity of the iconography in a lengthy cycle and to weigh it against another cycle whose purity in iconography may likewise be of varying degrees.

Among the documentary witnesses of a text, its translations into other

---

[3] *Ibid.*, pls. XXXVII, no. 204; XLVIII, nos. 287-289; LII-LIV, LXX-LXXIII, LXXVI-LXXVIII, etc.

languages must be taken into consideration. This applies also to those miniatures which are copied from one codex into another in a different language,
but although such a shift may result in stylistic alterations, it does not necessarily carry with it iconographic changes comparable to the changes of readings which inevitably occur in text translations. The shift of the constellation pictures of Aratus from Greek into Latin codices does not have, necessarily, a bearing on their iconography, and where alterations occur in later
western copies they are, in most instances, the result of changes other than
those caused by translation of the text. Or a text may be translated into the
vernacular without affecting the iconography of its illustration, as could be
seen in the Millstatt Genesis (figs. 124-125). This, of course, does not exclude the possibility that the vernacular has, on occasion, been the cause of
alterations in iconography.

Further documentary evidence in texts is supplied by quotations, where
all kinds of modifications, deliberate or unintentional, which writers make
in rapidly quoted passages, must be taken into consideration. Quotations can
be accompanied by miniatures which were taken over from the same source
as the quotations themselves, as e.g. the Vision of Isaiah in the homilies of
Jacobus Kokkinobaphus (fig. 138). But miniatures can also replace the text
quotations themselves, as we saw in the so-called monastic Psalters (cf. p.
121 and fig. 109), and in this case we can speak metaphorically of *pictorial
quotations*. They must be handled with the same care as text quotations with
regard to possible modifications. The painter of the Pseudo-Oppian who inserted, as quotations, scenes from the Alexander Romance (figs. 133-134)
was, of course, interested in the horse Bucephalas more than in any human
figure and this attitude may easily have produced slight modifications though
we are in no position to check them.

Sometimes it happens that various books are combined in one volume;
they may have different sources and these may be of different periods, so
that generalizations obtained from one book are not necessarily valid for
all the rest. Various miniature cycles, too, may be combined in one volume,
as in the well-known codex of Ademar in Leyden, cod. Voss. lat. oct. 15
from the eleventh century, a miscellaneous manuscript with various classical texts, of which three are illustrated, namely, the *Psychomachia* of Prudentius (fig. 79), Hyginus' *Astronomica* and Aesop's Fables according to
the redaction of Romulus. Though all three miniature cycles are assimilated
in their style, being apparently drawn by the same hand, each cycle, like its
corresponding text, has its own history, and while the date of the archetype
of the Prudentius drawings can be fixed in the fifth century, this date has
no bearing on the archetype of the Aesop Fables and of the constellation
pictures of Hyginus, both of which are much older.

Hort's third method concerns the *Genealogical Evidence*. It is the aim of each text critic to sum up all detailed observations of the mutual relationship of documents in a scheme which is generally called a stemma. Picture critics have often adapted this method from textual criticism in order to bring the mutual relationship of miniature cycles into a similar scheme, but they usually content themselves with making the text stemma, just as it is, the basis for the explanation of the pictorial relations, a usage for which the stemmata of the illustrated Prudentius and Terence manuscripts are well-known examples. Though text and picture stemmata which are concerned with the same recension ought not to contain mutually contradictory elements, they nevertheless should be worked out separately, and compared only afterwards. It will be observed, then, that they seldom coincide completely, and for the following reasons. First, the same text may have been illustrated twice by different artists unrelated to each other so that there are thus *two* archetypes for further copies, and a text stemma which can comprise both has to be split up in two separate picture stemmata. The two fully illustrated codices of the homilies of Gregory of Nazianzus, the one in Paris, cod. gr. 510 (figs. 137, 173), and the other in Milan, Ambros. cod. E. 49-50 inf. (fig. 105), may be quoted as examples; while their texts are united in the same stemma, their picture cycles are not. Secondly, the situation may be reversed and the picture stemma may include manuscripts which must be excluded from the text stemma. The miniature cycle of the Millstatt Genesis, for instance (figs. 124-125), belongs to the same recension and therefore has to be placed in the same stemma as the pictures of the Cotton Bible, while of course a Middle High German poem cannot be brought in any direct genealogical relationship to the Septuagint text. Thirdly, the accents in a picture stemma may be differently distributed from those in a text stemma. To begin with, the pictorial archetype may not coincide with the textual archetype since in most cases it is not even likely that the earliest text was already illustrated. Usually a certain time elapses before a text becomes canonical or popular enough to be illustrated. Moreover the pictorial archetype may be a manuscript which belongs to a rather remote side branch of the text stemma while more important text branches may remain unillustrated. Furthermore, the ramifications may be distributed in a picture stemma quite differently from the corresponding text stemma. Wherever a certain group of text errors makes the assumption of a ramification necessary, this may not have any effect on the pictures at all, and, vice versa, a break in the picture tradition may arise at a point where no textual changes have taken place. Thus it becomes clear that the possibilities for differences between a text and a picture stemma of the same recension are so manifold that a full coincidence between them cannot reasonably be

189

expected, though, to repeat, this does not imply a contradiction between them. Where such a contradiction exists, either the text or the picture critic must be wrong. Text and picture stemmata are complementary to each other and the evidence of the one strengthens that of the other.

Aside from these essential differences, however, there are many agreements in the way in which the method of genealogical evidence is to be applied. The distinction which textual criticism makes between *simple and divergent genealogy* is equally valid for picture criticism. In the latter the simple genealogy, in which the direct dependence of one miniature cycle upon another can be established, is just as rare as in text criticism, while the divergent one in which an unknown third is the common source, is much more frequent.

Concerning *genealogy and number*, textual criticism says that numerical preponderance may have to yield to qualitative preponderance. Though in general the majority has weight over the minority, the results based on this evidence can be upset by the smallest tangible evidence of another kind. How much the same is true for miniature cycles can be exemplified by the Greek Octateuchs. The codices Vatopedi 602, Seraglio 8, Smyrna A. 1 and Vat. gr. 746 form one branch while codex Vat. gr. 747 stands isolated as the single remainder of another branch. Iconographic analysis of their cycles, scene by scene, will very soon reveal that codex Vat. gr. 747 is a purer copy of the archetype than any manuscript in the rival group and therefore it has greater authority and weight than all the other manuscripts together.

The *manner of discovering genealogy* is likewise similar in text and miniature. As in texts we can assume that identical alterations in corresponding miniatures are hardly ever made independently from each other—though such a possibility cannot absolutely be excluded—and identical alterations can normally be taken as evidence of a common origin. This point is demonstrated by the three Aratus manuscripts which have the identical replacement of Engonasin, i.e. the kneeling Heracles, by the type of Bootes (p. 161). It is not likely that an alteration of this sort was made independently several times and therefore it can be taken for granted that those manuscripts which contain this error form a subordinate group of their own within the fuller stemma of the illustrated Aratea.

Complications of genealogy may originate by mixture. Two readings are sometimes conflated, and in this case we can always assume that the two simple readings are the basis for the third conflated one, and not vice versa that the two simple ones may be the result of independent impulses of simplification. The same problem arises also in picture criticism, where we have met a form of fusion which corresponds to *conflation* in textual criticism. The picture of the Isaiah Ode in the Psalter from Vatopedi (fig. 139) is a striking example of the conflation of two successive scenes: first the vision proper and second the receiving of the coal from a seraph, both being related to one and the same Isaiah figure. Behind this composition stands a miniature with two scenes like the one in the homily manuscript of Jacobus Kokkinobaphus in Paris (fig. 138), each of which has its own figure of the prophet. Just as in texts, there is no evidence or probability that the conflated version of the Psalter picture stood at the beginning of the development and that the two separate scenes were made up from it by doubling the figure of the prophet.

Another point essential in textual and picture criticism alike is the use of more than one model for a copy. The scribe may have realized that one model was not satisfactory to him in all its readings, so he used a second one from another branch of the stemma which likewise was not good enough to be transcribed exclusively, and consequently he chose variants from both models, combining their readings. In a stemma such a relation can be indicated by a line which connects the two branches. That miniaturists work in exactly the same way may be shown in a scene from the eleventh century Octateuch in Vatopedi, cod. 602 (fig. 195),[4] which illustrates the setting up of twelve stones in the midst of the Jordan (Joshua IV, 8-9). We see a group of workmen carrying on their shoulders stones to build an altar which stands, partly ready, in the center of the scene. They are guided by Joshua and a group of soldiers, and at the right a group of Israelites is watching the ceremony. There is a certain incongruity here in that Joshua appears to be passing by the very altar he is supposed to erect. This incongruity is the result of the conflation of two sources. The group of the stone carriers, the soldiers and the marching Joshua are copied from the corresponding scene of the Joshua Roll (fig. 193),[5] while the altar and the Israelites looking on at the right side are taken from another model which is preserved in its iconographic purity in an Octateuch like the codex Vat. gr. 746 (fig. 194).[6] Joshua stands in front of the onlookers and, by pointing at the altar, gives the order for its erection. As in textual criticism the creation of a new picture out of two variants not only leads further away from the archetype and makes its reconstruction more difficult, but it results in an iconographic corruption in spite of the copyist's intention to improve the scene.

In making a stemma of miniature cycles one point must be very strongly emphasized, namely, the necessity for a separation as strict as possible of iconography from style. Just as in text criticism the relationship between documents is determined by their differences in the readings and not by their

[4] Th. Ouspensky, *L'octateuque de la bibliothèque du Serail*, Sofia 1907, p. 162 and pl. XXXV, no. 229.

[5] *Il rotulo di Giosuè* (facsimile), pls. II-III.   [6] *Ibid.*, TEXT, pl. C, no. I.

palaeography which comes into play only secondarily for the fixing of the date and provenance of single documents, so likewise a miniature stemma should be based exclusively on iconographic and not stylistic evidence, which is only of subsidiary help for the dating of single documents and cannot be used for determining questions of descent. The transmissions of iconography and style often follow quite different paths, the style changing completely while the iconography remains stable, and vice versa. Two ninth century monastic Psalters, for instance, one in Moscow and the other in the Athos monastery Pantokratoros, show a characteristic style which, in the opinion of the writer, can be localized in Palestine or Syria[7] while other copies of the same recension from the eleventh century, like the Theodore Psalter in London, Brit. Mus., Add. 19352, and the Barberini Psalter in the Vatican, cod. Barb. gr. 372,[8] are painted in a very different style which has its roots in Constantinople. In other words, a Constantinopolitan illustrator was able to copy the iconography of an East Byzantine model quite faithfully but changed the style completely. The possibility of such complete stylistic transformations makes any conclusion as to the time of origin or locality of the archetype on stylistic grounds questionable. In reality iconography and style often parallel each other over long stretches of time, but it is an unstable association which easily and unpredictably can be broken off at any stage of the development so that the evidence gained from the one cannot be used indiscriminately as support for the evidence gained from the other. It is true that style, particularly in mediaeval art, can be very archaistic and reflect an earlier stage of development and thus have some bearing on genealogical problems, but the model which can be inferred from a copy on stylistic grounds seldom leads all the way back to the archetype but generally only to an intermediary copy. Thus in addition to the greater genealogical value of iconographic evidence in general, it normally spans larger periods and leads closer to the archetype than stylistic evidence can do. An iconographic stemma can in its ramifications comprise many groups of documents which stylistically may be very heterogeneous.

[7] Weitzmann, *op. cit.*, pp. 54ff. and pls. LIX-LXII (here further bibliography).
[8] J. J. Tikkanen, *Die Psalterillustration im Mittelalter*, p. 12 and *passim*.

V. THE CYCLE OF MINIATURES AS THE BASIC UNIT OF THE ILLUSTRATED BOOK

A. MONOCYCLIC AND POLYCYCLIC MANUSCRIPTS

JUST as a poem or treatise constitutes a unit, so the miniature cycle illustrating this poem or treatise forms a unit whose limits correspond with those of the texts. A work in which text and picture cycle fully coincide, we shall call a *monocyclic manuscript*, for which the Iliad manuscripts in Milan, the two Virgil codices in the Vatican and all Terence manuscripts are characteristic examples.

There are miscellaneous manuscripts or compendia where several text units, related or unrelated to each other, are bound together in a single volume, all of which may be illustrated. The textual units are determining factors for the grouping of the miniatures, insofar as the complement of pictures has to be divided in as many corresponding sections as there are different texts, and the history of each group of miniatures thus established has of course to be treated separately. Such a work may be described as an *addition of monocycles*, of which the codex Voss. lat. oct. 15 in Leyden with its drawings of the *Psychomachia* of Prudentius, the *Astronomica* of Hyginus and the Fables of Aesop is a typical representative.

Sometimes the literary and pictorial units vary and it is not altogether clear whether we deal with a large single cycle or a compilation of smaller cycles. This is particularly true for the Bible, which as a whole constitutes a unit though it is made up from various books of different origins. The earliest illustrated full Bibles preserved today are the Grandval and the Vivian Bibles, both products of the school of Tours,[1] and the one in S. Paolo-fuori-le-mura in Rome.[2] The iconographic source of their miniatures depends upon whether or not the archetype of these Carolingian Bibles, which Koehler placed in the fifth century in the period of Leo the Great, was illustrated by an homogeneous monocycle, invented for a full Bible to begin with, or whether the various books of the Bible had started separately with miniature cycles of their own so that the first illustrator of the full Bible could excerpt small sections out of them. In the latter case we would have an addition of abbreviated monocycles, each of them with its own archetype differing from the other in date and place of origin. Koehler has shown that the Genesis scenes in these Carolingian Bibles[3] are derived from a manuscript of the

---

[1] W. Köhler, *Die Schule von Tours*, pls. 50-53 and 69-76.

[2] S. O. Westwood, *The Bible of the Monastery of St. Paul near Rome*, Oxford 1876 (with 38 photos).—Boinet, *La miniature carolingienne*, Paris 1913, pls. CXXI-CXXX.—A. M. Friend, *Art Studies*, I, 1923, p. 70.

[3] Köhler, *op. cit.*, TEXT I, 2, pp. 186ff. and pls. 50 and 70.—Boinet, *op. cit.*, pl. CXXII.

same recension as the Cotton Bible in London. The source, then, must have been a Greek, probably Alexandrian, manuscript which, as far as we can judge, never contained more than just the Book of Genesis. If this is true, the following Exodus scenes[4] cannot be derived from the same source, and we must, therefore, treat the Genesis and Exodus pictures as remnants of two separate cycles whose iconographic archetypes may have different sources. A similar situation prevails with regard to the New Testament pictures in the Carolingian Bibles. Some of the scenes from the life of Paul in the S. Paolo manuscript[5] have an affinity with illustrations in the Greek manuscripts of the Cosmas Indicopleustes which, as we saw, had been taken over from an illustrated Acts of the Apostles (figs. 130 and 192), and thus an illustrated Greek Acts may be assumed as the ultimate source for the Life of Paul in the Latin manuscript. At the same time all three Bibles contain scenes from the Apocalypse,[6] a book which was not illustrated by the Greeks until the end of the Middle Ages. Again, the miniatures from the Acts and those from the Apocalypse go back to different monocycles.

Similar circumstances exist in Greek Bible illustration. With only one exception all Biblical miniature cycles are connected with single books of the Bible rather than with a full edition of it. The Vienna Genesis and the Cotton Bible never contained more than just the Book of Genesis, and the Octateuchs, as their name suggests, are limited to the first eight books of the Septuagint. Furthermore, the Four Books of Kings, the Book of Job and the Psalter are units with their own picture cycles. Of these we still possess illustrated copies, while other books like the Prophets, of which illustrated copies must also have existed (cf. p. 134), are today lost. Do all these books go back to one comprehensive illustrated Bible, in which the miniatures constituted an extensive monocycle which later was cut up into parts? It must be emphasized that some of the single books of the Bible are, or at least were before their mutilation, extremely rich in the number of their illustrations. If the Vienna Genesis or the Cotton Bible were still intact, we would see with amazement that each of them contained originally more than three hundred scenes. To illustrate the whole Bible on such a scale seems a practical impossibility. In the Octateuchs, in which the Genesis cycle is already an abbreviation compared with those we have to assume for the two Early Christian fragments quoted above, all eight books together with their several hundred pictures constitute such a thick volume that a full Bible illustrated on the same scale is unimaginable. The same is true for the Book of Kings in the Vatican, cod. gr. 333: its First Book alone comprises more

[4] Köhler, *op. cit.*, pls. 51 and 71.—Boinet, *op. cit.*, pl. CXXIII.

[5] Seroux D'Agincourt, *Histoire de l'art*, vol. v, pl. XLII, no. 8.

[6] Köhler, *op. cit.*, pls. 53 and 75.—Boinet, *op. cit.*, pl. CXXVIII.

than a hundred scenes, though later in the codex the copyist became tired and apparently abbreviated the miniature cycle of his model so that in the Fourth Book only a single miniature was executed. But the assumption that Books II-IV also were originally illustrated very extensively can be supported by the *Sacra Parallela* in Paris, cod. gr. 923, in which scenes from the later Books of Kings are much more numerous than in the Vatican codex. Thus the Four Books of Kings, which in their original stage must have comprised several hundred pictures, again could not have been a part of a fully illustrated Bible, but must have formed a unit in themselves from the very beginning. The only Septuagint Bible with illustrations we possess, cod. Vat. Reg. gr. 1—and its uniqueness can hardly be due to a fragmentary transmission of documents only—does not speak in favor of the existence of a fully illustrated Bible as archetype. Its miniature cycle distinctly lacks the homogeneity one would expect in a genuine monocycle. Miniatures divided into two or three superimposed strips with narrative scenes alternate with more hieratic full-page miniatures, some of which, as e.g. the Carrying of the Ark (fig. 158), were not even invented for the book to which they are at present attached. This clearly indicates that, as in the case of the Carolingian Bibles, the miniatures were not created for a full Bible, but were taken over as excerpts from the cyclic units of single books thereof.

It must be concluded, then, that the illustration of the Bible began with single books as the basic units and that the illustrated full Bible is a compilation of various excerpted monocycles. Therefore an iconographic analysis of an illustrated Bible must first determine the basic picture units and the distinctions between them. This raises the problem whether the cycle of the Octateuchs is a genuine monocycle, in which case the miniatures were all invented at the same time for this particular type of book, or whether the Octateuch is already composed of several cyclic units. Was the Pentateuch perhaps a basic unit to which the cycles of Joshua, Judges and Ruth were added or did the Genesis illustration constitute a cycle of its own within the Pentateuch? Or, to cite a similar example, did each of the major Prophets start with an independent cycle, or did the illustrations of the four major Prophets together form a monocycle, or was a homogeneous miniature cycle invented for all books of the Prophets, major and minor together? These and similar questions which remain to be investigated demonstrate sufficiently that the limits of a monocycle are not always easily defined.

As a result of the migration of miniatures, a pure monocycle may be enriched by infiltrations from other sources and, thus, described as an *infiltrated monocycle*. A good example is the Nicander manuscript in Paris in which the constellation picture of the Orion (fig. 131) was taken over into the basic monocycle from an Aratus manuscript. A further investigation of this manuscript will reveal that a few mythological scenes, whose source remains to be determined, also found their way into this codex. Another manuscript of this type is the Pseudo-Oppian in Venice, whose intrusions are manifold, some coming from a mythological source (fig. 72), others from the Alexander Romance of Pseudo-Callisthenes (figs. 133-134), and so on. A methodical study of these manuscripts should start first with the separation of all later infiltrations from the basic monocycle as far as the means of pictorial criticism permit. In the Paris Nicander this would mean limitation to the representation of plants with healing power against poisonous bites, of those animals like serpents, scorpions and other insects which cause the bites, and the implements connected with the manufacturing of remedies; and in the Pseudo-Oppian, after a similar extraction of its mythological scenes, there would be left the representations of the various groups of animals and the different techniques of hunting (figs. 61, 82, 122, 123) as the original monocycle. In order to determine the date of the pictorial archetypes of these and similar manuscripts, only the purified cycle can, of course, be used, and one must be careful not to base an argument about the date of the archetype upon an infiltrated miniature.

The intrusions may sometimes be not single miniatures, but a series of pictures coming from the same source, and though they may not constitute a complete cycle in itself, they may form at least a substantial part of it, either a section or an excerpt. An intrusion of this kind may at times be even more extensive in the number of its miniatures than the original monocycle. On occasion even *several* excerpted cycles may be taken over and be so predominant that the basic picture cycle remains only a small fraction of the total illustration. Such cases may be called *polycyclic manuscripts*. The initial step in the methodical study of such iconographically complex manuscripts must be the isolation of the various cycles involved, each of which has to be investigated separately with regard to the specific recension from which it was taken over. Polycyclic manuscripts are by no means rare, and as a matter of fact a considerable number of the most splendid Byzantine *cimelia* can be found among them.

In the Gregory manuscript in Paris, cod. gr. 510, the cycle of miniatures which is made up from the text of the homilies and constitutes the original set, is comparatively small, consisting, as a norm, of no more than one scene for each homily, decorating its title. At the same time not every title scene is made up from the homily text, because in cases where the homily deals e.g. with a Christian feast as the chief theme, a corresponding representation had already been taken over from a Gospel book or a lectionary, thus making it unnecessary for the artist to invent a new picture for the text of the homily. While the manuscript contains nearly two hundred scenes altogether, the number of genuine Gregory scenes is less than the number of homilies, which is forty-five. To this original set of miniatures belong scenes like Gregory and the monks embracing each other at the beginning of the homily *De Pace I*, the funerals of Caesarius, Gorgonia and Basil, the ordination of Gregory, Gregory preaching about the plague of hail,[7] and a few more of a similar character. For the intruded cycles, on the other hand, the various books of the Bible are the main source. From the scene with the sacrifice of Isaac (fig. 173) we have seen already that a Genesis cycle is involved, and if we search through the Gregory we will find that a substantial number of scenes from the same source had migrated into the Paris manuscript, sometimes even in larger sections, as e.g. the illustrations of the youth of Joseph.[8] Other Old Testament scenes are taken from Exodus and Joshua, and a section of scenes illustrating the adventures of Samson, from a Book of Judges.[9] Here again there is the problem of whether the source of the Old Testament scenes mentioned so far was an Octateuch, or whether separate Biblical books were used by the painter of the Gregory. The judgment of Solomon and the Ascension of Elijah[10] point to a Book of Kings, and the picture of Job with his wife and friends[11] to a Book of Job, which was one of the most popular illustrated texts in the Greek world. Quite a few scenes go back ultimately to an illustrated book of the major and minor Prophets, though some of them were copied from a Psalter manuscript as the intermediary step (cf. p. 149 and fig. 137). However, that a Prophet book also was used directly by the Gregory painter is indicated by the Vision of Ezekiel[12] which has no place in the Odes of a Psalter. By far the greatest complement consists of scenes from the life of Christ, most of which were taken, of course, from a Gospel book, but some of the full-size miniatures like the Metamorphosis and the Mission of the Apostles[13] may rather have been taken from a lectionary, in which such full-page pictures of the great feasts are more common. Furthermore, a series of martyrdom scenes is apparently based on a menologion, and a considerable number of pictures representing historical events, mostly from the period of Julian the Apostate, are taken from illustrated chronicles.[14] Here again the issue is complicated by the fact that the source was apparently not one single chronicle but several, which in our opinion were those of Sozomenos, Theodoret and Malalas.[15] Thus, in addition to the miniatures based on the text of the homilies, the cycles of more than ten dif-

---

[7] Omont, *Miniatures des plus anciens manuscrits grecs*, pls. XXIV, XXIII, XXXI, XXV, XXIX.

[8] *Ibid.*, pl. XXVI.   [9] *Ibid.*, pls. XL, LV, XLIX.   [10] *Ibid.*, pls. XXXIX and XLII.

[11] *Ibid.*, pl. XXVII.   [12] *Ibid.*, pl. LVIII.   [13] *Ibid.*, pls. XXVIII and LVI.

[14] *Ibid.*, pls. LII-LIV.

[15] K. Weitzmann, "Illustrations for the Chronicles of Sozomenos, Theodoret and Malalas," *Byzantion*, XVI, 1942-43, pp. 87ff.

ferent manuscripts were excerpted and their miniatures intermingled with genuine homily illustrations, making the Paris Gregory one of the most outstanding polycyclic manuscripts in existence.

A similar analysis of the Cosmas Indicopleustes manuscript in the Vatican, cod. gr. 699—and this applies, of course, also to the other Cosmas manuscripts in Florence and on Mt. Sinai (fig. 192)—reveals that the cycle of miniatures made up from this text itself is confined mainly to the schemes of the universe, while the great bulk of illustrations is once more taken over from the Biblical manuscripts. We have already discussed the miniature of the Sacrifice of Isaac (fig. 129) as a derivation from an Octateuch, and there are many more scenes and figures in the Cosmas which are derived from the same source, as e.g. the Moses as Shepherd, the group of Enoch and Thanatos, and several pictures from Exodus.[16] Other sources of the Cosmas painter were the Books of Kings, from which he copied Elijah's Ascension and the Babylonian Embassy sent to Hezekiah;[17] an illustrated Prophet book (cf. the Daniel picture, fig. 155); and an illustrated copy of the Acts of the Apostles, from which, besides the Conversion of Paul (fig. 130), he took over the Stoning of Stephen.[18] As each of these Biblical cycles may ultimately go back to archetypes of different dates and localities, the history of the polycyclic Cosmas illustration turns out to be very complex.

Furthermore, both groups of the illustrated Greek Psalters are polycyclic manuscripts. In the Psalter in Paris, cod. gr. 139, and other manuscripts of the so-called aristocratic recension the greatest single complement of miniatures has its source in the Books of Kings (figs. 93, 187); the illustrations of the Odes were taken over from the same sources from which the text itself is excerpted, namely an Octateuch (figs. 92, 113), a book of the major and minor Prophets (figs. 139, 157), and finally a Gospels from which the illustrations of the Theotokos, Zacharias and Simeon were taken. Besides these fragmentary cycles from various books of the Bible there are not many miniatures left which could be claimed as being genuine Psalter illustrations. These are confined to the title figure of David and a few scenes which are illustrations from his life, such as his Birth and his Education (figs. 140-141).

In the group of the so-called monastic Psalters with their considerably greater accumulation of miniatures even more cycles are involved. These Psalters, in contrast to the aristocratic group, contain first of all a considerable number of pictures which were made up from the text of the Psalms and illustrate verbally some phrases of the Psalter text. But these original Psalter illustrations are mixed and interwoven with other selective cycles which have penetrated into the Psalter from the outside. The primary sources of

[16] Stornajolo, *Miniature della Topografia Cristiana*, pls. 18, 19, 13, 14, 15, 17, 54.
[17] *Ibid.*, pls. 27 and 55.   [18] *Ibid.*, pl. 47.

these cycles are again an Octateuch, a Book of Kings, a Prophet book and the Gospels, and these sources are even more extensively exploited than in the aristocratic group; in addition, still other books were used, as the Book of Job, the Acts of the Apostles, a menologion, from which Saints, either as isolated figures or in a scenic context, were taken, and an illustrated Cosmas Indicopleustes from which a representation of the antipodes was copied.[19]

More polycyclic manuscripts will have to be investigated from the viewpoint of isolating their various cycles and connecting these with their respective recensions. Like the Paris codex gr. 510, in most illustrated Gregory manuscripts the basic stock of miniatures is enriched by others taken over from different sources. The painter of the Gregory manuscript in Milan (fig. 105) confined himself chiefly to the various books of the Bible, while the painter of the Gregory in the Panteleimon monastery (figs. 135-136) incorporated a whole cycle of mythological scenes the source of which can be determined as the commentary of Pseudo-Nonnus, and so forth. Polycyclic also is the well-known menologion of Basil II in the Vatican. Besides the scenes illustrating the lives of the saints, which constitute the original bulk of the pictures, for the scenes from the life of Christ, as we have already pointed out, a lectionary served as a model (cf. p. 181 and fig. 189); we shall see in the last chapter (p. 203) that a book of the Prophets was also used (figs. 198, 201-205).

Thus it becomes clear that for the study of iconography in illustrated manuscripts the basic unit is neither a single miniature nor a conglomeration of all the miniatures which happen to be accumulated between the two covers of a codex, but the monocycle of scenes which corresponds to a textual unit.

B. THE EFFECT OF THE CONCEPT OF THE CYCLIC UNIT ON STYLISTIC CRITICISM

The analysis of a polycyclic manuscript with regard to its basic units, though primarily an iconographic problem, has inevitably implications for its style. When, in the process of copying, an illuminator, either alone or in collaboration with fellow artists of his scriptorium, has to amalgamate several models in a polycyclic manuscript, he may or may not be able to unify the style of various models, for the power of tradition may be so strong that the style of the models remains distinguishable or may even dominate the personal style of the copyist. This is not, of course, peculiar to manuscript illumination; the problem arises in all media, wherever one or several artists seek to amalgamate different models in a complex monument. Byzan-

---

[19] Tikkanen, *Die Psalterillustration im Mittelalter*, p. 22.

tine book illumination offers a unique occasion for studying this problem in a manuscript, where not only are several models involved but also several artists who have attached their signatures each to his own pictures, so that iconographic units can objectively be confronted with the works of various artists, all of whom belong to the same scriptorium.

This manuscript is the well-known menologion of Basil II, cod. gr. 1613, which was written most probably in the first half of the long reign of this emperor (976-1025) and undoubtedly in the imperial scriptorium of Constantinople.[1] Its 430 miniatures, illustrating the first half of the calendar year from September to February, are executed by eight artists whose names are written on the margin beside each picture. Beginning with the one who apparently headed the scriptorium, their names are as follows: Pantoleon, Michael Blachernites (i.e. from the district of the Blachernae), Georgios, Symeon, Michael ὁ μικρός, Menas, Nestor and Symeon Blachernites. They all work together as a team, each of them painting usually no more than two or three miniatures at a stretch. Five or six in a sequence are exceptions. Kondakoff[2] and other scholars of his generation confine themselves to very general remarks about the style of the various artists, merely giving the preference in quality to one or the other. Venturi[3] was the first to attempt a definition of the style of each artist, and although his characterizations were not fully accepted and have been criticized by later scholars, no attempt has been made so far to revise them. According to Venturi, Pantoleon creates long figures and organizes the highlights so that they follow the motion of the drapery, but at the same time he is not consistent in his means of expression, and makes the figures now strait and geometrical (*strette e geometrizzate*), now jutting out and full (*larghe e piene*). Michael Blachernites is characterized as "*rozzo e materiale, grosso nel segno, largo e tondo, di proporzioni maggiori,*" Georgios as a painter who loves green shadows, round shoulders and prefers motions which make the figures pirouette, and Michael ὁ μικρός as an artist who depicts wry faces. To Menas is ascribed a predilection for classical elements seen in his representation of the Birth of the Virgin.[4] Nestor is supposed to be more individualistic than the others, showing a greater variety of draperies and costumes, while Symeon Blachernites is considered as not very elegant and as seeking forced effects.

The editor of the Vatican facsimile edition, accepting Venturi's stylistic analysis in principle,[5] nevertheless observes rightly that most of the charac-

---

[1] *Il menologio di Basilio II* (Codices e Vaticanis selecti, vol. VIII), Turin 1907.—K. Weitzmann, *Byzantinische Buchmalerei*, pp. 30ff.—S. Der Nersessian, "Remarks on the date of the Menologium and the Psalter written for Basil II," *Byzantion*, XV, 1940-41, pp. 104ff.

[2] *Histoire de l'art byzantin*, vol. II, p. 104.   [3] *Storia dell' arte italiana*, vol. II, p. 458.

[4] *Il menologio*, pl. 22.   [5] *Ibid.*, pp. XVI-XVIII.

terizations are not specific enough. Pantoleon's highlighting is found also in other painters' work and so is Georgios' green shadowing. He realizes that there are difficulties in the definition of the characteristics of the individual artists which are due not so much to Venturi's inadequacy of description as to actual incongruities within the works of each of the eight artists, difficulties which seem to frustrate any attempt to analyze their individual qualities. Moreover, the editor of the facsimile made the observation that several signatures were erased and incorrectly entered by a later scribe. If this is true, it might account for individual cases of incongruity, but hardly would explain the complete lack of stylistic unity within the work of each one of the eight painters.

In the following example, where three standing figures of the painter Pantoleon are shown side by side (figs. 196-198), we wish to point out the difficulties in trying to define this painter's style in such general terms as Venturi employed. Gregory of Nyssa (fig. 196), who holds a book in one hand and blesses with the other, is represented in frontal view and in a posture which indicates a differentiation between the bearing and the free leg. The free leg is marked by a slightly protruding knee and by some folds which gather at the knee, motifs which have little plastic value and which do not interfere with the straight and rigid outlines of the body. The highlights on the episcopal vestments form a two-dimensional pattern and do not aim at any modelling. In the figure of Joseph, who carries the doves as a sacrifice in the Presentation of Christ (fig. 197), Pantoleon seeks very different effects. The drapery lies tight on the body and every device is exploited to bring out its plastic values, as is apparent in the modelling of the upper thigh and particularly of the right arm, which is wrapped in classical fashion in the sling of the himation. At the same time the proportions are slim and the motions agile, even exaggerated as indicated by the small but expressive head which is thrust forward and exposes a long neck. A third figure, that of Zechariah (fig. 198), resembles, as far as the full plasticity and, in particular, the classical motif of the sling are concerned, the Joseph who holds the doves, but at the same time is far less manneristic. His body has more volume and, in spite of a slight swinging of the hip, stands more firmly on the ground. The normal-sized head is placed on a short neck and the proportions of the figure as a whole conform more to a classical canon. Judging by these three figure types, Pantoleon was apparently capable of expressing himself in different styles: sometimes he prefers an ascetic rendering and tries to hide the bodily values, at other times he uses manneristic formulae for forced motion, and then again he favors a plastic and well-proportioned figure style. How are these variations to be explained?

Can we assume that he had a free command of many different ways of expression, and that he applied them on the basis of mere artistic caprice?

Before answering this question, let us first examine from the same viewpoint three more examples by one of Pantoleon's collaborators, the painter Georgios (figs. 199-201). John the Faster, Bishop of Constantinople (fig. 199), is represented as an orans in frontal position, designed in straight outlines which give the figure the appearance of great firmness, and the slight differentiation between the bearing and the free leg does not impair the strong two-dimensional quality of the body, hidden under the garment. In describing this figure more or less the same terms can be used as for Gregory of Nyssa (fig. 196), painted by Pantoleon. In the Baptism of Christ, likewise signed by Georgios, the two disciples behind the baptizing John (fig. 200) are rendered in an entirely different way. Plastic effects are sought by means of a richly folded drapery and the classical formula of the sling is used again with good effect. Characteristic also is the protruding head and the long neckline of the foremost disciple and this reminds us again of the Joseph in the Presentation in the Temple (fig. 197), though on the whole the proportions are not quite so manneristic as in Pantoleon's picture. Moreover, in the figure of Nahum (fig. 201) the classical heritage is not confined to the plastic modelling of the drapery, but made visual by a free motion of the prophet in the surrounding space, a feature which Venturi fittingly describes as *"in moto così che sembra piroettare."* At the same time the prophet's head is firm on his neck and his slightly swinging attitude reminds us of the figure of Zechariah by Pantoleon (fig. 198). It is apparent that the range of possibilities of expressions is not only just as wide as in Pantoleon's work but—what is even more significant—the differentiations are of exactly the same nature, and consequently cannot be considered as the personal achievement of an individual artist.

The solution of the problem of conflicting styles within the *oeuvre* of one and the same artist lies, in our opinion, in the predominance of the style of the various models over the personal style of the menologion painters. Just as Gregory of Nyssa and John the Faster (figs. 196 and 199) have much in common, so have all figures of saints who belong to what might be regarded as the original stock of miniatures in the Vatican codex. Their style has in a long tradition of menologion illustration acquired ascetic qualities which are pictorially expressed by a two-dimensional, bodyless appearance of the saints.

Moreover, all pictures of the Vatican menologion which can be traced back to a lectionary as source, have essential stylistic features in common. Besides the Presentation in the Temple and the Baptism of Christ (figs. 197 and 200) we have mentioned previously the title miniature of Christ receiving the Book of Isaiah (fig. 189) as being copied from a lectionary, and this picture too shows a general classical appearance of its types and the same slightly manneristic elements, such as an inclination for slim bodies and small protruding heads on long necks. The same features can be seen also in the Birth of the Virgin by Menas, the Circumcision by Nestor, the Adoration of the Magi by Symeon Blachernites where we meet once more the long necks and protruding heads[6] and in all the other pictures which are derived from the same source. The lectionary, in the copying of which all the menologion artists participated except one,[7] must have been a manuscript not unlike the so-called Phocas Lectionary in the skevophylakion of Lavra on Mount Athos,[8] a manuscript characteristic for the advanced phase of the Macedonian renaissance. This means that the model which the menologion artists used could have been only slightly earlier than the Vatican codex itself.

Another group of miniatures which show a considerable homogeneity in style are the standing prophets. All the classical elements we saw in the Zechariah of Pantoleon and the Nahum of Georgios (figs. 198 and 201) can be found in the prophet figures of the other painters as well. Symeon, in his miniature of the prophet Haggai (fig. 202), reveals himself as an able artist by emphasizing strongly the distinction between the bearing and the free leg by which plasticity as well as motion of the body are competently expressed, and in this regard he apparently understood very well the essential qualities of the model he had before his eyes. In the manner in which the leg is modelled by the himation and the end of the garment is taken in repeatedly overlapping folds over the left shoulder the copyist tries to outdo a classical artist's devices for plastic rendering. Nestor's prophet Joel (fig. 203) shows perhaps less stress on plastic qualities compared with Haggai, but, being rendered in a less swinging motion, he stands more firmly on the ground and the effective use of the sling makes him appear no less classic. The Hosea of Michael ὁ μικρός (fig. 204) and the figure by Symeon Blachernites who is not accompanied by any text, but shows all the stylistic characteristics of a prophet (fig. 205), displays fundamentally the same classical elements though somewhat less conspicuously. All features which the figures of the prophets have in common can most easily be explained by the use as model of a Prophet book the decoration of which consisted of the frontispieces of the authors at the beginning of each book. This model must have been a renaissance manuscript of a purer classical style, and therefore some-

---

[6] *Ibid.*, pls. 22, 287, 272.

[7] There is no New Testament picture by Michael Blachernites.

[8] K. Weitzmann, "Das Evangeliar im Skevophylakion zu Lawra," *Seminarium Kondakovianum*, VIII, 1936, pp. 83ff.

what earlier than the lectionary, since in none of the prophets do we find the manneristic tendencies of the New Testament scenes. They are all sure in their proportions and have normal-sized heads. The Prophet book in the Vatican, cod. Chis. gr. R. VIII. 54,[9] represents more or less the stylistic phase to which we are inclined to attribute the model of the menologion prophets.

Though having emphasized so strongly the influence which the style of the models exerted upon the eight painters of the Vatican menologion, it should not be overlooked that the miniatures nevertheless possess also stylistic features which are due to the individual capacity of the eight copyists as well as to the influence of the Constantinopolitan style of the period in which the copy was made. A minute study of the original reveals that there are indeed differences in the linear design and in the technical treatment of the highlights which are used by one artist in a more smooth technique and by another in a harder and more geometrical way. Morelli's method of distinguishing different hands in a complex monument is not outruled but the characteristics of the individual copyists are only less conspicuous than those which are due to the conservative attitude towards the models.

The Gregory manuscript in Paris, cod. gr. 510, is another striking example in which various iconographic units have preserved stylistic features of their models. However, the cases of the Vatican menologion and the Gregory cannot be generalized. There are other polycyclic manuscripts in which the style of the different models is more and sometimes even completely amalgamated and unified by the copyists. It is natural that the more often a polycyclic manuscript is copied and the number of intermediary steps increases, the more will the stylistic differences between the various iconographic units gradually disappear. As for the Vatican menologion it seems quite probable that the eight artists themselves used a lectionary, a Prophet book and other manuscripts as direct sources, whereas the painters of later copies of the same menologion recension, like Moscow cod. 183[10] and Baltimore, Walters Art Gallery cod. 521,[11] apparently did not consult personally these sources again, but copied an already established polycyclic manuscript as an entity. This inevitably resulted in a levelling of the distinctions between the various cyclic units. Still another point, which has its bearing on the recognizability of the style of the models in a copy, is the degree of

[9] A. Muñoz, *I codici greci miniati delle minori biblioteche di Roma*, Florence 1905, pls. 1-5.— Weitzmann, *Byzantinische Buchmalerei*, p. 12 and pl. XII, no. 61.

[10] D. K. Tréneff, *Miniatures du ménologe grec du XIe siècle No. 183 de la Bibliothèque Synodale à Moscou*, Moscow 1911.

[11] Ricci-Wilson, *Census of Mss. in the U.S. and Canada*, I, p. 760, no. 16.—F. Halkin, *Analecta Bollandiana*, LVII, 1939, p. 225.

artistic sensibility of the copyist. For instance in the *Sacra Parallela* in Paris, cod. gr. 923, an iconographic compendium which is made up from a great number of models, the differences between the cyclic units are by far less conspicuous than in the Vatican menologion because the copyist simplified the models by reducing whatever their stylistic variety might have been to a limited number of fairly stereotype formulae for the figure style as well as for the architecture. It is in the works of higher quality only that the peculiarities of different models remain recognizable.

Returning once more to our starting point, it is now clear why Venturi's attempts to explain the stylistic differences of the miniatures of the Vatican menologion were bound to fail. His shortcoming lies in the exclusive appli-cation of the Morellian method of distinguishing various *hands*, a method which had been built up and so successfully employed for the Italian Ren-aissance, i.e. a period in which the personal style of the artist is indeed the decisive element in the evaluation of stylistic differences. But in the Middle Ages—and the same is true to a large extent also for the classical period— the style of the model as well as the style of the period in which the copyist works are preponderant and more conspicuous than the comparatively slight oscillations within the limited realm of personal expression. But the style of the model can only be determined after the model itself has been clearly defined in its iconographic character and limits. For this reason the icono-graphic study of a miniature cycle as well as of any classical or mediaeval work of art of great complexity is not only indispensable but has to *precede* stylistic analysis.

INDEX

ADDENDA

ABBREVIATIONS

1. GENERAL

U. Hausmann, *H.Rel.*=*Hellenistische Reliefbecher aus attischen und böotischen Werkstätten. Untersuchungen zur Zeitstellung und Bildüberlieferung*, Stuttgart, 1959.

R. Bianchi-Bandinelli, *Iliad*=*Hellenistic-Byzantine Miniatures of the Iliad* (*Iliad Ambrosiana*), Olten, 1955.

S. Der Nersessian, *D.O. Psalter*="A Psalter and New Testament Manuscript at Dumbarton Oaks," *Dumbarton Oaks Papers*, XIX, 1965, pp. 153ff.

K. M. Phillips, *Pers. and Andr.*="Perseus and Andromeda," in *Am. J. Arch.*, LXXII, 1968, pp. 1ff.

A. Sadurska, *Tab.Il.*=*Les Tables Iliaques*, Warsaw, 1964.

D.O.P.=*Dumbarton Oaks Papers.*

2. WRITINGS OF K. WEITZMANN

Ps.Vatop.="The Psalter Vatopedi 761. Its Place in the Aristocratic Psalter Recension." *Journal of the Walters Art Gallery*, X, 1947, pp. 21-51.

Josh.Roll=*The Joshua Roll. A Work of the Macedonian Renaissance*, Princeton, 1948.

Eur.Scenes="Euripides Scenes in Byzantine Art," *Hesperia*, XVIII, 1949, pp. 159-210.

Narr.Lit.="The Narrative and Liturgical Gospel Illustrations," *New Testament Manuscript Studies*, ed. M. M. Parvis and A. P. Wickgren, Chicago, 1950, pp. 151-174.

Gr.Myth.=*Greek Mythology in Byzantine Art*, Princeton, 1951.

Isl.Sc.Ill.="The Greek Sources of Islamic Scientific Illustrations," *Archaeologica Orientalia in memoriam Ernst Herzfeld*, New York, 1952, pp. 244-266.

Ill.Sept.="Die Illustration der Septuaginta," *Münchner Jahrbuch der bildenden Kunst* III/IV, 1952/53, pp. 96-120.

Kl.Erbe="Das Klassische Erbe in der Kunst Konstantinopels," *Alte und Neue Kunst* III, 1954, pp. 41-59.

Narr.="Narration in Ancient Art," *American Journal of Archaeology*, LXI, 1957. Narration in Early Christendom, pp. 83-91.

A.B.Ill.="Ancient Book Illumination." *Martin Classical Lectures*, XVI, Cambridge, Mass., 1959.

Survival="The Survival of Mythological Representations in Early Christian and Byzantine Art and their Impact on Christian Iconography," *Dumbarton Oaks Papers*, XIV, 1960, pp. 45-68.

G.Gr.="Geistige Grundlagen und Wesen der Makedonischen Renaissance."

Arbeitsgemeinschaft für Forschung des Landes Nordrhein-Westfalen, Heft 107, Köln-Opladen, 1963.

Ill.Fourth Cent.="Book Illustration of the fourth Century. Tradition and Innovation." *Akten des VII. Kongress für Christliche Archäologie*, Trier, 1965, Rome, 1969, pp. 257-281.

ADDENDA

The anonymous reviewer of *Roll and Codex* in the *Times Literary Supplement* (July 22, 1948, p. 480) stressed the pioneer character of this study and enumerated, with even more acumen than the author himself had done, the diversity of scholars on whose fields of interest it touches: "the classical philologist and the modern art historian, the papyrologist and the palaeographer, the literary historian and the ecclesiologist, the archaeologist and the student of iconography." He looked at the study in a certain perspective and placed it in a long line of writings which "tried to hammer out the differences between verbal and representational arts."

The majority of the reviewers were, as might have been expected, anchored in one of the various disciplines mentioned above and tended to isolate certain aspects of the book according to their individual interests. Yet three of them made serious endeavors to touch upon a multiplicity of problems and to do justice to the book as a whole: Katzenellenbogen, Bober, and Quain.

Of the more serious reviews two were written by classical archaeologists:

(1) A. W. Byvanck, in: *Erasmus*, II, 1949, col. 606-610.

(2) K. Schefold, in: *Orient, Hellas und Rom*, Bern, 1949, pp. 420-421.

Three were by Early Christian archaeologists:

(3) G. Bovini, in: *Rivista di Archeologia Cristiana*, XXIII-XXIV, 1947-48, pp. 389-392.

(4) G. de Jerphanion, in: *Orientalia Cristiana Periodica*, XIV, 1948, pp. 360-363.

(5) C. Cecchelli, in: *Doxa*, IV, 1951, pp. 5-10.

As anticipated the greatest number, four, were written by art historians:

(6) H. Bober, in: *Art Bulletin*, XXX, 1948, pp. 284-288.

(7) A. Katzenellenbogen, in: *Speculum*, XXIII, 1948, pp. 513-518.

(8) D. T. Rice, in: *Byzantinoslavica*, XI, 1950, pp. 108-110.

(9) D. Tselos, in: *Gazette des Beaux Arts*, XXXV, 1949, pp. 59-60.

One was written by a theologian:

(10) E. A. Quain, S.J., in: *Traditio*, VI, 1948, pp. 380-385.

Two were written by keepers of Library treasures:

(11) R. W. Hunt, in: *The Journal of Theological Studies*, L, 1949, pp. 126-127.

(12) K. Kup, in *Publishers Weekly*, Nov. 6, 1948, pp. 2011-2013.

Both archaeological reviews objected particularly to the thesis that the Hellenistic period could have created illustrated literary papyri; consequently, they questioned the thesis that the Megarian bowls, or more specifically the so-called Homeric bowls, and the Iliac tablets were reflections of miniature cycles. Although their arguments took different lines Byvanck and Schefold both concluded that the Romans, not the Greeks, invented the illustrated roll. Byvanck's argument hinges on the actual date of the Homeric bowls. Basing his assertion on the studies of C. W. Lunsingh Scheuerleer and other scholars, he contends that this particular group of terracotta relief bowls could not be earlier than the first century B.C. and that consequently the illustrated rolls, if indeed they existed, could likewise not be earlier. The same late date was also defended by Mrs. Quarles van Ufford-Byvanck ("Les Bols Homeriques," in: *Bull. van de Antieke Beschaving*, XXIX, 1954, pp. 34ff.). The most comprehensive and perceptive study of the Homeric bowls, however, was by U. Hausmann in 1959. By examining anew all the arguments, including the evidence from the Athenian agora (H. A. Thompson, "Two Centuries of Hellenistic Pottery," in: *Hesperia* III, 1934, pp. 311ff.) which excludes such a late date for the Megarian bowls, Hausmann arrives at a date around the second and third quarter of the second century B.C. for the subdivided group of the Homeric bowls. Thus it becomes clear that my own date, based on Robert and others, was too early. While accepting Hausmann's date of an origin of more than 100 years later and also his theory that the terracotta bowls are replicas of somewhat earlier metal bowls of the turn from the third to the second century, I still maintain that illustrated papyrus rolls were a creation of the Hellenistic age. An origin of such rolls in the later third century, i.e., prior to the Toreutic models of the terracotta bowls, rather than the turn from the fourth to the third century is more in agreement with the general situation of book collecting and book production in Alexandria under the Ptolemies. At the time of Ptolemy II (285-247) when, under the librarian Zenodotus, the first critical edition (ἔκδοσις) of the Homeric poems was made, rather than at the time of Ptolemy I (323-285) when books were collected under Demetrius of Phaleron, conditions were created for the first time which led to a more organized production and hence to the illustration of books. Hausmann (*op.cit.*, pp. 42, 43) accepts the thesis of the illustrated papyri as the ultimate, though not the immediate, models for the bowls, an opinion I fully share, and it is his regret as an archaeologist that this thesis did not find wider acceptance. He fully realized that illustrated editions of mythological literature have to be assumed as the basis for explaining the extraordinarily rich pictorial transmission from the Hellenistic East to the West.

Schefold admits only illustrated technical treatises for Greek antiquity, explicitly excluding the possibility of illustrated literary texts. Greeks, he argues, were used to listening to their poetry but not to seeing it in pictures. Poetry and representational arts were, according to him, two realms kept strictly separate. Schefold's definition of the Greek mentality seems to me to be an oversimplification which does not take into consideration trends which developed in Hellenistic

Egypt and show a clear deviation from or even contradistinction to fifth and fourth century Attica. When Zenodotus made an "ἔκδοσις" of the Homeric poems they were taken out of the hands of the minstrel or, in the case of dramas, out of the hands of the *chorodidaskalos*, and passed into the hands of the scholar whose interest was in codifying the text. This created a new desire to fix or to freeze the text so that it could no longer be changed. Such a belief in the unchangeability of the written word, coupled with its mass production and wide distribution, had not existed before in the culture of Greece and—to some extent—may even be considered un-Greek. It must be left to the literary historian to decide whether this effort to end textual modifications was due to an influence from the ancient Orient. It must be remembered that Hellenistic Alexandria had been touched by the Oriental literary tradition as the translation of the Septuagint from Hebrew to Greek proves, and this cosmopolitan center had taken over from the Egyptians the principles of the mass production of scrolls with pictures. To illustrate a literary text means to create a fixed iconography, which is a process analogous to the codification of the text; both activities are the expressions of the same mentality. Thus Hellenistic Alexandria had developed something new in the period between Attic Greece and Imperial Rome, and the juxtaposition of Greek and Roman art with regard to our special problems seems to me an over-simplification.

In a later article entitled "Origins of Roman landscape painting" (*Art Bull.*, XLII, 1960, pp. 87ff.), Schefold revised his position when he wrote (p. 88): "There is reason to believe that narrations in pictures with accompanying texts or without text . . . were widespread in the Greek world. We know such narrations from the Homeric bowls and from the so-called Iliac tablets," and (p. 89), "Weitzmann has shown that cyclic narration was a late achievement of Greek art." I, however, still maintain my reservations concerning illustrated rolls with a continuous narrative and a panoramic background in classical antiquity and Schefold's thesis (p. 90) that the yellow frieze of the Casa di Livia harks back to such an illustrated roll. All available evidence points to intercalated column pictures rather than continuous friezes in ancient rolls, and yet such friezes may have existed, after all, without leaving any traces. The main objection is that illustrations in or derived from manuscripts are basically narrative in character and must have an intimate relation to specific text passages, qualities which are not discernible in the yellow frieze. This objection is shared by M. L. Thompson, "Programmatic painting in Antiquity," *Marsyas*, IX, 1960-61, p. 57 note 97.

Among the reviewers in the Early Christian field, Bovini essentially accepts the derivation of the cups and the Iliac tablets from illustrated rolls; he also understands the implication of the adaptation of the codex around A.D. 100 for the history of book illumination. Jerphanion also accepts these tenets, but has one major point of criticism on a different plane. In his discussion of the miniature of the Rossano Gospels depicting the Healing of the Man Born Blind (p. 94 and fig. 76), he argues against the theory that the two phases of this scene were originally column pictures in a two-column text. By pointing at the miniature of the Communion of the Apostles in the same manuscript he assumes rather an influence from monumental art. Jerphanion is surely accurate in deriving the Communion miniature from a monumental source—the lay-out of this scene on two opposite pages is a clear indication that it could not have been invented for a manuscript—and he is quite correct in assuming this source to be one of the holy places of Palestine. The same applies equally to the two full-page miniatures with Pilate for which W. C. Loerke, in my opinion correctly, assumed monumental compositions in the Praetorium, one of the *loca sancta* of Jerusalem, as models ("The Miniatures of the Trial in the Rossano Gospels," *Art Bull.*, XLIII, 1961, pp. 171ff.). This does not mean, however, as Jerphanion seems to think, that *all* miniatures of the Rossano Gospels were derived from monumental art. I rather believe that there is an interpenetration of miniature and monumental painting. As a maxim, it can be stated that purely narrative scenes originate in manuscripts, while liturgical scenes not based on the Gospel text, like the Communion of the Apostles and scenes which imply *loca sancta*, are invented in monumental art. The same distinction applies to other manuscripts, notably the Rabula Gospels. Compositions like the Election of Matthias, the standing Hodegetria, the Crucifixion, the Ascension, the Christ enthroned between Saints, and Pentecost must be derived from monumental compositions—here again the connection with the *loca sancta* of Jerusalem remains to be investigated—whereas the narrative scenes alongside the Canon tables have the character of narrative Gospel scenes in the manuscript tradition. While writing *Roll and Codex*, I was aware of the existence of the reflection of monumental art in book illumination, but since this problem lies outside "a study of the origin and method of text-illustration" it was purposely omitted.

My not having dealt with the influence of monumental art on book illumination is also one of Cecchelli's criticisms, and he points explicitly at the frescoes of the Dura Synagogue. There is, as I believe, indeed a relation between the Dura frescoes and book illumination, but Carl Kraeling in his thorough and penetrating publication of the Synagogue frescoes had already come to the conclusion that at the root of the frescoes were "illustrated manuscripts that existed in antiquity in Jewish circles" (*The Excavations at Dura-Europos*, Final Report VIII, Part I, New Haven, 1956, pp. 392ff.). Thus the relationship is rather the other way around: with the help of the principles as developed in *Roll and Codex* one will be able to understand better the genesis of the Dura frescoes (K.W., *Narr.*, p. 89 and pl. 36,14. I am myself preparing a detailed study on the

Dura Synagogue and Christian Book illumination, which will appear in the same series as the present study). Cecchelli enumerates what he considers to be omissions in *Roll and Codex*, including the treatment of decorative, symbolic, and still other types of representations, whose pertinence to the problem of text illustration I admittedly fail to understand.

The relative extent of miniature cycles in ancient rolls has worried not only the archaeologist but also some art historians like Bober, although the *Imagines* of Varro with their 700 portraits "transmitted to all parts of the earth" clearly proves not only the existence of illustrated papyrus rolls but also their production on a vast scale at a time before the codex was invented. In addition, Bober takes issue with my theory that the column of Trajan is not derived from an ancient picture roll as Birt had believed; he supports his objection with the views of Hamberg (*Studies in Roman Imperial Art*, Copenhagen, 1945, pp. 129ff.) who made a strong case in defense of Birt's theory. All three—Birt, Hamberg, and Bober—see the best proof for the ancient picture roll in the Vatican Joshua Roll, claimed to be a survival of an ancient type of roll illustration. In *Roll and Codex* I could not yet provide the full evidence why the Joshua Roll is not, in my opinion, a direct copy of a classical model but a creation of the Macedonian Renaissance—evidence which was published only a year later in my book *The Joshua Roll*. I may, therefore, be permitted to repeat here briefly this evidence.

(1) The Joshua Roll never contained more than half the book of Joshua, i.e., it had only the chapters I-XII illustrated. The proof is that some of the later Octateuchs, manuscripts which belong to the same recension, have used the Vatican roll as the direct model for the illustration of only these twelve chapters; this is made clear by the adaptation of a rich landscape background and the numerous personifications, both of which are lacking in the rest of the Octateuchs. This means that the Joshua Roll is a special case and it cannot be used in support of the theory that the Bible as a whole was illustrated in the form of picture rolls with continuous friezes.

(2) Iconographically the Joshua Roll is, in the text-critical sense of the word, the most corrupt copy within the Octateuch recension; it is full of deviations from the Biblical text, which can be determined with considerable exactitude by comparison with the Octateuchs. The one closest to the text and, therefore, to the archetype is the Vat. gr. 747, an eleventh century manuscript which—as the only one of the later Octateuchs—is entirely free of the retroactive influence of the Vatican rotulus, i.e., it is without rich background and personifications, elements which are present in the Serglio Cod. 8, Vat. gr. 746, the lost one of Smyrna and Vatopedi 602. In addition, nowhere in Vat. gr. 747 is there an incorrect division of scenes as occurs occasionally in the other Octateuchs in that section which shows the impact of the Vatican Rotulus. Thus there is no reason

to maintain, from the inconographical point of view, that the Vatican Rotulus reflects an Early Christian model very closely.

(3) The Octateuch iconographically most reliable, Vat. gr. 747, is, as said before, without much landscape and practically without personifications and other classical elements with which the Vatican roll abounds. Moreover some of the classical elements as found in the later Octateuchs are precisely the same as those in the famous Paris Psalter gr. 139, i.e., they are intrusions made in the same scriptorium in the tenth century (cf. also K.W., *G.Gr.*, pp. 34ff.).

(4) The iconographical changes in the Rotulus are not mistakes but changes made purposely in order to militarize the pictorial narrative of the Conquest of the Holy Land, the content of the first twelve chapters of the Book of Joshua. These changes reflect the triumphal columns of Constantinople. In other words, no illustrated roll influenced the column of Trajan, but, vice versa, the columns of Theodosius and Arcadius influenced the Joshua Roll.

With the Joshua Roll removed as evidence for ancient book illumination with continuous friezes, the strongest support for the Trajan column's derivation from such a roll can no longer be taken for granted. Yet I wish to reiterate that in *Roll and Codex* (p. 129) I stated that "the continuous method in a papyrus roll for a special purpose should not entirely be excluded, although we have, at the present, no direct evidence for it."

Bober thinks that the establishment of the "papyrus style," i.e., of pictures interspersed within the writing columns, is based on too slender evidence, pointing to the Romance papyrus in Paris (fig. 40) as the only witness. This point of view disregards, however, the evidence of later manuscript copies of literary texts for which one has good reason to assume a classical archetype and which adhere to the principle of the papyrus style, such as the comedies of Terence, the Cynegetica of Oppian (figs. 59, 61) or the romance, *Apollonius of Tyre* (*A.B. Ill.*, p. 103 and fig. 110). Even more important is the newly found Heracles papyrus from Oxyrhynchus (p. 239 and fig. 40a), which frees the Paris Romance papyrus of its splendid isolation.

The searching review of Katzenellenbogen, which accepts most tenets, raises with great sagacity two points which need further clarification. If indeed the Milan Iliad harks back to an early roll, as he agrees, how can the complex battle scenes be explained? Do they not rather contradict the concept of the simple, concise column picture, which is claimed to be typical of the papyrus style? Bianchi-Bandinelli in writing the basic study on the Milan Iliad was very conscious of this problem and tried to solve it in the following way: He assumed the use of several models by the Milan Iliad artists of which only one, characterized by the simple conversation scenes, reaches back into the period of the papyrus rolls. The complex battle scenes, according to him, hark back to a later model when monumental art had begun to exert an influence on the parchment codex, which offered its larger and smoother surfaces for more panel-like pictures. In my review of Bianchi-Bandinelli's book (*Gnomon*, XXIX, 1957, pp. 606ff.), I have tried to modify his viewpoint by pointing out that according to his concept the papyrus model would have been without battle scenes, which does not seem very likely. More probably the original papyrus model included rather simple single-combat pictures which were later, under the impact of monumental art, enriched and enlarged. In other words, I envisage a kind of organic growth within a large miniature cycle rather than an assembly of smaller separate cycles. In a recent study (*Ill.Fourth Cent.*, pp. 261-62 and figs. 7-8) I have tried to demonstrate with a concrete example how a complex battle scene of the Milan Iliad has maintained the still recognizable nucleus of a single-combat group taken from the papyrus tradition.

Related to this problem is another issue raised by Katzenellenbogen. Accepting the four stages of development starting with the column picture and, as the result of gradual expansion, leading to the full-page miniature, he would like to add a fifth stage, the adaptation of monumental compositions, citing the Pentecost miniature of the Rabula codex as an example. As we have seen, Jerphanion also had raised the issue of the impact of monumental painting on book illumination. This affects not only Christian books like the Rossano and the Rabula Gospels, mentioned by the two reviewers, but also the miniatures with classical subjects. Being aware that here a lacuna had to be filled in order fully to comprehend all the possibilities of the codex after its invention, I wrote the brief study "Book Illustrations of the Fourth Century" which, taking up this issue in some detail, was meant to be supplementary to *Roll and Codex*.

There is only one review, that by Quain, which discusses the basic issue of the comparison between text criticism and picture criticism. Because he is a text critic, it was gratifying to notice that basically he accepts the analysis of the agreements and the differences between the methods of the two related and yet in some respects different disciplines. He does not lack a sense of humor when he raises the issue of who makes more errors in the process of transmission, the scribe or the miniaturist.

While some of the reviews, no doubt, brought out some stimulating criticism, it also must have become clear that the more fundamental discussions of the *Roll and Codex* problems are in books like those of Hausmann on the Hellenistic Relief cups and of Bianchi-Bandinelli on the Milan Iliad. The authors of these books were faced with the problem of whether or not *Roll and Codex* provided the basic explanation for the phenomenon of the rather sudden appearance of vast narrative picture cycles and of their "codification," or, in other words, of the establishing of a narrative iconography which is bound by principles similar to those by which text recensions are established.

A review of the reviews seemed appropriate as a starting point for a discussion of some of the more general problems. In the following there will be, with special reference to page and paragraph, brief comments on individual problems and some additional bibliography. It is not, however, my purpose to be complete in the bibliography, but rather to confine myself to the basic publications and to those writings that deal with the monuments from the point of view pertinent to "The Origin and Method of Text Illustration."

p. 11

The problem of classical and Early Christian book illumination has been discussed once more by H. Gerstinger in the *Reallexikon für Antike und Christentum* (s.v. *Buchmalerei*, vol. II, 1954, cols. 733ff.). Although *Roll and Codex* is quoted in the bibliography, the text conspicuously avoids any discussion of its tenets and in dealing with special problems, e.g., the Joshua Roll, the traditional views prevail.

About the same time R. Bianchi-Bandinelli (*Iliad*, pp. 25ff., which is essentially a translation of his "Continuità Ellenistica nella pitture di età medio- e tardo-Romana," *Riv. Ist. Naz. d'Arch. e Storia dell'Arte*, N.S. II, 1953, Rome 1954) sketches the development of classical book illumination and discusses its various problems, giving full consideration to the new approach in *Roll and Codex*, in order to find a place for the various groups of miniatures of the Milan Iliad in late classical painting. The group of miniatures which, according to him, reflects the earliest stage in the development harks back to the period of papyrus illustration. He accepts (p. 28) "the wide diffusion of ancient illustration," but suggests "that these were predominantly of a linear and not a pictorial character," a distinction with which I am in full agreement. He also agrees (p. 29) that the crucial Joshua Roll cannot be adduced as proof for the existence of continuous frieze illustration in rolls of the classical period because "none of the existing illustrated books of a profane character contain elements that could have derived from a continuous roll."

No comprehensive history of ancient book illumination has yet been written which takes into consideration all available evidence, i.e., the literary references, the preserved papyrus fragments, the reflection in other media of contemporary classical art and its survival in mediaeval manuscripts. In a series of printed lectures (*Ancient Book Illumination*), I have tried to supplement *Roll and Codex* by defining at least all the essential categories of texts which, in my opinion, had more or less extensive cycles of illustration in the Hellenistic and Roman periods. I am fully aware, however, that this study does not cover every ancient text which had pictures; the complete story will never be known because of the destruction of all great libraries of antiquity.

ADDENDA

In the years since the appearance of *Ancient Book Illumination* in 1959, new material has come to light which enhances the knowledge of illustrated texts in some specific cases. The first chapter, on the "Scientific and Didactic Treatises," deals chiefly with text categories already known to Bethe, but introducing some new monuments such as an Arabic translation of the *Mechanics* of Heron of Alexandria, and an illustrated *Works and Days* of Hesiod, to mention only two instances. The aim of the second chapter was to show that not only the Homeric epic poems but the whole epic cycle was richly illustrated and that even this is not the whole story of illustrated epic poems. There is evidence that there existed illustrated texts of a *Heracleia*, an *Achilleis*, and epic poems centered around Dionysos, Theseus, and other heroes. The Achilles cycle has recently been enriched by the magnificent silver plate in Augst, Switzerland (R. Laur-Belart, *Der Spätrömische Silberschatz von Kaiseraugst*, 1963). In chapter III the main intention was to demonstrate that not only the dramas of Euripides but also those of Aechylus and Sophocles were illustrated as evidenced by Megarian Bowls. The most unexpected evidence, regarding Menander illustrations, came in the form of a papyrus drawing, which E. Turner interpreted as a figure of Agnoia from the *Perikeiromene* (cf. p. 241); more important still is the excavation of a floor-mosaic on the island of Mytilene with scenes from Menander (cf. p. 237). The general character of these scenes is quite similar to the illustrations in the mediaeval Terence manuscripts (fig. 59).

In chapter IV I have tried to collect material that proves that prose texts were also illustrated on a vast scale. Most widespread, to judge from its reflections in later Byzantine manuscripts, must have been a mythological handbook, presumably the *Bibliotheke* attributed to Apollodorus, for which fuller evidence was presented in my *Greek Mythology in Byzantine Art*. Every type of ancient romance was illustrated with the love-romance being best exemplified by a romance entitled *Apollonius of Tyre*, of which there exists in Budapest a tenth century manuscript fragment. The historical romance is best demonstrated by the Alexander romance. Here our knowledge, based on later miniatures—the earliest ones being in the tenth century Pseudo-Oppian manuscript in Venice—is enhanced by a fourth century floor mosaic from a villa near Baalbeck (M. H. Chéhab, "Mosaiques du Liban," *Bull. du Musée de Beyrouth*, XIV, 1957, pp. 29ff., 49ff.). Further pertinent material may be expected to come from a variety of sources. In speaking about different types of portraits which existed in biographical and related texts I mentioned (*A.B.Ill.*, p. 131) that, aside from individual portraits, there must have existed in antiquity a type of miniature in which a teacher is depicted addressing a group of pupils. The evidence for this is a passage by Hunayn ibn Ishak, the ninth century Nestorian physician and lexicographer at the court of Baghdad, who states that in the old rolls from which he

233

translated the Greek authors into Syriac and Arabic, there appeared at the beginning of each philosopher's book a figure of him sitting on a high seat with his
pupils standing in front of him. In the Library of the Topkapu Sarayi, a thirteenth
century manuscript was recently discovered in which a whole series of classical
authors such as Socrates and Solon are depicted teaching disciples (R. Ettinghausen, *Arab Painting*, Skira 1962, p. 78 and figs. on pp. 76 and 77). Though transformed into the Arabic style they have, as Ettinghausen asserts, a long line of
antecedents and apparently are in the tradition of such illustrated texts as those
described by Hunayn. These few examples must suffice to make clear that we
are still at an early stage of collecting all the material pertinent to a comprehensive
history of ancient book illumination.

p. 13, note 3

After a period of primary interest in stylistic problems, classical archaeology
has recently become interested again in problems of iconographical interpretation,
especially of archaic art, cf. R. Hampe, *Die Gleichnisse Homers und die Bild-
kunst seiner Zeit*, 1952—E. Kunze, "Archaische Schildbänder," *Olympische
Forschungen*, vol. II, Berlin 1950—K. Schefold, *Frühgriechische Sagenbilder*,
Munich 1964—K. F. Johansen, *The Iliad in Early Greek Art*, Copenhagen 1967.

p. 18, §2

As for the revision of the date of the Megarian bowls, cf. my remarks p. 226
about Hausmann's book.

p. 18, fig. 6

Cf. also K.W., *Narr.*, p. 85 and figs. 4-5; *A.B.Ill.*, p. 40 and fig. 45.

p. 19, fig. 8

Cf. also K.W., *A.B.Ill.*, p. 41 and fig. 46—Blanckenhagen, *Narr. Am. Journ.
Arch.*, 61, 1957, p. 81 and pl. 30 fig. 8. The original of this Rondanini tablet,
long considered lost, has been found by Anna Sadurska. She made this plaque,
now in the National Museum of Warsaw, the point of departure for a new study
of the whole group. Sadurska, *Tab.Il.*, p. 61 and pl. XII. This important discovery
has made it possible to replace in the present volume the old line drawing of fig. 8
by a photographic reproduction. Mrs. Sadurska does not accept the derivation of
the Iliac tablets from illustrated rolls, but prefers to see them as derived from
monumental art. The iconographical relation of the Iliac tablets to the miniatures
of the Milan Iliad, one of the strong arguments in favor of a manuscript tradition,
is not discussed.

p. 20, figs. 9-10

K.W., *Eur.Scenes*, p. 186 and pl. 29, 14; *Narr.*, p. 86 and pl. 34, 6; *A.B.Ill.*, pp. 64f. and figs. 73-74. Hausmann, *H.Rel.* pls. 21-24. It is a great merit of Hausmann's book that it reproduces in photographs a great number of Megarian bowls which had hitherto been known only in line drawings. This enables the beholder to judge the style, and it remains to be regretted that not all of the bowls were reproduced in this manner in his book. For iconographical purposes, nevertheless, the drawings remain indispensable.

p. 22, fig. 12

It is not quite correct to say that all the scenes of the Heracles bowl in the Louvre fall within the limits of a single labor. The making of the club and its presentation to Heracles by Athena precedes the first deed whereas the subduing of the Erymanthian Boar is the fifth. Thus only the first two scenes are successive phases of the same episode and truly cyclic. The mixture of scenes from two episodes reveals the principle of an epitome, as occurs frequently in the Megarian bowls. The true cyclic method, with regard to a Heracles poem can now be more convincingly demonstrated by the newly discovered Heracles papyrus (cf. p. 239 and fig. 40a).

p. 24, §1

A Coptic textile in Frankfurt has conflated scenes, confined within a roundel, which are derived from the same cyclic archetype as the Iphigenia sarcophagi (K. Weitzmann, "Eine Darstellung der Euripideischen Iphigenie auf einem koptischen Stoff," in: *Antike Kunst*, VII, 1964, pp. 42ff. and pl. 12). The importance of this textile, besides contributing to the rounding out of the basic cycle, is twofold: (1) it strengthens the idea that the ultimate source is to be sought in the medium of painting and there is some evidence to relate the textile specifically to illustrated Greek manuscripts; (2) it was produced in Egypt, a fact which corroborates the thesis for an Alexandrian origin of the illustrated Euripides.

p. 25

Also scenes parallel to the Alcestis sarcophagi have come to light in the medium of painting. Two scenes from this myth have shown up among the predominantly Christian frescoes in the fourth century catacomb in the Via Latina (A. Ferrua, *Le Pitture della Nuova Catacomba di Via Latina*, Rome 1960, pp. 77-78, and pls. 76 and 79). In the first we see a person dying on a couch surrounded by mourners. Ferrua calls him *Admeto morente*, but, according to Euripides, Alcestis, not Admetus, is dying and is so represented on Roman sarcophagi like that of Cannes (my fig. 18a), which shows a very similar composition. So either the fresco does depict Alcestis—the bad state of preservation of the fresco makes it impossible to judge this on the basis of a photograh—or, if the dying person is indeed a male, he could only be the defunct in the role of Alcestis, although this does not seem very probable. The second scene depicts Heracles bringing Alcestis to the upper world. This scene also has its iconographical parallel in the Cannes sarcophagus (fig. 18c), but without the seated Admetus, who in the fresco is looking expectantly at the returning Alcestis. Here most likely two phases of the story are conflated so that the fresco would have an additional element of the basic cycle. What makes the frescoes of the catacomb in the Via Latina so important is that its largest cycle of representations, namely those from the Old Testament, can, according to an unpublished thesis by Liselotte Breitenbruch, not only be related to miniature painting in general but to very specific miniature recensions. This would greatly strengthen the thesis that the Alcestic cycle also ultimately harks back to an illustrated manuscript, presumably the *Alcestis* of Euripides.

p. 27, §1

For a fuller narrative cycle of the *Bacchae* of Euripides cf. the incised bronze disk of the late classical period in the Villa di Papa Giulio in Rome, K.W., *A.B.Ill.*, p. 77 and fig. 87.

p. 28, §3

In his *Antioch Mosaic Pavements*, D. Levi describes this Antioch floor mosaic at great length (pp. 68ff. and pls. XI-XIII). He agrees with the interpretation of the Hippolytus and Meleager panels, but proposes a different interpretation for the other three. He objects to my identification of the shepherd scene from Euripides' *Troades*, in which Helen approaches Paris (p. 76 note 54), on the ground that this scene does not illustrate an episode performed on the stage but recited by an actor. Yet, it was quite a common procedure to illustrate the content of a typical messenger report along with actual happenings on the stage (K.W., *A.B.Ill.*, pp. 71-72, figs. 78-79, p. 77 and fig. 87). Levi interprets the scene under consideration as Io and Argus, and, after an extensive discussion of vases and Pompeian frescoes, he has to admit that the mosaic artist does not seem to have copied it from an earlier composition. At first glance, the shepherd looked like Paris to him also, and any explanation which can make Paris the hero of this scene seems to me preferable to one where Argus, deviating from any of the known types in the Roman frescoes, is depicted like Paris. Aside from details, the general tenor of the mosaic is hardly that of Argus watching Io. Levi sees the panel I interpreted as Bellerophon rebuffing Stheneboea's advances as a representation of the Farewell of Adonis and he refers to Roman sarcophagi as the closest parallels. Yet while in the sarcophagi Adonis is actually about to leave, the hero in the Antioch mosaic makes no such move but is obviously taking a reticent attitude towards the advancing woman. On the other hand, Levi does point to the fresco in the Casa di Adonide (Reinach, *Repertoire de Peintures*, Paris 1922, 400,1) where Adonis is not turning away, though his languid seated attitude and Aphrodite's unveiling herself offer no further comparisons with our mosaic. As for the central panel, which I had explained as a scene from the *Medea* of Euripedes, Levi, after first weighing the same possibility, decides against it and prefers to identify the woman with Andromache from whom the little Astyanax is being taken away. The parallel he reproduces from a sarcophagus at Woburn Abbey, however, is hardly convincing as being "exactly the same situation." He prefers to leave his identification in quotation marks. Indeed, the ruinous state of the mosaic makes any certainty impossible.

The reason for choosing this Antioch mosaic as an example in *Roll and Codex* was to demonstrate that a single literary source, in this case the tragedies of Euripides, had determined the selection. Today this idea can be illustrated with a much richer and more precise monument: the previously mentioned (p. 233) floor mosaic found around 1962 at Mytilene where a considerable number of square panels are lined up each with a theatrical scene from a Menander play, repeating in each case the poet's name and adding the title of the play (Vanderpool in *Newsletter Am. Journ. Arch.*, LXVI, 1962, p. 390 and pl. III, figs. 9-10 where the scenes from the *Epitrepontes* and the *Messenia* are reproduced. The floor was excavated by the late Charitonides and will be published by Mrs. Lily Kahil).

p. 33, §1

The corroboration of evidence from the silver plates and various Psalter manuscripts of the aristocratic recension in order to achieve a clearer insight into a character of the common archetype has been discussed by K.W., *Ps.Vatop.*, pp. 20ff. Yet this article does not give the full evidence which will be presented by the author in a special study on the David plates.

p. 39, fig. 30-31

For a more recent discussion of the Iliac Tablets figs. 30-31, cf. A. Sadurska, *Tab.Il.*, pp. 24ff., 42ff., and the photographic reproductions on pls. I and IV.

p. 40, fig. 8

The original of the Rondanini plaque, as already mentioned (p. 234), has been rediscovered by A. Sadurska. I am grateful to her for the photograph which is here published by the courtesy of the National Museum in Warsaw.

p. 41, §1

Concerning a somewhat later date for the bowls and how it affects the dating of the archetypal papyrus scrolls, cf. p. 226.

p. 41, §4

For a fuller discussion of the form and arrangement of the 700 portraits in Varro's *Hebdomades*, cf. K.W., *A.B.Ill.*, pp. 116ff.

p. 42, §2

All writings on the Milan Iliad are now superseded by the basic studies of R. Bianchi-Bandinelli, who gave to this manuscript a secure place in the history of late classical painting, first in his study, "Continuità Ellenistica nella pittura di età medio- e tardo-Romana" (*Riv. Ist. Naz. d'Arch. e Storia dell'Arte*, N.S. II, 1953, Rome, 1954) and again in his book *Hellenistic-Byzantine Miniatures of the Iliad*, Olten 1955. He has succeeded in narrowing down the date to between the fifth and sixth centuries, i.e., somewhat later than had hitherto been assumed (third to the fifth centuries). In my opinion there still remains the question as to where the manuscript was made. Bianchi-Bandinelli proposes Constantinople, while I myself prefer Alexandria (K.W. review of Bianchi-Bandinelli's book in *Gnomon* XXIX, 1957, pp. 606-616). The Alexandrian origin is also discussed by K.W., "Observations on the Milan Iliad," *Nederl. Kunsthist. Jaarboek*, V, 1954, pp. 241ff.

p.42, note 8

A color reproduction of the Iliad miniatures, Calderini-Ceriani-Mai, *Ilias Ambrosiana* (Fontes Ambrosiani XXVIII), Olten 1953, reprints the Ceriani text of 1905 unchanged.

p. 43

Bianchi-Bandinelli, *Iliad*, p. 53, in describing the first miniature, distinguishes five episodes instead of my four. In the second scene he takes the shooting Apollo as an entity separate from the group of the slain Achaeans. Admitting that this is possible, I still prefer to see the two pictorial elements as belonging to one scene—in spite of a certain weakness in the spatial relation, which can easily be explained by the arranging of originally separate picture units in a common frame. Bianchi-Bandinelli identifies, quite correctly, the fragmentary figure at the right in the last scene as the speaking Achilles (v. 54-59) and not as Calchas (v. 74ff.). This would mean an even greater density of scenes in the archetype.

On the other hand, in describing the miniature III he distinguishes only two scenes where I assumed three by separating Athena flying to heaven (v. 221ff.) from the assembly into which Achilles throws down the shaft. We deal here, in my opinion, with a typical case of conflation of two originally separate entities into one.

p. 45

I have tried to reconstruct the missing third cup with the scenes from the end of the *Iphigenia at Aulis* (*Eur.Scenes*, pp. 177 and *Gr.Myth.*, pp. 169ff.) out of ancient marble reliefs and Byzantine ivory carvings. On monuments which I believe to be part of the same pictorial recension I found the following four scenes:

(1) Iphigenia reveals to Clytaemnestra, in the presence of Achilles, her decision to die (v. 1374f.). Relief in Termessus

(2) Agamemnon hides his grief (v. 1549). Florence, Ara of Cleomenes

(3) The preparation of the sacrifice (v. 1568f.). Ara of Cleomenes and Veroli-casket in London

(4) Artemis appears with the hind as a substitute for Iphigenia. Relief in Termessus and casket in the Louvre.

Whether the lost third cup, in conformity with the other two, had a fifth scene is impossible to say.

p. 49, §1-2
For both the Vienna mathematical papyrus and the Louvre astronomical papyrus, cf. K.W., *A.B.Ill.*, pp. 5ff. and pl. I, 1-2.

p. 51, §2
Add a papyrus in Leiden. *Aegyptus*, XXXII, 1952, pp. 45ff. with plate.

p. 51, note 12
Add: K.W., *Narr.*, p. 84 and pl. 33, fig. 1—*A.B.Ill.*, p. 100 and pl. LI, fig. 107.

p. 52, §1
The most important illustrated papyrus that came to light after the publication of *Roll and Codex* is the fragment of a Heracles poem (fig. 40a). (*The Oxyrhynchus Papyri*, vol. XXII, 1954, p. 85 no. 2331 and pl. XI, where the drawings are discussed by the writer. Also: *Narr.*, p. 84 and pl. 33, fig. 1—*A.B.Ill.*, p. 53 and pl. XXVI, fig. 59—*Survival*, p. 58, fig. 26. For the text, written in Ionic trimeter, cf. P. Maas, The ΓΡΥΛΛΟΣ Papyrus, in: *Greece and Rome*, II, ser. vol. V no. 2, October 1958, pp. 171ff. and pl. VII. However, I cannot agree with Prof. Maas that these drawings are meant to be caricatures.) There are three drawings intercalated in the text and two of them are within the same writing column. This points to a narrative cycle of even greater density than the one in the comparable romance papyrus in the Louvre (fig. 40). The interpretation of only the second scene is absolutely certain: it represents Heracles killing the Nemean lion. Of the other two scenes, which surely relate to the same πρῶτος ἆθλος, the first depicts, if we are not mistaken, Heracles pursuing the lion into a cave, and the third Heracles holding the lion's skin. The drawings have the character of quick sketches done with a broad brush, using some yellow and green

to enliven the scenes. The system of illustration is in complete accordance with the principles outlined on page 52.

p. 53, §1

Yet, ornamental decoration was not entirely unknown in papyri. In 1938 a papyrus whose text is a schoolbook, written about the third century B.C. and now in the Cairo Museum, was published by O. Guerard-P. Jouguet ("Un livre d'écolier du IIIᵉ siècle avant J.-C. Publication de la Société égyptienne de papyrologie. *Textes et documents*, II, Cairo, 1938.—Its importance for the history of book illumination has been demonstrated by C. Nordenfalk, *The Beginning of Book Decoration*, Essays in honor of Georg Swarzenski, Chicago-Berlin, 1951, pp. 9ff.). Its text columns are placed under arches which Nordenfalk (p. 12) correctly characterizes as "a forerunner of the Canon Tables." It is of great importance that the ornament occurs first in connection with the framing of writing columns, and not of pictures within a writing column. For this no evidence has yet appeared, and thus I believe the point (d) of the principles of the *papyrus style* is still valid.

p. 53, Note 14

Add K.W., *A.B.Ill.*, p. 132 and pl. LXIV, fig. 135—K.W., "Observations on the Cotton Genesis Fragments," *Late Classical and Mediaeval Studies in Honor of A. M. Friend*, Princeton 1955, p. 125 and pl. XVII, 22.

p. 54, note 17

Add K.W., *Narr.*, p. 84 and pl. 33 fig. 3—*A.B.Ill.*, p. 32 and pl. XVII, fig. 37. K. Weitzmann, "Observations on the Milan Iliad," *Nederl. Kunsthist. Jaarboek* V, 1954, p. 246 and fig. 2—A. Carandini, "La Secchia Doria: una 'Storia di Achille' Tardo-Antica," *Studi Miscellanei*, vol. 9, 1965, pp. 17, 18 and pl. IV, fig. 9.

p. 55, note 19

Add Weitzmann, *Nederl.Jaarb.*, p. 249, fig. 3, and the very detailed monograph on this situla by A. Carandini, *op.cit.*

p. 56, note 23

Add K.W., *A.B.Ill.*, p. 110 and pl. LVII, fig. 117.

p. 56, note 1

Four more papyrus drawings which surely once stood within text columns may be added here in order to demonstrate the ever widening range of literary texts which must have existed with illustrations.

(1) (fig. 41a) A fragment from the second century A.D. in Florence, Istituto Papirologico Pap. 1368 (A. Minto, "Frustulum Papyraceum con resti di figurazione dipinta: Hermes Psychopompos (?)," *Aegyptus*, XXXII, 1952, pp. 324ff. —in color; G. Piccardi, *Papiri Greci e Latini*, vol. XIII, fasc. II, 1953, p. 229 and pl. xv, no. 1368—in color; K.W., *A.B.Ill.*, p. 133 and pl. LXIV, fig. 136). It depicts a sketchily designed and colored figure of Hermes Psychopompos who seems to lead a soul into Hades. While Minto suggested that this miniature was inserted into a religious funerary text, in my opinion, a mythological test should also be considered as a possibility. The type of Hermes may be compared with that of the Psychopompos who, in a Vatican mosaic and on on some sarcophagi, leads Alcestis out of the lower world (*A.B.Ill.*, figs. 84-85, where they illustrate a scene from the *Alcestis* of Euripides).

(2) A fragment in the Laurentian Library in Florence, Pap. 847. (V. Bartoletti, *Studi Ital. Fil. Class.*, XXXIV, 1962, pp. 21ff. and pl. XXXIII; K.W., *A.B. Ill.*, p. 83 and fig. 72). The drawing is too fragmentary to determine its subject-matter, whereas the text has been identified as being from the Attic New Comedy and may be from a Menander play. Artistically worthless, this fragment is, nevertheless, of primary importance to prove the existence of illustrated dramas in papyrus scrolls.

(3) Two fragments from Oxyrhynchus nos. 2652 and 2653 belonging to the second or third century (E. G. Turner, "An Illustrated Papyrus of Menander?," *Atti dell' XI Congresso intern. di Papirologia*, 1965, Milan 1966, p. 591 and pl. XIII—The Oxyrhynchus Papyri, XXXII, 1967, p. 180 no. 2652 and pl. XV). The drawings in ink, of no artistic merit, depict a soldier wearing a helmet and a frontally standing woman inscribed Ἄγνοια. "Since Ἄγνοια is the prologue figure in Menander's *Perikeiromene*," to quote Turner, "it is tempting to suppose these sketches might have formed part of an illustrated roll of Menander."

p. 57, §1

Bianchi-Bandinelli ("Schemi iconografici nelle miniature dell' Iliade Ambrosiana," *Accad. Naz. Lincei Rendic.* Ser. VIII, vol. VI, fasc. 11-12, 1951, p. 430, note 1) gives a list of papyrus illustrations in which he mentions three not dealt with in *Roll and Codex*:

    No. 6 Florence P.S.I. 1294 - Ajax with discus
    No. 8 Florence P.S.I. 1295 - Military parade
    No. 9 Florence P.S.I. 920 - Christ in boat on lake Tiberias.

I had purposely left these three out because the large scale of the figures and the lack of writing makes it more than questionable that they ever formed part of an illustrated text. The same applies to two drawings in Berlin—nos. 5004 and 13982—which Bianchi-Bandinelli mentioned in a supplement to the above quoted list (*Iliad* p. 27, note 4).

p. 69, note 58

Add *A.B. Ill.*, p. 114 and pl. LIX, figs. 122-123.

p. 69, §1

At the 1955 meeting of the Archaeological Institute of America in Chicago, a symposium on Narration in Ancient Art under the direction of Carl Kraeling was held. The problem was discussed by a group of experts in the oriental and classical fields (*Am. Journ. Arch.* LXI, 1957, pp. 43ff.). The probabilities of the involvement of illustrated manuscripts, although this was only one and not even the main issue of the papers, was the present author's special interest. All three chapters on the Ancient Orient made it quite clear that narrative friezes existed in all cultures of the Ancient Orient on an even greater scale than in Greek art before the Hellenistic period. Helene Kantor (p. 44) shows how in Egypt, already in the Old Kingdom, funeral scenes were represented in cyclic fashion on the tombs of Saqqara and Giza, and how the principles of narrative friezes develop and change in the Amarna period and reach their zenith in the New Kingdom under Ramses II. Yet she saw no reason, correctly I believe, to connect the funerary and historical reliefs with illustrated papyrus rolls although the latter did exist contemporaneously. The most important group of monuments to be considered in connection with the illustrated roll is, of course, the Book of the Dead. Here Helene Kantor suggests (p. 52) that there is reason to believe that even before the period of the Rameseum papyrus, which I had quoted as the oldest illustrated papyrus in existence belonging to the end of the Middle Kingdom (my fig. 44), illustrated Books of the Dead existed. The evidence is in the vignettes which are depicted on the interior of coffins of the First Intermediate Period and the Middle Kingdom and which are considered to be reflections of illustrated papyri. She also discusses the illustrated satirical animal fables, and makes a welcome contribution to the continuation of their iconography by pointing (p. 54) to a ninth century Coptic painting showing a cat and three mice.

In the field of Babylonian art, Ann Perkins (pp. 54ff.) demonstrates how the "standard" of Ur of the middle of the third millennium B.C. shows progressive action in six registers, and how in some seals of the Akkadian period "for the first time Babylonian literature comes to the aid in interpretation," and how in the stela of Ur-Nammu from the twenty-first century B.C. a frieze principle had developed that comes "closest to Wickhoff's continuous" style. Yet she sees no reason to postulate at any point the existence of illustrated scrolls on which any of these representations may depend.

In his study of *Narration in Anatolian, Syrian and Assyrian Art*, Hans Güterbock (pp. 62ff.), especially in discussing the narrative principles of the extensive Assyrian reliefs, comes to the conclusion that in spite of the addition of inscriptions, they cannot be called text illustrations in the proper sense. A "fully developed continuous style is only found in the lion hunts of Ashurbanipal and the Phoenician bowls, both of the seventh century." These are the silver bowls which I had mentioned (pp. 36, 60) as forerunners of the Megarian bowls as far as their system of illustration is concerned. Güterbock makes it quite clear that within Assyrian art they are rather exceptional. Whether they really could have depended on illustrated rolls must be left open; if it were the case, the ultimate source might well have been Egyptian. Of special interest is Güterbock's discussion of the problem of whether cuneiform tablets had illustrations. There are, he asserts, tablets with signs of the zodiac and other sketches, but "such elaborate examples of real text illustrations come from the Hellenistic period."

This canvassing of the monuments of the Ancient Orient by these three experts makes it quite clear that there is no real evidence for illustrated texts in the strict sense of the word outside of Egypt, and that even in Egypt not all narrative works of art can be associated with the tradition of papyrus scrolls but only a limited group of monuments which illustrate the Book of the Dead and other ritual texts. Thus the restriction to Egyptian papyri in *Roll and Codex* appears fully justified as well as the thesis that the place of birth of Greek text illustration was Alexandria, the metropolis that was wide open to influences from Egypt.

George Hanfmann in his chapter on "Narration in Greek Art," on p. 73 deals with the "cyclic" method and defines it for the period he deals with somewhat differently from the way I used the term in *Roll and Codex*. In a sequence of metopes, e.g., the cyclic method, according to him, "divides the life of a hero into a succession of uniform isolated deeds." This is almost the opposite from the true narrative method used in the subsequent period in which the illustrator did everything to avoid isolation of scenes and to lead the eye quickly from one scene to the next for the sake of creating the impression of continuity. In order to accelerate this movement, the artist splits off one isolated episode into several phases. Thus the method as employed in the metopes was in *Roll and Codex* considered as a "preliminary step" leading to the fully developed cyclic method. Hanfmann's sensible analysis shows clearly that, compared with the later centuries, Archaic and High Classical art had a different focus with regard to narration in the representational arts. Moreover, his remark that "the Egyptians and Assyrians had applied themselves more attentively to the chronological portrayal of historic events" implies that the Hellenistic Greeks had more to learn about the method of storytelling in pictures from the Ancient Orient, especially Egypt, than from their own forebears.

Peter von Blanckenhagen's contribution to the "Narration in Hellenistic and Roman Art" (pp. 78ff.) centers on the continuous narrative which had been defined in *Roll and Codex* as one of several possibilities for the cyclic method.

Dealing chiefly with monumental friezes and single panels beginning with the Telephos frieze and focusing on Roman and Pompeian wall painting, he has clearly demonstrated that there existed, independent of the illustrated roll, a vast realm of monuments employing the continuous narrative. At the same time he does accept the derivation of the Iliac tablets from book illumination and he analyzes very correctly, I believe, the tablet with the Circe adventure (his fig. 8, my fig. 8) as a series of miniature scenes to which the Roman sculptor added the architecture. Blanckenhagen's essay has greatly contributed to a clear definition of where in Hellenistic-Roman narrative works of art book illumination was involved and where it was not.

The author's own contribution on "Narration in Early Christendom" (pp. 83ff.) starts out by summarizing *Roll and Codex* and then goes beyond it in certain aspects of the "extended" or "expanded cyclic method of narration" in Early Christian book illumination. Here I postulated, on the basis of the frescoes of the Dura Synagogue, the existence of Jewish book illumination. Especially in the Ezekiel panel the cyclic method typical for the illustrated book is employed, not slavishly but with certain alterations due to the change of the medium. But the value of the Dura frescoes lies not only in the fact that they are remnants of vast narrative biblical cycles prior to the Christians; they show that the Christians, as I demonstrated in the case of the scene of Jacob's Blessing, took over much of their iconography from the Jewish illustrated biblical texts. Richly illustrated books of the Old Testament thus form a link between classical and Christian book illumination.

The result of the symposium is a sharper definition of what constitutes narrative art at various periods and in various cultures, and it demonstrated clearly how little pre-Hellenistic monuments can be related to that kind of illustrated papyrus roll which we know existed in Egypt and exerted a decisive influence on the Hellenistic and Roman cultures.

p.70, §1

Much useful information about the gradual transition from roll to codex between the second and fourth centuries can be found in the very penetrating study of Colin H. Roberts, *The Codex* (*Proceed. Brit. Acad.*, XL, 1955, pp. 169ff.). He gives (p. 184) statistical evidence which makes it very clear that in the second century the codex was still a great rarity (2.31 per cent of the preserved documents of writing) and that it gained predominance (73.95 per cent) only in the fourth century. Roberts also discusses in detail (p. 191) the significance of the codex for the history of the Christian Canon and Christian writing in general. Obviously, the codex was used as early by the Christians as by the pagans.

p. 71, note 64

The Bern Physiologus has now appeared in a color facsimile by Christoph von Steiger and Otto Homburger, *Physiologus Bernensis*, Basel 1964. The archetype of the Physiologus text is here attributed to the turn from the second to the third century. Cf., p. 36, the description of the serpent miniature.

p. 71, note 65

For the critical text edition cf. F. Sbordone, *Physiologus*, Milan 1936.

p. 71, §2

It must be made clear that in the Paris Dioscurides the plant pictures are not only placed in open spaces at the *right* of the columns on recto pages, but are in the same position also on the verso pages (examples fols. 2^v and 5^v in K. Weitzmann, *Die Byzantinische Buchmalerei des 9. and 10. Jahrh.*, Berlin 1935, pl. LXXXVIII, 555-556). Thus we deal here, indeed, with the column principle (cf. H. Bober, *Art Bull.*, xxx, 1948, p. 287).

p. 72, §2

The beginning of the illustrations of constellation pictures in manuscripts has recently been discussed at length by Kyle M. Phillips, Jr., in *Pers. and Andr.*, an article which has broader implications for constellation pictures in general.

p. 73, §2

Cf. *A.B.Ill.*, pp. 86ff. and fig. 95.

p. 74, §2

For the principles of illustration in various treatises by Heron, including an Arabic manuscript of his *Mechanics*, cf. K.W., *Isl.Sc.Ill.*, pp. 245ff. and pl. XXXIII, 1-3—*A.B.Ill.*, p. 7ff. and pls. II, 4-IV, 9.

p. 75, §1

In my opinion the archetype of the *Cynegetica* contained only those pictures which illustrate the text precisely and have to do with animals and hunting. The numerous, chiefly mythological, miniatures which are based on other texts have been taken over from them, apparently for the first time in a manuscript of the Macedonian Renaissance. Cf. *Gr.Myth.*, pp. 141ff., where the sources are listed as Apollodorus' *Bibliotheke*, Pseudo-Kallisthenes' Alexander romance, *Iliad*, Euripidean tragedies, Dionysiac and bucolic poetry.

pp. 78, 80, 82

The reconstruction drawings of an illustrated *Odyssey*, Euripides, and *Iliad* have been repeated in *Ill.Sept.*, p. 115 and fig. 6—*Narr.*, p. 85 and ill. A—*A.B.*

Ill., p. 41 and fig. A; p. 67 and fig. B. For an additional reconstruction of a section of an illustrated *Little Iliad* cf. *Ill. Fourth Cent.*, p. 261 and fig. 8.

p. 83, §1
A typical case of flaking as the result of rolling of the parchment is the chryso-bul of Adronicus II Palaeologus in the Byzantine Museum in Athens; the head of Christ is completely gone. Cf. S. P. Lampros, Λεύκωμα Βυζαντινῶν Αὐτοκρατόρων, Athens 1930, pl. 79.

p. 83, note 2
Add: J. de Wit, *Die Miniaturen des Vergilius Vaticanus*, Amsterdam 1959.

p. 88, §3
For a detailed analysis of this Pseudo-Oppian miniature cf. *Eur.Scenes*, pp. 160ff. and pls. 25-26. Here all scenes are derived from illustrations of Euripidean tragedies, i.e., Theseus lifting the rock from the *Aegeus*, the slaying of Learchus by his father Athamas in a fit of madness (the inscriptions "Theseus" and "Atha-mas" are wrongly placed), and Themisto's killing of her own babe in the dark-ness of the bedchamber from the *Ino*, the boiling first of the ram and then of the cut-up Pelias by his own daughters in two successive phases from the *Peliades*, and finally the killing of her two children by Medea from the *Medea*. This miniature proves that illustrated Euripidean tragedies, some in addition to those known today, still existed and were available to the Pseudo-Oppian Illustrator in the Middle Byzantine period. Cf. also *Gr.Myth.*, pp. 131ff. and pl. XLIV, 159-163—*A.B.Ill.*, p. 78 and pl. XLI, fig. 88—*G.Gr.*, p. 20 and fig. 14.

p. 90
The reconstruction drawing has been repeated in *Ill.Sept.*, p. 115 and fig. A—*Narr.*, p. 87 and ill. B.

p. 94, note 26
A new facsimile in full color is now appearing in fascicules, of which three have so far come out, published by the Akademische Druck and Verlagsanstalt, Graz-Austria.

p. 95, §3
The nature of the Wolfenbüttel pattern book and the important role it played in transmitting Byzantine models to the Latin West has been expounded in sev-eral studies. K. Weitzmann, "Zur byzantinischen Quelle des Wolfenbüttler Mus-terbuches," *Festschrift Hans R. Hahnloser*, Stuttgart 1961, pp. 223ff.—*G.Gr.*, p. 49 and figs. 49-50—K.W., "Icon Painting in the Crusader Kingdom," *D.O.P.*, XX, 1966, pp. 75f. and figs. 53-55.

p. 96, §1
For further pages published of the unique cod. Vat. gr. 1087 cf. *Kl.Erbe*, p. 58 and fig. 25; Kyle M. Phillips, *Pers. and Andr.*, p. 19 and figs. 55, 59, 60; Prof. Ihor Ševčenko (oral communication) dates the manuscript in the middle of the fourteenth century.

p. 97, §4
The statement that the Milan Iliad is the earliest existing codex fragment with pictures must, in the light of Bianchi-Bandinelli's proof of a later date, be altered (the problem remains whether it is fifth or sixth century, cf. p. 238). Both the Vatican Virgil cod. lat. 3225 and the Quedlinburg Itala in Berlin, cod. theol. lat. fol. 485, dating around the turn from the fourth to the fifth centuries, are surely older.

p. 98, §2
Cf. *Gr. Myth.*, p. 115 and pl. xxxvi, 129. The wavering attitude of the illuminator is clearly shown by his framing of five consecutive miniatures depicting mythological hunters (including the two reproduced in our fig. 82), and then leaving a sixth with Orion and Atalanta hunting boars without a frame (*ibid.* pl. xxxv, 127 - xxxvii, 131).

p. 99, §1
A further study of the Octateuchs proved that the cod. Vat. gr. 747 is the one closest to the archetype and represents nearly always the better version (*Josh.Roll*, pp. 31ff.). Thus it seems likely that also in the present case, the lack of a dividing line between the two scenes is more in harmony with the earliest stage of the development; that in a second stage, as represented by the Smyrna Octateuch (D. C. Hesseling, *Miniatures de l'Octateuque grec de Smyrne*, Leiden 1909, pl. 69, fig. 227) and by the cod. Vat. gr. 746, a simple dividing line was added; and that only in a third stage, as seen in the Seraglio Octateuch and the latest one in Vatopedi, the two scenes became thoroughly separated and independently framed.

p. 99, §2
Cf. the color reproduction of the Bern miniature (v. Steiger-Homburger, *op.cit.*, fol. 7ᵛ).

p. 99, line 15
Instead of "in the earliest illustrated codex in existence" read "in one of the earliest...." (cf. the remark about the date of the Milan *Iliad*, p. 238).

p. 100, §1

Boeckler (note 42) argued that the miniatures of the Quedlinburg Itala were the first formulations of the subject they depict and he saw a proof of his theory in the precepts for the painter written on the empty parchment before it was painted over. In my opinion these precepts are sufficiently explained by a process of transforming column pictures of the papyrus tradition into panel-like pictures, a process which made rearrangement of the compositions necessary (cf. *Ill.Fourth Cent.*, pp. 263-64 and fig. 10). Similarly J. De Wit (*Die Miniaturen des Vergilius Vaticanus*, Amsterdam 1959) made the claims that the miniatures of the Vatican Virgil were original creations and that there never was another Virgil manuscript with the same cycle of illustrations. This opinion has been challenged, rightly I believe, by H. Buchthal in his review of De Wit's book (*Art Bull.*, XLV, 1963, pp. 372f.) and again in "A Note on the Miniatures of the Vatican Virgil Manuscript," *Mélanges Eugene Tisserant*, vol. VI [Studi e Testi 236], Vatican, 1964, pp. 167f.). As a concrete case in point, I have tried to demonstrate that the miniature with the wooden horse in the Vatican Virgil (*A.B.Ill.*, p. 60 and pl. XXXI, fig. 68) is taken over from an illustrated *Little Iliad* (*ibid.* pl. XXIII, fig. 54).

p. 100, §3

The problem of the impact of monumental painting on miniature painting after the invention of the codex has been more fully treated in *Ill.FourthCent.*, not only for scenic illustrations but also for pictures of constellations (p. 259 and fig. 3-4) and of the months (p. 265 and figs. 11 and 13).

p. 100, note 55

Add *A.B.Ill.*, p. 21 and fig. 25.

p. 104, §1

A. M. Friend's study on the Evangelist portraits was left at his death only in lecture form; I intend to publish it posthumously in this series, *Studies in Manuscript Illumination*. In the meantime I have tried to fill this lacuna in a sketchy way, not confining myself strictly to the Evangelist portraits, in *A.B.Ill.*, pp. 116ff. and pls. LX, 124-LXIV, 134—*G.Gr.*, pp. 45ff. and figs. 45-51—*Ill.FourthCent.*, pp. 271ff. and pls. CXLVI-CL.

p. 105, §1

The process of transformation of a narrative Gospel cycle into the full-page miniatures of a lectionary has been discussed at some length in *Narr. Lit.*, pp. 151ff.

p. 106, §2

De Wit, *op.cit.*, pp. 67-68, explains the strange building above the temple as a type of Baths, basing this identification on a Roman wall painting from the Esquiline, now lost, but known from Bartoli's engraving. Cf. Hülsen in *Röm. Mitt.*, XI, 1896, p. 213 and pl. IV-VII, esp. IV no. 4. This identification makes the building all the more incongruous in the Virgil miniature.

p. 107, §1

Not only in the Octateuchs, but also in several Psalter miniatures of the so-called aristocratic group the Crossing of the Red Sea is depicted in frieze form, as e.g., in the Psalter Vatopedi 761 from the eleventh century (*Ps.Vatop.*, p. 27 and fig. 11, cf. with fig. 23). This means that the rearrangement as seen in the Paris Psalter miniature was not made in the Psalter archetype, but at a later time within the development of this picture recension.

p. 107, note 67

Add *Ill.Sept.*, p. 110 and fig. 13.

p. 108, §2

For a discussion of the relation between the healing scenes and the framing arches cf. also: *Kl.Erbe*, p. 52 and pl. VII, 13—*A.B.Ill.*, p. 21 and pl. XIII, fig. 26—*G.Gr.*, p. 25 and fig. 20. Here, on fig. 21, is reproduced the Canon table of an Aethiopic Gospel book which surely is a close copy of a Byzantine model and shows the greatest similarity to the arches of the Apollonius manuscript.

p.110, §1

A.B.Ill., p. 86 and fig. 93, where the miniature is juxtaposed with a frameless picture of a mask of the Euripidean *Andromeda* from a Pompeian fresco. Cf. also the bronze disk in the Villa Giulia (*ibid.*, p. 76 and fig. 87) where in the lower left and right corners masks are depicted just as in the frontispiece of a manuscript.

p. 111, note 79

Add H. Schiel, *Codex Egberti der Stadtbibliothek Trier*, Basel 1960 (color facsimile).

p. 111, note 80

The codex Pantocrator 49 was acquired by the Dumbarton Oaks Collection in Washington, D.C. in 1962. Cf. S. Der Nersessian, *D.O.Psalter*, pp. 155ff.

p. 115, §3

A detailed study of all the miniature cycles involved in the illustration of the codex Paris gr. 923 is being prepared by the author as another study in this series,

Studies in Manuscript Illumination. The importance of this manuscript for the history of the Bible illustrations has been emphasized repeatedly. Cf. *Ps.Vatop.*, pp. 40ff. and figs. 25-26, and 29—*Ill.Sept.*, pp. 106 passim and figs. 8-9, 14, 16-17.—*A.B.Ill.*, p. 119 and pl. LXI, fig. 127.

p. 116, note 16

Add: C. Cecchelli—I. Furlani—M. Salmi, *The Rabbula Gospels*, Facsimile edition of the miniatures of the Syriac Manuscript Plut. 1, 56 in the Medicaean-Laurentian Library, Olten 1959 (in color).

p. 120, §1

In discussing the date when commentaries were first added to a text, I admit that I have relied too heavily on the authority of White and not given enough consideration to the study of G. Zuntz in *Zyzantion XIV*. In a detailed letter of April 25, 1951, in which he takes issue with my presentation of the problem, Zuntz reinforces his previous arguments with regard to a late origin of the combination of text and commentary. He correctly points out that the New York Papyrus (fig. 106) is a unique piece and too fragmentary to provide sufficient evidence for drawing far-reaching conclusions with regard to written commentaries between text columns. It indeed weighs in his favor that among the thousands of papyri known today no other example has come to light which would more clearly show the postulated combination of text and commentary. If, therefore, the New York Papyrus must be discarded as evidence, then Zuntz is right that the earliest extant documents are Christian manuscripts of which the Codex Zacynthius and the Job of Patmos cod. 171 are the earliest.

Since the former, dated by Hatch in the sixth century but by others like Zuntz around 800, is surely earlier than the latter, the precise date of the Patmos codex is of no consequence with regard to the commentary problem. Yet I may add that having had a chance to reexamine the Patmos Job during the Byzantine Exhibition in Athens in 1964, I have myself begun to doubt the seventh-eighth century date proposed in my various writings, while at the same time I am not prepared to date it as late as the end of the ninth or the first half of the tenth century as Zuntz proposes. I believe that the proposition pre- or post-iconoclastic is a fallacy since there is good reason to believe that the illustration of manuscripts (as well as the production of icons) continued during iconoclasm in those Near Eastern Orthodox countries which were not under the domination of the Byzantine emperor. The Patmos Job may well belong in the iconoclastic period.

Thus our present evidence points to a Christian origin for the combining of text and commentaries on the same page and at a time before A.D. 800. Since the earliest manuscripts with commentary illustrations—the so-called monastic Psalters—are not earlier than the ninth century, the above-stated controversy has no direct bearing on our basic problem of the various principles of illustration.

p. 121, note 33
The pictures of the Pantocrator Psalter have been fully published and described by S. Dufresne, *L'Illustration des Psautiers Grecs du Moyen Âge Pantocrator 61, Paris Grec 20, British Museum 40731*, Paris 1966.

p. 122, note 35
The chief miniature dealing with iconoclasm is that of the Council of 815 in the Pantocrator Psalter. Its accompanying, faded text which provides the explanation for the miniature has been read under ultraviolet light and been published by Ihor Ševčenko, "The Anti-iconoclastic poem in the Pantocrator Psalter," *Cah.Arch.*, xv, 1965, pp. 39ff., figs. 1-2.

p. 122, note 36
Add: There is, however, the Cairo school-book of the third century B.C. with ornamental arches. Cf. p. 210, addenda to p. 53.

p. 126, note 9
The tenth century date of the Joshua Roll has found wider acceptance in the last twenty years. Cf. esp. V. Lazarev, who in his *Istoriia vïzantiiskoi zhivopisï*, Moscow, 1947 (p. 55 and pls. IV, 18-20) still dated it in the seventh century but accepted the tenth century date in his revised Italian edition (*Storiea della pittura byzantina*, Turin, 1967, p. 138 and figs. 104-106).

p. 126, note 13
There is still a third case concerning a similar situation. The ciborium columns of San Marco in Venice have always been considered to be of Early Christian origin, whereas the Latin inscriptions on the dividing bands, which because of their paleography must be mediaeval, were assumed to have been added later. Here too the implication was that areas reserved for inscriptions were left empty for centuries until they were properly filled. Then E. Weigand ("Zur Datierung der Ciboriumsäulen von San Marco in Venedig," *Atti del V Congresso Internaz. di Studi Bizantini II* [Studi Bizantini e Neoellenici, vol. 6], Rome 1940, pp. 440ff.) and E. Lucchesi-Palli (*Die Passions-und Endszenen Christi auf der Ciboriumsäule von San Marco in Venedig*, Prague 1942) brought forth convincing arguments that the reliefs and the instructions are contemporary and must be dated around the middle of the thirteenth century.

p. 129, §3
For a full treatment of the author's explanation of the Vatican Rotulus cf. *Josh.Roll* and the summary remarks on p. 229.

p. 134, §2
John R. Martin ("An Early Illustration of *The Sayings of the Fathers*," *Art Bull.*, xxxii, 1950, pp. 291ff.) published a few miniatures of the cod. Paris. gr. 923 which prove that the *Apophthegmata patrum* existed with illustrations, thus adding another non-biblical text whose illustrations were excerpted by the illustrator of the *Sacra Parallela*.

p. 136, note 8
Add: *A.B.Ill.*, p. 19 and pl. xi, fig. 23.

p. 138, §1
For the classical sources of the miniatures of the *Marvels of the East* cf. also *A.B.Ill.*, p. 17-18 and fig. 21.

p. 138, note 20
Add: F. Sbordone, *Physiologus*, Milan 1936.

p. 140
H. Menhardt in a detailed study "Die Bilder der Millstätter Genesis und ihre Verwandten, Beiträge zur älteren europäischen Kulturgeschichte," *Festschrift R. Egger*, vol. iii, Klagenfurt 1954, pp. 248ff.) tried to connect iconographically the illustrations of the Millstatt Genesis with the Byzantine Octateuchs, but was contradicted by Hella Voss in her monograph (*Studien zur illustrierten Millstätter Genesis, Münchener Texte und Untersuchungen zur Deutschen Literatur des Mittelalters*, vol. iv, Munich 1962) who, by strongly reinforced arguments, proved convincingly that the Millstatt illustrations belong indeed to the same recension as the Cotton Genesis. Further proof may be found in two articles published in *Late Classical and Mediaeval Studies in Honor of A. M. Friend, Jr.*, Princeton 1955, one by K. Weitzmann, "Observations on the Cotton Genesis Fragments," pp. 121ff. and pl. xvi, 13-14, the other by R. B. Green, "The Adam and Eve Cycle in the *Hortus Deliciarum*," pp. 342ff. and figs. 4-13.

p. 142, note 35
Ainalov's book has, in the meantime, appeared in an English translation by E. and G. Sobolevitch, edited by C. Mango under the title *The Hellenistic Origins of Byzantine Art*, New Brunswick 1961.

p. 145, §2

For early illustrations of the Alexander romance in a miniature of Pseudo-Nonnus, *Oratio in Sancta Lumina*, in a whole series of miniatures in Pseudo-Oppian's *Cynegetica* and presumably in some Middle Byzantine ivories cf. *Gr. Myth.*, pp. 59ff., 85, and figs. 70-72; pp. 102ff., 144, and figs. 108-109; pp. 186ff. and figs. 250-253. Cf. also *A.B.Ill.*, pp. 105ff. and pl. LV, figs. 112-113. The earliest monument to be connected with the Pseudo-Kallisthenes is a fourth-fifth century mosaic recently found at Soueidie near Baalbeck (M. H. Chéhab, "Mosaïques du Liban," in: *Bull. Musée de Beyrouth* XIV, 1958, pp. 29ff. and vol. XV, 1959, pls. XXI-XXV). Its connection with the Alexander romance was fully recognized by D. J. A. Ross ("Olympias and the Serpent," *Journal Warburg and Courtauld Inst.* XXVI, 1963, pp. 1ff.), a scholar from whom we can expect a full treatment of the illustrated text of Pseudo-Kallisthenes.

p. 146, §1

If the interpretation of one of the so-called Iliac tablets as a scene from the Pseudo-Kallisthenes is correct, as proposed by Garrucci, then one would have to conclude that some text with Alexander stories, prior to the Pseudo-Kallisthenes, must already have had illustrations. *Gr.Myth.*, p. 105 and figs. 110-111; *A.B.Ill.*, p. 107 and pl. LV, fig. 114.

p. 147, §1

For a full treatment of the illustrations of the Pseudo-Nonnus text, cf. *Gr. Myth.*, pp. 6ff. I have tried to demonstrate that the main, though not the exclusive, source of its mythological scenes was an illustrated *Bibliotheke*, attributed to Apollodorus.

p. 149, §2

In a special study about the relationship of pictures and text in the cod. Paris 510, S. Der Nersessian ("The Illustrations of the Homilies of Gregory of Nazianzus, Paris gr. 510: A study of the connections between text and images," *D.O.P.*, XVI, 1962, pp. 195ff.) has come to the same conclusion with regard to our miniature (p. 218), namely, that it must be in the wrong place.

p. 151, §5

The idea that the illustrated Books of Kings was the source for the David cycle of aristocratic Psalter has been expounded at greater length, although not yet fully, in *Ps.Vatop.*, pp. 37ff. and *Ill.Sept.*, p. 110.

p. 152, §1

The Birth of David is not the only instance where a New Testament birth scene supplied the compositional scheme for an Old Testament one. In the Greek Octateuchs—like the twelfth century one in the Seraglio—the Birth of Moses in the manner of the Birth of the Virgin or of John the Baptist replaces a miniature of Pharaoh ordering the killing of the Jewish offspring as it is depicted in the Octateuch Vat. gr. 747, the one which is the closest to the archetype (K. Weitzmann, "The Octateuch of the Seraglio and the history of its picture recension," *Actes du X. Congrès Internat. d'Études Byzantines*, Istanbul, 1957, pp. 184-185 and pl. XL, fig. 5 and 6, where, unfortunately, the captions have been transposed). We are dealing here with a phenomenon, widespread in the Middle Byzantine period, to "Christianize" the Old Testament picture cycle.

p. 152, note 65
Add: P. A. Underwood, *The Kariye Djami*, New York, 1966, vol. I, pp. 71ff. and vol. II, pls. 114-115.

p. 155, §2
De Wit (*Die Miniaturen des Vergilius Vaticanus*, 1959, pp. 95f.) likewise derives the Neptune figure from a statuary type and assumes the same for the Venus figure, which he identifies as the type of the Venus Genetrix.

p. 157, §1
For the pictorial tradition of an ancient philosopher teaching pupils cf. the remarks on pp. 233-234.

p. 158, §1
For further illustrations of the constellation picture of Cassiopeia cf. K. M. Phillips, *Pers. and Andr.*, pp. 20ff. and figs. 52, 54-56, 62.

p. 161, note 13
Add: For an earlier Carolingian example of the constellation of Engonasin cf. the Aratus manuscript in the Cathedral Library of Cologne. *A.B.Ill.*, p. 25 and pl. XIV, fig. 30.

p. 162, § 2
For the miniature of Pantocratoros cod. 49, a manuscript which—as mentioned before—is now in the Dumbarton Oaks Collection in Washington, D.C., cf. S. Der Nersessian, *D.O.Psalter*, p. 171 and fig. 13, where it is placed alongside the better preserved miniature of the Psalter Paris suppl. gr. 610 (*ibid.*, fig. 14). The identical conflation of two events in both miniatures is proof that both manuscripts belong to the same branch within the stemma of the aristocratic Psalters.

p. 166, §1

The explanation that in the miniature of Joseph's Temptation by Potiphar's wife those elements which cannot be explained by the Bible text are mere decorative fillings can, in the light of some more recent studies of the Vienna Genesis, no longer be considered satisfactory. C. O. Nordström ("Some Jewish Legends in Byzantine Art," *Byzantion*, XXV-XXVII, 1958, p. 489) was the first to point out a Jewish element in the scene of Joseph on his way to his brothers. He explained the accompanying angel as the archangel Gabriel mentioned in a Jewish legend. Next, O. Pächt ("Ephraimillustration, Haggadah und Wiener Genesis," *Festschrift K. M. Swoboda*, Vienna, 1959, p. 217 and fig. 50) found further influence of Jewish legends in several miniatures, notably pict. 32 in which Potiphar hurries home to his wife in order to deliver the news of Joseph's exaltation. Then, I myself ("Zur Frage des Einflusses jüdischer Bilderquellen auf die Illustration des Alten Testamentes," *Mullus, Festschrift Th. Klauser*, Münster, 1964, p. 407 and pl. 13b) identified as Zuleika, the wife of Potiphar, the woman who in pict. 33 talks with the guardian of the prison.

Similarly, I would expect that in the present case also the elements which are supernumerous from the Biblical point of view are based on some legendary tradition. Jewish legends (Ginzberg, *The Legends of the Jews*, vol. II, 1946, p. 53) and also Flavius Josephus (*Ant.Jud.* II, IV, 3) stress the point that Potiphar's wife and Joseph were alone in the palace by adding that the temptation took place at a time when her retinue was attending an annual festival on the banks of the Nile. The tree in the miniature is a clear indication that the women of the household were not in the palace but outdoors. Admittedly this is not the whole explanation of the miniature, but may serve as a point of departure for further investigation.

p. 166, §3

For other examples of human figures represented in occupations with plants, not only in the Dioscurides of Lavra but in other herbals, Greek and Arabic, cf. *Isl.Sc.Ill.*, pp. 25off. and pl. XXXIV,7-XXXV,10. Cf. also *A.B.Ill.*, p. 13 and pl. VII, fig. 15.

p. 167, note 27

Add: *Isl.Sc.Ill.*, p. 259 and pl. XXXVI, 13—*Kl.Erbe*, p. 53 and pl. VII, 14—*A.B.Ill.*, p. 14 and pl. VIII, fig. 16.

p. 168, §1

For further miniatures in technical treatises with added figures cf. *Isl.Sc.Ill.*, p. 248 and pl. XXXIII, 3-4—*A.B.Ill.*, pp. 9ff. and pl. IV, figs. 7-9.

p. 170, note 37
Add: S. Der Nersessian, *D.O.Psalter*, p. 169 and fig. 10.

p. 170, §1
For the problem of the relation of some Psalter miniatures to the Octateuchs cf. *Ps.Vatop.*, pp. 32ff.

p. 171, §3
Bianchi-Bandinelli (*Iliad*, p. 66) explains the deviations from Homer's text as an influence of a theatrical scene. The pose of Hector and the disposition of the furniture, indicating an interior, speak in favor of such an assumption. However this source does not sufficiently explain the depiction of Astyanax as a youth in his prime, and I still prefer to think in this case of a conscious prolepsis of a kind which is not unique in miniature painting. In the Vatican Books of Kings, cod. gr. 333, there is a miniature (fol. 5ʳ) with Hannah praying for a child; in front of her stands a fully grown boy as a visualization of the fulfilment of her prayer, whereas the actual birth of Samuel is represented in a subsequent miniature (fol. 5ᵛ).

p. 173, §1
The conscious iconographic deviations in the Vatican Rotulus are fully discussed in the chapter of the "Triumphal Idea in the Joshua Roll" (*Josh.Roll*, pp. 100ff.).

p. 173, §2
Several cases of changes from narrative Gospel miniatures into more hieratic ones in lectionaries are discussed in *Narr.Lit.*, pp. 163ff. One of the most striking is the scene of the Mission of the Apostles which is depicted twice in the luxurious lectionary of Dionysiu, in one case in the narrative and in the other in the liturgical mode (*ibid.*, p. 166 and pls. xxiv-xxv).

p. 174, §2
For a photographic reproduction of the Phoenissae bowl cf. Hausmann, *H.Rel.*, pl. 12, fig. 3.

p. 175, §1
H.-J. Geischer ("Heidnische Parallelen zum frühchristlichen Bild des Isaak-Opfers," *Jahrbuch Antike und Christentum* x, 1967, pp. 127ff.) discusses a second type of the sacrifice of Isaac in which the victim is kneeling on both knees and Abraham is about to kill him with a knife. Also this type shows distinct features which point to a classical model, although a precise model which combines all

the classical features enumerated has not yet been found. As for the version derived from the sacrifice of Orestes cf. also *Survival*, p. 58 and figs. 27-28 (Early Christian ivory pyxis Trier).

p. 176, §1
The dependence of Bible illustrators on classical models is by no means confined to the Old Testament. We can cite an example from the New Testament, a miniature with the Massacre of the Innocents in the codex Munich lat. 23631, where several elements can be explained out of an illustrated Illiupersis. (*Survival*, p. 61 and figs. 32-33).

p. 176, §2
Add: *Ill.Sept.*, p. 115 and figs. 18-23.

p. 177, §1
H. Schade ("Das Paradies und die Imago Dei," *Probleme der Kunstwissenschaft*, vol. II, 1966, pp. 79ff.) deals at great length with the problem of the relation between the Creation of Adam and the Creation of Man by Prometheus (pp. 146ff.). For the first of my three phases, the Shaping of Adam, he concedes that there exists a similarity between Genesis and the Prometheus scene, but he goes to great lengths to reject the similarity for the second phase, the Enlivenment. He is correct in noticing certain differences between the corresponding scenes in the Grandval Bible and the Prometheus sarcophagus, notably, the fact that instead of placing his hand on a lifeless body the Christian Creator puts his hand under the head, and Schade interprets this difference as an intent to raise Adam up. Yet a lifting up of the body is not made visible by pictorial means since Adam still lies stiff on the ground in precisely the same position as the man in the Prometheus sarcophagus—a similarity too strong to be ignored. A change of meaning seems, indeed, to have been intended as suggested by the slight alteration of the gesture of the Creator, but this does not eliminate the comparable scene from the Prometheus myth as the ultimate source. We deal with a case where an interpretation based on a preconceived concept violates the visual evidence. Besides, it seems, *a priori*, unlikely that a Christian who used a Prometheus cycle as a model for the Shaping of Adam would have closed his eyes to the subsequent scene, which I called the Enlivenment, and would have invented, independently, a new composition and come out with a result remarkably similar to the one in the Prometheus cycle!

Moreover, one of Schade's statements should be corrected. On p. 125 he says: "Nun wollte K. W. die merkwürdige Darstellung der Oktateuche mit Hilfe des Prometheusmythos erklären." In *Roll and Codex* I have quite explicitly drawn a parallel only with the Cotton Genesis recension but nowhere with the Octateuchs which belong to another picture recension.

p. 178, fig. 183
Ps.Vatop., p. 42 and fig. 28.

p. 178, §2
In "Illustration for the Chronicles of Sozomenos, Theodoret and Malalas," *Byzantion*, XVI, 1942-43, pp. 87ff., I have tried to demonstrate that Greek Chronicles had been illustrated at an early (i.e., pre-iconoclastic) period.

p. 178, note 60
Recently all the miniatures of this manuscript have been published by S. Cirac Estopañan, *Skyllitzes Matritensis*, Barcelona-Madrid, 1965. For our miniature cf. p. 212, no. 568 and fig. on p. 413.

p. 179, note 61
Ps.Vatop., p. 9 and fig. 9.

p. 180, note 62
Cirac Estopañan, *op.cit.*, p. 50, no. 8 and fig. on p. 226.

p. 180, §3
Narr.Lit., p. 169 and pl. XXVIII, fig. 1.

p. 181
For similar examples of the substitutions of whole compositional schemes cf. K. Weitzmann, "The Octateuch of the Seraglio," *Actes du X. Congrès International d'Études Byz.*, Istanbul 1957, pp. 183ff. Abraham praying in proskynesis to the Lord is substituted by a composition in which a bust of Christ in heaven is blessing Abraham and Sarah standing opposite each other (pl. XL., 3-4). Another instance is the replacement of Pharaoh ordering the killing of the Jewish offspring by a more conventional scene of the Birth of Moses (pl. XLI, 5-6).

p. 190, §3
For a more detailed discussion of the genealogical relations among the Octateuchs and an emphasis on the excellence of the codex Vat. gr. 747 cf. *Josh.Roll*, pp. 30ff.

p. 191, §2
Cf. *Josh.Roll*, pp. 12ff. and pls. II, 5 and III, 9-12. The changes made by the Joshua Roll painters are only in the text-critical sense "errors," while from the

point of view of content and form they were made purposely with a definite idea in mind, namely, to infuse a triumphal idea, as has been explained *ibid.* on p. 107.

p. 192, note 7

While most scholars are today inclined to attribute the ninth century monastic Psalters—chiefly on iconographical and textual grounds—to a Constantinopolitan scriptorium, I still consider this problem unsolved as long as the stylistic discrepancy with contemporary miniatures that surely were made in Constantinople —like the Vatican Cosmas cod. gr. 699 and the Homilies of Gregory of Nazianzus in Paris cod. gr. 510—has not satisfactorily been explained.

p. 194, §1

The problem of the models of the Touronian Bibles, especially with regard to the four pictures which the Grandval Bible in London and the Vivian Bible in Paris have in common, has recently been discussed in an unpublished Ph.D. dissertation by Herbert L. Kessler, *The Sources and the Construction of the Genesis, Exodus, Majestas, and Apocalypse Frontispiece Illustrations in the Ninth Century Touronian Bibles* (Princeton, 1965). Following up a remark by R. Hinks (*Carolingian Art*, London 1935, p. 113) that the Maiestas picture could hardly be as early as the fifth century—i.e., the time of Pope Leo the Great, to whom Koehler attributed the archetype—Kessler has accumulated evidence for a later dating of this picture. But if one miniature is taken out of the set of four which, according to Koehler, were created as a coherent anti-Manichean program, then the whole reconstruction of the so-called Leo Bible of the fifth century becomes questionable. Kessler has come to the conclusion that the full-page multiscenic miniatures were excerpted from various illustrated books of the Bible during the Carolingian period. This ties in with my own observations concerning Bible illustration in the Byzantine East, namely, that the Early Byzantine period illustrated only individual books of the Bible with prolific miniature cycles and that the only Greek Bible in existence that is fully illustrated, the cod. Vat. Reg. gr. 1, is made *ad hoc* in the tenth century (*Sept.Ill.*, p. 100).

p. 194, §2

While the collation of the Cotton Genesis—made in 1700 before its destruction in 1731—listed 250 miniatures, I estimated that the 36 lacunae which existed already in 1700 amounted to about 50 folios with about 80 miniatures, thus arriving at the total number of 330 (K. Weitzmann, "Observations of the Cotton Genesis," *loc.cit.*, p. 117).

p. 195, §1

An example of a miniature of the *Sacra Parallela* manuscript in Paris, which was copied from the Fourth Book of Kings and has no parallel in the cod. Vat. gr. 333, has been published in *Ill.Sept.*, pp. 105ff. and fig. 8.

p. 195, §3

In the Nicander manuscript at least three additional sources have been brought into the discussion of its inserted mythological and other classical themes, in addition to an Aratus manuscript.

(1) The *Bibliotheke* of Apollodorus from which the miniatures of the Birth of the Giants seem to be derived (*Kl.Erbe*, pp. 54ff. and pl. VIII, figs. 15-16—*A.B.Ill.*, p. 98 and pl. L, fig. 105—*Survival*, p. 49 and figs. 7-8—*G.Gr.*, p. 16 and fig. 6).

(2) The mythological handbook of Conon which seems best to explain the miniature of Canopus bitten by a snake (*Isl.Sc.Ill.*, p. 261 and pl. XXXVI, 15—*A.B.Ill.*, p. 99 and pl. L, fig. 106).

(3) Bucolic poetry which seems to have been the source for more than one miniature. (*Kl.Erbe*, p. 53 and pl. VII, 14—*A.B.Ill.*, p. 109 and pl. LVI, fig. 116).

p. 196, §1

Contrary to the Nicander manuscript, in the case of the Pseudo-Oppian in Venice the various sources have been worked out in detail in *Gr.Myth.* (cf. p. 245 add to page 75).

p. 203, note 8

Add: *Narr.Lit.*, pp. 70ff. and pls. XXIX-XXXI—*G.Gr.*, pp. 39ff. and fig. 37.

p. 204

The controversy about the signatures of the eight miniature painters in relation to the pictures they accompany has recently been rekindled by Anatole Frolow ("L'Origine des miniatures du ménologe du Vatican," *Recueil des travaux de l'Acad. Serbe des Sc.* LXV," *Institut d'Études Byzantines* VI, 1960, pp. 29ff.). Because of the rather monotonous character of the miniatures, he doubts that they could be the works of eight different artists and he comes forth with a new theory that the signatures were copied from a model in which the style of the miniatures was more distinct and more individualistic. This idea has been repudiated by Ihor Ševčenko ("The Illuminators of the Menologion of Basil II," *D.O.P.*, XVI, 1962, pp. 245ff.) for two reasons. The first is codicological. He demonstrates that the system of the alternating signatures is in agreement with a working procedure according to which one artist, as a norm, worked on one sheet at a time and that six or seven illuminators usually worked together on two successive quires. In a mechanical process of copying, this coincidence between whole sheets and an individual artist could hardly have survived and, thus, he concludes that, indeed, the artists' names pertain to the actual miniatures of the Basil menologion. Secondly, by analyzing a few minor details, he uses the Morellian method in order to distinguish individual hands, claiming that previous attempts in this direction failed because the method was not applied with sufficient care and subtlety. I agree with Ševčenko as to the existence of personal traits in the style of each of the eight artists and that a further study of the style, more subtle and more thorough than has hitherto been attempted, remains to be made. Actually the style is not quite as monotonous as Frolow claims and this becomes clear if one compares the miniatures of the Vatican menologion with those of two slightly later copies, Baltimore cod. 521 and Moscow cod. 183, which are much more homogeneous. At the same time I still maintain that the major differences between the miniatures of the Vatican menologion are due less to the individuality of the artist than to the influence of the various models which may neither have been contemporaneous nor have necessarily belonged to the same scriptorium.

1. PARIS, BIBL. NAT. Cylix: Odysseus and Polyphemus

2. FLORENCE, MUS. ARCH. Crater: The Killing of Troilus

3. BERLIN, MUS. Scyphos: The Killing of the Wooers

a. Fight between Ajax and Odysseus

b. Achaeans Casting Dice

4a–c. VIENNA, MUS. OF DECOR. ARTS

c. Odysseus and Neoptolemus

5. MUNICH, ANTIQUARIUM. Amphora: The *Medea* of Euripides

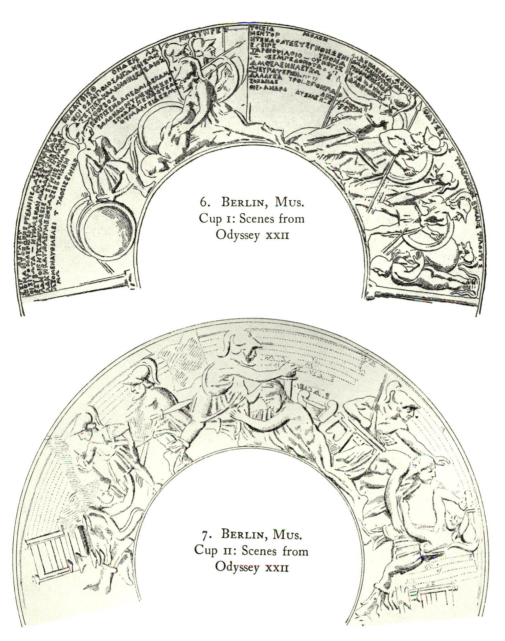

6. BERLIN, MUS.
Cup I: Scenes from
Odyssey XXII

7. BERLIN, MUS.
Cup II: Scenes from
Odyssey XXII

8. WARSAW, NAT. MUS. Tablet: Scenes from Odyssey X

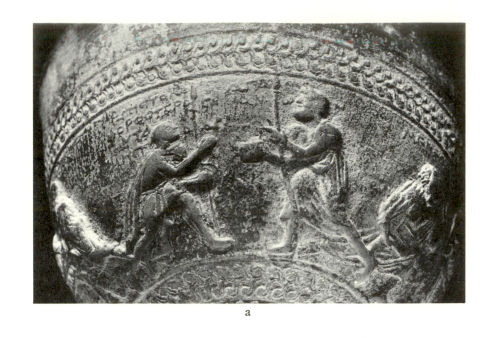

a

b

c

d

e

9a-e. NEW YORK, METROP. MUS. Cup: Scenes from *Iphigenia at Aulis*

10. BERLIN, MUS.
Cup: Scenes from *Iphigenia at Aulis*

11. BERLIN, MUS. Amphora: The Labors of Heracles

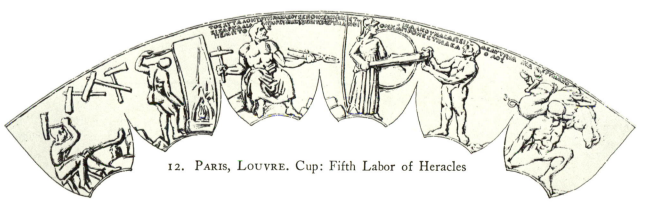

12. PARIS, LOUVRE. Cup: Fifth Labor of Heracles

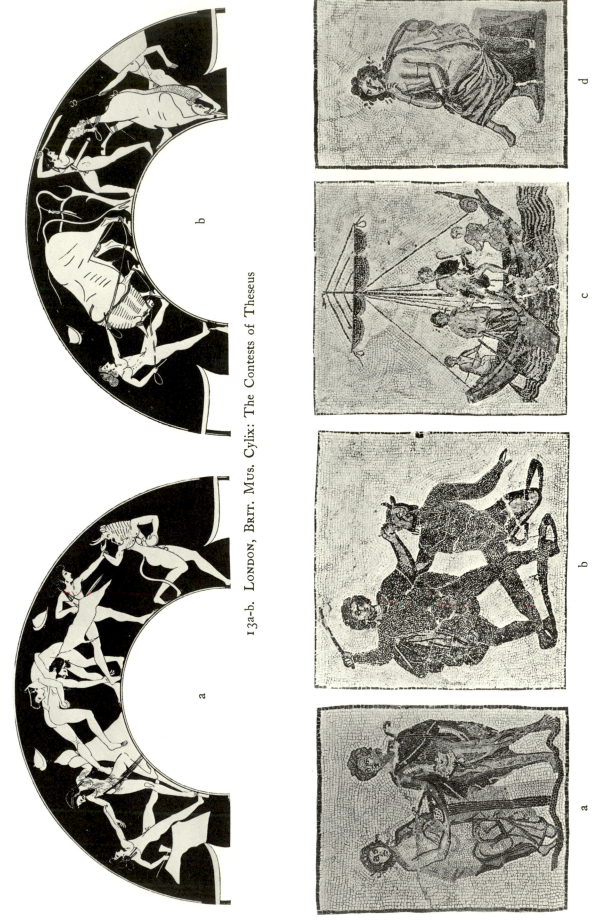

13a-b. London, Brit. Mus. Cylix: The Contests of Theseus

14a-d. Vienna, Kunsthist. Mus. Mosaic: Theseus and Ariadne

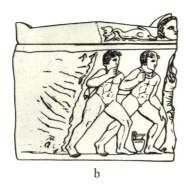

a

b
c

15a-c. MUNICH, GLYPTOTHEK. Sarcophagus: Scenes from *Iphigenia among the Taurians*

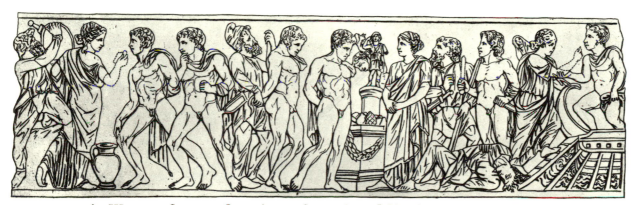

16. WEIMAR, SCHLOSS. Sarcophagus: Scenes from *Iphigenia among the Taurians*

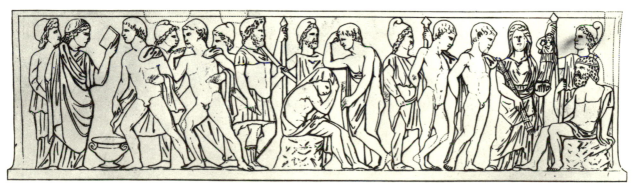

17. BERLIN, MUS. Sarcophagus: Scenes from *Iphigenia among the Taurians*

18a-c. CANNES, VILLA FAUSTINA. Sarcophagus: Scenes from the *Alcestis* of Euripides

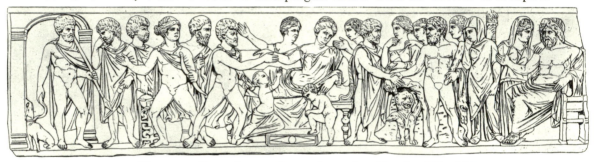

19. VATICAN. Sarcophagus: Scenes from the *Alcestis* of Euripides

20. BERLIN, Mus. Cup: Scenes from Iliad XIX-XXI

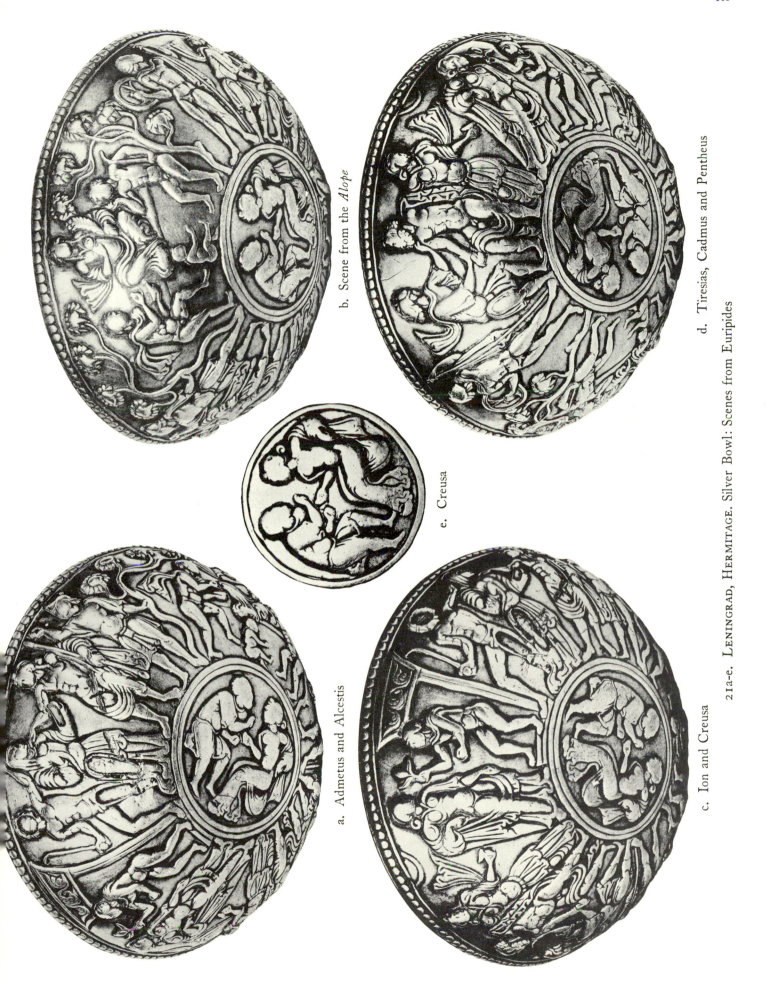

b. Scene from the *Alope*

d. Tiresias, Cadmus and Pentheus

e. Creusa

a. Admetus and Alcestis

c. Ion and Creusa

21a-e. LENINGRAD, HERMITAGE. Silver Bowl: Scenes from Euripides

22. ROME, PAL. CONSERV. Tensa: Scenes from the Life of Achilles

23. BERLIN, MUS. Pergamon Altar: Telephus Frieze

25. ROME, MUS. CAPIT. Tablet: Scenes from Iliad XXII

24. LONDON, BRIT. MUS.
Lamp Handle: Achilles

26. ROME, PAL. CONSERV. Tensa: Scenes from the Life of Achilles

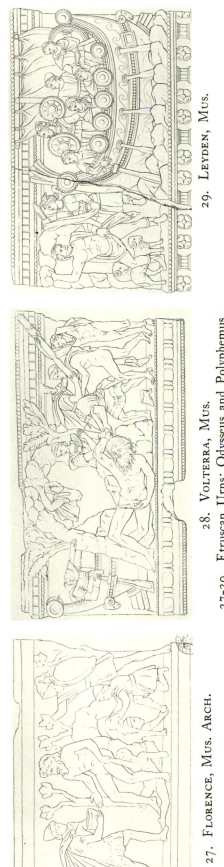

27. FLORENCE, MUS. ARCH.

28. VOLTERRA, MUS.

29. LEYDEN, MUS.

27-29. Etruscan Urns: Odysseus and Polyphemus

30. PARIS, CAB. DES MED. Tablet: Scenes from Cypria and Iliad I

31. ROME, MUS. CAPIT. Tablet: Scenes from Iliad I

32. MILAN, AMBROS. LIB. COD. F. 205 inf. *Pict.* I: Revenge of Chryses

33. MILAN, AMBROS. LIB. COD. F. 205 inf. *Pict.* II: Achilles' Wrath

34. MILAN, AMBROS. LIB. COD. F. 205 inf. *Pict.* IX: The Council of the Gods

35. BERLIN, MUS. PAP. 11529: Mathematical Text

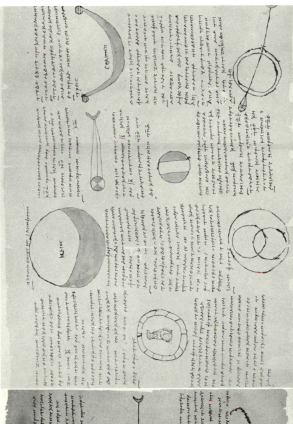

36. CHICAGO, FIELD COL. MUS. PAP. 1: Mathematical Text

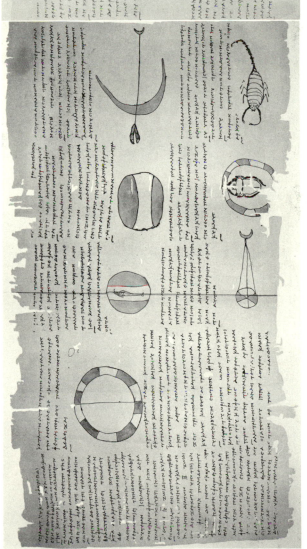

37. PARIS, LOUVRE. PAP. 1: Instructions about the Spheres

38a-c. LEYDEN, MUS. PAP. I. 384: Magical Text

39. OSLO, UNIV. LIB. PAP. I: Magical Text

40a. OXFORD, Pap. gr. Oxy. 2331: Herakles

40. PARIS, BIBL. NAT. Cod. suppl. gr. 1294: Romance

41. OXFORD, JOHNSON COLL.
Papyrus: Charioteers

42. MUNICH, STATE LIB. Pap. gr. mon. 128: Briseis

41a. FLORENCE, IST.
PAPIROL. Pap. 1368

43. FLORENCE, MUS. ARCH. Papyrus: Amor and Psyche

44. The Ramesseum Papyrus: Accession to the Throne of Sesostris I

b

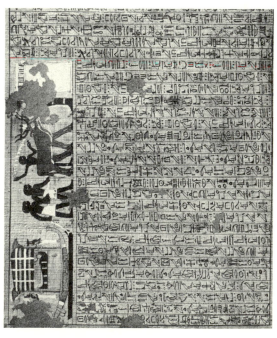

a

45a-b. The Book of the Dead of Iouiya

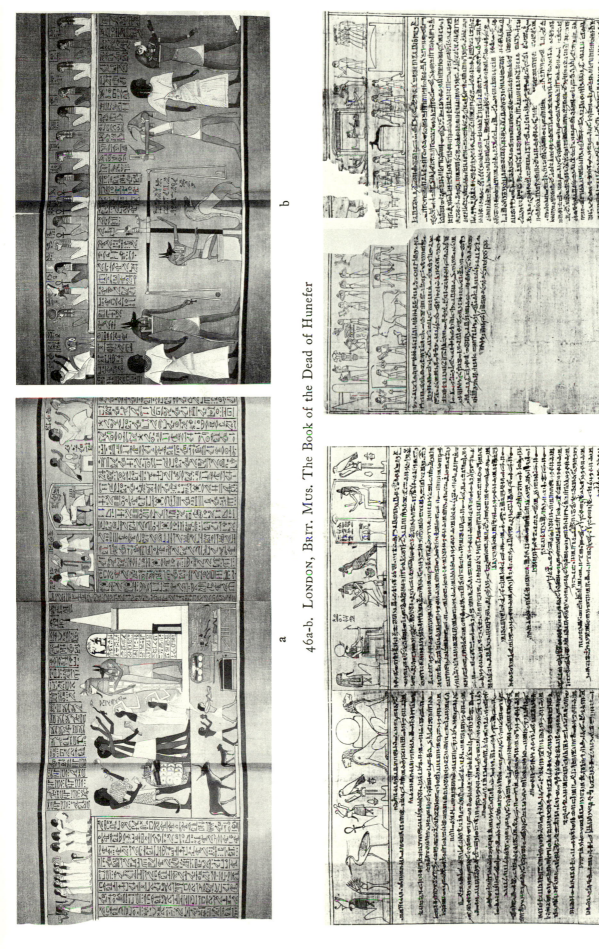

46a-b. London, Brit. Mus. The Book of the Dead of Hunefer

47a-b. London, Brit. Mus. The Greenfield Papyrus: Book of the Dead

48. CAIRO, Mus. The Book of the Dead of Nesikhonsu

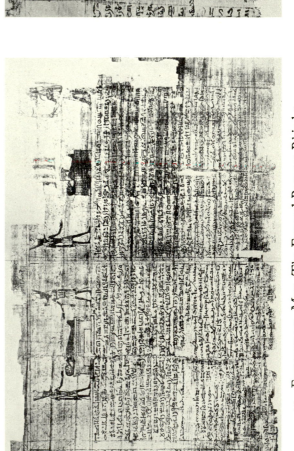

50. EDINBURGH, Mus. The Funeral Papyrus Rhind II

49. EDINBURGH, Mus. The Funeral Papyrus Rhind I

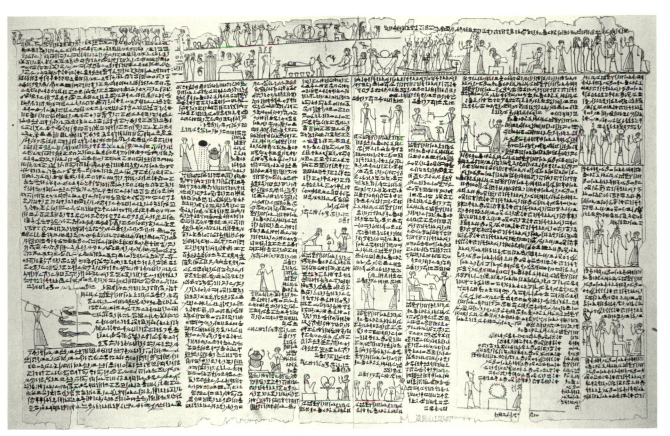

51. PARIS, LOUVRE. Pap. 3079: The Book of the Dead

52. PRINCETON, N.J., UNIV. LIB. The Book of the Dead

53. LONDON, BRIT. MUS. PAP. 10051: Magical Text

54. LONDON, BRIT. MUS. PAP. 10016: Satirical Fables

55. BERLIN, MUS. Relief Cup: Satirical Fables

56. Berne, City Lib.
Cod. 318. Fol. 12ᵛ: Serpent

57. Paris, Bibl. Nat.
Cod. gr. 2179. Fol. 124ʳ: Plants

58. Munich, State Lib. Cod. 210. Fols. 119ᵛ-120ʳ: Constellations

59. VATICAN. Cod. lat. 3868. Fols. 60ᵛ-61ʳ: The *Adelphoe* of Terence

60. FLORENCE, LAURENT. LIB. Cod. Plut. LXXIV, 7. Fols. 232ᵛ-233ʳ: Soranus on Bandaging

61. VENICE, MARCIANA. Cod. gr. 479. Fol. 15ᵛ:
Oppian's *Cynegetica*

62. PARIS, BIBL. NAT. Cod. lat. 8085. Fol. 57ʳ:
Psychomachia of Prudentius

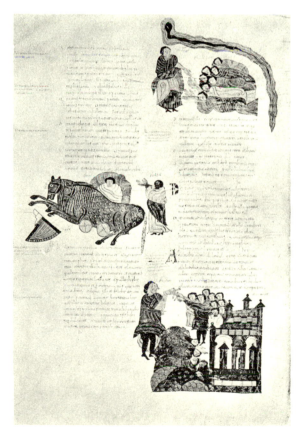

63. MONTECASSINO, LIB. Cod. 132. Pag. 451:
Hrabanus Maurus

64. LEON, SAN ISIDORO. Bible, Fol. 146ᵛ:
Story of Elijah

65. BERLIN, STATE LIB. COD. PHILL. 1832.
Fol. 83ʳ: Constellations

66. LONDON, BRIT. MUS. COD. Cotton Tib. B.V.
Fol. 38ᵛ: Aquila

67. BASEL, UNIV. LIB. COD. A.N.IV.18.
Fol. 31ᵛ: Aquarius and Capricornus

68. MT. ATHOS, LAVRA. COD. Ω 75.
Fol. 45ᵛ: Plants

69. VATICAN. Cod. lat. 3868. Fol. 70ᵛ: The *Hecyra* of Terence

70. FLORENCE, LAURENT. LIB. Cod. Plut. VI, 23.
Fol. 172ʳ: Scenes from the Gospel of John

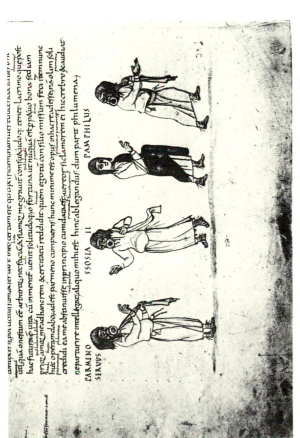

71. FLORENCE, LAURENT. LIB. Cod. Plut. VI, 23.
Fol. 192ʳ: Scenes from the Gospel of John

72. VENICE, MARCIANA. Cod. gr. 479. Fol. 47ʳ: Jealousy

73. VIENNA, NAT. LIB. Cod. theol. gr. 31.
Pict. 11: Story of Abraham

74. VIENNA, NAT. LIB. Cod. theol. gr. 31.
Pict. 10: Story of Lot

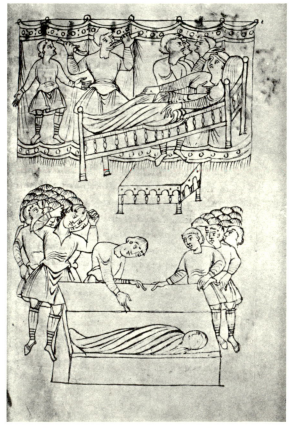

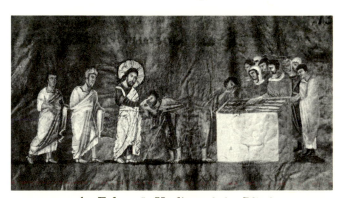

76. Fol. VII^r: Healing of the Blind

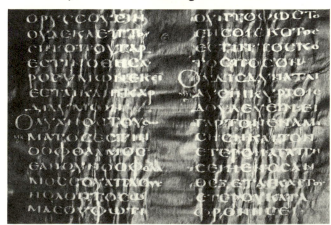

75. LEYDEN, UNIV. LIB. Cod. Perizoni 17.
Fol. 25^r: Death of Antiochus

77. Fol. 113^r: Matthew, Chap. VI
76-77. ROSSANO, CATHEDRAL. Cod. Purp.

78. Vienna, Nat. Lib. Cod. med. gr. 1.
Fol. 483ᵛ: *Ornithiaca* of Dionysius

79. Leyden, Univ. Lib. Cod. Voss. lat. oct. 15.
Fol. 40ᵛ: *Psychomachia* of Prudentius

80. Vatican. Cod. gr. 1087. Fol. 304ᵛ:
Constellations

81. Durham, Cathedral. Cod. Hunter 100.
Fol. 119ᵛ: Cauterizing

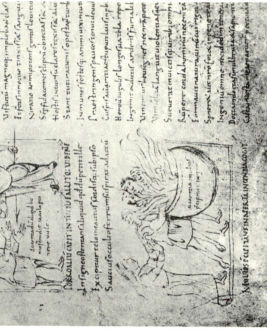

83. PARIS, BIBL. NAT. COD. LAT. 8318. Fol. 59ᵛ:
Psychomachia of Prudentius

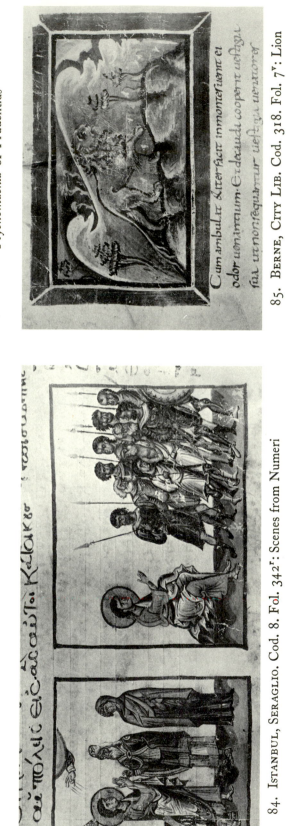

85. BERNE, CITY LIB. COD. 318. Fol. 7ᵛ: Lion

82. VENICE, MARCIANA. COD. GR. 479. Fol. 20ʳ: Hunting with Dogs

84. ISTANBUL, SERAGLIO. COD. 8. Fol. 342ʳ: Scenes from Numeri

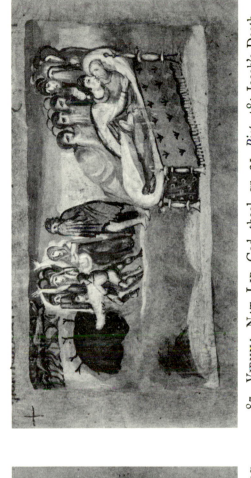

86. Vienna, Nat. Lib. Cod. theol. gr. 31. *Pict.* 45: Jacob's Blessing

87. Vienna, Nat. Lib. Cod. theol. gr. 31. *Pict.* 48: Jacob's Death

88. London, Brit. Mus. Cod. Sloane 1975. Fol. 21ʳ: Camelia

89. Rome, Bibl. Casanatense. Cod. A.II.15. Fol. 2ᵛ: Cauterizing

90. LEYDEN, UNIV. LIB. Cod. Voss. lat. quart. 79.
Fol. 54ᵛ: Aquila

91. VATICAN. Cod. lat. 3225. Fol. 24ᵛ:
Sacrifice of Aeneas

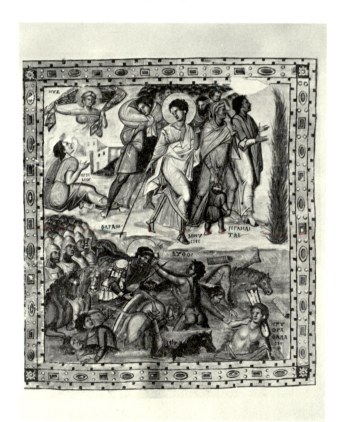

92. PARIS, BIBL. NAT. Cod. gr. 139.
Fol. 419ᵛ: Crossing of the Red Sea

93. PARIS, BIBL. NAT. Cod. gr. 139.
Fol. 136ᵛ: Repentance of David

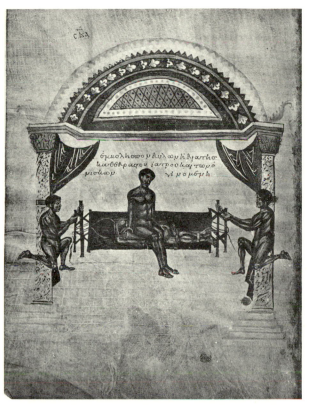

94. FLORENCE, LAURENT. LIB. COD. PLUT. LXXIV, 7.
Fol. 202ᵛ: Treatment of Dislocated Bone

95. VATICAN. Cod. lat. 3868. Fol. 3ʳ:
Masks of the *Andria* of Terence

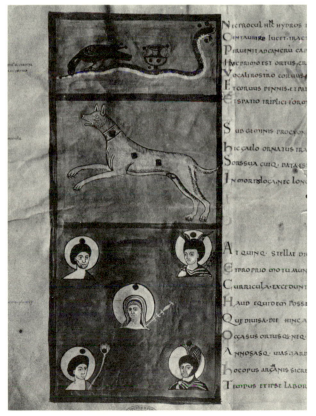

96. AACHEN, CATHEDRAL. Gospels of Otto.
Pag. 249: Annunciation

97. BOULOGNE-SUR-MER, BIBL. MUN. COD. 188.
Fol. 29ᵛ: Constellations

98. VATICAN. Cod. gr. 699. Fol. 80ʳ: Luke

99. PATMOS. Cod. 70. Fol. 40ᵛ:
Healing of the Blind

100. ETSCHMIADZIN. Cod. 229.
Fol. 222ᵛ: Mary at the Tomb

101. MOSCOW, MUS. OF FINE ARTS.
Alexandrian World Chronicle. Fol. VIᵛ

102. PARIS, BIBL. NAT. Cod. gr. 115.
Fol. 43ʳ: Scenes from the Gospel of Matthew

103. PARIS, BIBL. NAT. Cod. gr. 923.
Fol. 212ʳ: Scenes from the Gospels

104. FLORENCE, LAURENT. LIB. Cod. Plut. I, 56.
Fol. 6ʳ: Canon Table

105. MILAN, AMBROS. LIB. Cod. E. 49-50 inf.
Pag. 597: Portraits and Scenes from Kings

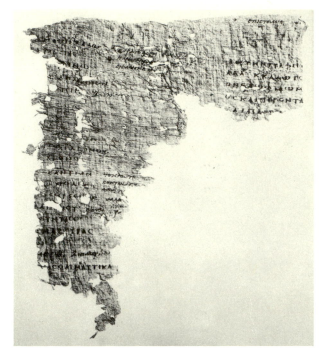

106. NEW YORK, MORGAN LIB.
Amherst Pap. XIII: Text of Comedy

107. OXFORD, BODL. LIB. Cod. d'Orville 301.
Fol. 260ʳ: *Elements* of Euclid

108. VATICAN. Cod. gr. 752. Fol. 261ʳ:
Christ, Asaph and Korah

109. MT. ATHOS, PANTOKRATOROS. Cod. 61.
Fol. 42ᵛ: Scenes from the Gospels

110. ROME. Column of Trajan

111. VATICAN. Cod. Palat. gr. 431: Joshua Rotulus

XXXV

115. PARIS, BIBL. NAT. COD. gr. 923.
Fol. 227^r: Scenes from Flav. Josephus

114. PARIS, BIBL. NAT. COD. gr. 923.
Fol. 31^r: Scenes from the Old Test.

112. VATICAN. COD. gr. 747. Fol. 212^v: Song of Moses

113. MT. ATHOS, VATOPEDI. COD. 760. Fol. 270^r:
Song of Moses

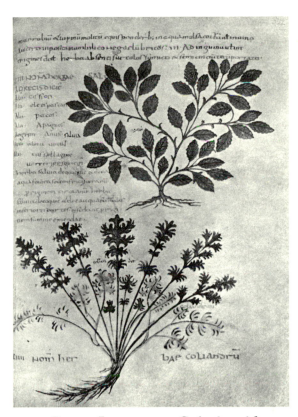

116. Munich, State Lib. Cod. lat. 337.
Fol. 121ʳ: Plants

117. Cassel, Landesbibl. Cod. phys. fol. 10.
Fol. 27ʳ: Plants

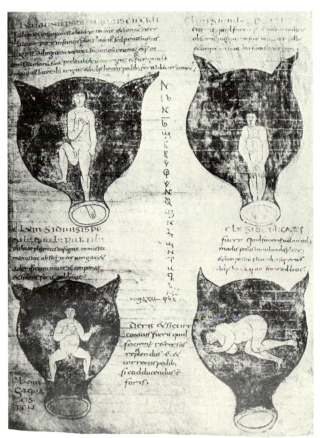

118. Brussels, Bibl. Royale. Cod. 3714.
Fol. 28ʳ: Positions of the Embryo

119. London, Brit. Mus. Cod. Cotton Vit. A.xv.
Fol. 100ʳ: Cynocephalus

120. OXFORD, BODL. LIB. COD. BODL. 764.
Fol. 17ᵛ: Deer and Snake

121. CAMBRIDGE, UNIV. LIB. COD. K.k.IV.25:
Swimming Deer

122. VENICE, MARCIANA. Cod. gr. 479. Fol. 27ᵛ: Deer and Snake

123. VENICE, MARCIANA. Cod. gr. 479. Fol. 27ʳ: Swimming Deer

124. Fol. 3ᵛ: Creation of Adam

125. Fol. 35ᵛ: Isaac's Blessing

124-125. KLAGENFURT, MUS. Genesis of Millstatt

126. Fol. 87^r: Sacrifice of Isaac

127. Fol. 87^v: Sacrifice of Isaac

128. Fol. 88^r: Sacrifice of Isaac

126-128. ISTANBUL, SERAGLIO. Cod. 8

129. VATICAN. Cod. gr. 699. Fol. 59^r:
Sacrifice of Isaac

130. VATICAN. Cod. gr. 699. Fol. 83^v:
Conversion of Paul

131. PARIS, BIBL. NAT. Cod. suppl. gr. 247.
Fol. 2ᵛ: Orion and the Scorpion

132. VATICAN. Cod. gr. 1087.
Fol. 303ʳ: Orion

133. VENICE, MARCIANA. Cod. gr. 479. Fol. 8ʳ: Alexander Romance

134. VENICE, MARCIANA. Cod. gr. 479. Fol. 8ᵛ: Alexander Romance

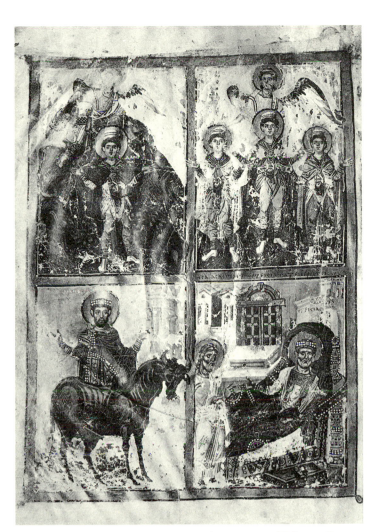

135-136. Mt. Athos, Panteleimon. Cod. 6. Fols. 162ᵛ-163ʳ: Birth of Zeus

137. Paris, Bibl. Nat. Cod. gr. 510. Fol. 435ᵛ: Scenes from the Canticles

138. Paris, Bibl. Nat. Cod. gr. 1208. Fol. 162ʳ: Vision of Isaiah

139. Mt. Athos, Vatopedi. Cod. 760. Fol. 280ᵛ: Vision of Isaiah

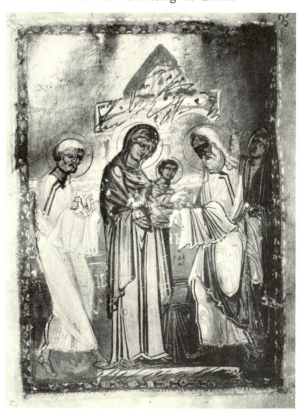

140. WASHINGTON, DUMBARTON OAKS, COD. 3
Fol. 5ʳ: Birth and Anointing of David

141. ROME, PAL. DI VENEZIA. Ivory Casket:
Birth and Caressing of David

142-143. MT. ATHOS, PANTELEIMON. COD. 2. Fol. 228ʳ-228ᵛ: Presentation in the Temple

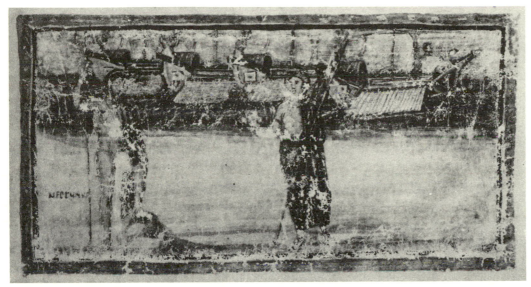

144. VATICAN. Cod. lat. 3225. Fol. 44ᵛ: Neptune and Venus

145. ROME, LATERAN.
Neptune (reversed)

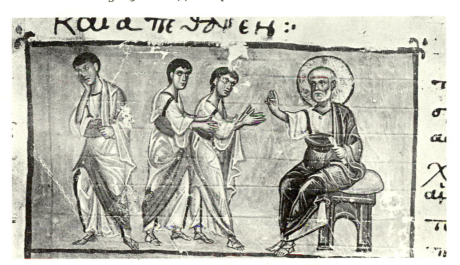

146. VATICAN. Cod. gr. 746. Fol. 59ᵛ: Curse of Noah

147. VATICAN. Cod. gr. 746. Fol. 134ᵛ: Joseph and the Egyptians

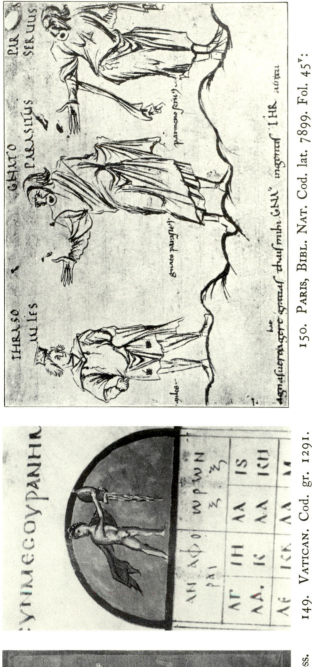

150. PARIS, BIBL. NAT. COD. LAT. 7899. Fol. 45ᵛ:
The *Eunuchus* of Terence

153. OXFORD, BODL. LIB. COD. AUCT. F.II.13: Fol. 45ᵛ:
The *Eunuchus* of Terence

149. VATICAN. COD. gr. 1291.
Fol. 22ʳ: Aquarius

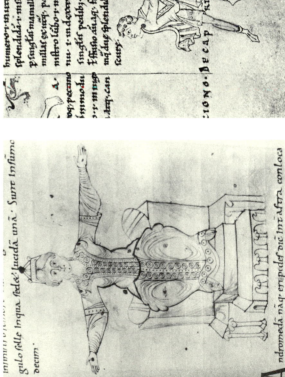

152. DURHAM, CATHEDRAL.
COD. Hunter 100. Fol. 62ᵛ: Aquarius

148. LEYDEN, UNIV. LIB. COD. VOSS.
lat. quart. 79. Fol. 28ᵛ: Cassiopeia

151. ST. GALL, STIFTSBIBL.
COD. 250: Cassiopeia

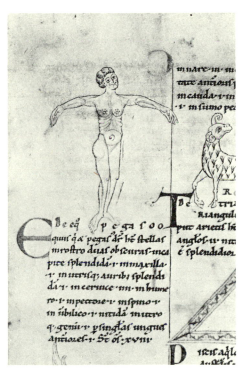

154. DURHAM, CATHEDRAL.
Cod. Hunter 100. Fol. 62ʳ: Andromeda

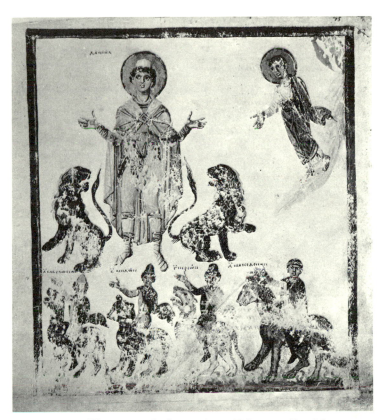

155. VATICAN. Cod. gr. 699. Fol. 75ʳ: Daniel

156. BOULOGNE-SUR-MER,
BIBL. MUN. Cod. 188. Fol. 21ʳ:
Engonasin and Corona

157. WASHINGTON, DUMBARTON OAKS, Cod. 3
Fol. 76ʳ: Habakkuk

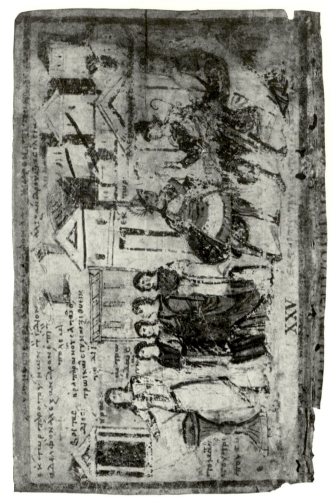

159. MILAN, AMBROS. LIB. COD. F. 205 inf. *Pict.* xxv:
Hecuba in the Temple; Hector with Paris and Helen

160. MILAN, AMBROS. LIB. COD. F. 205 inf. *Pict.* xxxiii:
Assembly of the Achaeans

158. VATICAN. COD. REG. gr. I. Fol. 85ᵛ:
Ark of the Covenant

161. VIENNA, NAT. LIB. Cod. theol. gr. 31. *Pict.* 31: Joseph and Potiphar's Wife

162. PARIS, BIBL. NAT. Cod. suppl. gr. 247.
Fol. 45ʳ: Salamander

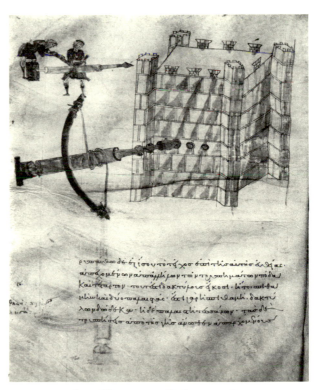

163. VATICAN. Cod. gr. 1605.
Fol. 14ᵛ: Bow-drill

164. WASHINGTON, DUMBARTON OAKS, Cod. 3
Fol. 73ʳ: Moses Receiving the Law

165. VATICAN. Cod. gr. 747. Fol. 114ᵛ:
Moses Receiving the Law

166. VATICAN. Cod. gr. 747. Fol. 223ʳ: Destruction of the City of Ai

167. VATICAN. Cod. Palat. gr. 431: Destruction of the City of Ai

168. Milan, Ambros. Lib. Cod. F. 205 inf. *Pict.* xxvi: Hector and Andromache

169-170. Vatican. Cod. gr. 747. Fol. 224ʳ-224ᵛ: The Gibeonites before Joshua

171. Vatican. Cod. Palat. gr. 431: The Gibeonites before Joshua

172. LONDON, BRIT. MUS.
Cup with Scenes from
the *Phoenissae*

173. PARIS, BIBL. NAT. COD. gr. 510.
Fol. 174ᵛ: Sacrifice of Isaac

174. VATICAN. COD. gr. 333. Fol. 24ʳ:
David with the Head of Goliath

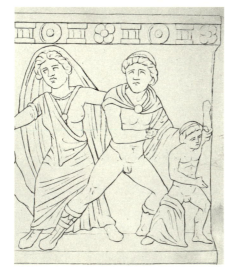

175. FLORENCE, MUS. ARCH.
Etrusc. Urn: Telephus

176. MILAN, AMBROS. LIB. COD. F. 205 inf. *Pict.* XLIII:
Peneleos with the Head of Ilioneus

179. VENICE, SAN MARCO.
Mosaic: Animation of Adam

182. ROME, MUS. CAPIT. Sarcophagus:
Animation of Man

178. LONDON, BRIT. MUS. Cod. add. 10546.
Fol. 5ᵛ: Enlivenment of Adam

181. NAPLES, MUS. NAZ. Sarcophagus:
Enlivenment of Man

177. VENICE, SAN MARCO.
Mosaic: Shaping of Adam

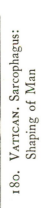

180. VATICAN. Sarcophagus:
Shaping of Man

183. VATICAN. Cod. gr. 333. Fol. 44ʳ:
Coronation of David

184. VATICAN. Cod. gr. 333. Fol. 14ᵛ:
Anointing of Saul

185. MADRID, BIBL. NAC. Cod. 5-3N-2. Fol. 230ʳ:
Coronation of Leo Tornikios

186. VATICAN. Cod. gr. 333.
Fol. 15ᵛ: Anointing of Saul

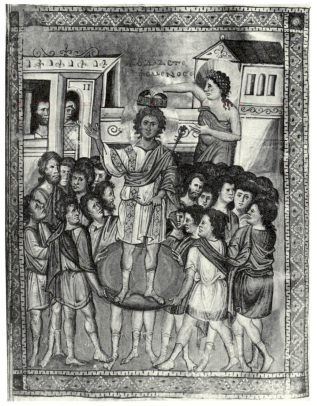

187. PARIS, BIBL. NAT. Cod. gr. 139.
Fol. 6ᵛ: Coronation of David

188. MT. ATHOS, VATOPEDI. Cod. 761.
Fol. 14ʳ: Coronation of David

189. VATICAN. Cod. gr. 1613. Pag. 1: Christ Reading from Isaiah

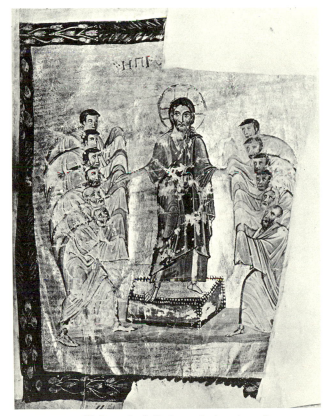

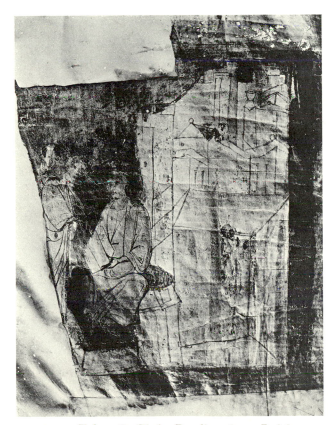

190. Fol. 11ʳ: Mission of the Apostles   191. Fol. 11ᵛ: Christ Reading from Isaiah

190-191. LENINGRAD, PUBLIC LIB. Cod. gr. 21

192. Mt. Sinai. Cod. 1186. Fol. 128v: Conversion of Paul

193. Vatican. Cod. Palat. gr. 431. Joshua on the March

195. Mt. Athos, Vatopedi. Cod. 602. Fol. 345v:
Joshua Erecting an Altar and on the March

194. Vatican. Cod. gr. 746. Fol. 443v:
Joshua Erecting an Altar

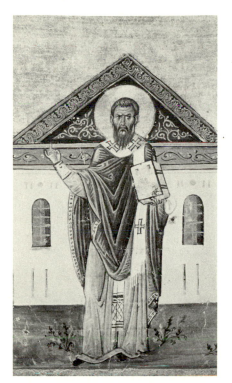

196. Pag. 305: Gregory of Nyssa   197. Pag. 365: Joseph   198. Pag. 382: Zechariah

199. Pag. 6: John the Faster   201. Pag. 216: Nahum

200. Pag. 299: Peter and Andrew

196-201. VATICAN. Cod. gr. 1613

202. Pag. 248: Haggai

203. Pag. 124: Joel

204. Pag. 119: Hosea

205. Pag. 286: A Prophet

202-205. VATICAN. Cod. gr. 1613